Achevé d'imprimer en octobre 2010
dans les ateliers de Normandie Roto Impression s.a.s.
61250 Lonrai
N° d'édition : 13017

N° d'impression : 103883
Dépôt légal : septembre 2004

Imprimé en France

Teaching Gender

Teaching Gender

*The British University and the Rise of
Heterosexuality, 1860–1939*

SAMUEL RUTHERFORD

OXFORD
UNIVERSITY PRESS

OXFORD
UNIVERSITY PRESS

Great Clarendon Street, Oxford, OX2 6DP,
United Kingdom

Oxford University Press is a department of the University of Oxford.
It furthers the University's objective of excellence in research, scholarship,
and education by publishing worldwide. Oxford is a registered trade mark of
Oxford University Press in the UK and in certain other countries

Published in the United States of America by Oxford University Press
198 Madison Avenue, New York, NY 10016, United States of America

British Library Cataloguing in Publication Data
Data available

Library of Congress Control Number: 2024946303

ISBN 9780198937494

DOI: 10.1093/9780198937524.001.0001

Printed and bound by
CPI Group (UK) Ltd, Croydon, CR0 4YY

Links to third party websites are provided by Oxford in good faith and
for information only. Oxford disclaims any responsibility for the materials
contained in any third party website referenced in this work.

The manufacturer's authorised representative in the EU for product safety is Oxford
University Press España S.A. of El Parque Empresarial San Fernando de Henares, Avenida de
Castilla, 2 – 28830 Madrid (www.oup.es/en or product.safety@oup.com). OUP España S.A.
also acts as importer into Spain of products made by the manufacturer.

Acknowledgements

This book began life as a PhD dissertation that I defended at Columbia University in April 2020. But in the years since, it has taken on a life of its own. I am grateful to teachers, mentors, and interlocutors who have influenced the book's conceptual framing and my wider outlook as a historian in especially foundational ways. My PhD supervisor, Susan Pedersen, gave me a training that meant that this could be a book concerned with politics and the state as well as gender. Though he had no formal role in my education, Ben Griffin has also substantially shaped my thinking about the politics of gender in modern British history. One of my first college professors, Margot Canaday, introduced me to the history of sexuality, as well as showing me for the first, pivotal time that it was possible to make a life in academia as a queer person doing queer research. It was a pleasure to return to, and to understand anew, her foundational work on sexuality and the state in the course of writing this book. Tony Grafton gave me an early grounding in intellectual and cultural history, as well as in how to be a humane and generous colleague and teacher. I continued to develop my thinking about the relationship of intellectual history and the history of education to the history of gender and sexuality in conversations with Paul Babinski and Ben Bernard. Camille Robcis pushed me to think beyond Britain, and Mo Moulton to think more queerly and transly; I am indebted to them both for feedback that challenged me at important moments in the development of this project.

The North American Council for British Studies, the Columbia University Graduate School of Arts and Sciences, and the Heyman Center for the Humanities at Columbia provided generous research funding that allowed me to visit archives across England and Scotland. Librarians and archivists at the Columbia Rare Books and Manuscripts Library, the University of Glasgow Archives, Royal Holloway College Archives, Edinburgh University Special Collections, Manchester University Special Collections, Liverpool University Archives, King's College London Archives, University College London Archives, Durham University Archives, the Cadbury Research Library at the University of Birmingham, King's College, Cambridge Archive Centre, Girton College Archives, Christ's College Archives, Somerville College Archives, Magdalen College Archives, Corpus Christi College, Oxford Archives, the Manuscripts Department at the Cambridge University Library, the Weston Library at Oxford, the Women's Library collection in the LSE Special Collections department, and the National Archives at Kew offered invaluable assistance. I am especially grateful to Julian Reid at Corpus Christi College, Oxford; Patricia McClure at King's College, Cambridge; Catherine Smith at Manchester; Clare Daniel at Glasgow; and Anne-Marie Purcell at Royal Holloway.

I wrote this book while a Junior Research Fellow at first Merton College and then Corpus Christi College, Oxford. Merton and Corpus gave me a kind of time, space, and (not least) money to which few early-career academics have access. That time, space, and money enriched the book in countless ways. I am deeply grateful to both colleges for their support. But more importantly, my privileged experience made me aware of the inequity of how academic resources are distributed. We should all have access to the working conditions that allow us to produce research of which we can feel proud at the pace that is necessary to treat important subjects with the depth that they deserve.

The thinking that informed this book would also not have been possible without my Oxford students. Students' demands for teaching provision in queer and trans histories brought me back to the LGBTQ+ history field and made this into a book about the history of sexuality. At the same time, my teaching in British social and political history 1680–present crystallized my sense of the book's contribution to its national field. I would especially like to thank the History and English undergraduates with whom I read *The Well of Loneliness* in winter 2021, the first four master's students who took my course Approaches to Queer and Trans Histories in winter 2022, and the Corpus second-year undergraduates whom I taught Disciplines of History in autumn 2023, for moments in the classroom that touched me profoundly. I am also grateful to Oxford colleagues—especially Christina de Bellaigue, Eli Bernstein, Matt Cook, Jane Garnett, Matthew Grimley, Dan Healey, Conrad Leyser, Sloan Mahone, James McDougall, Katherine Paugh, Catherine Phipps, Alice Raw, Mori Reithmayr, John Watts, and William Whyte— who offered mentorship, guidance, support, and collegiality. More recently, my colleagues at the University of Glasgow have given me a warm welcome and a smooth landing, and it has been a delight to finish the book here.

At Oxford University Press, Tom Stottor and Jo Spillane were informative, responsive, and reassuring guides to the editorial and production processes; I am especially grateful to Tom for his early enthusiasm for the project. The feedback from the two anonymous reviewers did much to shape the final manuscript, and credit must especially be given to Reviewer 2 for suggesting what is now the book's subtitle. Alma Igra organized a pandemic-era Zoom writing group, with members Nimrod Ben-Zeev, Freddy Foks, Devon Golaszewski, Zac Levine, Brianna Nofil, Jake Purcell, Andrew Seaton, Halimat Somotan, and Chika Tonooka. This group made all the difference in the book's early stages, and many of its members provided invaluable editorial feedback and moral support at subsequent points as well. Lucy Delap and Peter Mandler have been wise and supportive interlocutors about this project for many years. Any number of historians on social media came to my rescue time and again with bibliographic recommendations that made it possible to venture into a much wider range of fields and give my subject the scope that it deserves.

Long ago, Nancy Retter at Marshall Middle School and Margo Bergen, Joan Gass, Brady Kelso, and Irene Segade at Scripps Ranch High School believed in me as a historian and a writer when such ambitions seemed very remote. My most constant sources of support on every front have been Madeleine Picciotto, Don Rutherford, and Miranda Rutherford. My mother, Madeleine Picciotto, read the entire manuscript, but that is only a tiny slice of a lifetime in which she has always been there for me. It has been a gift to remain connected across time and distance to friends, including Nicholas Bellinson, Ben Bernard, Mette Bundvad, Maddy Case, Jack Doyle, Lynton Lees, Oren Lurie, George Morris, Brianna Nofil, Jake Purcell, and Emily Sung, who have taught me so much about what it means to live alongside and to love one another.

This book has a different name on the cover than I thought it would when I began to write it. Though it is not principally a work of trans history, it nevertheless has been shaped by the fact that I began to transition as I wrote it. Transition has been a leap of faith and it has been a great gift of grace. I am especially grateful to Jack Doyle and Zavier Nunn, who in a variety of ways made it all seem possible. The fight for trans liberation here in the UK and around the world continues. This book—for what it's worth—is dedicated to my comrades in that struggle.

Contents

Abbreviations

Archives

Birmingham	Cadbury Research Library, University of Birmingham
Bodleian	Bodleian Library, University of Oxford
BL	British Library
CUL	Cambridge University Library
Christ's	Christ's College, Cambridge Archives
Columbia	Rare Books and Manuscripts Library, Columbia University
CCC	Corpus Christi College, Oxford Archives
DUA	Durham University Archives
EUSC	University of Edinburgh Special Collections
Girton	Girton College, Cambridge Archives
GUA	Glasgow University Archives
KCC	King's College, Cambridge Archive Centre
KCL	King's College London Archives
LUA	Liverpool University Archives
LSE	Women's Library, London School of Economics
Magdalen	Magdalen College, Oxford Archives
MUA	Manchester University Archives
RHUL	Royal Holloway, University of London Archives
Somerville	Somerville College, Oxford Archives
TNA	The National Archives
UCL	University College London Archives

Other Abbreviations

AEW	Association for the Education of Women
BFUW	British Federation of University Women
CIE	Confédération Internationale des Étudiants
ELEA	Edinburgh Ladies' Educational Association
IFUW	International Federation of University Women
KCHSS	King's College for Household and Social Sciences
KCL	King's College London
KCW	King's College for Women
LSE	London School of Economics
NUS	National Union of Students
QMC	Queen Margaret College, Glasgow
SRC	Students' Representative Committee
UCL	University College London
UGC	University Grants Committee

Introduction

When Margery Fry was twenty-eight, she turned down a proposal of marriage. The year was 1902, and educated middle-class women like her typically understood the choice of a career versus marriage and family to be mutually exclusive. Instead of becoming an Oxford academic's wife, Fry became a university administrator in her own right: the warden of the first women's hall of residence at the University of Birmingham. And instead of marrying, she entered into a thirteen-year domestic partnership with a woman colleague that ended only with her partner's sudden and premature death.

Twenty-five years later, Fry had become the most powerful woman in UK higher education. Principal of Somerville College, Oxford, she was also the only woman on the seven-person University Grants Committee, the government agency that administered universities. After her partner died, she did not pursue any other relationships. Having claimed a career in higher education and a social niche on the basis of her unmarried status, she expressed scepticism about married women working in academia. She celebrated the women's college as a distinctive, gender-segregated space, even as she helped to administer a national higher education system organized around the model of the large, urban, non-residential, gender-integrated research university. Yet despite this longstanding commitment to college and career, by the time she was in her eighties, in the 1940s and 1950s, she often commented in interviews that the great tragedy of her life was that she had never had a heterosexual relationship and a family.[1]

Margery Fry's long life spanned a transformative period for higher education, for gender and sexuality, and for British politics and society more widely. When she was born in 1874, not only women but most men could not vote, and no university in the British Isles would grant women a degree. By the time she died in 1958—after universal suffrage and two world wars, at the height of the postwar welfare state—25 per cent of undergraduate students were women, but marriage and birth rates were also at their height. The norms that governed British society by the 1950s left Fry feeling alienated from her own life trajectory.

---

[1] Typescript transcript of interview of Fry on the BBC's Asia Programme, 1956, Margery Fry Papers Box 41, Folder 4, Somerville; Margery Fry, *The Single Woman* (London: Delisle, 1953); Sir James Marchant, ed., *What Life Has Taught Me: By Twenty-Five Distinguished Men and Women* (Long Acre and London: Odhams Press, 1948), 50–64. Fry's life is discussed in detail in Chapter 6.

This book is about how that happened: how, amid the many other transformations in British politics and society in the late nineteenth and early twentieth centuries, the material conditions of a newly expanded and gender-integrated university system helped to bring a pervasive norm of heterosexuality into being. In committee rooms, classrooms, dormitories, and nightclubs, ideals about what higher education was for and who should have access to it ran up against day-to-day realities: funding priorities, institutional governance, and the negotiation of interpersonal interactions within the shared space of a university community. Though early activists for women's higher education had assumed it would take place in separate institutions designed with women in mind, the gender integration of existing universities quickly emerged as a pragmatic, more efficient solution. As women and men students, faculty, and administrators worked out how to relate to one another in these mostly urban, non-residential universities, they tried out various models of gender-integrated sociability, but ultimately landed upon a highly ritualized, but also highly sexualized, model of complementary heterosexuality as offering a clear script through which to organize cross-gender interaction. In the process, they affirmed binary gender difference as central to what it meant to live in a mixed-gender society. On university campuses, people brought heterosexuality into being when women student government leaders at the University of Manchester installed a new electric lighting system to prevent their peers from turning out the lights during dances, when the *Glasgow University Magazine* published reviews critically appraising the grace and beauty of men students' drag performances, and when economics lecturer Margaret Miller's campaign to challenge a marriage bar at the University of Liverpool became a national cause célèbre.

As they went out dancing, gossiped about each other's sex lives, and fought for women to not have to make the choice Fry did between marriage and career, university students, faculty, and administrators elevated heterosexuality and the gender binary as normal and natural, more desirable than other ways of organizing intimacy, desire, and community. In the process, they made alternatives not impossible, but certainly less visible and less realizable. Historians continue to discuss the success or failure, the possibilities or limits, of women's inclusion in previously all-male institutions. This book, however, is about how norms for gender and sexuality were produced and reproduced: through the messy interactions of everyday institutional life, and at a historical moment when anxiety accrued around gender and sexuality as symptomatic of wider political and social instability.

Why Universities?

Universities offer us a space in which we can understand how middle-class British women and men worked out how to relate to one another across gender lines, how they created the hetero/homo and the male/female binaries in the process, and how these developing norms were part of the modern British state's changing conception of citizenship, to which gender difference, the male breadwinner ideal, and heterosexuality were central. In Britain over the course of the period 1860–1939, an eclectic patchwork of postsecondary institutions, with a range of governance and funding structures, missions, and student populations, became a substantially centralized and state-funded—and, incidentally, gender-integrated—national higher education system. Though only a small minority even of middle-class young adults attended university in this period, policy questions and cultural anxieties about higher education and about students loomed large in government and the media. Universities were increasingly conceptualized as key sites of contestation around state power and its limits, of intergenerational tension and conflict, and of acculturation into norms for middle-class adulthood, not least around gender and sexuality. As the first book-length study to consider English and Scottish universities alongside each other as elements of an increasingly cohesive national higher education system, this book connects both higher education reform and the construction of the hetero/homo and male/female binaries to the making of the twentieth-century British state.

Higher education expansion began in the early nineteenth century, with the founding of two new universities, the University of London in 1828 and the University of Durham in 1832, which joined the medieval foundations of Oxford, Cambridge, St Andrews, Glasgow, and Aberdeen and the early modern foundations of Edinburgh and Trinity College Dublin (see Table 0.1). The Scottish universities were formally nondenominational, with a long tradition of educating working- as well as middle-class students for careers in medicine, ministry, and the law.[2] But London was England's first non-Anglican and first non-residential university, beginning a slow movement towards opening up English higher education to students from a wider range of backgrounds. In the mid-nineteenth century, the explosion of population and accumulation of industrial capital in cities such as Bristol, Birmingham, Manchester, Liverpool, Leeds, and Sheffield led local elites to seek to found new institutions to meet demand for postsecondary education in these cities. Like London, these institutions saw access as part of their mission: keeping fees affordable, not requiring the extra expense and logistical hurdle of residence, and offering courses in more scientific and technical subjects with obvious professional applications in England's industrial cities.[3] While government sought to limit the number of chartered universities (a charter, granted through an Act of Parliament, allowed a university to confer degrees),

---

[2] Jennifer J. Carter and Donald J. Withrington, eds., *Scottish Universities: Distinctiveness and Diversity* (Edinburgh: John Donald, 1992), 7.

[3] William Whyte, *Redbrick: A Social and Architectural History of Britain's Civic Universities* (Oxford: Oxford University Press, 2015); R.D. Anderson, *Education and Opportunity in Victorian Scotland* (Edinburgh: Edinburgh University Press, 1989).

anyone could set up a college or institute, and offer non-degree certificates or allow students to sit the exams of the University of London as 'external' students.

But from the late nineteenth century, government began to take a more active role in developing a systematic higher education policy and accrediting institutions it deemed worthy of university status. In the 1890s and 1900s, several of the now-decades-old English 'civic' or 'redbrick' universities received charters. Government intervention also led to the founding of public university systems in Wales and Ireland. By this time, the typical UK university was an urban, non-residential research university, offering bachelor's degree courses in humanities, natural sciences, and applied sciences subjects, and in professional fields such as law and medicine. Though this model in some ways resembled the German 'Humboldtian' research university model that in the nineteenth century was seen as the gold standard worldwide, it also built on a longstanding tradition of urban, non-residential higher education in Scotland. It did, however, contrast with the Oxford and Cambridge model: these two universities, which traced their educational philosophy back to a monastic ideal, consisted of federations of residential colleges, required residence and celibacy as key elements of university life for both students and faculty, and required all students to study the Greek and Latin classics. In the late nineteenth century, Oxford and Cambridge enjoyed, if anything, increasing cachet as sites for the cultivation of an imperial governing elite. But within the larger context of UK higher education, they were also increasingly anomalous. By the late 1930s, two-thirds of men university students in England attended a London or 'redbrick' university.[4]

The London colleges and the civic universities brought higher education within reach of those in England and Wales who could not afford Oxford or Cambridge, and Scottish universities maintained their tradition of access. In 1890, the Board of Education introduced full scholarships for all English and Welsh university students who signed a pledge saying they would pursue teaching as a career upon graduation, and in 1901 Andrew Carnegie endowed a fund that made tuition free for all Scottish students attending Scottish universities. By the 1920s, the typical male Scottish or English redbrick student was middle- to lower-middle-class, with fathers in clerical or commercial occupations. As many as 20 per cent of non-Oxbridge students came from working-class backgrounds. In 1930, approximately half of the students at redbrick English, Welsh, and Scottish universities received some form of financial aid.[5] The London colleges and

---

[4] Carol Dyhouse, *Students: A Gendered History* (London: Routledge, 2006), 9; Whyte, *Redbrick*; Georgia Oman, *Higher Education and the Gendering of Space in England and Wales, 1869–1909* (Basingstoke: Palgrave Macmillan, 2023); Paul Deslandes, *Oxbridge Men: British Masculinity and the Undergraduate Experience* (Bloomington: Indiana University Press, 2005).

[5] BFUW Committee on Standards (1927–34), 5BFW/5/2/23, LSE; University Grants Committee, 'Report Including Returns from Universities and University Colleges in Receipt of Treasury Grant Academic Year 1928–1929', UGC/3/10, TNA, 7.

Oxbridge skewed somewhat more elite, with students' fathers more likely to work in the traditional professions.[6] With the cost of attending Oxford or Cambridge three times that of attending a Scottish university and twice that of an English redbrick, students with greater financial resources were over-represented there. But approximately 36 per cent of Oxbridge students received some form of scholarship as well.[7] The typical university student was middle-class, with social norms among students reflecting those common among other middle-class young people.[8] However, even most middle-class adolescents did not go to university. In the late 1930s, about 11 per cent of young people who pursued at least some secondary education did, or about 2 per cent of the overall eighteen-to-twenty-five age cohort—reflecting limited access to secondary education and the extent to which university degrees remained closely associated with qualification for specific professional careers, as well as the fact that the UK population was at this time overwhelmingly working-class.[9]

These middle-class students brought with them expectations for extracurricular life that they had encountered at secondary school, but also took advantage of the greater independence that adulthood and postsecondary education afforded. From the late nineteenth century, they founded student unions, sports teams, debating societies, theatre ensembles, Christian organizations, and Officers' Training Corps regiments. They also visited pubs, coffeehouses, theatres, cinemas, and brothels, the majority living either at home or in private rented accommodation where they experienced a relative lack of surveillance. Student culture—and, for that matter, faculty culture—could inhere in specific fields of study, as when rivalries arose between arts and sciences students, or the close-knit social ties of subject communities fostered socialization between students and faculty.[10] But it also increasingly became identified with life outside the classroom, with both students and outside observers perceiving 'the student' as a class-specific and lifecycle-specific category of person with a distinctive way of life.

---

[6] Dyhouse, *Students: A Gendered History*, 7–16; R.D. Anderson, *Universities and Elites in Britain since 1800* (Cambridge: Cambridge University Press, 1992).

[7] Anderson, *Universities and Elites*, 10–11; M.C. Curthoys and Janet Howarth, 'Origins and Destinations: The Social Mobility of Oxford Men and Women', in *The History of the University of Oxford, Volume VII: Nineteenth-Century Oxford, Part 2*, ed. M.G. Brock and M.C. Curthoys (Oxford: Clarendon Press, 2000), 571–95; Carol Dyhouse, *No Distinction of Sex? Women in British Universities 1870–1939* (London: University College London Press, 1995), 27–8; BFUW Committee on Standards.

[8] For a useful characterization of this from a different but related national context see Paul Axelrod, *Making a Middle Class: Student Life in English Canada during the Thirties* (Montreal and Kingston: McGill–Queen's University Press, 1990).

[9] Dyhouse, *Students: A Gendered History*, 4; Gillian Sutherland, 'Education', in *The Cambridge Social History of Britain, 1750–1950, Volume 3*, ed. F.M.L. Thompson (Cambridge: Cambridge University Press, 1990), 119–69, at 162.

[10] For some examples of discipline-specific cultures see Laura Kelly, *Irish Medical Education and Student Culture, c. 1850–1950* (Liverpool: Liverpool University Press, 2020); Caroline M. Barron and Joel T. Rosenthal, eds., *Thomas Frederick Tout (1855–1929): Refashioning History for the Twentieth Century* (London: Institute of Historical Research, 2019).

Another critical aspect of the national integration and state-funded expansion of universities is that politicians and policymakers increasingly conceived of higher education as having strategic importance for Britain's place in the world. Historians have tended to treat the higher education systems of the four home nations in isolation, or else have situated English higher education within the context of the universities of the British Empire, especially those in the settler colonies of Canada, Australia, New Zealand, and South Africa.[11] Many university administrators and policymakers were certainly ardent imperialists who valued the role that metropolitan British higher education played in strengthening imperial ties. Imperial networks ensured that faculty and students circulated between colonies and metropole. The most elite universities within Britain attracted the greatest numbers of overseas students—by 1910, a quarter of Oxford students came from beyond the British Isles, owing in part to the Rhodes Scholarships—but throughout the period the average national percentage of overseas students stayed steady at around 10 per cent, most from India and the settler colonies but also including some from other parts of the British Empire, the United States, Europe, and East Asia.[12] Administrators and policymakers were preoccupied with international comparisons and the role of higher education in geopolitics, especially with reference to Germany and the United States.

At the same time, higher education policy directed from Westminster had a UK rather than a wider imperial scope. Faculty and students increasingly understood themselves as belonging to a community—as well as formal professional and student organizations—that spanned the UK. Efficient communication and transportation networks knit together faculty, students, and administrators across the British Isles. The expanding mass media, including tabloid newspapers and newsreels with national reach, disseminated a cohesive vision of 'the student' as an engaging subject of human-interest reporting. What is more, from the turn of the twentieth century, the Treasury increasingly heeded calls for financial intervention from civic university vice-chancellors worried about their institutions' solvency. As new conceptions of the strategic importance of a national higher education system began to emerge in the context of the Edwardian political ideology of 'national efficiency', and as international competition escalated before the First World War and geopolitical realignment followed in its wake, Liberal policymakers called for this case-by-case funding to be formalized and systematized. By the time of the founding of the University Grants Committee, the first national

[11] Tamson Pietsch, *Empire of Scholars: Universities, Networks and the British Academic World, 1850–1939* (Manchester: Manchester University Press, 2013); Deslandes, *Oxbridge Men*. For systemic accounts of English higher education see Whyte, *Redbrick* and Keith Vernon, *Universities and the State in England, 1850–1939* (Abingdon: Routledge, 2004); for Scotland see Anderson, *Education and Opportunity*. Oman's *Higher Education and the Gendering of Space* treats England and Wales together. For Ireland, see Kelly, *Irish Medical Education*.

[12] Hilary Perraton, *A History of Foreign Students in Britain* (Basingstoke: Palgrave Macmillan, 2014).

Table 0.1 Chartered universities in the United Kingdom and the Republic of Ireland, 1935.

University	Year of foundation	Year women admitted to degrees
University of Oxford	c.1200	1920
University of Cambridge	c.1225	1948
University of St Andrews	1411	1892
University of Glasgow	1451	1893
University of Aberdeen	1495	1892
University of Edinburgh	1583	1892
Trinity College Dublin	1592	1904
University of Durham	1832	1895
University of London (11 constituent colleges and numerous Schools)	1836	1878
University of Wales (4 constituent colleges)	1893	1894
University of Birmingham	1900	1901
University of Manchester	1903 (founded as Owens College, 1846)	1897 (as Owens College, part of Victoria University)
University of Liverpool	1903	1897 (as part of Victoria University)
University of Leeds	1904	1897 (as part of Victoria University)
University of Sheffield	1905	1905 (coeducational from receipt of university charter)
Queen's University Belfast	1908	1882
National University of Ireland (3 constituent colleges)	1908	1908
University of Bristol	1909 (founded as Bristol University College, 1876)	1876
University of Reading	1926	1926 (coeducational from foundation)

government higher-education policy body, in 1919, politicians and senior civil servants conceptualized UK higher education as a national system that served national strategic needs. To illustrate this, in this book I focus on the universities of Glasgow, Edinburgh, Manchester, Durham, Liverpool, and Birmingham; several University of London colleges; and Oxford and Cambridge. I argue that the increasing cohesion of British higher education has something to tell us about the national history of the UK and the making of the twentieth-century British state, while still recognizing that this national history unfolded in an imperial and global context.

This process of expansion, reform, and nationalization was also substantially structured by questions of gender. In the late nineteenth and early twentieth centuries, higher education systems across western Europe and North America faced the question of whether and how institutions that had for centuries been normatively masculine might include women. In places like France, Germany, and Scandinavia with fully public university systems, and in the context of the significant expansion of public higher education in the United States following the 1862 Morrill Act, women's formal admission to universities on equal terms to men was one part of a larger process of gendered reconfiguration of the state and citizenship.[13] In a wider European context, Britain was relatively early in making at least limited provision for the higher education of women.[14] But what is especially distinctive about the British case was how closely this was entwined with a particular trajectory of wider systemic higher education reform, in keeping with a larger mid-nineteenth-century worldview that saw liberal education as intimately connected with claims to citizenship and the franchise.[15]

The early-to-mid-nineteenth-century wave of expansion of higher education in England also saw several experiments to provide for the higher education of women. As early as the 1840s, some London education activists leveraged the relative lack of regulation in the sector to establish small, independent women's colleges, some residential and some non-residential. Others campaigned for women to be admitted to classes at existing non-residential universities in Scotland and England. From the 1870s, still others founded residential colleges in Oxford and Cambridge patterned on the model of the men's colleges, and lobbied for university recognition. They achieved some measures of inclusion as early as the 1880s,

[13] R.D. Anderson, *European Universities from the Enlightenment to 1914* (Oxford: Oxford University Press, 2004), 256–73; Patricia M. Mazón, *Gender and the Modern Research University: The Admission of Women to German Higher Education, 1865–1914* (Stanford: Stanford University Press, 2003); Ning de Coninck-Smith, 'Gender Encounters University—University Encounters Gender: Affective Archives, Aarhus University, Denmark, 1928–1953', *Women's History Review* 29, no. 3 (2020): 413–28; Christine D. Myers, *University Coeducation in the Victorian Era: Inclusion in the United States and the United Kingdom* (Basingstoke: Palgrave Macmillan, 2010); Lynn D. Gordon, *Gender and Higher Education in the Progressive Era* (New Haven: Yale University Press, 1990).

[14] Anderson, *European Universities*, 257.

[15] Oman, *Higher Education and the Gendering of Space*, 10.

though Oxford and Cambridge would not grant women and women's colleges completely equal membership until 1920 and 1948 respectively. But this was atypical. Other universities readily admitted women on the same terms as men, beginning with the University of London in 1878—though this was not always the desired outcome of women's-education activists, who sought to provide for what they saw as women's distinct educational needs. By the time Trinity College Dublin admitted women to degrees in 1904, all universities in the British Isles except Oxford and Cambridge were formally gender-integrated (see Table 0.1).

Yet the earliest cohorts of women students were small. Britain still had a rigidly gender-segregated labour market with very limited professional opportunities for women, and it was not considered possible for middle-class women to both marry and pursue a career. By 1910, women were a quarter of those graduating with bachelor's degrees, but that percentage would not increase substantially until the 1970s.[16] Due in part to quotas that Oxford and Cambridge imposed on women students, over 80 per cent of English women students attended non-Oxbridge universities.[17] But even in these institutions that advertised their formal equality, the first generation of women students did not always in practice have equal access to classes and university facilities. They were subject to onerous restrictions around matters such as curfews and chaperonage, and often chose to lead largely gender-segregated social lives.[18]

After the turn of the twentieth century, as social mores changed, women and men students increasingly sought (albeit not always successfully) to relate to one another across gender lines. But themes of adversity have remained pervasive in secondary literature. Early activists for women's higher education, especially in Oxford and Cambridge, were effective chroniclers of their own movement, establishing a narrative of struggle to overcome sexist obstacles to inclusion that culminated in the triumphant admission of women to degrees.[19] Subsequent historians have variously emphasized the homosocial cultures that flourished in gender-segregated women's colleges and their relationship to the women's movement of the late nineteenth and early twentieth centuries, or women faculty's and students' experiences of the gender inequalities that persisted in formally gender-integrated institutions.[20] The rise of the history of masculinities has also led to important studies of student masculinities and their role in the perpetuation

---

[16] Dyhouse, *No Distinction of Sex?*, 248.   [17] Dyhouse, *Students: A Gendered History*, 8–9.

[18] Oman, *Higher Education and the Gendering of Space*; Dyhouse, *No Distinction of Sex?*

[19] Emily Davies, *The Higher Education of Women* (London: Alexander Strahan, 1866); Annie M.A.H. Rogers, *Degrees by Degrees: The Story of the Admission of Oxford Women Students to Membership of the University* (Oxford: Oxford University Press, 1938); Vera Brittain, *The Women at Oxford: A Fragment of History* (London: Harrap, 1960).

[20] For the former see Rita McWilliams-Tullberg, *Women at Cambridge: A Men's University— Though of a Mixed Type* (London: Victor Gollancz, 1975); Martha Vicinus, *Independent Women: Work and Community for Single Women, 1850–1920* (London: Virago, 1985); Gillian Sutherland, *Faith, Duty and the Power of Mind: The Cloughs and Their Circle* (Cambridge: Cambridge University Press, 2006); Gillian Sutherland, *In Search of the New Woman: Middle-Class Women and Work in*

of patriarchal power structures, largely in the context of gender-segregated institutions and especially egregious displays of misogyny.[21] This book connects many of these dots: between the different experiences of gendered sociability that women and men historical actors had, both within and across gender lines; between individual institutions and national structures and cultures of higher education; between historical actors' aspirations for university life and the compromises made in day-to-day existence.

In so doing, it demonstrates that the expansion and reform of British higher education was fundamentally structured by questions of gender. Such questions arose when women fought for inclusion in all-male institutions against masculine opposition, but also when women's higher-education activists sought to preserve gender-segregated spaces, as many did, rather than cooperate with men administrators who wished to move towards more 'efficient' gender-integrated institutions. The evidence of daily life on urban non-residential campuses in particular suggests that women faculty, students, and other reformers intentionally leveraged gender norms to further a wide range of personal and political goals, as likely to affirm and work within structures of power as to challenge them. As they did so, they proved active participants in a pivotal moment for the creation of new, extremely influential and consequential, ways of thinking about gender and sexuality.

Gender and Sexuality Trouble in Interwar Britain

This book braids together several different stories one could tell about what happened to gender and sexuality in early-twentieth-century Britain: a story about the gendered logics at the heart of the nascent welfare state; a story about how expanded educational opportunities opened up new career and life trajectories for middle-class women; a story about urbanization, youth culture, and youth sexuality; and a story about the coalescence of new expert discourses, subjectivities, and communities that alternately pathologized and offered possibilities for non-normative gender and sexual expression. It brings political, economic, and social histories of women and gender into conversation with the history of heterosexuality and the 'new British queer history' to show, through the lens of universities and

---

Britain 1870–1914 (Cambridge: Cambridge University Press, 2015); for the latter see Dyhouse, *Students: A Gendered History*; Oman, *Higher Education and the Gendering of Space*.

[21] Dyhouse, *Students: A Gendered History*; Deslandes, *Oxbridge Men*; Sonja Levsen, 'Constructing Elite Identities: University Students, Military Masculinity and the Consequences of the Great War in Britain and Germany', *Past & Present*, no. 198 (2008): 147–83; Thomas Weber, *Our Friend 'The Enemy': Elite Education in Britain and Germany before World War I* (Stanford: Stanford University Press, 2008); Kelly, *Irish Medical Education*. For a key comparison from the US case see Nicholas Syrett, *The Company He Keeps: A History of White College Fraternities* (Chapel Hill: University of North Carolina Press, 2009).

with a more critical approach to the construction of the male/female binary, that the increasing centrality of heterosexuality to British politics and society was entwined with the impulse to shore up essentialized conceptions of gender difference as against anxieties about their demise.[22]

Historians working across national contexts such as France, Germany, and the United States, as well as Britain, have shown that assumptions about gender difference undergirded late-nineteenth- and early-twentieth-century politics, especially when it came to anxieties about citizenship and democratization, efforts to establish political stability after wars or other moments of extreme upheaval, and the expansion of the state into the realm of social policy.[23] In Britain in particular, an ideal of respectable masculinity that inhered in the capacity for disinterested rationality and the ability to provide for one's dependents had informed claims to citizenship and the expansion of the franchise from the early nineteenth century.[24] In this context, women's activists who sought to make claims for women's economic independence, access to education, and inclusion in the state and citizenship often did so in terms that assumed fundamental differences between the sexes. In the years before the First World War, the New Liberal governments introduced new social policies such as health insurance, unemployment insurance, and pensions that made unprecedented state commitments to funding welfare benefits but linked those benefits to employment status and, implicitly, respectable masculinity. When an increasingly visible and radical women's suffrage movement lobbied for the vote, it also capitalized on gendered discourses of citizenship, staking claims to the franchise on the basis of women's moral purity, martyrdom to the cause, and ability to contribute a gendered perspective to policy questions such as maternal and child welfare.[25] For some middle-class women, education and new feminized professions—teaching, social work, politics and local government— offered a space for new forms of intimacy and community between women that could prove a powerful, radical challenge to the imperatives of marriage and

---

[22] On the 'new British queer history' see Chris Waters, 'Distance and Desire in the New British Queer History', *GLQ: A Journal of Lesbian and Gay Studies* 14, no. 1 (December 2007): 139–55; Brian Lewis, ed., *British Queer History: New Approaches and Perspectives* (Manchester: Manchester University Press, 2013).

[23] Judith Surkis, *Sexing the Citizen: Morality and Masculinity in France, 1870–1920* (Ithaca: Cornell University Press, 2006); Mary Louise Roberts, *Civilization without Sexes: Reconstructing Gender in Postwar France, 1917–1927* (Chicago: University of Chicago Press, 1994); Laurie Marhoefer, *Sex and the Weimar Republic: German Homosexual Emancipation and the Rise of the Nazis* (Toronto: University of Toronto Press, 2015); Margot Canaday, *The Straight State: Sexuality and Citizenship in Twentieth-Century America* (Princeton: Princeton University Press, 2009).

[24] Anna Clark, *The Struggle for the Breeches: Gender and the Making of the British Working Class* (Berkeley: University of California Press, 1995); Kathryn Gleadle, *Borderline Citizens: Women, Gender, and Political Culture in Britain 1815–1867* (Oxford: Oxford University Press, 2009); Catherine Hall, Keith McClelland, and Jane Rendall, *Defining the Victorian Nation: Class, Race, Gender and the Reform Act of 1867* (Cambridge: Cambridge University Press, 2000); Elaine Hadley, *Living Liberalism: Practical Citizenship in Mid-Victorian Britain* (Chicago: University of Chicago Press, 2010).

[25] Sandra Stanley Holton, *Feminism and Democracy: Women's Suffrage and Reform Politics in Britain 1900–1918* (Cambridge: Cambridge University Press, 1986).

motherhood, but one that saw gender segregation as the primary avenue of escape from patriarchy's logics.[26]

The First World War licensed further expansion of the role of the state in the economy and planning. It also seemed to many contemporaries to lead to profound challenges to gender norms: from the entry of women into new occupations to replace men serving in the military, to servicemen's experiences of disability and trauma. This fed into perceptions of the immediate postwar years as a time of radical upheaval. Industrial action, anticolonial uprisings in Ireland and elsewhere in the British Empire, and economic crisis generated fears about the stability of the political and social order. Conservatives projected their anxieties about this upheaval onto some of its most visible symbols: single, independent young women who earned their own living; people of colour, including colonial ex-servicemen; and people who visibly transgressed gender norms, both those who belonged to queer subcultures and those who did not.[27] Landmark legislation in the immediate postwar era was entwined with efforts to restore gender norms. The Representation of the People Act 1918 enfranchised some women, but also all men over twenty-one except conscientious objectors and all men over eighteen who had fought in the war, thus placing military masculinity at the centre of claims to citizenship. The Restoration of Prewar Practices Act removed women from skilled industrial occupations in order to give ex-servicemen these kinds of jobs. Family allowances and pensions for the widows of servicemen were the first state benefits to be distributed directly to women—but women qualified for them based on their husbands' wartime sacrifice.[28]

By the late 1920s, desire for restoration of national political and social order fed into the ascendancy of a new kind of consensus Conservative politics under the leadership of Prime Minister Stanley Baldwin: avowedly anti-Communist, populist, offering a fantasy of stability and domestic peace; but also distinctively modern, aided by the ability of a new mass media to mobilize a new mass electorate. Women, who achieved the franchise on the same terms as men in 1928,

---

[26] Vicinus, *Independent Women*.

[27] Jon Lawrence, 'Forging a Peaceable Kingdom: War, Violence, and Fear of Brutalization in Post-First World War Britain', *Journal of Modern History* 75, no. 3 (September 2003): 557–89; Lucy Bland, 'White Women and Men of Colour: Miscegenation Fears in Britain after the Great War', *Gender & History* 17, no. 1 (2005): 29–61; James J. Nott, '"The Plague Spots of London": William Joynson-Hicks, the Conservative Party, and the Campaign against London's Nightclubs, 1924–29', in *Classes, Cultures, and Politics: Essays on British History for Ross McKibbin*, ed. Claire V. Griffiths, James J. Nott, and William Whyte (Oxford: Oxford University Press, 2011), 227–46; Stuart Middleton, 'The Crisis of Democracy in Interwar Britain', *The Historical Journal* 66, no. 1 (February 2023): 186–209.

[28] Nicoletta F. Gullace, *'The Blood of Our Sons': Men, Women, and the Renegotiation of British Citizenship during the Great War* (Basingstoke: Palgrave Macmillan, 2002); Susan Kingsley Kent, *Making Peace: The Reconstruction of Gender in Interwar Britain* (Princeton: Princeton University Press, 1993); Susan Pedersen, *Family, Dependence, and the Origins of the Welfare State: Britain and France, 1914–1945* (Cambridge: Cambridge University Press, 1993).

overwhelmingly voted Conservative.[29] The literary critic Alison Light has offered the framework of 'conservative modernity' to characterize the cultural politics of this moment, highlighting how middle-class women in particular participated actively in the reaffirmation of the feminine domestic sphere.[30] When the war-time coalition and then postwar Labour governments planned an expanded welfare state during and after the Second World War, they built on this longer history of norms for responsible citizenship organized around the male breadwinner ideal.[31] Throughout the first half of the twentieth century, then, as government incorporated universities into an expanded state, they also became part of a gendered state, in which claims to citizenship were entwined with adherence to norms for masculinity and femininity.

This story—of a state that came to incorporate (white, middle-class) women into citizenship while reinscribing the logic of gender difference—has often been told in a way that highlights the importance of gender as a central analytic. But queer historians and queer theorists have long understood that the categories into which societies organize gender and sexuality change over time. In particular, they have shown that the categories of 'homosexuality', 'heterosexuality', and 'sexual orientation' are distinctively modern inventions, whose rise to become dominant frameworks must be explained.[32] As the field of British queer history has developed over the last several decades, it has examined the complex interplay between normative regulatory structures and individual subjectivities, drawing attention to the variety and historical specificity of different models for making sense (or not) of queer sex, desire, relationships, and intimacies.[33]

---

[29] David Jarvis, 'Mrs Maggs and Betty: The Conservative Appeal to Women Voters in the 1920s', *Twentieth Century British History* 5, no. 2 (January 1994): 129–52; Philip Williamson, *Stanley Baldwin: Conservative Leadership and National Values* (Cambridge: Cambridge University Press, 1999); Ross McKibbin, *Classes and Cultures: England 1918–1951* (Oxford: Oxford University Press, 1998); Ross McKibbin, *Parties and People: England, 1914–1951* (Oxford: Oxford University Press, 2010).

[30] Alison Light, *Forever England: Femininity, Literature, and Conservatism between the Wars* (London: Routledge, 1991).

[31] Adrian Kane-Galbraith, 'Male Breadwinners of "Doubtful Sex": Trans Men and the Welfare State, 1954–1970', in *Men and Masculinities in Modern Britain: A History for the Present*, ed. Matt Houlbrook, Katie Jones, and Ben Mechen (Manchester: Manchester University Press, 2024), 49–66; Teri Chettiar, *The Intimate State: How Emotional Life Became Political in Welfare-State Britain* (Oxford: Oxford University Press, 2022); Carolyn Steedman, *Landscape for a Good Woman: A Story of Two Lives* (New Brunswick, NJ: Rutgers University Press, 1986); Ina Zweiniger-Bargielowska, 'Rationing, Austerity and the Conservative Party Recovery after 1945', *The Historical Journal* 37, no. 1 (March 1994): 173–97; Pedersen, *Family, Dependence.*

[32] For foundational framings of this see Eve Kosofsky Sedgwick, *Epistemology of the Closet* (Berkeley: University of California Press, 1990); David Halperin, 'How to Do the History of Male Homosexuality', *GLQ: A Journal of Lesbian and Gay Studies* 6, no. 1 (2000): 87–121; Jonathan Ned Katz, *The Invention of Heterosexuality* (New York: Penguin, 1995).

[33] Jeffrey Weeks, *Coming Out: Homosexual Politics in Britain, from the Nineteenth Century to the Present* (London: Quartet Books, 1977); Jeffrey Weeks, *Sex, Politics and Society: The Regulation of Sexuality since 1800* (London: Longman, 1981); H.G. Cocks, *Nameless Offences: Homosexual Desire in the Nineteenth Century* (London: I.B. Tauris, 2003); Lewis, ed., *British Queer History*; Waters, 'Distance and Desire'; Laura Doan, *Disturbing Practices: History, Sexuality, and Women's Experience*

Putting the approach of the 'new British queer history' into conversation with a literature about the political and social history of women and gender, however, affords new insights that extend but in some ways depart from a focus on sexual subjectivities. In this book, rather than zeroing in on minority gender and sexuality subjectivities and communities, I show that the normative and the anti-normative were mutually constitutive, and that the contingent circumstances that contributed to the rise of heterosexuality concomitantly marginalized alternatives. I also foreground the relationship between sexuality and gender: showing—in part through giving trans stories about gender equal weight with queer stories about sexuality, and in part through reading queer history alongside the social and political history of women and gender—that the hetero/homo binary emerged from widespread cultural anxiety about managing the boundaries of the male/female binary.[34] In so doing, I focus on two themes that historians have highlighted as especially important for the making of modern gender and sexuality paradigms: urbanization and the development of consumer culture and youth culture; and the early 1920s as a moment of exceptional anxiety and moral panic around the perceived instability of the gender order.

Lesbian and gay history and theory has established the growth of cities and capitalism from the mid-nineteenth century as foundational to the emergence of self-conscious gay identity and community in many western national contexts.[35] In the British case, historians have shown that the growth of London as an imperial metropolis from the late nineteenth century was important to the formation of queer masculine subcultures: as a site of contact, including across lines of class and race, and as a site of sexual scandal and crisis around the definition of regulatory categories.[36] So, too, did the city afford a space for the development of queer feminine intimacies, as new opportunities to leave home and enter education and

of Modern War (Chicago: University of Chicago Press, 2013); Matt Houlbrook, Queer London: Perils and Pleasures in the Sexual Metropolis, 1918–1957 (Chicago: University of Chicago Press, 2005); Anna Clark, Alternative Histories of the Self: A Cultural History of Sexuality and Secrets (New York: Bloomsbury, 2017); Sharon Marcus, Between Women: Friendship, Desire, and Marriage in Victorian England (Princeton: Princeton University Press, 2007); Helen Smith, Masculinity, Class and Same-Sex Desire in Industrial England, 1895–1957 (Basingstoke: Palgrave Macmillan, 2015); Mo Moulton, '"Both Your Sexes": A Non-Binary Approach to Gender History, Trans Studies and the Making of the Self in Modern Britain', History Workshop Journal, no. 95 (Spring 2023): 75–100.

[34] On trans approaches to a more expansive history of gender see Kit Heyam, Before We Were Trans: A New History of Gender (London: Basic, 2022); Moulton, 'Both Your Sexes'.

[35] John d'Emilio, 'Capitalism and Gay Identity', in The Lesbian and Gay Studies Reader, ed. Henry Abelove, Michèle Aina Barale, and David M. Halperin (New York: Routledge, 1993), 467–76; George Chauncey, Gay New York: Gender, Urban Culture, and the Making of the Gay Male World 1890–1940 (New York: Basic, 1994); Samuel Delaney, Times Square Red, Times Square Blue (New York: New York University Press, 1999).

[36] Matt Cook, London and the Culture of Homosexuality, 1885–1914 (Cambridge: Cambridge University Press, 2003); Morris Kaplan, Sodom on the Thames: Sex, Love, and Scandal in Wilde Times (Ithaca: Cornell University Press, 2005); Houlbrook, Queer London; Nadia Ellis, 'Black Migrants, White Queers and the Archive of Inclusion in Postwar London', Interventions 17, no. 6 (November 2015): 893–915; Katie Hindmarch-Watson, 'Sex, Services, and Surveillance: The Cleveland Street Scandal Revisited', History Compass 14, no. 6 (June 2016): 283–91. Cf. British queer history that has

work disrupted middle-class women's ties to their families of origin, provided contexts in which desire and domestic partnerships between women could flourish, and led to new, if fraught, kinds of intimacy across class lines.[37]

At the same time, historians have also identified the changing structure of the economy and society in the early twentieth century as central to the development of heterosexual identities and communities. If the city became figured as a newly frightening site of sexual predation for white middle-class women, it could also—especially after the turn of the twentieth century—be a site for the creation of new kinds of sexual autonomy and independence.[38] Among middle-class British young people, a nineteenth-century norm of idealized romantic courtship in which family members and wider social convention carefully surveilled and regulated physical contact between couples gave way, by the First World War, to more sexualized conceptions of dating and courtship.[39] Across lines of class and region, the migration of young adults to cities, new employment opportunities for young women in particular, rising school-leaving age and age of marriage, and rising wages all allowed for the development of a commercial youth leisure culture centred on pleasure-oriented dating and sex outside of and in a life stage prior to marriage.[40] Seeing the city—including cities other than London—as a space for young-adult independence and self-fashioning (albeit mediated through structures such as capitalism) can help us to apprehend not only discrete histories of homosexuality and heterosexuality, but also how homosexual and heterosexual cultures developed alongside each other as a mutually constitutive, distinctively modern formation for organizing sex and sociability. I show in this book that the expansion of urban, non-residential, gender-integrated universities is a part of this story.

As in a wider literature that has highlighted the political and social instability of the years immediately following the First World War, British queer history has identified the early 1920s as a key moment of disjuncture or crisis for the British gender order, when to many observers sexual deviance and gender

---

sought to reorient analysis away from London, e.g. Smith, *Masculinity, Class and Same-Sex Desire* and Matt Cook and Alison Oram, *Queer beyond London* (Manchester: Manchester University Press, 2022).

[37] Sutherland, *In Search of the New Woman*; Vicinus, *Independent Women*; Seth Koven, *The Match Girl and the Heiress* (Princeton: Princeton University Press, 2014).

[38] On sexual anxieties in nineteenth-century London see the foundational work of Judith Walkowitz: *City of Dreadful Delight: Narratives of Sexual Danger in Late-Victorian London* (Chicago: University of Chicago Press, 1992); 'Going Public: Shopping, Street Harassment, and Streetwalking in Late Victorian London', *Representations* 62 (April 1998): 1–30.

[39] Maggie Kalenak, '"Consider Yourself Kissed": Intimacy, Engagement, and Material Culture in Nineteenth-Century Middle-Class English Love Letters', *Journal of Victorian Culture* 28, no. 2 (April 2023): 243–62; Nancy Christie and Michael Gauvreau, *Bodies, Love, and Faith in the First World War: Dardanella and Peter* (Basingstoke: Palgrave Macmillan, 2018).

[40] Claire Langhamer, *Women's Leisure in England 1920–1960* (Manchester: Manchester University Press, 2000); Simon Szreter and Kate Fisher, *Sex before the Sexual Revolution* (Cambridge: Cambridge University Press, 2010); Selina Todd, 'Young Women, Work, and Leisure in Interwar England', *The Historical Journal* 48, no. 3 (2005): 789–809.

nonconformity seemed like palpable expressions of political and social instability. A newly powerful popular press directed the public's attention to sensationalist stories of obscenity trials, 'sex changes', and dens of vice like drag balls and night-clubs. Though historians have hitherto largely told these stories with a focus on the emergence of gay and lesbian identities and communities—on sexuality—a closer examination of many key cases suggests that 1920s moral panic tended to revolve more around threats to the stability of the *gender* order: an 'obscene' novel about a gender-crossing 'invert'; sensationalist newspaper stories about 'women' who 'masqueraded' as men; 'painted boys' whose use of cosmetics signified their degeneracy.[41] The fear that, in the words of a 1926 popular song, 'It's hard to tell 'em apart today' seemed expressive of a moment in which many felt that traditional social structures were under threat.[42]

Backlash against gender nonconformity and gender crossing took a variety of forms. In student culture as more widely, some young men, many of them ex-servicemen, turned to misogynistic violence to 'reclaim' their society from what they saw as feminine degeneration: with cis women, trans women, and feminine men all becoming targets of a form of aggression that, for some, also lent itself to fascist and fascist-adjacent politics.[43] But for a larger group, including many women, the ethos of 'conservative modernity' offered a respectable, reassuring avenue through which to assert values of 'normality' and 'decency' and the stabil-ity of the gender binary.[44] In universities, young adults drew on tropes from lit-erature and film as well as from expert medical and psychological discourses to idealize norms for cross-gender interaction that emphasized complementary sexual relationships founded on a stable gender binary. Amidst uncertainty about how to negotiate cross-gender social interaction, both women and men students landed on heterosexuality as a practical solution. Its heavily ritualized, scripted

---

[41] Doan, *Disturbing Practices*; Laura Doan, *Fashioning Sapphism: The Origins of a Modern English Lesbian Culture* (New York: Columbia University Press, 2001); Houlbrook, *Queer London*; Matt Houlbrook, '"The Man with the Powder Puff" in Interwar London', *The Historical Journal* 50, no. 1 (2007): 145–71; Alison Oram, *Her Husband Was a Woman! Women's Gender-Crossing in Modern British Popular Culture* (London: Routledge, 2007); James Vernon, '"For Some Queer Reason": The Trials and Tribulations of Colonel Barker's Masquerade in Interwar Britain', *Signs* 26, no. 1 (2000): 37–62.

[42] For a discussion of the song see Doan, *Fashioning Sapphism*, xiv. Emma Heaney has identified the trans woman as a characteristic signifier of this anxiety about modernity and degeneration, a read-ing that Matt Houlbrook echoes (if within a queer rather than a trans framework) in his analysis of the 'man with the powder puff'. Emma Heaney, *The New Woman: Literary Modernism, Queer Theory, and the Trans Feminine Allegory* (Evanston: Northwestern University Press, 2017).

[43] Julie Gottlieb, 'Britain's New Fascist Men: The Aestheticization of Brutality in British Fascist Propaganda', in *The Culture of Fascism: Visions of the Far Right in Britain*, ed. Julie Gottlieb and Thomas P. Linehan (London: I.B. Tauris, 2004), 83–99; Julie Gottlieb, 'Body Fascism in Britain: Building the Blackshirt in the Inter-War Period', *Contemporary European History* 20, no. 2 (May 2011): 111–36; Tony Collins, 'Return to Manhood: The Cult of Masculinity and the British Union of Fascists', *The International Journal of the History of Sport* 16, no. 4 (1 December 1999): 145–62.

[44] Laura Doan, 'Marie Stopes's Wonderful Rhythm Charts: Normalizing the Natural', *Journal of the History of Ideas* 78, no. 4 (October 2017): 595–620.

tropes offered an accessible paradigm: less threatening both than masculine violence and than more amorphous conceptions of 'Platonic friendship', and neutralizing the threat of more radical challenges to the gender order. Students' articulation of heterosexual scripts—through sex and relationships, as well as through fiction, theatre, and gossip columns—enshrined this norm of pleasure-oriented sex and dating, founded on an essential complementary gender binary, as central to the purpose of university life.

In the interwar period, this paradigm became so hegemonic as to marginalize and silence other forms of sociability and intimacy: those that prioritized homo-sociality and gender segregation, those that allowed for non-sexual cross-gender friendship, and those that allowed for gender diversity and gender crossing. This especially affected the extent to which women academics and students could conceptualize academia as a life path offering an alternative to the imperatives of marriage and reproduction. But there was one exception to this rule: the category of male homosexuality. As the men's colleges of Oxford and Cambridge became outliers within the wider landscape of gender-integrated higher education, some men within these colleges turned to theorizing erotic desire between men as a way of articulating the value of intimate, gender-segregated residential education as against the encroachment of gender integration and heterosexuality. Their formulation of homosexuality was reactionary, conservative, and invested in ideas of essential differences between the sexes. Both heterosexuality and male homo-sexuality, I suggest, gained new salience in the interwar period as paradigms for conceptualizing gender and sexuality that could reassert the stability of binary gender difference, at the expense of a wider set of possibilities for sex, relation-ships, desire, intimacy, and gender expression.

Teaching Gender, then, situates the story of the making of the male/female and the hetero/homo binaries in the interwar period in the context of life on university campuses, with a focus on the kinds of sociability and intimacy that came to seem desirable in urban non-residential gender-integrated universities as opposed to gender-segregated residential colleges. I suggest that it was when individuals' intimate lives and subjectivities ran up against the institutional frameworks that shaped their daily lives that they actively fashioned new forms of intimacy and relationality—but that often the result of this was to reaffirm norms of gender and sexual difference, rather than fundamentally to challenge or to think beyond them. The rise of heterosexuality did not eradicate all other ways of conceptualizing sex, desire, and intimacy.[45] But it did make it more difficult to imagine life paths outside the heterosexual norm. As faculty, students, and other historical actors

---

[45] Sedgwick, *Epistemology*, 9; Doan, *Disturbing Practices*, 22; Anna Clark, 'Twilight Moments', *Journal of the History of Sexuality* 14, no. 1 (2005): 139–60; see also Houlbrook, *Queer London*; Smith, *Masculinity, Class and Same-Sex Desire*; George Morris, 'Intimacy in Modern British History', *The Historical Journal* 64, no. 3 (June 2021): 796–811.

navigated sex, relationships, friendships, and the everyday business of teaching and learning amidst a gender order that they perceived as shifting and unstable, they contributed to making sexual orientation the primary paradigm through which British people would understand gender and sexual diversity in the twentieth century.

Love Letters, Meeting Minutes, and Necking in Nightclubs

Teaching Gender is organized into three parts that, respectively, tell a political and institutional story about the structure of British higher education; a social history story about student sociability; and an intimate and emotional story about academics' personal lives and their relationship to normative structures of gender and sexuality. It focuses less on curriculum or research and more on the teaching and learning that took place in day-to-day institutional life, but outside of the classroom: in committee meetings, halls of residence, the letters pages of student newspapers. I suggest that we might think of the university—principally, the urban, non-residential, publicly funded university—as a semipermeable institution wherein the normative force of state structures and individuals' intimate lives come into contact. Following the lead of other historians who have examined the relationship between intimacy and the state, I show how the everyday experience of life on a university campus in early-twentieth-century Britain could expose the limits of pervasive norms for gender and sexuality and individuals' efforts to escape them—but also how individuals demonstrated agency in reworking, if ultimately reinscribing, such norms to suit their needs.[46]

Part I, 'Making the Coeducational University', explains how reformers initially conceptualized independent women's colleges to suit women's distinct educational needs, but how the combination of practical logistical constraints and increased state involvement in higher education funding and policy led to the centralization of higher education and the rise of urban, non-residential research universities that were incidentally gender-integrated. Part II, 'Gendering the Student', shows how students' efforts to resist administrative surveillance of cross-gender social interaction and develop new gender-neutral paradigms for 'corporate life' foundered on social awkwardness and, after the First World War, a widespread misogynistic backlash against women students and assertion of an invented tradition of masculine student sociability. Instead, students landed upon a vision of sex and

---

[46] For the British case see work such as Jordanna Bailkin, *The Afterlife of Empire* (Berkeley: University of California Press, 2012) and Deborah Cohen, *Family Secrets: Shame and Privacy in Modern Britain* (New York: Oxford University Press, 2013); for a US history perspective with an especially helpful conceptual framework see Margot Canaday, Nancy F. Cott, and Robert O. Self, eds., *Intimate States: Gender, Sexuality, and Governance in Modern US History* (Chicago: University of Chicago Press, 2021).

romance that emphasized casual sex and binary gender norms as offering a workable script for negotiating cross-gender sociability and for containing more radical challenges to the gender order. Part III, 'Lost Causes', explores what happened to gender-segregated women's and men's colleges as they became increasingly marginal in the higher education landscape, and to a wider range of possibilities for gender and sexuality that the rise of heterosexuality occluded. Over the course of the book, we learn how British higher education became gender-integrated, how students within gender-integrated universities landed upon heterosexuality as the most workable paradigm for organizing cross-gender interaction, and how, although some men developed conceptions of male homosexuality in reaction to the trend towards heterosexuality, the hetero/homo binary ultimately became dominant at the expense of alternative conceptualizations of gender and sexual diversity.

In the chapters to come, we will meet Margery Fry, who by the 1950s struggled to conceptualize her own non-normative life trajectory outside of the paradigm of heterosexuality. But through government reports, student union meeting minutes, fiction, photographs, and love letters, we will also meet dozens of other historical actors, such as the Scottish MP who single-mindedly worked to reorganize the national higher education sector on the principle of 'efficiency', the wealthy widow who tried to sue the University of Glasgow for using her donations to fund gender-integrated classes, the polymathic intellectual who saw his Cambridge college as fertile ground on which to theorize the nature of sexual desire between men, and the dozens of anonymous students at Scottish and northern English universities who wrote in to their university magazines to say that necking in nightclubs was a more pleasurable part of their university experience than 'Platonic friendship' between the sexes. In realms from budgets and course scheduling to student theatre and nightlife, universities were sites in which middle-class British people of all ages learned how to do gender and sexuality—in the process bringing some of the most pervasive social structures of the twentieth century into being.

Teaching Gender: The British University and the Rise of Heterosexuality, 1860–1939. Samuel Rutherford, Oxford University Press. © Samuel Rutherford 2025. DOI: 10.1093/9780198937524.003.0001

PART I
MAKING THE COEDUCATIONAL UNIVERSITY

1

Inventing Higher Education for Women

What is higher education for? Is it for the benefit of the students who pursue it, the faculty and administrators who make careers within it, the wider polity, economy, and society in which they live? Is it for the production of advanced, highly specialized research, or undergraduate education? Is it for the best and the brightest, or all who need to be inducted into rational, disinterested citizenship? Is it for young adults, or those of all ages? Does it train students for specific professional careers, or might it best prepare talented young people to contribute to society by offering a more general education? Ought it to produce an elite, and if so, how ought that elite to be defined? What responsibilities does it have with respect to religious or moral education? Ought it to serve the economic and social needs of the local area, or of a wider nation or empire?

In the early nineteenth century, the prevailing answer to these questions would have been that the purpose of higher education was either to prepare promising young men for careers in specific professions such as ministry, law, and medicine; or to acculturate these young men into the norms of elite adult masculinity. Higher education had a specific, narrowly defined social role, and it was a classed and gendered one. These assumptions dictated the subjects students could study, the ways that their qualifications were assessed, the career and life trajectories that professional academics pursued, and the routines that structured academics' and students' daily lives.[1]

From the mid-nineteenth century, the growth and increasing wealth of the industrial middle class, coupled with questions about the expansion of the franchise and the importance of educating citizens for their role in democracy, opened up the possibility that universities might teach a wider range of subjects to a wider range of people, foster social mobility, hold their students and faculty to more exacting academic standards, and play a wider role in acculturating middle-class young people into appropriate adult social roles. The founding of new institutions, and the expansion and reform of existing ones, followed.

This widening conception of the purpose of higher education opened the door to the inclusion of middle-class women, alongside calls for women to gain access to other markers of middle-class respectability such as the traditional professions

---

[1] Matthew Andrews, *Universities in the Age of Reform: Durham, London and King's College, 1800–1870* (Cham: Palgrave Macmillan, 2018); A.J. Engel, *From Clergyman to Don: The Rise of the Academic Profession in Nineteenth-Century Oxford* (Oxford: Clarendon, 1983).

and the national franchise. But unlike some of these other causes, support for women's higher education was never especially controversial. By the late nineteenth century, it was a mainstream, common-sense view that drew in women and men, Liberals and Conservatives, suffragists and anti-suffragists. But in a context in which it was assumed that women and men would pursue very different life trajectories, almost all university faculty, administrators, education reformers, donors, and politicians imagined that women's higher education would necessarily have to take place in distinct institutions and be organized along distinct lines, to suit women's distinct educational, professional, and personal needs. Women would need education for specific, feminized professional careers, but also perhaps for futures in which they, unlike men, did not work outside the home. They would need education for femininity, marriage, and motherhood.

Reformers disagreed about the forms that this might take, and how best to negotiate the logistics. Some drew on examples from the United States, where women's higher education was already well-established, but others innovated new home-grown models, with financial backing from local citizens in cities across the country. New, purpose-built institutions, and programmes for women within existing institutions, took different approaches to questions such as whether women should study full-time, whether they should live in residential colleges or at home, whether they should pursue a general liberal-arts degree or more specialized study, and whether higher education was for everyone or only for the most talented or those who intended to pursue specific professional careers. Yet, despite garnering support, many of these new initiatives ran up against challenges relating to funding, institutional governance, and national government's increasing interest in regulating higher education. In the process of trying earnestly to meet women's educational needs amid the prevailing ideological currents of late-nineteenth-century politics and the practical constraints of existing educational provision, university reformers across the country came to see integrating women into existing institutions on equal terms to men as practical, efficient, and ideologically preferable—albeit an imperfect solution to the challenges that women students and academics faced.

Previous historians have pointed to the unevenness of women's inclusion and to the informal forms of segregation that persisted in formally gender-integrated institutions, especially in the early years of coeducation in the late nineteenth century.[2] This is undoubtedly true, but it does not necessarily help us to understand

---

[2] Carol Dyhouse, *No Distinction of Sex? Women in British Universities 1870–1939* (London: University College London Press, 1995); Christine D. Myers, *University Coeducation in the Victorian Era: Inclusion in the United States and the United Kingdom* (Basingstoke: Palgrave Macmillan, 2010); Georgia Oman, *Higher Education and the Gendering of Space in England and Wales, 1869–1909* (Basingstoke: Palgrave Macmillan, 2023); cf. Julie S. Gibert, 'Women Students and Student Life at England's Civic Universities before the First World War', *History of Education* 23, no. 4 (December 1994): 405–22.

the nature of the gendered assumptions that undergirded reformers' visions: assumptions that did not always map readily onto a Liberal/Conservative or a male/female divide, and that led to contingent and sometimes unexpected outcomes amid other political constraints. The expansion of educational opportunities for girls and women must be understood in the context of a wider moment of liberal education reform, steeped in questions about citizenship, the role of the state and the church in education, and the status of charitable institutions.[3] At the same time, such questions were implicitly structured by assumptions about gender difference that guided the logic of higher education reform, women's and otherwise.[4]

The following two chapters explain the circumstances that led to the large, urban, centralized, publicly funded, and incidentally coeducational research university becoming the normative model of higher education in Britain: first, in the context of the eclectic patchwork of higher education provision that existed in the nineteenth century; and subsequently, amid the centralization and nationalization that took place in the sector as a result of the dramatic shift in conceptions of the role of the state that occurred more widely in early-twentieth-century politics. These transformations sidelined institutions that, whether for women or for men, promoted distinct gender-segregated visions of higher education. While powerful men higher-education administrators and policymakers led this process, it did not solely break down on predictable gendered lines. Moreover, it laid the groundwork for those studying and working in formally coeducational institutions to innovate, through their daily lived experience, new patterns of middle-class cross-gender interaction. This resulted neither in the eradication of gender distinctions nor in mere continuity of a universal unreconstructed misogyny, but in a new way of understanding, and living, binary gender difference as a fundamental structuring principle of British society.

Liberalism and Education Reform at Mid-Century

Expanding women's access to secondary and higher education had been an aspiration of some British feminists and social reformers from at least the late

---

[3] Gillian Sutherland, 'The Movement for the Higher Education of Women: Its Social and Intellectual Context in England, c. 1840–80', in *Politics and Social Change in Modern Britain: Essays Presented to A.F. Thompson*, ed. P.J. Waller (Sussex: The Harvester Press, 1987), 91–116; Gillian Sutherland, *Faith, Duty and the Power of Mind: The Cloughs and Their Circle* (Cambridge: Cambridge University Press, 2006).

[4] On assumptions of gender difference structuring the logic of political reform see Ben Griffin, *The Politics of Gender in Victorian Britain: Masculinity, Political Culture and the Struggle for Women's Rights* (Cambridge: Cambridge University Press, 2012), 7–8; Ben Griffin, 'Paternal Rights, Child Welfare and the Law in Nineteenth-Century Britain and Ireland', *Past & Present* 246, no. 1 (February 2020): 109–47.

seventeenth century.[5] But the idea gained new support and salience in the context of the liberalism that undergirded British thought, politics, and society throughout the nineteenth century, and especially in the century's middle decades. Regardless of whether the Liberal Party itself was in power in any particular moment, liberalism offered a pervasive set of principles for thinking about the role of the state and of local government in the lives of individuals, encompassing issues as wide-ranging as empire, trade, and foreign policy; the relationship of the state to the established church; the status of the franchise; poverty and social equality; corruption and good governance; and the individual, the family, and the community as units of society.[6]

Education sat at the heart of many of these considerations. The prospect of expanding the parliamentary franchise generated new concerns about how best to educate the electorate for the responsibilities of citizenship—as well as a desire to restrict the franchise only to those who had attained the capacity to cast a rational, disinterested vote.[7] While newly enfranchised working- and lower-middle-class supporters of the Liberal Party gravitated to a politics grounded in ideals of masculinity, Nonconformist Protestantism, economic populism, nationalism, and imperialism, members of an upper-middle-class professional elite drew on liberal ideals to articulate new roles for 'merit', expertise, and 'the intellectual' in politics and civil society.[8] For such thinkers, both the pursuit of higher learning for its own sake and the application of advanced knowledge to practical social problems had the potential to revitalize the nation. This was one route towards a new understanding of teaching, research, and the institutions in which they took place not merely as sites for training in the traditional professions of law, medicine, and the clergy, but rather as part of the spirit of civic life. New calls for 'liberal education' began to proliferate in this context, as education reformers and

---

[5] Deirdre Raftery, 'The Opening of Higher Education to Women in Nineteenth Century England: "Unexpected Revolution" or Inevitable Change?', *Higher Education Quarterly* 56, no. 4 (2002): 331–46.

[6] Peter Mandler, ed., *Liberty and Authority in Victorian Britain* (Oxford: Oxford University Press, 2006).

[7] J.P. Parry, 'Liberalism and Liberty', in Mandler, *Liberty and Authority*, 71–100, at 76; Sandra M. den Otter, *British Idealism and Social Explanation: A Study in Late-Victorian Thought* (Oxford: Clarendon Press, 1996); J.S. Mill, 'Considerations on Representative Government', in J.S. Mill, *On Liberty, Utilitarianism and Other Essays*, ed. Mark Philp and Frederick Rosen (Oxford: Oxford University Press, 2015), 181–405; Catherine Hall, Keith McClelland, and Jane Rendall, *Defining the Victorian Nation: Class, Race, Gender and the British Reform Act of 1867* (Cambridge: Cambridge University Press, 2000); Elaine Hadley, *Living Liberalism: Practical Citizenship in Mid-Victorian Britain* (Chicago: University of Chicago Press, 2010).

[8] Eugenio F. Biagini, *Liberty, Retrenchment and Reform: Popular Liberalism in the Age of Gladstone, 1860–1880* (Cambridge: Cambridge University Press, 1992); Christopher Harvie, *The Lights of Liberalism: University Liberals and the Challenge of Democracy 1860–86* (London: Allen Lane, 1976); Stefan Collini, *Public Moralists: Political Thought and Intellectual Life in Victorian Britain 1850–1930* (Oxford: Oxford University Press, 1991); H.S. Jones, *Intellect and Character in Victorian England: Mark Pattison and the Invention of the Don* (Cambridge: Cambridge University Press, 2007).

intellectuals sought to consider how institutional structure and curriculum could lend themselves to a new kind of educational project.[9]

The political and intellectual life of nineteenth-century Britain was also inextricable from questions about appropriate sources of truth and moral authority and the status of the established Church.[10] New theological currents prompted conversations about what higher education was for and what its place was in the life of the nation. John Henry Newman's efforts to found a national Catholic university for Ireland in the 1840s and 1850s led him to articulate an influential statement about the value of liberal education for its own sake that was taken up by Christian and secular education reformers alike.[11] A desire to preserve the stature of the established Church, on the other hand, drove a group of Anglican clergy to establish King's College London (KCL) in 1831 as an orthodox response to the secular institution that would come to be known as University College London (UCL); and the Cathedral Chapter of Durham to establish a new university under its aegis in 1832. KCL and Durham became centres of experimentation, with KCL pioneering teaching in English literature and natural sciences, and Durham striving to meet the local demand for more affordable and accessible higher education in applied sciences in the industrial north-east of England.[12] In a moment when traditional sources of truth and knowledge seemed fundamentally up for debate, education reformers sought to give practical expression to their questioning through new educational institutions with new curricula.

These high-minded aspirations nevertheless unfolded within specific practical constraints that dictated how intellectuals and activists could reform centuries-old institutions and found new ones, as well as what the relationship would be of private educational entrepreneurs to both the government's and the established Church's roles in secondary and higher education. In the first half of the nineteenth century, the reform of the funding and governance of endowed educational institutions was central to Whig and, later, Liberal campaigns against corruption, and proved a vital testing ground for the expanded authority of the state to challenge entrenched interests and to regulate private enterprise.

[9] See e.g. F.W. Farrar, ed., *Essays on a Liberal Education* (London: Macmillan, 1867); J.S. Mill, *Inaugural Address Delivered to the University of St Andrews* (London: Longmans, Green, Reader, and Dyer, 1867).

[10] For a general statement of this principle see Mandler, *Liberty and Authority*, 10. See also Boyd Hilton, *The Age of Atonement: The Influence of Evangelicalism on Social and Economic Thought, 1795–1865* (Oxford: Clarendon Press, 1988); *Essays and Reviews* (London: John W. Parker & Son, 1860); Ieuan Ellis, *Seven against Christ: A Study of 'Essays and Reviews'* (Leiden: Brill, 1980).

[11] Sheldon Rothblatt, *The Modern University and Its Discontents: The Fate of Newman's Legacies in Britain and America* (Cambridge: Cambridge University Press, 1997), Chs. 1–2; Stefan Collini, 'The Useful and the Useless: Newman Revisited', in *What Are Universities For?* (London: Penguin, 2012), 39–60. On the reception of Newman among higher education reformers in his lifetime see Jones, *Intellect and Character*.

[12] William Whyte, *Redbrick: A Social and Architectural History of Britain's Civic Universities* (Oxford: Oxford University Press, 2015), 43–5; Andrews, *Universities in the Age of Reform*.

Church, charity, guild, and educational endowments—many medieval or early modern in origin—were all subject to government inquiries and commissions between the 1820s and the 1870s, an issue that substantially structured political fault lines between Liberals and Conservatives in the period.[13]

Following one such government inquiry, Parliament passed a Charitable Trusts Act in 1853. It established the Charity Commission, the first permanent independent regulatory body for charities (with jurisdiction in England and Wales), and granted the commission sweeping powers to inquire into the running of charitable trusts, arbitrate disputes, and mandate more financially efficient schemes for charities' management.[14] However, lobbyists ensured that the Act explicitly excluded the universities of Oxford, Cambridge, London, and Durham and many endowed secondary schools from the commission's purview. This omission led, in the 1860s, to a wide-ranging Schools Inquiry Commission into the funding and governance of secondary education for both boys and girls across Britain, which recommended systemic reorganization of private secondary education. Endowed Schools Acts of 1869 and 1873 established that educational endowments (with, still, the exception of Oxford and Cambridge) came under the purview of the Charity Commission, and established a specific body of Schools Commissioners with sweeping powers to appropriate and redistribute educational endowments—in particular, to remove some schools from the control of the Church of England and to use funds established for boys' schools to found new girls' schools.[15] Subsequent judicial rulings also determined that newly founded higher education institutions were, unlike Oxford and Cambridge, subject to the Charity Commission's regulatory powers.[16] Though this approach to state involvement in education was restrained by comparison to those that would be taken a decade or two later in Third Republic France and unified Germany, it was controversial within the British political context.[17] Not only did these developments lay the groundwork for sweeping expansion and reform of British higher education,

---

[13] H.S. Jones, 'The English Civic Universities: Endowments and the Commemoration of Benefactors', in *Dethroning Historical Reputations: Universities, Museums and the Commemoration of Benefactors*, ed. Jill Pellew and Lawrence Goldman (London: Institute of Historical Research, 2018), 25–34, at 26.

[14] Richard Edmund Mitcheson, *Charitable Trusts: The Jurisdiction of the Charity Commission, Being the Acts Conferring Such Jurisdiction, 1853–1883* (London: Stevens and Sons, 1887).

[15] Charity Commission, *Charitable Trusts Acts, 1853–1894, Analytically Arranged* (London, 1896); Colin Shrosbree, *Public Schools and Private Education: The Clarendon Commission, 1861–1864, and the Public Schools Acts* (Manchester: Manchester University Press, 1988).

[16] Mitcheson, *Charitable Trusts*, 248.

[17] Lawrence Goldman, 'The Defection of the Middle Class: The Endowed Schools Act, the Liberal Party, and the 1874 Election', in *Politics and Culture in Victorian Britain: Essays in Memory of Colin Matthew*, ed. Peter Ghosh and Lawrence Goldman (Oxford: Oxford University Press, 2006), 118–35, at 127. For the French and German comparisons see George Weisz, *The Emergence of Modern Universities in France, 1863–1914* (Princeton: Princeton University Press, 1983); Emily J. Levine, *Allies and Rivals: German–American Exchange and the Rise of the Modern Research University* (Chicago: University of Chicago Press, 2021).

they also revealed the form and content of academic secondary and higher education to be central to conceptions of the state and citizenship in this period.

It was in this context of liberal political thought, religious ferment, and legal reform that higher education for women became thinkable. Religion, politics, and the law shaped ideas about who and what higher education was for: whether it was for only the most academically exceptional students, or a wider population; whether it was for the pursuit of higher learning for its own sake, or for training and acculturation in the professions. At the same time, these were necessarily gendered questions: how might a practical, vocationally oriented form of higher education for women differ from that for men? Was there a market for women's higher education that would make new institutions profitable, and what did that market want? As reformers put forward schemes for women's education and sought to put them into practice, their small-scale, at times quixotic, experiments in designing higher education for what they saw as a new and distinct population would have far-reaching impacts on universities as a whole.

The Women's College

In the mid-nineteenth century, few of those who sought to expand educational opportunities for women did so on the basis of straightforwardly feminist principles—or, for that matter, from a perspective that emphasized the pursuit of knowledge for its own sake. Instead, both women and men reformers were often influenced by evangelical Protestant ideas about the value of advanced general education as preparation for a purposeful Christian life. Many held that improving academic education for women would prepare them to fulfil their God-given roles as wives and mothers, serving as intelligent and sympathetic companions to their husbands and managing their households efficiently. Though this argument proceeded from the principle of essential differences between the sexes, it also stemmed from a desire to take women's capabilities seriously, to treat them with dignity, and to give them equivalent, if different, opportunities to men. Some, too, appreciating the reality that many middle-class women would not marry and could not depend on their parents for financial support, recognized the urgent economic need for advanced education that would train women to work in professional occupations, albeit in the context of a gender-segregated labour market in which the main profession accessible to women was schoolteaching.[18]

---

[18] Christina de Bellaigue, *Educating Women: Schooling and Identity in England and France, 1800–1867* (Oxford: Oxford University Press, 2007); Carol Dyhouse, *Girls Growing up in Late Victorian and Edwardian England* (London: Routledge, 1981); Laura Schwartz, 'Feminist Thinking on Education in Victorian England', *Oxford Review of Education* 37, no. 5 (October 2011): 669–82; Gillian Sutherland, *In Search of the New Woman: Middle-Class Women and Work in Britain 1870–1914* (Cambridge: Cambridge University Press, 2015), 23–6. For a comparable account of evangelicalism

Though these evangelical reformers' practical approach to education contrasted with the deliberately unworldly perspective of a theologian like Newman, they were like other intellectuals and reformers of the mid-century liberal moment in seeing the expansion of educational opportunities as a necessary foundation for self-development and for an ethical approach to civil society and community life. At their outset, then, most concrete efforts to create higher education for women proceeded from the assumption that this would take place in separate institutions, to suit women's distinct educational needs; and also that it would be practically oriented, preparing women primarily for careers as wives and mothers and secondarily for a limited range of gender-segregated professional occupations.

These commitments resulted in the proliferation of girls' day and boarding secondary schools, as well as Church of England-sponsored teacher-training colleges.[19] The 1840s saw two attempts in London to found independent colleges for women offering an academic higher education: Queen's College, the project of Anglican theologian F.D. Maurice; and Bedford College, the project of evangelical Nonconformist activist and social reformer Elizabeth Jesser Reid. Both colleges aspired to teach an advanced, wide-ranging liberal-arts curriculum to upper- and middle-class 'ladies' who would likely not go on to work outside the home, but they also hoped to set higher standards for the training of governesses and women teachers. These were highly respectable institutions, enjoying patronage from prominent women members of London society who provided financial support and enforced the colleges' class exclusivity.[20]

But there was an important difference: while at Queen's women supporters had only an advisory role, reporting to an all-male Committee on Education comprised of academics and clergymen, at Bedford Reid insisted that the majority of the college's governing body be women. This was to be a longstanding tension in women's higher education, as women's desire to control institutions for women—and, sometimes, to enforce norms of propriety for the younger women in their care—clashed with, and remained subordinate to, the competing visions of men administrators and donors who could leverage their greater professional experience in higher education administration to assert their authority. Reid, in canvassing financial and logistical support from other middle-class London women, called for a small group of unmarried women to work together in secret to further the cause of women's higher education. She described her college as an

and women's education in the US context, see Andrea L. Turpin, *A New Moral Vision: Gender, Religion, and the Changing Purposes of American Higher Education, 1837–1917* (Ithaca: Cornell University Press, 2016).

[19] de Bellaigue, *Educating Women*; Janet Howarth, 'The Church of England and Women's Higher Education, c. 1840–1914', in Ghosh and Goldman, eds., *Politics and Culture in Victorian Britain*, 153–70.

[20] Margaret J. Tuke, *A History of Bedford College for Women, 1849–1937* (London: Oxford University Press, 1939); Hilda Kaye, *A History of Queen's College, London, 1848–1972* (London: Chatto and Windus, 1972).

'underground railway': a highly charged turn of phrase for someone who had begun her activist career in the antislavery movement.[21] Not only does this considerably overstate the marginality of a project that, though it often struggled financially, was in fact relatively uncontroversial, Reid and her colleagues in any event felt obliged to ask for guidance from men faculty at University College London about matters such as curriculum design, hiring faculty, and fundraising. Mutual distrust between women activists and men faculty and administrators remained a common element of initiatives for women's higher education. This often allowed women activists to reaffirm essential differences between the sexes and to represent themselves as the only ones speaking up in the best interests of the younger women students for whom they were advocating, even when the political reality was more complex.

Both Queen's and Bedford struggled to attract students: without more and better girls' secondary schools, there were not enough students capable of moving on to university-level work to keep the institutions viable. Both colleges struggled to mediate among students of varied abilities and academic backgrounds. And without affiliation to a degree-granting university, they lacked the power to enforce common academic standards or issue qualifications. Within a few years, both institutions were instead teaching a secondary-level curriculum to a mix of teenagers and adult women. It would take the expansion of girls' secondary education that followed the Schools Inquiry Commission to create a viable market for women's colleges.

To be sure, within the exceptional institutions of Oxford and Cambridge the discussion about women's higher education unfolded differently: entwined not only with ideas about religion, self-development, and new intellectual opportunities for respectable Christian ladies, but also with how to reform institutions whose structure and curriculum seemed ill-suited to the needs of nineteenth-century students. Within these two institutions, prominent liberal reforming academics and administrators perceived that seeking to provide for women students' distinct capacities and needs could be a route to challenging the old-fashioned and inflexible curriculum—narrowly focused around theology, classical languages, and (at Cambridge) mathematics—within which men students were taught. These reformers welcomed the opportunity to work informally with women students on a volunteer basis, trying out new subjects of study and new modes of examination.[22] They saw the creation of new courses of study to suit women's needs as a route to creating a more modern and more flexible curriculum for all. But they clashed with those who argued that, in the name of formal equality, women ought to be

---

[21] Tuke, *A History of Bedford College*, 99.
[22] Rita McWilliams-Tullberg, *Women at Cambridge: A Men's University—Though of a Mixed Type* (London: Victor Gollancz, 1975), 28, 42–3; Jones, *Intellect and Character*, 91; Samuel Rutherford, 'Arthur Sidgwick's *Greek Prose Composition*: Gender, Affect, and Sociability in the Late-Victorian University', *Journal of British Studies* 56, no. 1 (January 2017): 91–116, at 110–13.

educated in accordance with the existing standards for men; and with those who primarily sought courses of study that met practical, career-oriented needs, including around the professionalization of marriage and motherhood.

It was in this context that the evangelical-Anglican women's-rights activist Emily Davies conceived of and founded what was arguably the most exceptional institution in the nineteenth-century women's higher education landscape: Girton College, Cambridge, the first fully residential college for women, founded on the Oxford and Cambridge model. Davies had perceived education to be foundational to improving the lives of middle-class women ever since she and her sister had been denied any formal education beyond basic literacy while her brothers went to Cambridge. In the 1860s, she became an active member of campaigns to expand girls' secondary education and to admit women to the examinations of the University of London, to the 'Local Examinations' that Cambridge had established in 1857 as a school-leaving qualification, and to medical study at a range of universities. Not only did Davies perceive that furthering women's equality must begin with education, she saw the challenge of reforming women's education as systemic, not solved through fighting on a case-by-case basis for individual exceptional women's admission to specific courses of study and specific exams.[23]

Like other reformers of the period, Davies imagined the typical woman university student to be an upper- or middle-class lady of leisure, whose daily domestic duties were primarily performed by servants. She hoped that higher education would save such women from boredom and idleness, help them to manage their households and domestic staff efficiently, and provide them with both the motivation and the practical skills to undertake socially beneficial voluntary work. The greater analytic faculties and wider perspective on life that higher education would provide might foster in women greater sympathy with those unlike themselves, and instil a more fully realized sense of Christian charity and mission. In her 1866 treatise *The Higher Education of Women*, she argued that 'it is in fact as a means of bringing men and women together, and bridging over the intellectual gulf between them, that a more liberal education and a larger scope for women are chiefly to be desired'.[24] But her hoped-for end result was not to dissolve distinctions between men and women, but rather to allow them to work more cooperatively together within an ideal complementary marriage. Like other reformers, Davies recognized the economic reality that some women would need to earn their own living. But she primarily framed higher education as making it *more*

---

[23] Sarah Delamont, 'Davies, (Sarah) Emily (1830–1921), suffragist and promoter of higher education for women', *Oxford Dictionary of National Biography*, 23 September 2004, accessed 10 July 2022, https://www.oxforddnb.com/view/10.1093/ref:odnb/9780198614128.001.0001/odnb-9780198614128-e-32741; Emily Davies, 'Special Systems of Education for Women', *London Student*, June 1868, GCPP/Davies/11/19, Girton; Emily Davies, 'The Application of Funds to the Education of Girls', paper given to the National Association for the Promotion of Social Science, 3 May 1865, GCPP/Davies/11/6, Girton.

[24] Emily Davies, *The Higher Education of Women* (London: Alexander Strahan, 1866), 123.

likely that women would marry, marry well, and be intelligent and sympathetic companions to their husbands. Rather than lives of isolation, loneliness, and frustration, Davies hoped that higher education would give married upper- and middle-class women lives of curiosity, sympathy, and social purpose.

Where Davies differed significantly from other reformers was in the institutional structure she imagined to be best suited to achieving this. She thought that the best way to ensure the quality and rigour of women's education was not to think from first principles about the kinds of curriculum and institutional structure best suited to women, but to model women's colleges after existing prestigious men's institutions. She thought the residential Cambridge college of the kind that her brothers attended, with a curriculum grounded in subjects such as mathematics and classics and assessed through competitive examinations, to be the gold standard. She sought to make a political case that women were intellectually and physically capable of pursuing exactly the same higher education as men, and she perceived that this would only be possible within a fully residential institution, in which students had their material needs provided for and were insulated from the domestic responsibilities that their families might demand of them. Importantly, she believed that residence was an integral part of what higher education, in its most abstract philosophical sense, was for: it would allow students to meet and make friends with new people, thus expanding their capacities for sympathy—an opportunity that was at the time rare for upper- and middle-class young women who lived at home.[25] At the same time, her commitment to residence tapped into broader contemporary trends in institutional reform within Oxford and Cambridge, where academics in men's colleges also increasingly saw the residential college as a site in which young people might be acculturated into norms of middle-class adulthood, including around marriage and family.

Girton College accepted its first students in 1869. It was situated in a village outside Cambridge, at a safe distance from the temptations of the university town. Nevertheless, it took the Cambridge men's college as its model. Though the university did not recognize the new college, it prepared its students to excel at the same university examinations as men Cambridge students, pushing them to work at the same pace despite many students' lack of an adequate secondary education. Davies fundraised for a grand, purpose-built campus designed by distinguished architect Alfred Waterhouse, known for his work at several Oxford and Cambridge colleges as well as Manchester, Leeds, and Liverpool universities—an indication of her aspirations for the college despite the challenges of financing such a large

---

[25] Davies, *The Higher Education of Women*, 130, 136, 140–1, 150; Emily Davies, 'Some Account of a Proposed New College for Women', paper presented at the National Association for the Promotion of Social Science, 1868, GCPP/Davies/11/7, Girton; Emily Davies, 'College Education for Women', paper delivered at the Literary and Philosophical Society of Nottingham, 8 February 1872, GCPP/Davies/11/18, Girton.

building project. From the outset, she made clear her intention to campaign vigorously and insistently for Girton students to be admitted to Cambridge degrees.[26]

In promoting the college, Davies distinguished her model explicitly from Queen's College and Bedford College in London.[27] Over the next decade, she would also become a critic of other Cambridge women's-education activists like married couple Henry and Eleanor Sidgwick, whose own project, Newnham College, was nondenominational, critical of the existing Cambridge curriculum, sought to meet women students where their academic abilities were, and was less rigidly adherent to norms of propriety for students. Newnham designed a bespoke curriculum for each of the small number of students it accommodated in a rented house in central Cambridge. Sometimes these students did take Cambridge exams, but they did so at their own pace and in the order they chose, and it was not a condition of study at Newnham. In further contrast to Davies, the Sidgwicks understood themselves to be equipping their students for the formal labour market, primarily as teachers—and, in the process, to be improving the standard of girls' education nationwide.[28] In 1887, Eleanor Sidgwick undertook a survey of the life trajectories of the first fifteen years of Newnham and Girton alumnae, finding that 70 per cent of them had not married and over three-quarters were working as teachers.[29] But Davies continued to regard Newnham's pragmatic approach as a betrayal of the principle of abstract equality, and of the transformation in personal relations that she had hoped such equality might bring about. If women were educated primarily to be teachers in gender-segregated secondary schools—a career which, if pursued long-term, foreclosed the possibility of marriage—they could not also be complementary partners in intellectually and emotionally satisfying marriages.

Despite their differences, what Girton and Newnham did have in common was their emphasis on residence as a condition of women students' higher education. This was at once normative and radical. It ensured that women students' lives could be regulated and surveilled, propriety enforced, and their contact with men limited. But it also ensured that students had quiet places to study and were isolated from practical and emotional demands that their families might make upon them. They could put their studies first. This dual connotation meant that residential higher education for women could attract support from a variety of sectors—becoming common nationally much earlier than residential higher education for men, which until the 1930s remained confined to Oxford and Cambridge. At the same time, Davies's and the Sidgwicks' visions closely echoed

---

[26] McWilliams-Tullberg, *Women at Cambridge*, 51–3.
[27] Davies, 'Special Systems of Education for Women'; Anne Austin, letter to Miss Richardson reporting on town hall meeting advertising Girton, 31 March 1868, GCPP/Davies/15/1/5, Girton.
[28] McWilliams-Tullberg, *Women at Cambridge*, 44–6.
[29] Eleanor M. Sidgwick, 'Proposed Degrees for Women' (flysheet, 12 February 1896), GCPP/Davies/13/2/9/6, Girton.

how Oxford and Cambridge academics and administrators in the mid- to late-nineteenth century conceptualized the men's college: as a kind of intergenerational family environment in which social norms, including around appropriate gendered behaviour, could be transmitted. However, the idea that the college might rival the biological family as a primary site of middle-class women's attachments seemed threatening to many observers. In the twentieth century, the women's college would increasingly become a target of suspicion in a way that the men's college did not.

Historians have devoted disproportionate attention to the efforts of Oxford and Cambridge women and their allies to gain a foothold in these two idiosyncratic and conservative institutions. But to focus only on this story is to misapprehend the national political landscape around women's higher education in the mid- to late nineteenth century. The founding of Girton and Newnham illuminated some of the most pressing issues at the heart of what higher education for women was for and how it should be structured, issues that also suffused discussions about women's higher education nationwide. But for the most part the early conceptualization of women's higher education took place elsewhere, fitting into a framework that was easily compatible with class-based ideas of propriety and respectability and with an exalted, but distinct and essentialist, conception of women's role in the household, religion, and society. This lent campaigns for women's higher education mainstream legitimacy, and made them popular causes among philanthropists and members of high society.

Testing the Women's College Model:
The Case of Royal Holloway

Educational endowment had long been an effective way for the wealthy and powerful, from royals and bishops to merchants, to express their charitable bona fides. But in the nineteenth century, the expanded wealth of the industrial middle class and the growth of industrial cities led to capital investment in higher education on an unprecedented scale.[30] Donors who had made their money in industry typically had no prior experience in higher education policymaking. In an era when the national student body numbered only a few thousand, most had not even been students themselves.[31] But many had firm ideas about what higher education *should* provide: the roles that colleges and universities might play within the economies and societies of their local regions, the subjects that were valuable

---

[30] Whyte, *Redbrick*, 111, 115, 127.
[31] Gillian Sutherland, 'Education', in *The Cambridge Social History of Britain, 1750–1950*, Volume 3, ed. F.M.L. Thompson (Cambridge: Cambridge University Press, 2000), 119–69, at 137–9.

for students to study, the kinds of students who might go to university and what their lives should be like while they were there.

In the case of women's colleges, founders elaborated distinctive visions grounded in the assumption that—whether for reasons of essential sex difference or simply the reality of different career and life paths—women's higher education would necessarily need to take different forms to men's. Their wealth gave them the power to put those visions into practice. Although government was in the mid-nineteenth century becoming increasingly interested in regulating charities, it still believed that funding and administering higher education fell largely outside the state's remit. Furthermore, in England and Wales (though not in Scotland), longstanding legal precedent held that it was the responsibility of charitable trustees to ensure that the income from their trusts was spent in accordance with the benefactor's wishes.[32] In other words, by the 1870s, the independent, endowed women's college—an outcome of the intellectual and social developments of the previous decades that had made some forms of higher education for women seem respectable, socially progressive, and inevitable—was well placed to become a lightning rod for debates about the competing authority of donors, the state, and educational experts; the purpose of higher education, both in general and for women in particular; and the future direction of UK higher education as a whole.

No institution better exemplifies these themes than Royal Holloway College, the grandiose project of pharmaceuticals magnate Thomas Holloway. Holloway was the son of a baker-turned-publican and left school at sixteen to work in the family business, before making a fortune in patent medicines. In the 1860s, he retired to a country house in Berkshire.[33] Struggling to make social headway with the county's elite families, he landed on philanthropy as a way to secure his reputation, and his wife suggested a women's college as a respectable project. In the spring of 1874, he purchased 94 acres at the top of Egham Hill, south of the Thames and east of Windsor Great Park—a site large enough for a monumental college building and grounds, far from the perceived health risks and moral dangers of the metropolis.[34]

Holloway set about managing the details of the college's design and construction, but he also sought to familiarize himself with more abstract questions: what a women's college was for, how it should be run, what objectives it might seek to achieve for its graduates and for the wider society in which they lived, what kinds

---

[32] Mitcheson, *Charitable Trusts*, 71, 245, and *passim*.

[33] T.A.B. Corley, 'Holloway, Thomas (1800–1883), manufacturer of patent medicines and philanthropist', *Oxford Dictionary of National Biography*, 23 September 2004, accessed 12 July 2022, https://www.oxforddnb.com/display/10.1093/ref:odnb/9780198614128.001.0001/odnb-9780198614128-e-13577.

[34] Caroline Bingham, *The History of Royal Holloway College, 1886–1986* (London: Constable, 1987), 36–48.

of women should attend the college, and what feminine values the curriculum and culture of the institution should convey. He consulted with experts, including Emily Davies, and read and took notes on the deeds of foundation of other privately funded English colleges.[35] But as he was drawing up his plans, a chance meeting with a member of the board of trustees of American women's college Vassar drew his attention to a different model. Vassar College had been founded in 1861 in Poughkeepsie, New York by Matthew Vassar, an Anglo-American brewer who, like Holloway, desiring to secure his legacy as a philanthropist, had put his fortune into a women's college.[36] Holloway saw in Vassar a kindred spirit on whom he might model himself and his institution.

The Vassar model entailed the combination of a high academic standard with a relatively conservative approach to students' residential and social life. Promotional materials explained that, after some consideration among 'thinking men', the college had decided on a rigid curriculum with only two tracks, arts and sciences, both demanding a high level of pre-existing classical education from incoming students; and a residential environment that imitated the kinds of homes from which it imagined its ideal students might come, with a ladylike and non-sectarian, but adamantly Christian, tenor.[37] Assurances about the appropriately feminine and domestic character of residential education for women were commonplace among the several 'female seminaries' that had been founded on the American East Coast from the 1840s, but Matthew Vassar made two important innovations. First, he held that his college should be to women 'what Yale and Harvard are to young men': it should teach an advanced liberal-arts curriculum, emphasizing classical studies and experimental science (though also adding the feminine subject of fine art). Second, it should be contained within a single, monumental building: a lasting testament to Vassar's beneficence, and also a total institution in which the daily lives of both the students and the women faculty (who held subordinate positions to men professors) could be intensely regulated.[38] Vassar's ambition, and his desire to craft his own legacy, led unexpectedly to a new model for women's higher education, one that combined the curriculum of the American men's liberal-arts college—a type of institution that had no exact equivalent in Britain—with ideals of feminine domesticity. Residence was important to Vassar, but for different reasons than it was to Davies or the Sidgwicks.

Vassar's ideas captivated Holloway, buttressing his decision to situate his college not in connection with neighbours in London or in Cambridge, unlike

[35] Bingham, *History of Royal Holloway*, 42–3; 'Deed of Foundation of Josiah Mason's Scientific College', n.d., RHC/2/14, RHUL; 'The Owens College', n.d., RHC/2/20, RHUL; 'Girton College—Memorandum and Articles of Association and Bye-Laws', n.d., RHC/2/10, RHUL.

[36] Helen Lefkowitz Horowitz, *Alma Mater: Design and Experience in the Women's Colleges from Their Nineteenth-Century Beginnings to the 1930s* (New York: Knopf, 1984), 29.

[37] *Historical Sketch of Vassar College*, 1876, RHC/2/4, RHUL; see also 'Vassar College: Its Foundations, Aims, Resources and Courses of Study', May 1873, RHC/2/8, RHUL, 75–6.

[38] Horowitz, *Alma Mater*, 28–42.

Reid or Davies, but rather in splendid isolation on Egham Hill, analogous to Vassar's location on the outskirts of Poughkeepsie in New York's Hudson Valley. He directly copied phrasing from Matthew Vassar's letters into the deed of foundation for his own college.[39] He also copied Vassar's approach to student finance—a few need-based scholarships, but an assumption that most students were of a social class that could afford to pay their own way—and its governance structure, including its 'board of gentlemen governors' and its 'lady principal', the college's only senior woman employee. Conceived of as a helpmate to the trustees but subordinate to them, her duties primarily concerned domestic matters and discipline.[40] This was similar to the model of Queen's, but it differed from Bedford and Girton, which both included women on the board of governors and in other senior leadership roles. By looking to pre-existing models, a philanthropist like Holloway with no practical experience in higher education could find out how to run a higher education institution. By drawing so heavily on an American model, though, he unwittingly started new conversations in Britain about the future direction of women's higher education that would ultimately resolve in opposition to the independent women's college.

In an 1883 will, Holloway formally founded the college, established a trust through which it would be funded, and appointed the first board of governors (three years later, they named the college 'Royal Holloway' in honour of Queen Victoria, another indication of their claims to respectability). He died only two months later, with his vision yet to be realized. The college building was still under construction, and there was as yet no prospect of staff or students. But there was a board of governors—all men, as stipulated by the deed of trust, and all prominent in business, politics, the Church, and high society—dedicated to complying with Holloway's vision.[41] In imitation of Vassar, they hired a residential academic staff composed of young, unmarried women, overseen by three non-resident male lecturers in mathematics, zoology, and classics and moral sciences. They hired as 'lady principal' M.E. Bishop, the forty-four-year-old headmistress of pioneering girls' day school Oxford High School, a deeply religious Anglican who believed strongly in gender-segregated education.[42]

Holloway had chosen his governors for their social standing, not for their expertise in higher education or women's issues. Perhaps unsurprisingly, therefore, they struggled to translate the American liberal-arts college into an English context. They did not understand that Matthew Vassar intended his college to

---

[39] 'Communications to the Board of Trustees of Vassar College by Its Founder', n.d., RHC/2/7, RHUL. Holloway underlined passages he wished to use, and struck out those he did not. 'Deed of Foundation of Royal Holloway College', 11 October 1883, RHC/1/1/2, RHUL. Bingham has also drawn attention to similarities in the language of Vassar's and Holloway's bequests: *History of Royal Holloway*, 54–5.

[40] 'Vassar College: Its Foundations, Aims, Resources and Courses of Study'; 'Laws and Regulations of Vassar Female College', n.d., RHC/2/5, RHUL.

[41] Bingham, *History of Royal Holloway*, 64.   [42] Bingham, *History of Royal Holloway*, 72.

rival Yale or Harvard, instead perceiving the liberal-arts curriculum as a smatter-
ing of general education suited to elite women's presumed futures as managers of
households, sympathetic wives, and mothers of children. To this end, in addition
to academic subjects, they provided for instruction in cookery, hygiene, wood-
work, dressmaking, and gym. Concerned about subjecting psychologically fragile
women to undue strain, they did not require students to sit any exams, but this
left Royal Holloway students outside the prevailing British mechanism of assuring educational quality and credentialling student success.[43] The college, then,
seemed not to fit: it was neither school nor college, neither American nor British.
It was much more than a finishing school, but its ideal student was evidently a
marriageable young lady.

This incongruity also had implications for whether the college could and
would want to confer undergraduate degrees. Thomas Holloway had intended
that his college become an independent, degree-granting institution like Vassar.
But he did not realize that the poorly regulated landscape of mid-nineteenth-
century US higher education, in which institutions did not need any formal
licence in order to award degrees, did not pertain in the UK.[44] In mid-nineteenth-
century Britain, concern about state overreach and about whether new institutions would water down existing standards of higher education had led prevailing
legal and political opinion to resist the proliferation of chartered universities.
Instead, reformers supported the creation of 'federal' universities: drawing on the
model of Oxford and Cambridge, in which numerous colleges with their own
endowments, statutes, personnel, and distinct identities were loosely federated
under the aegis of a university that had the power to set examinations and award
degrees. Outside of Oxford and Cambridge, this model enjoyed only brief
popularity. But it was in vogue in the 1860s–80s, structuring at that time the
constitution of the University of London (with affiliated colleges including UCL
and KCL) and the Victoria University (comprising colleges that would eventually
become the universities of Manchester, Liverpool, and Leeds). The college, with
responsibility for teaching, had the autonomy to meet the needs of its own local
population of students; the university had the responsibility to uphold common
academic standards regardless of the differences between colleges' student bodies.
The college could be privately funded and governed, with the legal status either
of a limited company or a charitable trust; the university was ultimately responsible
to the state and the public good.[45]

---

[43] James Elwick, *Making a Grade: Victorian Examinations and the Rise of Standardized Testing*
(Toronto: University of Toronto Press, 2021).

[44] John R. Thelin, *A History of American Higher Education*, 3rd edition (Baltimore: Johns Hopkins
University Press, 2019), 43–4.

[45] Sheldon Rothblatt, 'Historical and Comparative Remarks on the Federal Principle in Higher
Education', *History of Education* 16, no. 3 (1987): 151–80; Keith Vernon, *Universities and the State in
England, 1850–1939* (Abingdon: Routledge, 2004), 73–83.

The question of degrees had not much troubled Bedford and Queen's. If the education they provided was primarily intended for elite women who sought generally to broaden their intellectual horizons, it mattered less whether they could provide their students with a piece of paper that said 'Bachelor of Arts'. To the Cambridge women's colleges, by contrast, degrees—and standardized, accredited examinations—were essential. In addition to the symbolism, important to Davies, of women students pursuing an identical course of study to men students, there were practical considerations. In reality, as Eleanor Sidgwick had found, the women enrolling at colleges were not the ladies of leisure that education reformers had initially imagined, but rather middle-class women who needed to earn their own livings and who saw higher education as a route to employment in the new academic girls' secondary schools that the Schools Inquiry Commission had ushered into being. Would-be schoolteachers needed a credential that their prospective employers would recognize and respect. In the entrepreneurial higher-education climate of the mid-nineteenth century, the difficulty of obtaining a charter was no barrier to founding a college. But the lack of degree-granting powers limited a college's ability to grow and to attract students. At the same time, seeking affiliation to a degree-granting university constrained a college to follow that university's requirements concerning examinations and therefore curriculum. What path would the governors of Royal Holloway take?

By the late 1890s, the college had slowly become more academic, using Oxford and London examinations as a guide to an appropriate university-level curriculum that emphasized the increasingly common 'single honours' model of advanced study in an individual subject, instead of a general liberal-arts degree. But some of the governors saw this as a missed opportunity to take the college in a direction that they thought more befitting to the class of 'ladies' they hoped to attract. One governor in particular, Sir M.E. Grant-Duff, argued that, in increasingly responding to the demands of students who sought a credential that would allow them to go into teaching, Royal Holloway had fallen afoul of Thomas Holloway's wish that the college not offer a narrowly vocational education. Leveraging the power that an appeal to the founder's wishes could have in a system of charities law designed to protect donors' intentions, Grant-Duff argued that Royal Holloway had a unique opportunity to develop a new kind of women's education. Those 'girls' who wished merely to pass examinations 'on account of the market value which attaches to having passed them' might study with coaches who would help them cram for exams, he wrote in an October 1897 memorandum. But those who had 'an interest in the things of the mind' might pursue an alternative curriculum. He proposed that Royal Holloway jettison its use of Oxford and London exams in favour of this alternative path.[46]

---

[46] M.E. Grant Duff, 'Memorandum', October 1897, RHC/1/7/9, RHUL, 2–3; Board of Governors' Minute Book, 1892–9, RHC/1/2/2, RHUL.

Yet in fact, Grant-Duff's proposal was exceptionally vocational in its orientation: not vocational in the sense of preparing students for a profession outside the home, but organized entirely around preparing students to be wives, mothers, and housekeepers. Grant-Duff held that the only subject 'indispensable' to Royal Holloway students was 'household management'. He recommended that students study only enough arithmetic to undertake household bookkeeping, that they be able to write good English essays and appreciate modern English literature, speak conversational French, have some acquaintance with history and geography, and be accomplished in art and music. He held that philosophy and higher mathematics were unlikely to be of interest to any women students. While they might learn first aid and gardening, advanced study of natural sciences would result in the production of overly specialized knowledge, working contrary to the aim of 'produc[ing] highly cultivated women'.[47] Underscoring the idea that Royal Holloway's education should be intended for the highest class of young women, he recommended the abolition of most scholarships. In one sense, then, his vision for the college was merely an elitist one, removing it from the reach of women who needed to earn their own living. But it was in another sense strikingly original. As Eleanor Sidgwick's data had demonstrated, women who went to college in order to seek professional qualifications and pursue careers were overwhelmingly also remaining unmarried. Grant-Duff's vision for Royal Holloway held out hope for an alternative: a women's college that would make its students more marriageable, not less.

Indeed, while Grant-Duff wrote that his scheme might be considered complementary to the efforts of other colleges to offer young women more academic forms of education, he also expressed the hope that it might in time come to be seen as the *best* way of educating women, and that Royal Holloway might be the cornerstone of a national women's university that would prepare students for a future not as 'assistant schoolmistresses', as he dismissively wrote, but as 'daughters, sisters, wives and mothers'.[48] Henry Sidgwick had originally conceptualized the idea of a federal women's university, uniting Oxford, Cambridge, and London women's colleges, in the 1860s. At a time when no university in the UK granted degrees to women, the idea seemed both pragmatic and innovative. But after the University of London admitted women to degrees in 1878, and UCL, as one of its constituent colleges, in turn admitted women on the same terms as men, starting an entirely new university came to seem less necessary. Rather, the minority who continued to believe that women's higher education must be fundamentally different and separate from men's began to hold tenaciously to the idea, even as their views came to seem increasingly outmoded.[49] Thirty years previous, Grant-Duff might have found common ground with many progressive reformers, including

---

[47] Grant-Duff, 'Memorandum', 4–9.   [48] Grant-Duff, 'Memorandum', 11–12.
[49] McWilliams-Tullberg, *Women at Cambridge*, 43, 120.

Reid, Maurice, Davies, and Sidgwick. But by the 1890s, his views were increasingly out of step with the mainstream, and the future of Royal Holloway as an independent institution looked uncertain.

Seeking to secure the college's financial future, the governors continued to believe that there was an untapped market of less academically inclined women students, whom the college might attract by offering two-year courses in modern languages, art, and music and one-year courses in hygiene, domestic economy, and needlework, instead of three- or four-year degree courses.[50] At the same time, in the 1896–7 academic year, the university senates of Oxford and Cambridge both rejected proposals to admit women to degrees. This was an opportunity for Royal Holloway to capture the market—but how? Deciding to consult outside opinion, the governors planned a conference and sent out invitations.

On Saturday, 4 December 1897, eighty delegates descended upon a rented conference room in central London. They included representatives from Oxford, Cambridge, and the London colleges; from local women's-education initiatives throughout the country; and from London girls' secondary schools. Almost half were women. Though some were Liberals and some Conservatives, some in favour of women's suffrage and some against, they shared a set of baseline assumptions. All took for granted that women university students were a population distinct from men whose needs should be considered separately—even if some ultimately came to the conclusion that women could and should be taught the same subjects on the same lines as men. Everyone assumed that residential and social life would remain gender-segregated, even in a mixed university, and accepted that women who wished to pursue a career instead of marriage were necessarily entering a different labour market from men. The college governors asked the delegates to consider three concrete options: whether Royal Holloway ought to become a standalone institution with the power to grant its own degrees; to affiliate with other women's colleges, such as those at Oxford and Cambridge, into a larger women's university; or to seek recognition as a constituent college of the University of London, meaning its students would sit London exams and receive London degrees.[51]

The delegates quickly discarded the notion of Royal Holloway becoming an independent institution. Although this had originally been the path Thomas Holloway envisioned, it became apparent that it was impractical within the existing structure of higher education in Britain.[52] On the other hand, several leaders of the Oxford anti-women's-degrees campaign attended the conference in order to propose that Royal Holloway become the cornerstone of a new national

---

[50] 'Financial Position and Future Development of Royal Holloway College', 1896, RHC/1/7/9, RHUL.

[51] 'University Degrees for Women: Report of a Conference Convened by the Governors of the Royal Holloway College and Held at the House of the Society of Arts on Saturday, 4th December, 1897' (London, 1898), RHC/1/7, RHUL, 7–8.

[52] 'University Degrees for Women', 8–10.

women's university. Though they spoke primarily about the importance of keeping women out of Oxford and Cambridge, they also concurred with Grant-Duff in seeing an opportunity for Royal Holloway to design a new kind of university education that would fit women for their distinctive role as wives and managers of households.[53]

These campaigners introduced their proposal early in the proceedings, and it sparked a backlash that shaped the rest of the conference. Twenty-one speakers focused their remarks on opposition to the scheme, arguing that education experts, women students, and their parents preferred degree courses that resembled as closely as possible men's university education. The heads of Oxford and Cambridge women's colleges, including Henry and Eleanor Sidgwick and Emily Davies, declared that they would never collaborate with such a project. Sophie Bryant, headmistress of North London Collegiate School for Girls, observed, 'I have never met with a woman who for herself wanted a Women's University. I have never even met with a woman who knew any other woman who desired to make use of such a University.'[54] Several other speakers observed that most women students were not ladies of leisure looking to broaden their cultural outlook. They were middle-class women seeking qualifications for professional careers that would allow them to support themselves, and who thus relied on the credentialling function of a diploma from a widely recognized university. There was so little demand for non-degree, non-university courses that even institutions that did offer such courses, like Queen's, suffered from declining enrolments.[55] Royal Holloway would have to adhere to the credentialling model in order to enrol enough students to remain financially viable.

As delegates discarded first the notion of Royal Holloway becoming an English Vassar and then, resoundingly, the proposal for a women's university, they arrived by default at the third option, becoming a constituent college of the University of London. Most of the delegates did believe that women would benefit from segregated residential and social lives, but also maintained that advanced single-honours courses in standard academic subjects were the most practical route to women's intellectual, professional, and social equality. The idea that Royal Holloway might be able to retain its identity as a women's college while still accessing London degrees and the university's wider resources seemed promising. At the same time, it raised further questions: for example, would Royal Holloway participate in the university's intercollegiate lecture scheme, which could see men students from other London colleges attending Royal Holloway lectures? And would subordination to the university senate limit the governors' ability to dutifully carry out their founder's wishes? Following the conference, Royal Holloway

---

[53] 'University Degrees for Women', 13–16.
[54] 'University Degrees for Women', 18–19.   [55] 'University Degrees for Women', 40, 46–7.

did seek affiliation with the University of London. But cultural and constitutional clashes between college and university would be a source of ongoing friction.

What was clear, however, was that the American women's-college model had not successfully translated to the British context. Liberal-arts education had become so associated with the ideas of men who felt that education in feminine accomplishments and housewifery was best suited to women's needs, that feminists and progressive education reformers found themselves rallying behind a model that looked more like Emily Davies's imitation of the Cambridge men's college. Furthermore, women seeking careers, especially as schoolteachers, needed qualifications that would be recognizable to hiring committees familiar with the names of institutions like Oxford, Cambridge, and London and with single-honours degrees in specific subjects, assessed through competitive examination; but not with the American model or with nascent, experimental institutions.[56] After the turn of the twentieth century, these pragmatic reasons for supporting the assimilation of women's education to the single-honours model began to intersect with new trends in national and imperial politics—producing, as we will see, new experiments in women's liberal-arts education, but ultimately even more momentum behind coeducation and the single-honours curriculum. Holloway's quixotic dream of an English Vassar, and Grant-Duff's aspiration to fulfil that vision after Holloway's death, were left behind in the face of these considerations.

The AEW: A Success Story?

As the Royal Holloway conference's ultimate decision to recommend affiliation to the University of London suggests, the 1890s were a tipping point, away from independent women's colleges and towards the affiliation of women's colleges to larger universities and, ultimately, those universities' formal gender integration. This happened before it was entirely clear that UK higher education would become increasingly homogenized, centralized, and organized around the model of the large, urban, primarily non-residential research university, but coeducation presaged this larger shift.

In part, this transition was shaped by the resounding defeat of women's degrees campaigns at Oxford and Cambridge in 1896–7, which shifted women's-education activists' focus away from these institutions and towards more winnable battles elsewhere. But it was also a product of several decades' worth of steady activism and institution-building elsewhere in the country, which the Royal Holloway

---

[56] See also memorials submitted to the 1896–7 Cambridge University Degrees for Women Syndicate, arguing that women who had studied at an Oxford or Cambridge women's college but could not take a BA from the university were disadvantaged in hiring. UA/Min.VI.23 and UA/Synd. II.7, CUL.

governors' heavy emphasis on Oxford and Cambridge as suitably socially elite reference points had led them to overlook. On the high tide of liberal education reform in the 1860s, activists had founded Associations for Promoting the Higher Education of Women (AEWs) in towns and cities across the country. AEWs were women-led, drawing on upper- and middle-class women activists' experience in political campaigning and charitable fundraising. But AEW leaders also recognized the limits of their knowledge about and access to higher education institutions, and sought to forge partnerships with sympathetic men allies who worked in local colleges and universities. AEWs had a dual role: they directly provided educational opportunities for women by arranging lecture series, administering exams, advising individual women how to construct their own university-level curricula through these lecture series and independent study, and organizing and supervising accommodation for women students; and they lobbied universities and government to admit women to formal university classes and degrees and to increase women's access to higher education.

Over the course of the 1860s–80s, the AEWs in cities such as Edinburgh, Glasgow, Manchester, Leeds, London, and Oxford became fully fledged parallel universities that operated seamlessly alongside the pre-existing men's colleges and universities in those cities. But they did so on different lines to the women's colleges like Queen's, Bedford, Girton, and Royal Holloway. Flexibility and ease of access were cornerstones of the AEW model: students could register for just one lecture series, or for an entire course of study assessed through accredited examinations and equivalent to a degree; they could study full-time or part-time; they could piece together a curriculum suited to their own personal or career goals; they could study while living at home or in a licensed hostel approved by the AEW. Studying part-time and at a non-residential institution could make higher education more accessible to many students who struggled to balance their studies alongside domestic responsibilities, or who could not afford the considerably higher cost of residence. AEWs provided access to classes and lectures that local men university faculty taught on a volunteer basis, offering a guarantee of quality and of equivalence to the education those faculty provided to their men students. At first, these were separate classes just for AEW students, but increasingly for reasons of efficiency faculty began simply to allow women to sit in on their regular lectures. At the same time, women AEW staff offered academic and pastoral advising tailored to women students, combining equality of opportunity with recognition of what most continued to believe were women students' necessarily distinct academic, professional, and personal needs.[57]

Perhaps the most distinctive element of the AEWs—and the factor that was most decisive in leading them to become the normative model of women's higher

---

[57] Dyhouse, *No Distinction of Sex?*, 14–16; Sutherland, *Faith, Duty, and the Power of Mind*, 90–3.

education—was their governance structure. The women who founded AEWs brought vision and administrative and fundraising experience to the projects, but they understood their success to be dependent upon collaboration with men academics and university administrators who offered experienced counsel on how to run a higher education institution. These collaborations were effective in providing women access to opportunities, but they were not without conflict. For example, the Edinburgh Ladies' Educational Association (ELEA), founded in 1867, initially limited its membership to women, with men only able to join as non-voting honorary members. The organization, its academic offerings, and its campaign for women to be admitted to degrees at the University of Edinburgh were expertly run by Mary Crudelius, the wife of a wool merchant with no previous administrative or campaigning experience. But Crudelius and her colleagues also sought carefully to manage the involvement of enthusiastic men allies such as Edinburgh English professor David Masson. Masson assumed a large share of the early teaching burden of the ELEA, liaised between the organization and the university, and recruited more of his university colleagues to join the ELEA's faculty. Masson and his colleagues argued that it was democratic to give the teaching faculty a share in the ELEA's governance, but ELEA women worried about ceding too much power to men. In the association's early years, they kept its organizing committee women-only and insisted on only canvassing women in fundraising appeals.[58] By 1876, though—when the association had expanded significantly and the University of Edinburgh was offering a non-degree certificate to women who pursued its curriculum—it ultimately yielded to Masson's and his colleagues' insistence that men be allowed onto the governing body and that a new committee be formed of professors who would oversee the curriculum.[59]

In this way, the ELEA's relationship with the university became gradually closer, but also gradually out of the hands of its women leaders. In the early 1870s, Crudelius perceived the AEW model to be a cautious and pragmatic one. The ELEA campaigned for women's admission to degrees, but remained content to run a parallel academic programme rather than address what Crudelius termed 'the vexed question of mixed classes'.[60] By the late 1870s, though, as men faculty took a more active role in directing this organization and organizations like it across Britain, it was they who simply opened their university classes to women registered with the AEWs, frustrated with the scheduling burden of having to give the same classes twice.[61]

---

[58] Letters from ELEA faculty to Crudelius, 1876, Coll-42/5/8, EUSC; 'Minutes of Meetings of the Edinburgh Ladies Educational Association', 1867–75, Coll-42/3/5, EUSC.

[59] Correspondence between Crudelius and Masson, 1868–76, Coll-42/5/1, EUSC; Report of the Edinburgh Ladies' Educational Association, 1876–7, Coll-42/1/4, EUSC.

[60] Report of the Edinburgh Ladies' Educational Association, 1869–70, Coll-42/1/4, EUSC.

[61] See the example of UCL, discussed in Negley Harte, John North, and Georgina Brewis, *The World of UCL* (London: UCL Press, 2018), 89. See also Elwick, *Making a Grade*, 12, 184.

In Glasgow, by contrast, activists did not found an AEW until 1877. But thanks to a £12,000 donation from Isabella Elder, the widow of a Clydeside shipping magnate, in 1884 the Glasgow AEW bought a large house and grounds, hired a teaching staff, established an endowment, and became Queen Margaret College (QMC), Scotland's only independent women's college.[62] QMC enjoyed close relations with the University of Glasgow, with university faculty teaching and examining on QMC courses and advising the college's governing council.[63] When the Scottish Universities Act 1889 granted Scottish universities the power to award degrees to women students, university administrators assumed that the University of Glasgow would simply absorb QMC.[64] But this became the subject of a long-running legal battle with Elder, who argued that she had endowed QMC on the basis that the teaching provided in the college would be completely separate and yet completely identical to the teaching provided to men at the university.[65] Yet the all-male faculty not only, as at Edinburgh, resented the burden of having to teach the same class twice over on two different campuses, many felt that they could treat their women students more fairly if they were not separated out as a distinct class of person.[66] Without the same obligation to comply with the conditions that donors attached to their donations that existed in English law, university administrators ultimately decided to ignore Elder and to fully integrate teaching—although QMC remained a hall of residence, student union, and centre for academic and pastoral advising for women students. Elder, who had previously been a major donor to the university, was deeply offended, and never donated again.[67] But her conviction that women's educational interests could only be safeguarded through a separate institution was coming to seem out of step with the times: as one senior male university administrator argued, the new generation of women students wanted 'to compete...with the men'.[68]

Formal equality had been the goal of most AEWs. Upon achieving admission to classes and to degrees, several—such as those in London and Manchester—voted to dissolve themselves. But the women activists who had founded the organizations remained ambivalent about the chain of events they had set in motion. In many cases, they continued to work in partnership with universities,

---

[62] Michael Moss, J. Forbes Munro, and Richard H. Trainor, *University, City and State: The University of Glasgow since 1870* (Edinburgh: Edinburgh University Press, 2000), 106.

[63] Queen Margaret College Annual Reports, 1885–93, DC 233/2/3, GUA.

[64] 'Memorial (Printed) and Drafts of the Council of Queen Margaret College to the Court of Glasgow University on Affiliation', 1890, DC 233/2/4/4/17, GUA.

[65] 'Correspondence between John Caird, Principal of Glasgow University and Mrs Isabella Elder concerning the separate teaching of women at Queen Margaret College', October 1892, GUA 62398, GUA.

[66] 'Statement by the Dean of the Faculty of Arts', DC 233/2/4/4/37, GUA, 5; 'Report (Printed) of Faculty of Arts, Glasgow University', 1896, DC 233/2/4/4/42, GUA, 1–3.

[67] Letters from Isabella Elder to Robert Story, 2 April, 5 April, and 15 April 1899, DC 21/290–292, GUA.

[68] David Murray, letter to Sheriff Barry, 11 July 1897, GUA 62445, GUA.

advocating for the establishment of new (often voluntary) administrative positions called 'tutors for women' in order to safeguard women students' interests within formally coeducational institutions. Conflicts between women activists and volunteers and men academics and administrators persisted in coeducational universities through the 1890s–1920s, reinscribing assumptions of essential differences between men and women students within coeducational institutions and structuring the terms on which the first generations of women students experienced higher education. Colleges and universities would never find the untapped market of women students seeking a practical higher education for marriage and motherhood that those like Grant-Duff had imagined. Instead, as we will see, students in coeducational universities discovered that, while pursuing the same courses of study alongside each other, they could relate to one another through a more pleasure-oriented vision of sex and romance—transforming how young people thought about marriage, heterosexuality, and the purpose of higher education.

Historians of women's higher education have long recognized the importance of AEWs in opening up the Scottish and the English 'civic' universities to women.[69] But what has been less well understood is how the apparent success of the AEWs, both at meeting the immediate practical needs of prospective women students and at working in tandem with existing institutional structures, foreclosed an alternative set of possibilities that, until the 1890s, seemed like a possible direction for women's higher education. When women's higher education first became thinkable in the mid-nineteenth century, amid the nexus of liberalism, evangelicalism, and a changing institutional and financial landscape for secondary and higher education, reformers imagined that it would take place in separate institutions, to suit the distinctive personal and academic needs of upper- and middle-class women who would become wives and mothers. While liberal reformers took the lead on establishing new independent women's colleges, these ventures enjoyed broad support (including substantial financial support) from members of high society of all political persuasions. Though they had differing visions of what it might mean in practical terms, founders of independent women's colleges saw themselves as offering practical solutions to the problems that women faced in developing their minds, broadening their cultural horizons, training for careers, and accessing expanded social opportunities. They drew on existing English ideals of residential collegiate higher education historically reserved only for men, American models of residential collegiate higher education for women, and novel models of their own, including the dream of a national federal women's university to rival Oxford and Cambridge.

---

[69] Dyhouse, *No Distinction of Sex?*, 15.

That the national federal women's university never came to be owes itself to a set of contingent circumstances of the 1860s–90s that saw women's-education activists turn away from the residential college as an expensive, resource-intensive model increasingly associated with a conservative and narrowly class-bound conception of education for 'ladies', and towards what came to be seen as the more expedient solution of the AEW. This did not mean that women's-education activists necessarily perceived formal coeducation as the ideal way to guarantee women students' equality of opportunity. Many, perhaps most, remained committed to the idea that some gender segregation was necessary, even in the formally gender-integrated university. But their institutional visions increasingly became marginalized, as men faculty, university administrators, and national politicians and civil servants all, for different reasons, threw their support behind the AEW model. In the process, the vision of a higher education that would elevate and professionalize the feminine role of the wife and mother also fell by the wayside. The next chapter takes this story into the twentieth century, which saw the emergence of a national higher education sector organized around the norm of the large, urban, public research university that also, incidentally, became coeducational.

Teaching Gender: The British University and the Rise of Heterosexuality, 1860–1939. Samuel Rutherford,
Oxford University Press. © Samuel Rutherford 2025. DOI: 10.1093/9780198937524.003.0002

2

Efficiency, Centralization, and Integration

Between 1878 and 1904, every degree-granting university in the United Kingdom except Oxford and Cambridge admitted women to degrees. In 1901, over half of full-time men students and three-quarters of full-time women students attended a coeducational university, a figure that would rise to almost 70 per cent of men students and 85 per cent of women students by the late 1930s.[1] This rapid transformation in the constitution of British higher education was not, primarily, owing to the efforts of feminist activists, or even those who took any interest at all in the principle of gender equality. Rather, it was a byproduct of enthusiasm for the principle of 'efficiency' that took over Liberal intellectual life and institutional administration in the early twentieth century, coupled with a revolution in Liberal intellectuals' and politicians' conception of the capacity of the state to organize institutions and solve social problems. These political shifts resulted in the efficiency-driven nationalization of British higher education in the years around 1910–20, and the incidental absorption of women into a centrally coordinated, largely state-funded higher education system.

University reform in Scotland presaged these wider developments. In Scotland there had for centuries been a tradition of the university as a source of social mobility, civic pride, and national identity.[2] The urban universities in Edinburgh, Glasgow, and Aberdeen enjoyed support from local civic leaders, and from the late nineteenth century all four Scottish universities collectively received a modest grant from the Treasury in Westminster at a time when no English university was receiving such state funding. Legislative reforms in 1858 and 1889 standardized governance structures and curricula across the Scottish universities, effectively creating a national system decades before anything similar was contemplated in England or across the four home nations.[3] Coeducation was an incidental part of this process: the Scottish Universities Act 1889 clarified that Scottish universities had the power to determine their own admissions policies, opening the door to the admission of women, which universities welcomed due to their existing good

---

[1] Carol Dyhouse, *Students: A Gendered History* (London: Routledge, 2006), 4.

[2] R.D. Anderson, *Education and Opportunity in Victorian Scotland* (Edinburgh: Edinburgh University Press, 1989), 124, 149–57.

[3] Robert Anderson and Stuart Wallace, 'The Universities and National Identity in the Long Nineteenth Century, c. 1830–1914', in *The Edinburgh History of Education in Scotland*, ed. Robert Anderson, Mark Freeman, and Lindsay Paterson (Edinburgh: Edinburgh University Press, 2015), 265–85; Robert Anderson, 'Professors and Examinations: Ideas of the University in Nineteenth-Century Scotland', *History of Education* 46, no. 1 (January 2017): 21–38.

relations with AEWs. In 1901, a $10 million donation from Andrew Carnegie established a fund that made tuition free for all Scottish students attending Scottish universities, transforming the conditions of higher education in Scotland and underscoring the Scottish universities' status as institutions serving the public good of the Scottish nation.

From the turn of the twentieth century, leading politicians and civil servants drew on the Scottish model and brought it south: seeking to develop this kind of civic higher education throughout England, Wales, and Ireland, but also to make the University of London and the government in Westminster anchors for a more centralized and substantially state-funded university system. In the process—though without necessarily meaning to—reformers, as in the Scottish case, incidentally made UK higher education coeducational. Those donors, activists, and intellectuals who continued to support independent women's institutions found their views sidelined and ignored, as university administrators and national politicians threw their weight behind a nationally integrated, state-funded higher education system in which the paradigmatic institution was the large, urban, non-residential research university that was incidentally coeducational. Between the 1890s and the 1920s, a long and hard-fought campaign for institutional reform within the University of London unfolded against the backdrop of these changing politics, with significant consequences for independent women's colleges—especially those with more idiosyncratic administrative structures or curricula, such as Royal Holloway and a new venture, Kensington-based King's College for Women. In an economic climate in which state funding for higher education became increasingly necessary to universities' survival, leading after the First World War to the establishment of the first permanent government agency to administer higher education funding and policy, those who sought to promote the gender-segregated residential college—whether for women or for men, though especially for women—struggled to make themselves heard.

To politicians and civil servants, nationalization was a victory, though their plans also took care to safeguard institutional and academic freedom. Yet this did not go far enough for some conservatives, who cast themselves in resistance to government-imposed logics of efficiency, modernization, and the gender integration that efficiency and modernization implied. To some women academics and activists, coeducation of the sector was a positive outcome, allowing for expanded academic opportunities for a younger generation increasingly able to pursue advanced research in traditional academic disciplines. But to others, it was a profound loss: eradicating the freedom that they had experienced earlier in the nineteenth century to undertake experiments in curriculum and institutional structure, as well as the prospect that higher education might be able to enrich the lives of women who did not intend to pursue careers outside the home. Coeducation happened incidentally, imperfectly, and at the expense of a variety of earlier efforts to establish spaces for women's higher education. It was this set

of contingent political circumstances, unexpected alliances, and uneasy compromises that structured the terms on which faculty and students remade gender
and sexuality within the space of the coeducational university.

New Liberalism and National Efficiency

The years between 1885 and 1914 saw the emergence of important new strands in
political thought, politics, and public policy that emphasized expanded conceptions of the role of the state to direct the economy and society; an increased role
for technocratic 'expertise'; and popular appeals to national and imperial patriotism
amid both the growth of mass democracy in Britain and a changing geopolitical
order that saw empires such as Germany, the United States, and Japan challenging
Britain's pre-eminence. These political changes, which reached their fullest
expression in the Liberal government that came to power following a landslide
victory in the 1906 general election, significantly affected national higher education policy and established a place for a new kind of university within British
public life.

The historian Keith Vernon has identified a nexus of 'idealism and efficiency'
shaping national education policy at the turn of the twentieth century.[4] British
idealism was an academic philosophical movement that enjoyed a moment of
remarkable popularity specifically in Oxford and the Scottish universities in the
1870s–80s, influencing a generation of elite young people (at that point overwhelmingly men) who subsequently went into politics and public policy. It perceived community as the most fundamental level of human organization, and the
self-development of the individual as a moral calling that tended towards the
benefit of society as a whole. Though idealists disagreed about the appropriate
extent of the powers of the state and its intervention into people's lives, they
tended to view the state as a moral agent with the capacity and the duty to allevi-
ate the social problems of industrial modernity.[5] This was an important challenge
to the individualism and faith in the free market of the earlier Victorian period.
Idealism was therefore consistent with a belief in the value of higher education as
a public good and as an agent of individual self-development and social renewal.

The ideology of 'national efficiency', by contrast, arose in the context of anxiety
about the British Empire's ability to compete with other world powers that
emerged from Britain's pyrrhic victory in the South African War of 1899–1902.
Informed in part by social-Darwinist ideas about competition between different
races or civilizations, a cross-party group of public intellectuals with close ties to

---

[4] Keith Vernon, *Universities and the State in England, 1850–1939* (Abingdon: Routledge, 2004), 136–7.
[5] Sandra M. den Otter, *British Idealism and Social Explanation: A Study in Late-Victorian Thought* (Oxford: Clarendon Press, 1996).

government argued that building a more 'efficient' British Empire would involve greater centralized planning of the economy and the military, greater physical fitness of the general population, and a centralized national higher education system that would emphasize scientific research. All of this would be managed by a technocratic elite of experts.[6] Both the social sciences and the applied sciences therefore assumed greater importance in the minds of national efficiency enthusiasts. Drawing on models from Germany and the United States, they advocated the founding of new departments and institutions that would promote advanced research in these fields, and emphasized that research's strategic importance.

No individual better exemplifies the fusion of idealism and efficiency, and its impact upon the development of a national higher education system, than the long-serving Liberal MP Richard Burdon Haldane. Born in 1856 in Edinburgh, Haldane studied philosophy at the University of Edinburgh. He spent a pivotal term studying abroad at the University of Göttingen, during which he became a fluent German speaker and an enthusiastic proponent of idealism. After university, he built a successful legal career before being elected as the MP for East Lothian, a constituency east of Edinburgh, in 1885. He was an enthusiastic liberal imperialist, as eager to expropriate resources from the colonies in order to secure Britain's position on the world stage as to advance social reformist projects in the metropole. He was a skilled politician who worked hard behind the scenes to further his personal enthusiasms, none more so than higher education. Drawing both on Scottish and on German models, Haldane made important contributions to expanding higher education in Ireland and in the North of England, promoting university extension and adult education. Above all, he led the way in making London into a centre of research and teaching in fields meeting imperial strategic needs, from engineering and economics to teacher training. Haldane sought on a practical level to systematize and centralize higher education, but at the same time he saw universities as an organic expression of the spirit of the British nation and empire and as a source of moral and social uplift.[7]

The conception of higher education's role in the life of the nation and empire that resulted from this moment was profoundly gendered, and entwined with the question of how women would be incorporated within the newly systematized structure. At the same time that a group of mostly men politicians, civil servants, and university administrators were contributing to this reconceptualization of higher education, the movement for women's inclusion in the national franchise

---

[6] G.R. Searle, *The Quest for National Efficiency: A Study in British Politics and Political Thought, 1899–1914* (Berkeley: University of California Press, 1971); Bernard Semmel, *Imperialism and Social Reform: English Social-Imperial Thought, 1895–1914* (London: Allen & Unwin, 1960).

[7] H.C.G. Matthew, 'Haldane, Richard Burdon, Viscount Haldane (1856–1928), Politician, Educationist, and Lord Chancellor', *Oxford Dictionary of National Biography*, 6 January 2011, accessed 24 May 2024, https://www.oxforddnb.com/view/10.1093/ref:odnb/9780198614128.001.0001/odnb-9780198614128-e-33643?rskey=FNmqOG&result=3; Eric Ashby and Mary Anderson, *Portrait of Haldane at Work on Education* (London: Macmillan, 1974).

was gaining in visibility, popularity, and radicalism. As both the 'constitutionalist' and 'militant' wings of the women's suffrage movement became more radical, leading suffragists' justifications of women's claim to the political sphere became increasingly grounded in essentialist rhetoric: advocating women's entitlement to the franchise on the basis of their moral purity, status as mothers, and systematic oppression as a sex class.[8] To a striking extent, sex essentialism was something suffrage activists shared with anti-suffrage women, with whom they had often worked together previously on issues such as women's education. Both suffrage and anti-suffrage activists accorded women a vital role in social reform, and perceived higher education for women as a means to develop women's capacities to act in that sphere.[9]

A disconnect emerged between this wider political context and Haldane's ambitions for British higher education, even as suffrage militancy escalated in the years before the First World War. As Haldane and his allies took it upon themselves to redesign higher education in London, they professed themselves ardent supporters of women's rights. But they barely took into consideration the views of women academics, administrators, and activists, who often sought to defend gender-segregated women's higher education. This resulted in unexpected alliances and divisions that, ultimately, brought women into large, urban research universities on the same formal terms as men, but at the expense of the gender-differentiated conceptions of higher education that had emerged in the nineteenth century. It is possible to understand in more detail how this occurred by turning to the examples of some London women's colleges that were casualties of the reorganization of the University of London and the subsequent fuller nationalization of higher education.

Applied Sciences for Women?

In 1907, despite this tendency towards centralization, an eclectic group of education reformers decided to undertake an ambitious but idiosyncratic experiment: a university-level degree course in 'domestic science'. A new academic discipline that had begun to take shape in the United States at the end of the nineteenth century, domestic science sought to find new ways of rationalizing and systematizing housework; to educate mothers, social workers, policymakers, and the public about health and sanitation; to undertake experimental, laboratory-based research into food, hygiene, and public health; and to elevate the role of the

[8] Sandra Stanley Holton, *Feminism and Democracy: Women's Suffrage and Reform Politics in Britain 1900–1918* (Cambridge: Cambridge University Press, 1986), 12–28; Susan Pedersen, 'A Knife to the Heart', *London Review of Books* 40, no. 16 (30 August 2018).

[9] Julia Bush, *Women against the Vote: Female Anti-Suffragism in Britain* (Oxford: Oxford University Press, 2007).

housewife as a manager of a household who was an expert in her own field. The reformers who sought to import domestic science to British higher education thus looked back to the work of earlier women's education reformers who had conceptualized gender-differentiated higher education as making more meaningful the distinct life paths that middle-class women already pursued, whether within or outside the home. At the same time, they were part of the turn to national efficiency, imagining that domestic science research might have national strategic importance in the same way that engineering or agricultural science research did: thus justifying state funding in higher education and tending toward a healthier, fitter, more efficient nation and empire that would remain strategically competitive with other world powers.[10]

Yet however vociferously domestic science advocates made the case for the academic rigour of their subject, and for its contrast with old-fashioned ideas of feminine 'accomplishments', the field was never able to escape the perception that it was too feminized to be a serious course of academic study or professional training. Although borne out of the national efficiency movement, it—like other conceptions of gender-segregated women's higher education—also became a victim of it.[11] Though there was never a moment at which domestic science was part of the mainstream of British higher education, its fate is illustrative of how the structure and culture of higher education were changing in this moment—and why an important consequence of this was to marginalize women's colleges within the larger national higher education landscape.

The group who conceptualized the domestic science degree course represented a range of perspectives about the purpose and structure of higher education for women. Arthur Smithells was a chemistry teacher at the rigorously academic Manchester High School for Girls, who had become nationally recognized for designing a new science curriculum that connected the abstract principles of physics and chemistry to 'practical' applications such as baking, successfully engaging girls who had previously been bored or intimidated by science. Alice Ravenhill, a Co-operative Society hygiene lecturer who had recently returned from undertaking a Board of Education-funded study of American home economics courses, was an anti-suffragist who thought that women's distinct capacities and social roles meant that domestic science was the primary contribution they could and should make to public life. Thereza Rücker, a highly educated and religious woman who had assisted her geologist father with his research before

[10] Nancy L. Blakestad, 'King's College of Household and Social Science and the Household Science Movement in English Higher Education, c. 1908-1939' (PhD thesis, University of Oxford, 1994), 95-100; Anna Davin, 'Imperialism and Motherhood', History Workshop, no. 5 (April 1978): 9-65.

[11] Samuel Rutherford, 'Higher Learning and Contestations', in The Cultural History of Higher Learning in the Age of Industry, ed. Heather Ellis and Tamson Pietsch (London: Bloomsbury, 2025). An earlier version of some of the material about domestic science in this chapter originally appeared in my chapter in The Cultural History of Higher Learning in the Age of Industry. I am grateful to Bloomsbury Academic for permission to reproduce this material.

marrying the principal of the University of London, thought that a university course in domestic science would provide new, but appropriately feminine, opportunities for women's employment. She also saw domestic science education as fundamental to a eugenicist project '[f]or the future of a nobler race' that would 'arrest decay and enable our Nation to hold its own', as she wrote in a fundraising appeal.[12] Smithells, Ravenhill, and Rücker found a home for the course at King's College for Women (KCW), a small, somewhat conservative, Anglican institution that had begun life as an AEW scheme associated with King's College London and remained closely linked to KCL.

All the members of the organizing committee must have agreed to use Rücker's social-Darwinist language in the fundraising appeal, indicating the extent to which racist, imperialist logic suffused the project. At the same time, the last founder of the domestic science course came to support it from a different perspective. Hilda Oakeley, the daughter of a schools inspector, had a first career working in settlement houses in London before entering Somerville College, Oxford in 1894, at the age of twenty-seven. She excelled at Oxford's distinctive 'literae humaniores' classics and philosophy course, leaving Oxford with a faith in liberal education as a route to self-development and as something that would, by enriching students' intellectual and ethical capacities, endow them with the cast of mind to solve practical social problems. After helping to found a new women's college at McGill University in Montreal, Oakeley returned to England. She taught briefly at Manchester before taking up a position as vice-principal at KCW, in which capacity she encountered Smithells, Rücker, and Ravenhill.[13] Her experiences in the residential collegiate environments of Somerville and McGill, and the liberal-arts curriculum she had encountered at McGill and when visiting other universities in North America, were personally transformative, going on to shape her ambitious yet open-ended aspirations for women's higher education in Britain.[14]

Like Haldane, then, Oakeley brought a background in academic philosophy and a passionate faith in liberal idealism to her work in educational reform and administration. But unlike Haldane, Oakeley singled out women's higher education as especially in need of revitalization. And unlike both Haldane and her colleagues in the domestic science scheme, she was a strident critic of efficiency logics. An interdisciplinary humanities education grounded in philosophy,

[12] 'King's College for Women Department of Home Science and Economics', 1910, Q/EPH/SYL/3, KCL; 'National Fund for Endowment of Home Science', n.d. (c.1913), Papers of Sir John Adkins, Q/PP1, KCL.
[13] Janet Howarth, 'Oakeley, Hilda Diana (1867–1950), Educationist and Author', Oxford Dictionary of National Biography, 23 September 2004, accessed 6 August 2022, https://www.oxforddnb.com/display/10.1093/ref:odnb/9780198614128.001.0001/odnb-9780198614128-e-48502.
[14] Letters from Hilda Oakeley to S. Margery Fry, 1898–1904 (see esp. 25 August 1904), Margery Fry Papers, Box 27 Folder 8, Somerville College, Oxford; Hilda Oakeley, History & Progress, and Other Essays and Addresses (London: George Allen & Unwin, 1923).

she thought, would give students the necessary tools for 'dealing with social and political problems' while combating 'the doctrinairism of the statesman who has dabbled in political science'.[15] Though initially sceptical when she learned that her role at KCW would involve helping to establish the domestic science course, Oakeley came to see domestic science as part of her overall mission as a philosopher and educator 'to make a further contribution to the solution of that supreme practical problem, the problem of the right relation of knowledge to life'.[16] She argued that combining education in the abstract principles of fields as diverse as organic chemistry, economics, child development, and ethics with their practical applications offered radical new possibilities for the development of self and society.[17]

Though they may have come to their views for different reasons, Rücker, Ravenhill, and Smithells agreed with Oakeley that the time was right for experimentation in the form and content of women's education. In their initial brainstorming, the organizing committee sought to ensure that subjects such as philosophy and economic history featured alongside hygiene and 'practical chemistry' (i.e. cooking and baking). They also envisioned a hall of residence that would provide students with practical experience in skills such as cooking, laundry, and managing a budget.[18] The concept of a degree course in domestic science thus had an innovative, experimental appeal that could unite suffragists and anti-suffragists, humanities scholars and social reformers, those who believed in the ideology of separate spheres and those who had spent their careers overcoming it. It was much more than a curriculum of feminine 'accomplishments' like that which Grant-Duff had imagined for Royal Holloway—though it contained enough of those elements to attract the interest of those who held traditional ideas about women's social roles. To those who designed, implemented, and supported the scheme, it was distinctively modern, rising to meet the challenges of twentieth-century workplaces, motherhood, and national and imperial competition.

In autumn 1907, KCW officially launched a three-year degree-level course in 'Home Science and Economics'. Though the University of London, through which KCW awarded degrees, had not yet approved the course as qualifying for the BSc degree, KCW proposed to issue a diploma certifying that the student had passed a set of degree-level examinations. In their first year, students would study biology, chemistry, economics, hygiene, cookery, and their choice of divinity, philosophy, or literature; over the course of the degree, study would become increasingly specialized and practically oriented towards household management,

---

[15] Hilda Oakeley, 'History and Progress' (a lecture given at McGill in 1900), in *History & Progress*, 13.
[16] Oakeley, 'Home Science', in *History & Progress*, 227.   [17] Oakeley, 'Home Science', 228.
[18] 'Report on the Scheme for a Diploma in Household Science', n.d. (c.1912), QAP/GPF/1, KCL.

food and cookery, business affairs, and child development. The syllabus stated that the course might be especially useful to 'young women whose position in life is likely to call them in the future to the management of a great household or a large estate'; to women planning to emigrate to the colonies and who therefore might be expected to manage without domestic help; and to those who planned to pursue careers as matrons of hostels or hospitals or as teachers of domestic science.[19] By the course's third year, sixty of KCW's 167 students were studying domestic science.[20] The initiative attracted significant interest from prestigious donors—including Queen Mary, the wife of King George V; the Duke of Devonshire; the Goldsmiths' and Clothworkers' Companies; and the Rothschilds—allowing the college to begin to plan a new purpose-built campus in Kensington.[21] As in the case of Royal Holloway, an institution invested in a specific, gender-differentiated vision of higher education for women could attract significant support from high society. But this did not necessarily translate into support from intellectuals and academics, who often argued that, however scientifically robust, no course called 'domestic science' should have a place in higher education.

In 1910, in an effort to promote the course, Oakeley wrote a series of articles in which she made a case for domestic science's humanistic qualities, its appeal to a large potential audience, and its power to help rather than hinder the cause of women's education. In an article in *Common Cause*, the magazine of the constitutionalist wing of the suffrage movement, she criticized those women's rights activists who argued that domestic science detracted from efforts to secure women's status in traditional academic subjects. Women's right to study mathematics or classics at the women's colleges in Oxford and Cambridge was now well established, she wrote, but 'To accept the older established as the only valuable methods, because the movement for the Higher Education of women found them already in the field, would surely be incompatible with the spirit of that movement.' It was short-sighted to suggest that university study was incapable of encompassing such fields of knowledge as hygiene and household management. If women education reformers turned their attention to the study of the household, moreover, surely they would improve it, just as they had more traditional forms of higher education.[22]

Oakeley's essays referenced Plato and Aristotle, John Henry Newman and John Dewey; to her, domestic science was just one more piece of evidence for education's potential to contribute to human flourishing. But this was a striking claim

---

[19] 'The Higher Education of Women. Proposed Scheme for Establishing Courses of a University Standard in Home Science and Economics', 1907–8, KW/SYL/15a, KCL.

[20] 'Reports and Memoranda on Application to the University Grants Committee for a Grant for the Development of the College' (1910), KWA/GPF/9, KCL; 'Minutes of the Committee of Management of King's College for Women' (1907–11), KW/M/5, KCL.

[21] 'Donations to the Household and Social Science Department of King's College for Women, University of London', December 1915, QAP/GPF/1, KCL.

[22] Hilda D. Oakeley, 'Home Science and Economics', *Common Cause*, 13 October 1910, 428–9.

to put forward in a suffrage publication in 1910, at a time when the 'constitutionalist' and 'militant' wings of the suffrage movement were united in attempting to work with a cross-party group of MPs to craft legislation. Oakeley's essays generated furious debate, with opponents doubting whether gender-essentialist conceptions of women's education were compatible with those that prioritized formal equality, and worrying that domestic science would set back the cause of women's higher education for which they had spent decades fighting.[23] The debate over domestic science thus demands to be read in the context of wider discussions over vision and strategy in the women's movement at this moment, with the high political stakes of the suffrage campaign making Oakeley's more catholic stance difficult to maintain.

One of the most outspoken and persistent voices in opposition to Oakeley was that of Ida Freund, a chemistry fellow at Newnham College, Cambridge and a prominent advocate for girls' science education. To Freund, single-honours degrees in physics, chemistry, and biology were the gold standard of higher education in science, and the goal of an undergraduate science degree for a student of any gender should be to prepare her or him to undertake advanced pure scientific research. Domestic science's interdisciplinary approach was too eclectic to be the basis of a comprehensive science curriculum, and thus would prepare students neither for life nor for university.[24] It might train a woman to bake a perfect chocolate cake, Freund wrote, but it would hardly allow her to 'succeed in adding something, however small, to the stock of the world's knowledge' in the way that study at Cambridge might.[25] As Oakeley and Freund debated each other in the letters pages of Common Cause and in other venues throughout 1911 and 1912, Freund continued to label domestic science a 'pseudoscience', arguing that it was deleterious to efforts to raise standards in women's higher education and risked enforcing a distinction between subjects of study appropriate for men and for women.[26]

To be sure, Freund had reason to believe that domestic science might prove detrimental to the cause of women's education. Some defences of domestic science in the education press did have more in common with Grant-Duff's vision of education for marriage at Royal Holloway than with Oakeley's avant-garde

---

[23] See esp. Walter Winter, 'Domestic Science and the Universities', Common Cause, 3 November 1910, 491; Margaret McKillop, 'Domestic Science and the Universities', Common Cause, 24 November 1910, 543–4.

[24] Ida Freund, 'Domestic Science–A Protest', The Englishwoman, May 1911, 149–63.

[25] Ida Freund, 'Domestic Science—A Protest. II.', The Englishwoman, June 1911, 279–96.

[26] Hilda Oakeley, 'Letter to the Editor', Common Cause, 22 February 1912, 789; Oakeley, 'Home Science and Economics: A Note on Miss Freund's Article', Common Cause, 7 March 1912, 817–18; Oakeley, 'Domestic Science', Common Cause, 28 March 1912, 872. Oakeley's notes on the debate and manuscript copies of her letters to the editor are collected in 'Out-Correspondence of Warden Concerning Establishment of Home Science Course', 1911–12, KWA/GPF/11, KCL. Ida Freund, 'Letter to the Editor', Common Cause, 29 February 1912, 195–7; Freund, 'A Degree Standard in Home Science', Common Cause, 14 March 1912, 832–4.

experiments in liberal education.[27] Having excelled in her studies at Girton in the 1880s—at a time when women science students in particular were extremely marginalized in Cambridge—Freund knew advances in women's higher education to be tenuous and hard-won, and may well have feared their erosion.[28] But so too must have Oakeley, who was four years younger than Freund and had also been extraordinarily successful in the most competitive academic examinations then open to women. While their disagreement was in part about how best to advance the cause of women's equality, it was also about how best to design an undergraduate degree course. Freund, who had studied at Davies's Girton and then spent her entire career in Cambridge, saw the single-honours model and its emphasis on competitive examinations as a way to ensure high standards and thus gender equality. But Oakeley had spent a formative period of her career in Canada. She had thus gained familiarity with the North American general-education model and its ability to provide a common foundation for students whose secondary education had been more varied and uneven. Oakeley, unlike Freund, thought that higher education should be open to everyone, not only the most talented.[29]

But Oakeley and her colleagues continued to face problems in explaining how their vision would fit in with the overall structure of UK higher education, and in confronting the reality of prospective students' academic ability. Prospectuses listed the names of domestic science graduates pursuing high-profile professional careers, but the more typical student could not pass first-year University of London exams in basic general science.[30] Academically rigorous girls' secondary schools encouraged students who demonstrated potential in science to apply to courses in the traditional science disciplines at more prestigious colleges and universities, while those who were attracted by the idea of a degree in domestic science often were not especially academically gifted at science, or had not had the opportunity to attend the kind of school that might have prepared them for university-level science work. The course's advocates had hoped that it would be a way of 'providing women who had less opportunity to develop their scientific interests with an entry point into university and a professional life which might otherwise have been closed to them'.[31] But this could not happen if teachers continued to believe, like Freund, that domestic science was not a real science course, and that only those students who had previously demonstrated talent at science should study it at university. This left domestic science, like other

[27] 'Secondary Schools Association. Conference at Bradford', Education 17, no. 428 (10 March 1911): 142–5, at 145; see also e.g. Hubert Curtis, 'Home Science Teachers in Secondary Schools. To the Editor of Education', Education 17, no. 444 (30 June 1911): 410–11.

[28] On the experience of women science students in late-nineteenth-century Cambridge see Marsha L. Richmond, '"A Lab of One's Own": The Balfour Biological Laboratory for Women at Cambridge University, 1884–1914', Isis 88, no. 3 (1997): 422–55.

[29] Hilda Oakeley, My Adventures in Education (London: Williams and Northgate, 1939), 69–73.

[30] 'Minutes of Staff Meetings', 1902–9, KW/M/9, KCL.

[31] Blakestad, 'King's College of Household and Social Science', 330.

gender-differentiated conceptions of women's higher education, in an uncertain position, even as more masculinized applied sciences were coming to seem central to reformers' vision for a reimagined University of London.

Reforming the University of London

At this time, significant changes were underway within the University of London. The university had been founded in 1825 essentially as an examination board to regulate degree examinations at colleges across Britain and the empire, including two London-based colleges, University College and King's College. But as the number of higher education institutions in London proliferated, reformers began to call for the university to become a teaching institution, with London-area colleges incorporated as constituent schools. This would mean that the same faculty would both teach classes and set exams, and grant teaching faculty representation in university governance—leading to greater professional autonomy and academic freedom for faculty. But some national efficiency enthusiasts also saw the reform process as an opportunity to enact their ideal of a rationalized, unified institution, located on a central campus, with a budget controlled by a central university council with extensive executive powers. These included Haldane, at the time a rising star on the left wing of the Liberal party, and his friend Sidney Webb, who was involved in London education reform in his capacity as chair of the London County Council's Technical Education Board.[32] Together, Webb and Haldane masterminded a scheme for reform of the university, and Haldane steered it through Parliament over considerable opposition and despite a Conservative government being in power.

Webb and Haldane did not achieve the full centralization for which they had hoped, but the University of London Act 1898 instituted a standing commission to oversee the work of the university; a new constitution which centralized governance in a court, council, and senate along the Scottish model becoming common at non-Oxbridge English universities; faculties and boards of studies that would regulate curriculum and examinations; a distinction between 'internal' students who would attend courses and 'external' students who could sit London exams anywhere in the world; and a formal statement of non-discrimination on the basis of sex and religion. It also made important determinations about what counted as a university subject, which would have consequences for London colleges and their students and teachers. Music and law were out (the latter because the Inns of Court, with closer ties to Oxford and Cambridge, had refused to be included in the scheme), but Haldane's and Webb's great personal preoccupations,

---

[32] Vernon, *Universities and the State*, 69–88.

the new subjects of engineering and political science, were in. Each man had also played a central role in the foundation of a new college—Haldane, the engineering-focused Imperial College; Webb, the London School of Economics (LSE)—for which they sought to establish a prominent position in the restructured university.[33]

Haldane and Webb were able to gain a still more prominent role in higher education policy with the help of a new ally, Robert Morant, permanent secretary at the Board of Education from 1903 and another disciple of the efficiency movement. Universities around the country—especially in Wales and Scotland—had been receiving some Treasury funding since the mid-nineteenth century, but it was small and sporadic. Following calls from a group of vice-chancellors from northern English universities for larger and more systematic grants, as well as the altered political circumstances that followed the 1906 general election, the Treasury appointed a committee, with Haldane as chair, to investigate the grants system. It was not yet possible to reach agreement between the Treasury, the Board of Education, and university vice-chancellors about how best to institutionalize state funding for higher education, but grants increased steadily.[34]

London women's colleges, including KCW and Royal Holloway, struggled in the changing policy environment. Increasing centralization of the University of London and of national higher education policy would not safeguard the interests of small institutions that served specific constituencies and had reasons to keep their governance structures and curricula different from the norm. When, after its 1897 conference, Royal Holloway decided to apply for affiliation to the University of London, the small-town women's college did not fit easily within the metropolitan university. The older, conservative voices overrepresented on the board of governors increasingly began to object to cooperation with the University of London, worrying that university curricula were too narrowly career-oriented, that collaborating in initiatives such as an intercollegiate lecture scheme eroded the college's gender-segregated identity, and that it was being dragged far from Thomas Holloway's original vision. Adhering to the original intent of the founder became a refrain on the part of governors who feared that the expansive reach of the University of London was turning their college into something alien over which they had no control.[35]

The position of KCW's domestic science department was even more fraught. To KCW administrators, the domestic science students' membership in a college that offered access to classes in the humanities and social sciences allowed them to pursue a truly liberal education. Administrators also asserted the value of having a women's college in Kensington, a part of the city without other educational

[33] Vernon, *Universities and the State*, 89, 163–4.
[34] Vernon, *Universities and the State*, 134–59.
[35] Board of Governors minute books, 1899–1907 and 1907–12, RHC/1/2/3–4, RHCA.

opportunities for women, for students whose parents did not wish them to take public transportation to college. But to the newly empowered University of London Senate, having several small women's colleges throughout the city was inefficient, and KCW's plan for a residential campus in Kensington where domestic science students could practise their skills by running the college's hall of residence was not in keeping with the academic standardization, enforced through competitive examinations, that the reformed teaching university sought to institute.[36]

In 1909, the government authorized a Royal Commission to determine the best way to rationalize the many different institutions of higher education in London and to provide the University Senate with the means to govern them. To that date the largest-ever state inquiry into higher education, the commission was again chaired by Haldane, then serving as Secretary of State for War in H.H. Asquith's Liberal government. Haldane had recently concluded a successful project to modernize and rationalize the organization of the army. He returned to his pet project of the University of London with greater fervour, and what was to become known as the Haldane Commission clearly bore the stamp of his thinking.[37] In addition to Haldane's old collaborator Robert Morant, shortly to leave the Board of Education to head the new National Insurance Commission, the other members of the committee included Alfred Milner, who had been governor of the Cape Colony during the South African War and was now a Unionist member of the House of Lords and trustee of the Rhodes Trust; Robert Romer, a retired judge; Laurence Currie, a banker; William Symington McCormick, an English literature scholar, university administrator, and secretary of the Carnegie Trust that funded Scottish higher education; Edmund Beale Sargant, who had reformed the South African education system under Milner's governorship; and the commission's only woman member, Louise Creighton, widow of a Bishop of London, a long-time moderate women's and social reform activist and a recent convert to women's suffrage.[38] This collection of individuals sat at the nexus of imperialism and social reform, and articulated a place for higher education within that distinctively early-twentieth-century political project.

The Haldane Commission gathered evidence for four years, interviewing dozens of witnesses, before reporting in 1913. Historians have justly recognized the wide-ranging ambition of the reforms it proposed.[39] But they have overlooked how a consequence of this vision was the systematic sidelining of women's

---

[36] 'Executive Committee and Council Minutes', July 1911–December 1914, QA/C/M1a, KCL.

[37] Matthew, 'Haldane, Richard Burdon', *ODNB*. On the intersection of war mobilization and higher education reform see David Edgerton, *Warfare State: Britain, 1920–1970* (Cambridge: Cambridge University Press, 2006).

[38] 'Royal Commission on University Education in London. First Report of the Commissioners', 1910, *Parliamentary Papers* Vol. 23, Cd. 5165, ii.

[39] Vernon, *Universities and the State*, 166–8; F. M. L. Thompson, *The University of London and the World of Learning, 1836–1986* (London: Hambledon, 1990).

education. Considering that almost a third of students studying for London degrees in 1910 were women—much higher than the national average—issues pertaining to women and women's colleges were notably absent from the testimony the commission gathered.[40] A few witnesses, especially those from coeducational UCL and LSE, did not include gender as a category in their evidence because they saw women as fully integrated into a mixed institution to which gender difference was irrelevant.[41] But most simply assumed that the default university student was a man, especially when discussing fast-developing fields of professional education such as medicine and engineering that were a central concern of the commission. If issues specific to women did appear in the evidence, it was often as an afterthought, or else in a dismissive light, as witnesses described the standard of teaching in women's colleges as inferior to that in men's and coeducational colleges.[42]

During the consultation period, Oakeley submitted a 'Memorandum on the University Education of Women in London' to the commission. She argued that it was necessary to write such a document because many seemed to believe that, since the University of London granted degrees to women, there was no need 'for a special consideration of the interests of women'. The memo stated that women's colleges fulfilled specific needs that meant that they deserved a place in the university alongside coeducational colleges. It also included a defence of domestic science as a robust field of study which sought, among other things, to elevate the importance of 'the work and occupations which fall to the majority of women'. She ended with a plea that the commission's evident interest in engineering and medicine not preclude provision within the University of London for students who seek 'knowledge and culture as ends in themselves', thus linking gender-differentiated study and career paths for women to the question of the role of liberal education in the modern university.[43]

Late in the evidence-gathering period, the commission did invite a small number of representatives from women's colleges to testify, and their comments echoed Oakeley's. For example, E.C. Higgins, principal of Royal Holloway, and Royal Holloway classics lecturer M.E.J. Taylor, chair of the University Board of Studies in Classics, both spoke in favour of a wide-ranging matriculation examination requiring competency in arts and science subjects, including classical languages—in contrast to male colleagues from London's medical schools who testified in

---

[40] Partial data appears in Carol Dyhouse, *No Distinction of Sex? Women in British Universities 1870–1939* (London: University College London Press, 1995), 248.

[41] See e.g. the testimony of Sidney Webb, 'Royal Commission on University Education in London. Appendix to First Report of the Commissioners. Minutes of Evidence, July 1909–April 1910; with Appendices and Index', 1910, *Parliamentary Papers* Vol. 23, Cd. 5166, 21–8.

[42] See e.g. 'Royal Commission on University Education in London. Appendix to Final Report of the Commissioners. Minutes of Evidence, February 1912–December 1912; with Appendices and Index', 1913, *Parliamentary Papers* Vol. 40, Cd. 6718, 143.

[43] 'Appendix to Second Report of the Commissioners', 192–3.

the same session and who suggested that matriculation ought to focus more specifically upon the qualifications necessary for a specific subject.[44] The principals of the other London women's colleges, Bedford and Westfield, also spoke about the value of separate women's colleges and the market for them among students and their parents: not only could they offer a guarantee of safety and respectability, they provided students in male-dominated fields such as the natural sciences with more supportive environments, and 'more unrestrained and more natural' opportunities for social life than might be the case in a mixed college. KCW and Westfield, both Anglican foundations, and fully residential and otherwise idiosyncratic Royal Holloway, perceived themselves to have a different student base from secular, primarily non-residential Bedford, which had close ties with progressive, secular, coeducational UCL. Some families would feel more comfortable sending their daughters to more socially conservative, small, exclusive women's colleges close to their homes, witnesses said, and there was no reason why such women should not also have the opportunity to attend university in London and receive an accredited London degree.[45]

But representatives from these institutions met with sceptical questions from the commissioners about the efficiency of running a full range of degree courses. If small colleges were to continue being a part of the university, the commissioners asked, might it not be better for them to specialize more narrowly, and to rely more on collaboration with larger institutions and the intercollegiate lecture system? Men administrators such as the Provost of UCL welcomed this suggestion. But the heads of women's colleges continued to defend the value of their distinctive offering.[46] The debate about the London women's colleges thus unfolded on similar lines to earlier disagreements between universities and AEWs, when men faculty had observed that teaching mixed classes was more efficient than teaching women and men separately. But it also gave concrete expression—and gendered significance—to questions about the benefits of liberal-arts versus single-honours curricula and about small, undergraduate-teaching-focused colleges versus large, multivalent research universities. Was it the business of the state to accredit and fund small, often somewhat conservative women's colleges because they met the needs of some students, even if they were not in keeping with the institutional priorities of a modern, forward-looking, efficient university for the imperial metropolis?

The Haldane Commission published its final report in 1913. Probably largely written by Haldane himself, the report began by defining 'The Essentials of a University Education', quoting John Henry Newman at length in order to describe an ideal community of teachers and students in close association with each other,

---

[44] 'Appendix to Second Report of the Commissioners', 148–9.
[45] 'Appendix to Third Report of the Commissioners', 106–12, 171–7.
[46] See e.g. 'Appendix to Third Report of the Commissioners', 230.

in which all made studying their main business. It then assessed how far the University of London bore out these values and what had to be done to bring it closer to embodying them. The commissioners felt that the university should leave more elementary and more practical forms of education to secondary schools and technical colleges, and should prioritize the needs of the full-time, traditional-age undergraduate. Research and teaching should take place in the same institutions and in close relation to one another. The university should make ample provision for postgraduate study, but the teaching of undergraduates should still be its primary aim.[47] These principles led the commissioners to recommend centralizing the university's administration to a much greater extent, with a representative senate but with all the governance and finance of the constituent colleges under the ultimate control of an unelected executive council.

Appeals to Newman and other idealist expressions of the value of liberal education had undergirded discussions of university reform since the mid-nineteenth century. But Haldane departed substantially from previous higher education policy experts in arguing that the best way to put his ideals into practice was by reorganizing the University of London on efficiency principles. Newman's nineteenth-century Catholic conception of the purpose of a university made a strange bedfellow with the ideology of national efficiency. The effort to square this circle—to describe an efficient research and teaching university for the twentieth century situated at the centre of the imperial metropolis, whose curriculum would run from classics to medicine and art to engineering, but nothing 'of a narrow utilitarian kind'—had consequences above all for London's women's colleges.[48]

Many London institutions objected to the proposed subjection of their governing bodies to the university council and senate. But women's colleges in particular worried that they would lose their ability to offer an educational environment designed especially for women, whatever precisely they took that to mean. Bedford had long feared that it would become merely 'a Woman's Department of University College'—a betrayal of the wishes of its founder, Elizabeth Jesser Reid—and in the minds of some faculty, incorporation within the university only made that prospect more likely.[49] At Royal Holloway, too, opposition took shape around the perceived need to remain faithful to Thomas Holloway's vision for his college. The Haldane report had come down harshly on Royal Holloway's conservatism, insisting that incorporation within the university be conditional not only on the governors subjecting themselves to university authority but also on other modernizing measures: introducing women onto the board of governors, eliminating a significant gender pay gap, and instituting a staff pension scheme.

---

[47] 'Final Report of the Commissioners', 26–9.   [48] 'Final Report of the Commissioners', 32.
[49] Margaret J. Tuke, *A History of Bedford College for Women, 1849–1937* (London: Oxford University Press, 1939), 207; see also Janet Sondheimer, *Castle Adamant in Hampstead: A History of Westfield College, 1882–1982* (London: Westfield College, 1983), 82.

In response, 'lady principal' E.C. Higgins organized a delegation of one hundred students—about half the student body—to travel to London to vote against a University of London Students' Representative Council motion in support of the Haldane report, ironically leveraging the structures of the wider university in order to express opposition to them.[50]

The report's impact upon KCW was greater still. An entire section of the final report was dedicated to the problems the college caused for the plan for a more centralized and academically robust university. KCW's location in Kensington made it difficult to incorporate it into the commission's proposals for a university centre in Bloomsbury. The women's college was 'inconvenient'. Its benefits to Kensington were not worth the cost of its maintenance. One university college, Bedford, was sufficient to serve the needs of women who desired a liberal education in a single-sex college.[51] The only question was what to do about domestic science, which no other college in the university offered. Late in the evidence-gathering period, Thereza Rücker's husband Arthur, the former principal of the University of London, a member of the governing body of Imperial College, and a champion of the KCW domestic science scheme, had returned to the commissioners for a second interview in order specifically to make the case that domestic science was a university-level applied science, a feminine equivalent of the engineering work undertaken at Imperial.[52] The commissioners appear to have been convinced by this argument—but not by Oakeley's case that domestic science's success hinged on it being part of a larger liberal-arts college. They recommended that KCW be dissolved and all but one of its departments merged into a newly coeducational KCL. The domestic science department might become a separate university research institute for 'Household and Social Science'.[53]

In Kensington, faculty, administrators, and students greeted the news with shock and outrage.[54] In a report prepared for the University of London Senate in response to the commission's recommendations, KCW presented extensive data to suggest that it would be a waste to close the college at a time when its academic offerings were becoming steadily stronger and it had just begun building its new, privately funded Kensington campus. They observed that the centralizing mind-set of the commissioners risked steamrolling over smaller institutions that were nevertheless making a valuable contribution to higher education in London.[55] But they were overpowered by the leadership of KCL and the university senate,

---

[50] Bingham, *History of Royal Holloway*, 120–4.
[51] 'Final Report of the Commissioners', 75–6.
[52] 'Appendix to Third Report of the Commissioners', 201.
[53] 'Final Report of the Commissioners', 83.
[54] 'Warden's Memorandum in Response to the Final Report of the Royal Commission on the University of London', 1913, in Papers of Sir John Atkins, Q/PP1, KCL.
[55] 'Future Policy in Regard to King's College for Women and the Home Science Department, and Their Relation to King's College', 1913, and 'Memoranda and Reports Relating to Royal Commission on the University of London', 1912–14, KWA/GPF/12, KCL, 11–12.

who felt that, in the name of efficiency, the women's college could no longer be maintained as a separate institution.[56] Over the protests of alumnae, current and former faculty, and donors, KCL absorbed KCW. The women lecturers moved into offices on the Strand campus, and some old classrooms were hastily renovated into a women's common room.[57] In 1914, the domestic science department alone took up residence at the still-under-construction campus as King's College for Household and Social Science (KCHSS).[58]

Although Bedford, Westfield, and Royal Holloway all ultimately decided that greater integration with the University of London was in their best interests, the fate of KCW, and the difficulty Royal Holloway continued to have in fitting into the University of London, indicate how the rise of the urban research university went hand in hand with the marginalization of the women's college. Those who promoted coeducation, the research university, and the single-honours degree course could cast themselves as the modern and forward-thinking party, while those who advocated the women's liberal-arts college appeared hopelessly old-fashioned: tarred by their association with policies such as Royal Holloway's all-male board of governors, and with the anti-women's suffrage movement that many domestic science advocates, like Ravenhill, supported, at a time when suffrage militancy was at its most radical and visible. The domestic science course ensured its survival by staking a claim of equivalence to masculine applied sciences—in the process simply underscoring further that domestic science was for women and engineering was for men. But Oakeley lost her campaign for a wide-ranging liberal education suited to the practical needs of at least some women students. After KCW was dissolved, she left academia to pursue a different type of institutional administration, and spent the rest of her working life as the head of an East London women's settlement house.

The Nationalization of British Higher Education

The outbreak of war in August 1914 forestalled the further implementation of the Haldane recommendations. Haldane himself returned to the War Office, taking a leading role in mobilization and military strategy for the first year of the war, before his intellectual and personal connections to German academia forced him out of a formal role in British politics. Morant planned and became the first permanent secretary of the new Ministry of Health in Lloyd George's wartime coalition government. Sidney Webb also contributed to postwar planning in his

---

[56] 'Future Policy in Regard to King's College for Women', 7–8.

[57] Oakeley, 'King's College for Women', in *The Centenary History of King's College London, 1828–1928*, ed. F.J.C. Hearnshaw (London: George G. Harrap & Co., 1929), 489–509, at 507–9.

[58] 'Minutes of the King's College for Women Delegacy', November 1913, KW/M/6, KCL; Rutherford, 'Contestations'.

capacity as one of the intellectual leaders of the Labour Party. Thanks in part to the efforts of these figures, both the teaching and the research missions of universities came to be seen as integral to the war effort and to postwar planning. Several branches of government channelled large grants to university science departments to support research with military applications, and scientists consulted for the government and the armed forces directly.[59]

KCHSS was no exception to this policy reorientation: in Kensington, lab space and the time of staff and students were dedicated to inquiries such as how to feed soldiers most efficiently and nutritiously.[60] Many faculty worked as government consultants, on topics such as designing the kitchens of council houses and finding the most effective substitutes for staples in the face of food shortages.[61] The war created a sense of urgency, utility, and demand for scientific research that domestic science staff and students were especially qualified to provide. Before the war, the domestic science department had won a grant from the Carnegie Trust to build a library—but in 1916, KCHSS applied for permission to use the grant for laboratory equipment instead.[62] The philosophy that Oakeley had so emphasized in the original plans for the degree course became an optional subject immediately following KCHSS's independence, and was eliminated altogether in 1916. In 1920, as a result of this move to an exclusively scientific curriculum, the University of London finally granted KCHSS the right to grant the BSc for its three-year course.[63]

By the end of the war, however, the institution was like other colleges and universities in facing a substantial budget deficit.[64] The economic instability of war left colleges and universities that were funded largely through endowments and private subscription in a fragile position. At the same time, a wave of ex-servicemen students whose studies had been interrupted by their military service returned to higher education, leading to twice as many students in the system in 1919 as in 1914.[65] A more systematic approach to state funding was becoming essential to

[59] Edgerton, *Warfare State*, 111–23.

[60] 'Executive Committee Minutes', December 1914–January 1920, QA/C/M1, KCL.

[61] 'Home Science Executive Committee Minutes', November 1915–November 1918, QAP/GPF/4/1, KCL.

[62] 'Executive Committee Minutes', 17 February 1916.

[63] Among many other examples, see 'King's College for Women Department of Home Science and Economics [Syllabus]', 1912, Q/EPH/SYL/6, KCL; 'Household and Social Science Department, King's College for Women [Syllabus]', 1915–16, KW/SYL/17; 'Household and Social Science Department—University Diploma Course [Syllabus]', 1916, Q/EPH/SYL/15; 'KCHSS [Syllabus]', 1926, Q/EPH/SYL/20. See also 'Rough Notes Summarizing Contents of a Course of Lectures on Hygiene and Sanitation', 1913, KW/LECT/1, KCL.

[64] Challenges faced by maintenance costs are discussed in 'Minutes of the Hostel Management Committee', K/HOS/1, KCL. See also discussion in 1916 about filling places in the hostel in 'Executive Committee Minutes', December 1914–January 1920, QA/C/M1. See also 'Report from the Academic Board—One Year Special Course', in Executive Committee Minutes, July 1929, QA/C/M4. See also 'Special Investigation Sub-Committee Minutes', November–December 1922, QA/CS/M4.

[65] University Grants Committee, 'Returns from Universities and University Colleges in Receipt of Treasury Grant', 1919–20 and 1920–1, UGC/3/1–2, TNA.

higher education's survival. Moreover, to some politicians the war had demonstrated that state-sponsored scientific research, and the support of higher education more generally, should be central to postwar planning. At the same time, however, policymakers feared that coupling universities too directly to national strategic interest would make Britain too much like Germany. Though British higher education reformers both before and after the war would admire the coherence of Germany's national public university system, in the immediate postwar years safeguarding academic freedom from state incursion appeared paramount.[66]

A 1918 Treasury committee, on which Haldane, Morant, and Sidney Webb's wife and collaborator Beatrice served, led to a solution: the University Grants Committee (UGC), a standing independent committee that would distribute government funds to universities across the UK and ensure that those funds were being spent responsibly. The decision to house the UGC under the aegis of the Treasury, which had jurisdiction over the entire UK, instead of the Board of Education, which only had jurisdiction over England and Wales, spoke to the committee's national ambitions. While the Treasury would allocate the UGC's budget, how the UGC distributed those funds to universities would be entirely independent from government, thus safeguarding academic freedom. For the first time, funding for higher education could be equalized across the four home nations and conceptualized as a truly national system. To be sure, collaboration with the universities of the settler colonies did remain symbolically important to many politicians and higher education administrators who sought to promote imperial unity.[67] But the institutionalization of state support for higher education in the home nations—and only them—represented an important step in the construction of a specifically national university system.

William McCormick, the Scottish administrator who had served on the Haldane Commission, was the UGC's first chair, and the other members were distinguished academics and university administrators, primarily but not only from a research science background. In its early years the committee comprised between six and nine members. Margery Fry, who had previously been tutor for women at the University of Birmingham and was soon to become principal of Somerville College, Oxford, was the only woman member and served from the committee's inception until 1948. The committee quickly developed a working system: it would award grants to individual universities on a quinquennial basis, responding to universities' applications for funds to support operational costs and capital projects. It would visit each institution within the five-year period to ensure that the funds were being spent responsibly.[68]

---

[66] Vernon, *Universities and the State*, 176–8.

[67] Tamson Pietsch, *Empire of Scholars: Universities, Networks and the British Academic World, 1850–1939* (Manchester: Manchester University Press, 2013).

[68] Vernon, *Universities and the State*, 188; Margery Fry, 'The University Grants Committee: An Experiment in Administration', *Universities Quarterly* 2, no. 3 (May 1948): 221–30; Ashby and Anderson, *Portrait of Haldane*, 152; Christine Helen Shinn, *Paying the Piper: The Development of the University Grants Committee 1919–1946* (London: Falmer Press, 1986).

Its independence from government notwithstanding, the UGC had its own policy priorities, and these profoundly shaped the structure of British higher education in the interwar period. The committee's first priority was to help institutions to balance their books: by persistently lobbying the Treasury for increased funding, even despite repeated periods of government austerity; but also by insisting that universities cultivate diverse revenue sources, such as from private donors and local government.[69] They urged the expansion and improvement of existing institutions rather than the foundation of new ones: hiring more faculty and improving their salaries and benefits; hiring more clerical staff to allow faculty to focus on teaching and research instead of administration; upgrading facilities, especially laboratories and libraries; and improving opportunities for student 'corporate life' through the construction of residence halls, student unions, and athletic facilities.[70] The UGC established standards that new institutions had to meet in order to be considered for a university charter, including demonstrated demand for an institution of higher learning in that city or region, a stable financial model that did not depend entirely on state support, and a constitution that provided for a high degree of faculty governance and safeguarded against undue influence from donors and other local political and commercial interests.[71] Though the committee articulated beliefs in the value of higher learning for its own sake and in the importance of academic freedom, it also emphasized national strategic reasons for state investment in universities: to meet workforce needs for more teachers and for 'University trained men in commerce and industry'; and to pursue research in new technical fields such as electrical and aerospace engineering and agricultural science.[72] Despite repeatedly underscoring their commitment to universities' institutional autonomy, then, in the interwar period the members of the UGC played an outsized role in developing a unified national higher education policy that saw unprecedented sums of money funnelled to a specific set of expenditures, as well as establishing an influential set of standards according to which the sector might expand.

Though it was not their foremost priority, the UGC understood a successful national higher education sector to be one that fully incorporated women faculty and students and promoted gender equality. As we will revisit in Chapter 6, Fry, as the committee's long-serving woman member, may have disproportionately informed this stance. But it was evidently an investment shared to some extent by the whole committee, who took care in their visits to institutions around the

[69] 'Returns from Universities and University Colleges in Receipt of Treasury Grant', 1922–3, UGC/3/4, TNA, 8; 'Returns from Universities and University Colleges in Receipt of Treasury Grant', 1924–5, UGC/3/6, TNA; University Grants Committee, Minutes, 1919–33, UGC/1/1, TNA, see esp. minutes of meetings 5 February 1925, 7 November 1929.

[70] 'Report Including Returns from Universities and University Colleges in Receipt of Treasury Grant', 1923–4, UGC/5/27, TNA, 11–12, 29; 'Report for the Period 1929–30 to 1934–35', UGC/3/16, TNA, 40–1; see also Vernon, *Universities and the State*, 190–3.

[71] Shinn, *Paying the Piper*, 96–7.

[72] 'Report of the University Grants Committee', 1921, UGC/5/26, TNA, 4.

country to ensure that they met with mixed-gender groups of faculty and students as well as understanding women's specific institutional needs. In statements about the student population, the committee consistently referred to 'young men and women', a striking departure from previous writing about higher education policy, including that of the Haldane Commission, that had assumed a normative male student.

Overall, the UGC found that 'The needs and interests of men and women both as students and teachers are largely the same', but that it was necessary to do more actively to ensure that women faculty were working under equal conditions and that their voices were represented in institutional governance. The committee advocated for equal pay, for increased promotion of women faculty to more senior roles, and for better representation of women on university committees, especially but not only those that dealt with women students' disciplinary and pastoral needs.[73] What is more, they enforced these priorities through their disbursal of grants. In 1920, for example, after the first year of Treasury grant disbursal, the UGC informed Royal Holloway that they would only put the college forward for a grant if it included women representatives, including women faculty, on its board of governors; and if it committed to promoting more women faculty to senior positions. In need of the money, Royal Holloway changed the constitution of its board accordingly.[74] The UGC were happy to agree that small residential women's colleges had a place within the wider higher education system, especially as in the immediate postwar period women's colleges were helping to ameliorate a significant shortage of secondary school teachers.[75] But these colleges needed to demonstrate their willingness to adapt to sector-wide norms of formal gender equality in the context of a system that, as it expanded, was becoming increasingly gender-integrated.

As overall national enrolments nearly doubled from prewar levels, the proportion of students who were women also expanded somewhat, reaching a high of over 30 per cent of all undergraduates nationally by the late 1920s.[76] Student expansion was concentrated overwhelmingly in Scotland and the North of England, meaning that in the interwar period the typical experience of higher education was of a large, urban, non-residential university that combined teaching and research, and that made no formal distinctions between women and men, either for its faculty or its students. The UGC's massive and unprecedented distribution of Treasury funding helped to make permanent the shift of women students away from small residential women's colleges to large coeducational universities. This put an end to the aspirations of many earlier education reformers that women's colleges

---

[73] Report, 1923–4, 21.   [74] Minutes, UGC/1/1, at 22 July 1920 and 21 October 1920.
[75] See comments on Westfield, Minutes, UGC/1/1, at 10 December 1919.
[76] However, after 1929 the proportion of women students fell slightly, owing to the economic crisis of the early 1930s. 'Returns from Universities and University Colleges in Receipt of Treasury Grant', 1926–7, UGC/3/8, TNA.

might offer higher education suited to the feminized career of wife, mother, and household manager; or even that they might teach a particular kind of feminized applied science or help to save the liberal arts from the logics of efficiency.

In 1924, once the University of London's finances had stabilized, a new committee convened to consider implementing the Haldane Commission's pre-war recommendations. It took a middle ground: upholding many of the Haldane Commission's ideas about the centralization of university funding and governance but reserving greater autonomy for individual colleges regarding hiring, curriculum, and other academic matters. While the university site in Bloomsbury never became the fully centralized campus Haldane had envisioned, grants from the London County Council and the Rockefeller Foundation made it possible to construct a large new building in which central administrative offices and new university departments such as the Institute for Historical Research did take up residence.[77]

Neither Royal Holloway nor KCHSS found a successful long-term identity as a women's college within the University of London. The Royal Holloway governors felt that their institution was held at arm's length from the university, always last on the list for preferments, and that the college's physical distance from central London made it challenging to make their presence felt in the capital. Yet they also continued to find it difficult to reconcile their identity as a women's institution with the norms for higher education set by the central university. The college's culture had not moved with the times, and in the 1930s, strict rules about curfews and chaperones and gender inequalities in governance put it out of step with other women's colleges. Ultimately, change came suddenly: in 1945, the college admitted a few men graduate students who were studying for University of London PhDs with supervisors who happened to be Royal Holloway faculty. It thus became the first women's college in the UK to admit men, and undergraduate coeducation soon followed.[78]

As a specialized institute dedicated to the study of a subject whose academic legitimacy many doubted, KCHSS seemed even more marginal. Graduates found that the household science BSc had little name recognition in the professional world. The perception that the wide-ranging course was too 'superficial' endured. By the early 1930s, 45 per cent of KCHSS graduates were pursuing postgraduate training, because employers did not view the degree as a sufficiently serious qualification on its own.[79] In 1953, when an increased demand for domestic science teachers after the Second World War that administrators had confidently predicted never materialized, KCHSS decided to admit men students. The college gradually moved away from the 'household management' emphasis, focusing on

---

[77] Vernon, *Universities and the State*, 205; 'Report for the Period 1929–30 to 1934–35', 9.
[78] Bingham, *History of Royal Holloway*, 152–3, 157.
[79] Blakestad, 'King's College of Household & Social Science', 374–8.

industrial food science and on nutrition and other para-medical fields. It closed its doors in 1985.[80] It had never inaugurated the movement for renewal of national motherhood, or simply for valuing expertise in domestic work, for which early promoters such as Rücker, Ravenhill, and Smithells had hoped. Instead, it seems to have become increasingly marginalized as later developments in higher education and in women's issues passed it by.

To be sure, the coeducation that followed on the heels of centralization was uneven. While financial exigency, changing norms, and the policy priorities of senior university administrators, local and national politicians, and civil servants resulted in the erosion of independent women's colleges, the same did not necessarily apply to institutions for men. Despite considerable pressure from the University of London Senate and from public opinion, most of the London medical schools (affiliated not to colleges but to teaching hospitals) remained opposed to the admission of women. Most temporarily admitted women for the duration of the First World War, but backtracked on this policy in the 1920s. This was embarrassing for the university, which prided itself on its commitment to gender equality. But the university senate did not go any further than to issue a series of reports making a case for the benefits of coeducation and for the need to train more women doctors.[81]

Policymakers widely perceived Oxford and Cambridge, too, as exceptional institutions that merited exceptional treatment. Oxford and Cambridge had originally been excluded from the terms of reference of the UGC, reflecting the unease many in those universities felt about government interference. But post-war financial exigency—evidenced by the findings of a Royal Commission into Oxford and Cambridge, chaired by former prime minister H.H. Asquith, which reported in 1922—resulted in the two universities agreeing to cooperate with the UGC. In return, they received enormous grants, vastly out of proportion to those awarded to other universities, in particular to support staff salaries and laboratories.[82] The commission also found that the financial position of the Oxford and Cambridge women's colleges was 'totally inadequate', leading the UGC to recommend the award of exceptional grants to them—the only institutions not of university status to which it distributed funds.[83]

In a 1923 memorandum to the Treasury on the financial status of the Oxford and Cambridge women's colleges, the UGC commented on the limited attention

---

[80] Blakestad, 'King's College of Household & Social Science', 175–90.

[81] Dyhouse, *Students: A Gendered History*, 137–54.

[82] Vernon, *Universities and the State*, 198; John Prest, 'The Asquith Commission, 1919–1922', in *The History of the University of Oxford*, Volume 8: *The Twentieth Century*, ed. Brian Harrison (Oxford: Oxford University Press, 1994), 26–43, at 43; University Grants Committee, 'Returns from Universities and University Colleges in Receipt of Treasury Grant 1925–1926', UGC/3/7, TNA; 'Report Including Returns from Universities and University Colleges in Receipt of Treasury Grant Academic Year 1928–1929', UGC/3/10, TNA; UGC Minutes, UGC/1/1, TNA.

[83] UGC Minutes, at 22 March 1923.

given to them in the Asquith Commission's report.[84] Though there were representatives from the women's colleges on the commission, their needs fell down
the priority list, and the commission's report was cautious, deferring to the two
universities' right to govern their own affairs. Oxford had, in 1920, decided to
admit women to degrees and to equal membership in the university, a relatively
uncontroversial decision worked out in closed-door committee negotiations in
acknowledgement of the fact that, with the extension of the national franchise to
some women in 1918, women's role in society was changing.[85] But in Cambridge,
a similar effort in 1921 had been met, once again, with backlash, from academics
and especially from alumni. Many felt that, as the last single-sex university in the
UK, it was all the more important for Cambridge to be able to offer a gender-
segregated option to men. The Asquith Commission validated this opinion,
advocating 'that Cambridge should remain mainly and predominantly a men's
University'. It recommended that Oxford, too, impose a quota on women students,
which it did in 1925, thus ensuring that women would remain in a marginal position
in the university for decades to come.[86] But as a greater proportion of the
university-going population, men as well as women, attended the rapidly expanding
'civic' universities, Oxford and Cambridge held a still prestigious, but increasingly
anomalous, position within the national higher education landscape.

   When, in the latter stages of the First World War, politicians had begun to moot
the possibility of a Royal Commission into Oxford and Cambridge, a minority of
faculty and administrators feared that this spectre of state intervention represented a
threat to their academic and administrative freedom.[87] Some conservatives who
distrusted the statist reforming zeal of Lloyd George's wartime government
hoped that the cultivation of private sources of income would allow Oxford and
Cambridge to resist a host of changes that they feared the state would exact in
exchange for its financial investment—not least, the admission of women. For
example, A.E. Shipley, master of Christ's College, Cambridge, who served a term
as university vice-chancellor in 1917–19, was a prominent opponent of women's
admission to Cambridge. In the years after the First World War, he argued that
cultivating a private donor base was a better approach than state funding to
stabilizing Cambridge's finances.[88] Shipley took an active interest in US higher
education, including chairing a 1918 diplomatic delegation that toured US
universities in order to explore wartime strategic collaboration between US and
UK higher education. Tellingly, the American model to which he hoped Cambridge

[84] UGC Minutes, at 22 March 1923.
[85] Prest, 'The Asquith Commission', 39, 43; Janet Howarth, 'Women', in *The History of the University of Oxford*, Volume 8, ed. Harrison, 344–75, at 349–50.
[86] Prest, 'The Asquith Commission', 39; Rita McWilliams-Tullberg, *Women at Cambridge: A Men's University—Though of a Mixed Type* (London: Victor Gollancz, 1975).
[87] Prest, 'The Asquith Commission', 30.
[88] 'Scrapbook Concerning Christ's College and A.E. Shipley', n.d., Box 196 (i), Christ's College, Cambridge.

might aspire was Princeton, a wealthy private institution proud of its identity as a men's university.[89] Like Thomas Holloway's trustees, who perceived that they could resist institutional change by invoking their legal responsibility to comply with their benefactor's wishes, Shipley may have hoped that private money could help Cambridge not only to free itself from government dependence, but also to attach conditions to funding that would secure a lasting commitment to single-sex education. Indeed, as we will see in Chapter 7, some Oxford donors were successful in doing just that, carving out men's spaces within the formally coeducational university.

To Shipley, the continued success of private single-sex liberal-arts colleges in the US was proof that UK higher education should also continue to prioritize gender segregation.[90] But while Shipley idolized Princeton and Yale, one of his colleagues on the 1918 delegation, Birmingham history lecturer Rose Sidgwick, was most impressed by large coeducational universities, both public and private. She toured women's dorms at the University of Michigan; admired that the law, medical, and dental schools at the University of Pennsylvania were open to women; and agreed with a woman professor at Northwestern who dismissed 'household science' as a 'fad'.[91] Sidgwick, one of the first British women to be hired into a standard faculty job also open to men applicants at a large coeducational research university, had more in common with colleagues at Michigan, Penn, or Northwestern than with the women she met who taught at Bryn Mawr or Wellesley. Her career path, much more than Shipley's, indicates where British higher education was by the 1920s. Michigan was increasingly the model, not Thomas Holloway's vision of Vassar.

Like their mid-nineteenth-century forebears, the educationists on the UGC asked searching questions about the purpose of a university education. They asserted that, whatever the social and economic value of advanced training in the professions, a university education ought also 'to bring its own reward of an enlarged and more balanced mind' and 'to provide a background of values for after-life', regardless of the profession or the social class of the student. They funnelled millions of pounds into improving facilities for advanced teaching and research in the natural and applied sciences; at the same time, they warned against 'premature specialisation'. They argued that 'The measure of a University's performance is not the number of students to whom it gives degrees, but the number to which it gives a university education, with all which that term should imply'.[92]

---

[89] Arthur Everett Shipley, *The Voyage of a Vice-Chancellor* (Cambridge: Cambridge University Press, 1919).

[90] A.E. Shipley, 'Women at Cambridge', *The Times*, 17 October 1921, 6.

[91] Rose Sidgwick, 'Diary of US Trip', October–December 1918, Margery Fry Papers, Box 30 Folder 3, Somerville.

[92] 'Report Including Returns from Universities and University Colleges in Receipt of Treasury Grant Academic Year 1928–1929'; 'Report for the Period 1929–30 to 1934–35'.

In addition to the idealism of these claims, what is striking about them is how non-gendered they were: gone was the idea that, in order for women students and faculty to achieve these ends, they might need separate institutions designed specifically for their needs. As an increasing proportion of women and men studied and taught within large, urban, coeducational research universities, the idea of a distinct education designed for women's distinct paths and responsibilities in life came not only to fade into the background, but also to seem retrograde. So thoroughly discredited was the idea of a university-level education that would professionalize housekeeping and childcare that even recent historians have not been able to appreciate the ways that 'domestic science' might at the time have seemed ambitious and innovative, if also troublingly imperialist and eugenicist.[93] To be sure, the sex essentialism that suffrage militancy had reaffirmed continued to play a major role in the women's movement in the interwar period. Eugenicist feminists still held sway in early-twentieth-century British politics and society, their ideas continuing to shape many middle-class young women's conceptions of their values and life trajectories. But within the higher education sector, its policy substantially directed by a small group of mostly men with their own statist Liberal and Labour politics, gender integration came to seem part of a larger agenda of efficiency and centralization coextensive with 'progress'.

It has been argued that the civic universities admitted women reluctantly, because financial pressures meant that they needed to attract the tuition fee payments of this additional category of students.[94] But to place the causal burden there underrates the extent to which the nationalization of UK higher education was also, if somewhat unintentionally, the re-gendering of UK higher education: at once part of significant changes to women's participation in politics and public life in the decades around the turn of the twentieth century, and a shift in the structure and culture of educational institutions that prioritized the flexibility and accessibility of the urban public university over the exclusive, intimate community of the private residential college.

The private residential college's promise of the value of gender-segregated community did not disappear in the interwar period, not least because of the outsize prestige of still almost fully residential, and overwhelmingly masculine, Oxford and Cambridge. As we will see, while academics and administrators continued to struggle to make a case for the distinctive value of the women's college, the men's college continued to produce new, self-consciously countercultural, theorizations of the value of masculine intimacy and community. Yet for the vast majority of

---

[93] Gillian Sutherland, 'The Plainest Principles of Justice: The University of London and the Higher Education of Women', in Thompson, *The University of London*, 35–57; Dyhouse, *No Distinction of Sex?*, 45–8, 140–1; Christine D. Myers, *University Coeducation in the Victorian Era: Inclusion in the United States and the United Kingdom* (Basingstoke: Palgrave Macmillan, 2010), 75–8.

[94] Dyhouse, *No Distinction of Sex?*, 9.

academics, administrators, policymakers, and, above all, students, the challenge was how in practical terms to negotiate the social relations inherent to life on an urban, coeducational campus. That the UGC chose to articulate its views about the purpose of higher education in non-gendered terms did not mean that students in coeducational universities did not experience gender as a category that profoundly structured their day-to-day lives. In fact, despite broad support for coeducation and gender-integrated sociability for most of the period from the 1890s to the 1930s, cross-gender relations remained fraught. Part II of this book shows how students tried and failed to remake both formal student government and the informal invented tradition of student ritual mayhem as gender-neutral institutions, instead arriving at the ritualized social norms of heterosexuality, and the essential differences between the sexes that heterosexuality affirmed, as offering the most workable script for social relations in the coeducational university.

Teaching Gender: The British University and the Rise of Heterosexuality, 1860–1939. Samuel Rutherford, Oxford University Press. © Samuel Rutherford 2025. DOI: 10.1093/9780198937524.003.0003

PART II
GENDERING THE STUDENT

3
'Corporate Life'

In 1870, thirteen years before the University of Manchester would admit women to degrees, a student named H. Kirk introduced a motion in the university debating society in favour of coeducation. It passed by twenty-two votes to seven. In 1887, eight years before the University of Durham admitted women, a student magazine editorial lamented the slowness of the 'misogynistic and hard-hearted Senate' to open degrees to women. In 1890s Glasgow, while the university was still working out the details of women's admission to degrees, men students moved ahead of university administrators to elect women to student government positions and otherwise include them in student life, speaking dismissively of those men who still harboured outdated prejudices about the academic capabilities of women students.[1] In the 1890s, as northern English and Scottish universities admitted women to degrees, men students expressed their support for the principle of women's equality and their excitement at the prospect of increased social contact with women of their own age and social status.

Yet this early, and resounding, enthusiasm for gender integration only rarely matched up with the reality of life in a coeducational university. By the 1930s, long after every university in the British Isles save Cambridge had admitted women to degrees, entrenched divisions between men's and women's student unions, students' practical difficulties in relating to one another across gender lines, and a wider cultural perception of the 'student' as an essentially masculine category of person were more typical. Students turned to paradigms for cross-gender interaction that affirmed essential differences between women and men, instead of attempting to include women within previously all-male forms of student life.

Women never exceeded 30 per cent of all British undergraduates throughout this period, and a story about the precarity that both women students and academics felt in coeducational institutions and about the persistence of gender-segregated forms of sociability is well known to historians.[2] But less well understood

---

[1] 'Female Education', *Owens College Magazine*, January 1870, UMP/2/1, MUA, 13–19; see also 'Women at College', *Owens College Magazine*, May 1870, 129–33; 'Editorial', *The Undergrad*, 30 November 1887, SC12348/3, DUA; 'Notes from Queen Margaret', *Glasgow University Magazine*, 21 December 1892, DC198/1, GUA, 50; 'Our Sister College', *Glasgow University Magazine*, 3 December 1891, 59–60.

[2] Carol Dyhouse, *No Distinction of Sex? Women in British Universities 1870–1939* (London: University College London Press, 1995); Carol Dyhouse, *Students: A Gendered History* (London: Routledge, 2006);

is why. The majority of men students were not unreconstructed misogynists, nor, by the turn of the twentieth century, were academics and administrators very invested in closely regulating social contact between women and men. Rather, in the first instance, students' ideals of gender-neutral community life, however enthusiastically expressed, foundered on the realities of day-to-day interaction. Students' secondary-school experiences had accustomed them to gender-segregated friendships, extracurricular activities, and distinct institutional cultures. Women students in particular, in the minority and frustrated with the gap between men's stated support for equality and a reality of clumsiness and condescension, often declined men students' overtures, forming their own gender-segregated organizations and social circles instead.

Furthermore, these dynamics intensified after the First World War, when many ex-servicemen re-entering higher education sought to 'restore' an imagined, romanticized pre-war masculine student culture. As in British society more widely, by the late 1920s and early 1930s, right-wing backlash against the perceived instability of the social and political order often fixated on gender as a particular source of anxiety, asserting in response a binary, essentialist conception of masculinity to which virility, militarism, misogyny, and violence were central. Though very few students became outright fascists—and these were often derided by their peers—mainstream student culture did become associated with aggressive displays of masculine excess, played out on the streets of university cities as much as in student magazine offices and debating society chambers. This led some women, though certainly not all, to opt out of gender-integrated student life still further. It became difficult to imagine a common student culture that could offer a single, gender-neutral ideal of what university might be for—entrenching perceptions of an essentialized gender binary.

To some students, the coalescence of a 'student movement' engaged in internationalist leftist politics seemed to offer one vision of collective identity that could overcome gender divides. As universal suffrage and a new kind of mass politics emerged in the early twentieth century, the adult norms and values into which a period spent at university might induct students changed. Where nineteenth-century colleges and universities might have prepared both women and men for their roles in the family—as wives and husbands, mothers and fathers; for men, as breadwinners—interwar universities sought instead to inculcate civic responsibility. This was bottom-up just as much as top-down, with students themselves taking the lead in defining the terms of youth social and political engagement. Students became an increasingly visible category of person with an

Laura Kelly, *Irish Medical Education and Student Culture, c.1850–1950* (Liverpool: Liverpool University Press, 2018); Georgia Oman, *Higher Education and the Gendering of Space in England and Wales, 1869–1909* (Basingstoke: Palgrave Macmillan, 2023). For statistics about women's higher education participation see Dyhouse, *No Distinction of Sex?*, 17.

increasingly important voice in politics, social reform, and wider discourses about generational divides and social change. At the same time, active engagement in liberal and left-wing political activism and social service remained minority interests on campuses.[3] Instead, mainstream student life, especially at urban, non-residential universities, foregrounded apolitical activities such as sport, as well as a burgeoning off-campus commercial youth leisure culture centred on venues such as dance halls and nightclubs.

Challenges around navigating cross-gender relations were central to how students experienced these aspects of university life. Given the resurgence and entrenchment of ideas about essential differences between men and women, and a wider climate of cultural anxiety around perceived challenges to the gender binary, students often found themselves at an impasse, unable to find workable strategies for relating to one another across gender lines. Over the course of the 1920s and 1930s, as students tried out and discarded other possibilities, a relatively casual, sexualized culture of heterosexuality emerged as the most viable paradigm through which women and men might socialize: offering a reassuringly clear-cut set of rules that could enable cross-gender interaction while still affirming the stability of the gender binary. For pre-First World War students, university had served as an artificially gender-segregated space and time prior to, and preparatory for, a later life stage centred on marriage and family. But for interwar students, the ways that campus life interacted with a profoundly shifting social and political landscape beyond the university meant that dating and sex became central aspects of what university was for—with important consequences for how middle-class British people more widely made sense of gender and sexuality.

Part II of this book explains how students at urban, non-residential, gender-integrated universities sought to make meaning of their time at university; how this was shaped both by the dramatic national political and social upheavals of the period after the First World War and by students' relationship to an emergent urban, commercial youth leisure culture; and how, given the failure of alternatives, students landed upon heterosexuality as a viable means of relating to one another across gender lines. Chapter 3 considers organized student government and extracurricular life, while Chapter 4 discusses masculine student traditions grounded in ritual mayhem, disorder, and violence. In the context of backlash in the 1920s against the perceived disintegration of gender roles (as symptomatic of the disintegration of the social order more widely), claims that women students might participate in student traditions on the same terms as men seemed a provocative challenge. Ex-servicemen students in particular defensively rejected the

---

[3] On interwar student politics see Georgina Brewis, *A Social History of Student Volunteering: Britain and Beyond, 1880–1980* (Basingstoke: Palgrave Macmillan, 2014); Mike Day, *National Union of Students, 1922–2012* (London: Regal Press, 2012); Jodi Burkett, ed., *Students in Twentieth-Century Britain and Ireland* (Basingstoke: Palgrave Macmillan, 2018); Brian Simon, 'The Student Movement in England and Wales during the 1930s', *History of Education* 16, no. 3 (September 1987): 189–203.

idea that women could be students in the same way that men were students. As Chapter 5 will show, heterosexuality, instead, seemed to offer students a route to gender-integrated sociability while still affirming complementarity and essential differences between the sexes.

The Beginnings of Student Self-Governance

From the late nineteenth century, liberal idealist conceptions of education, self-development, self-governance, and their relationship to a revivified society gained new urgency in the context of the development of a mass electorate. Many intellectuals and educationists supported the expansion of elementary education and the professionalization of teacher training both in the metropole and in the empire, in order to prepare the population for the responsibilities of citizenship.[4] But many—including students themselves—also perceived a special relationship between university campus citizenship and national citizenship. Students' engagement as campus citizens could prepare them to exercise responsibly their roles as citizens in the nation and empire, and they might set an example of civic engagement to others. These values were reflected in longstanding formal political structures such as the MPs for university constituencies who sat in the Westminster Parliament, elected by university graduates; and the Scottish tradition of university rectors elected through a popular vote of current students.[5] But they also reflected an equally longstanding tradition of bottom-up student resistance to universities' disciplinary authority, which students drew on and refashioned in response to changing relations between urban universities and the cities in which they were located, and to the growing presence of women in previously all-male institutions.

In the late nineteenth century, of the thousands of students enrolled at universities in cities like Glasgow, Edinburgh, Manchester, Liverpool, and London, half lived at home; of the rest, although women were more likely to live in halls of residence, most men lived in private lodgings.[6] Typical experiences of student life involved a lengthy public transit commute to campus and continuing ties to one's home community and childhood friends, but also new kinds of independent access to urban leisure spaces.[7] John Smith Flett, who attended the University of Edinburgh in the 1880s and 1890s, remembered that on weekends he and his

---

[4] Lynton Lees, 'Democracy's Children: Education, Childhood, and Citizenship in Britain and the Empire, c. 1918–1955' (PhD thesis, Columbia University, 2024).
[5] Catriona M.M. Macdonald, '"To Form Citizens": Scottish Students, Governance and Politics, 1884–1948', *History of Education* 38, no. 3 (May 2009): 383–402.
[6] Dyhouse, *Students: A Gendered History*, 9.
[7] Thomas Kelly, *For Advancement of Learning: The University of Liverpool, 1881–1981* (Liverpool: Liverpool University Press, 1981), 181; Brewis, *Student Volunteering*, 73; Oman, *Higher Education and the Gendering of Space*, 88.

friends, who lived in lodgings in the city, would attend concerts and football matches, hike and swim, and spend time together 'discussing everything under heaven'.[8] Flett's experiences gesture to the existence of a youth leisure culture that defined studenthood beyond the confines of the classroom.

At the same time, Flett and his friends were subject to a strict disciplinary regime that governed their behaviour both on and off campus. In an era when undergraduate study typically began between the ages of seventeen and nineteen (and sometimes younger in Scotland) but the legal age of majority was twenty-one, universities understood themselves to have a responsibility *in loco parentis* to regulate student behaviour. Before the First World War, university senates took an active role in day-to-day student discipline. The Durham University Senate was an extreme example, handing down regulations about the hours during which it was acceptable to play billiards in the Union and the advisability of punting in shirtsleeves.[9] But other universities, such as Glasgow and Edinburgh, also banned pastimes perceived to be immoral such as drinking, card-playing, and dancing, and fined or suspended students who did not comply.[10] These rules served to inculcate norms of respectability in students who aspired to gain qualifications for the traditional professions and join the middle class. They were also—especially in older institutions—part of a parallel justice system that had for centuries insulated students from the real force of the law and had granted licence to youthful masculine misbehaviour. The Scottish universities had long traditions of violence and misrule associated with graduation ceremonies, the hazing of first-year students, and rectorial elections, practices that students at newer foundations like Durham and University College London also adopted.[11] Like other western European traditions of misrule, these sought to assert the power of the collective and to signal that authorities governed by consent. In 1913, for example, when the Glasgow University Senate fined a student £5 for 'kick[ing] a bench', the student body threatened to protest by disrupting graduation ceremonies—which succeeded in causing the senate to rescind the fine.[12] When students hazed first-years or kidnapped a prominent visiting speaker, they also enforced—through violence, if necessary—norms of university masculinity, initiating outsiders into the culture of the institution.

---

[8] Sir John Smith Flett, 'My Student Days at Edinburgh University, 1886–1894', Coll-100/Dc.6.116, Edinburgh University Special Collections, 22–3.

[9] 'Editorial', *The Undergrad*, 30 November 1887, 3–4; 'Senate Minutes', 1888–94, UND/BA1/7, DUA, 116; Edgar Jones, *University College Durham: A Social History* (Aberystwyth: self-published, 1996).

[10] See e.g. 'Senate Minutes', 1878–86, UND/BA1/6, DUA, 155; Letter from the Senate to the Union, 10 February 1893, in 'Union Board of Directors Minute Book', 1890–7, DC 94/2/2, GUA, 191; 'SRC Women's Committee Minutes', EUA/IN20/SRC/d, EUSC.

[11] Macdonald, 'To Form Citizens', 389–91; 'Meeting of the Students' Representative Council', *Glasgow University Magazine*, 4 December 1889, 4–5; C.E. Whiting, *The University of Durham, 1832–1932* (London: The Sheldon Press, 1932), 155; 'Council Minutes', 1875–85, UCLCA/CC/1, UCL.

[12] 'Editorial: "The Case Is Altered"', *Glasgow University Magazine*, 17 December 1913, 212–13.

Once women began to enter previously all-male universities, new forms of *in loco parentis* discipline emerged, in order to protect the reputations of women students living away from home and to regulate contact between women and men. Fully residential independent women's colleges enforced appropriate middle-class feminine behaviour through emphasis on religious worship, curfews, and chaperonage. This was the case, too, in halls of residence for women at coeducational universities.[13] The wardens of women's halls—who by the interwar period tended to be academics, but earlier were more likely to have had experience running boarding houses—took an active role in directing student life. At universities such as UCL, Durham, and Manchester in the 1890s and 1900s, where the first women students and faculty had founded separate women's student unions, wardens chaired women's union meetings. They intervened in elections and decision-making processes when they felt that students had not reached the most desirable outcome.[14]

Students experienced these restrictions as stifling and unfair, and were attentive to double standards in the treatment of women versus men. At Durham, for example, men as well as women spoke out against a university senate regulation that if a woman student and a man student were seen walking together unchaperoned, the woman—and only the woman—would be expelled.[15] The renegotiation of gender norms and cross-gender sociability within coeducational universities was entwined with the development of collective student identity, as students asserted their ability to enforce democratically their own norms of respectable behaviour independent of administrative oversight. This was especially the case for communities of women students. In 1911, the Durham Women's Union, finding that 'several periodicals of objectionable character' had begun appearing in the union, ruled that the union committee would henceforth need to approve all periodicals brought into the union.[16] That same year, the Manchester Women's Union expelled two members who had sequestered themselves alone in a dark room with their dates during a union event, and it enforced strict limits on men visitors. In 1917, when Manchester administrators permitted the women's union to take bookings from university societies and external groups without the approval of the vice-chancellor, the union secretary attributed this victory for self-governance to the union's success in demonstrating its concern for members' respectability.[17]

[13] Oman, *Higher Education and the Gendering of Space*, 60–9.

[14] See e.g. 'Women's Union Society', n.d. (*c.*1920s), MEM/III/B, UCL; 'Women's Union Minutes', 1899–1930, UND/GE2/AA1, DUA; Phoebe Sheavyn, 'Socials and Excursions in 1913–14', AWS/2/1, MUA; 'Women's Union Minute Book', 1913–17, SUA/1/3/5, MUA.

[15] 'Senate Minutes', 1901–6, UND/BA1/9, DUA, 141; 'Women's Union Minutes', 1899–1930, UND/GE2/AA1, DUA; 'Sent Down', *The Palatine* 1, no. 2 (March 1923), SC+04522, DUA, 1–2.

[16] 'Union Committee Minutes', 1902–12, UND/GE1/AC1, DUA, 153.

[17] 'Women's Union Minute Book', 1908–12, SUA/1/3/1/3, MUA; 'Resolution Passed at the Mass Meeting of Women Students on Wednesday October 30th', 30 October 1913, AWS/2/1, MUA; 'Women's Union General Meetings Minute Book', 1916–21, SUA/1/3/2/1, MUA.

Despite a general tendency to work within the system, at times students also undertook more confrontational actions. At Edinburgh just after the First World War, residents of the women's hall bristled at the strict disciplinary expectations of a new warden, who had previously been a matron at a secondary school. In summer 1920, they submitted to the hall's management committee a unanimous petition demanding her resignation. Astonished and appalled, the committee resolved that they had 'no alternative but to ask all the residents...to vacate their rooms' at the end of term unless they withdrew the petition and acknowledged the warden's authority. Some students did apologize, others chose to leave the hall instead, and the warden ultimately admitted that the job was probably not right for her and resigned. At the start of the new academic year, the committee offered concessions to the students, inviting them to elect a representative who would attend committee meetings and allowing them to host a dance for the first time.[18] Through asserting their own capacity for collective self-governance, then, women students in particular won representation on university committees and the ability to deal internally with a wide range of student disciplinary matters.

In the process, women and men students alike began for the first time to articulate a generational difference between the interests of different members of the university. Nineteenth-century philosophies about student life had held that students would benefit from the salutary moral influences of being in close contact with older university-educated people, a theory that to some extent still endured in fully residential Oxford and Cambridge into the twentieth century.[19] When the newer civic universities had been smaller, it had seemed more likely that students, faculty, and alumni would have shared interests and would benefit from shared associational life. University unions initially included many non-student members: men's unions were often funded through alumni subscription, the funds managed by a board of alumni trustees; women's unions, on the other hand, often began life as organizations for all women affiliated to the university because there were no pre-existing alumnae associations, women's staff common rooms, or social organizations for the wives of male faculty.[20] But in the early twentieth century, students began to complain that staff- and alumni-dominated unions were anti-democratic. Student leaders argued that, as representative political organizations and as the hosts of events, unions ought to reflect the expectations that a younger generation brought to student life. Scottish universities had long had a tradition of student representation in university governance in the form of students' representative committees (SRCs), and from the 1890s students

---

[18] 'Minutes of Masson Hall Committee', 1894–1935, EUA GD58/1, EUSC; see also Dyhouse, *No Distinction of Sex?*, 114–16.

[19] Samuel Rutherford, 'Arthur Sidgwick's *Greek Prose Composition*: Gender, Affect, and Sociability in the Late-Victorian University', *Journal of British Studies* 56, no. 1 (January 2017): 91–116, at 107–9.

[20] See e.g. 'Glasgow University Union: Board of Directors Minute Book', 1890–7, DC94/2/2, GUA; 'Women's Union General Committee Minute Book', 1900–4, SUA/1/3/1/1, MUA; 'Wives of the University Staff, Who Are Members of the Women's Union Session 1919–20', AWS/2/2, MUA.

at English and Welsh universities also began to establish SRCs.[21] In managing student life, union committees and SRCs proposed to learn from best practices developed by their peers at other institutions, instead of from those members of their own universities who offered age and experience.[22] Gradually, the influence of older adults upon organized student life began to decline. In the years before the First World War, students at different institutions began more readily to communicate with each other, leading to the coalescence of a cohesive national student culture that faced a common set of challenges regarding what it might mean for that culture to be mixed-gender.

Gender and the Shape of Student Associational Culture

Even in earlier decades, organized student life was similar across different institutions and different types of institution, but this increased still further over the course of the period. Student culture drew on forms of associational life that would have been familiar to students from secondary school, but developed on a larger and more autonomous scale that also reflected the growth of civil society organizations more widely in the early twentieth century.[23] Students could join debating societies, political clubs, sports teams, charitable organizations, subject-specific academic societies, and groups for every conceivable Christian denomination. The Student Christian Movement (founded 1889), a national organization with local campus chapters, attracted an especially wide cross-section of students.[24] Union committees organized 'smoking concerts', 'at-homes', and dances ranging from balls to informal 'flannel dances', and complained that turnout at events was never high enough. Union meetings were dominated by discussions regarding budgets and the upkeep of the union's physical space alongside constant negotiations over newspaper and magazine subscriptions. Student magazines printed reports of student government meetings, editorials, and letters to the editor commenting on campus current affairs, but also fiction and poetry, gossip columns, formal photographs of union committees and sports teams, cartoons caricaturing popular professors, and in-jokes whose meaning is lost to readers a century later. Across thousands of pages of union records and student magazines, the tone can seem monotonously repetitive, indicative of how consistent the shared repertoire of language for talking and writing about student life was.

---

[21] Kelly, *For the Advancement of Learning*, 95.

[22] 'Women's Union General and Committee Minutes', 1903–7, REC/2005/61/2, UCL; 'Women's Union Minute Book', 1913–17, SUA/1/3/5, MUA; 'SRC Minutes', 1913–27, UND/GB1/AA1, DUA.

[23] Helen McCarthy, 'Whose Democracy? Histories of British Political Culture between the Wars', *The Historical Journal* 55, no. 1 (March 2012): 221–38.

[24] Brewis, *Social History of Student Volunteering*, 19–20.

School spirit was a paramount value in campus life. This involved not only visible pride in one's institution—coalescence of campus culture went hand-in-hand with the proliferation of blazers, caps, badges, and ties for every conceivable academic, athletic, or social affiliation or distinction—but a willingness to pitch in, participate, and socialize.[25] Students writing in campus publications tended to agree that those who took their studies too seriously were boring killjoys. But those very involved in organized student life often affected a high-minded tone, supporting charitable initiatives, Christian organizations, and the Officers' Training Corps.[26] At Durham, where disproportionate numbers of men students came from the elite boys' 'public' schools, they brought with them customs regarding the violent hazing of freshmen, but also orderly sports-centric rituals that emphasized public-school links, such as an annual cricket match against the Old Harrovians and a procession of boats similar to that associated with Eton's Fourth of June celebrations.[27] At other universities, too, men students sought to inculcate values of fair play, good character, and citizenship through activities like sport and debate. They inveighed against 'hooliganism' that went too far, and asserted that the student community was capable of disciplining offenders themselves without interference from university authorities.[28] This stood in contrast to, and at times in tension with, less institutionalized forms of student culture—which featured bawdy humour, practical jokes, more sexualized entanglements with the opposite sex, and participation in off-campus urban nightlife; and which may, as we will see, have done more to influence gender and sexuality norms than did organized on-campus extracurricular activities.

When women began to enter the universities, they found a welcome in the more organized, institutionalized form of student culture. As in the case of boys' schools, girls' secondary schools had prepared students to take an active role in institutional civic life through student government and extracurricular activities such as debate, while also expecting that through student government students would learn how to self-regulate norms of appropriate gendered behaviour.[29] But in gender-integrated universities, students also used formal student civic

---

[25] On the importance of badges and blazers see e.g. 'Women's Union Society', MEM/III/B, UCL, 5, 11; 'Women's Union Minutes', 1899–1930, UND/GE2/AA1, DUA.

[26] See e.g. *The Undergrad*, 18 February 1886, DUA; 'Men's Union General Committee Minute Book', 1861–81, SUA/1/2/1/1, MUA; 'SRC Minutes', 1913–27, UND/GB1/AA1, DUA; 'Letters to the Editor', *Glasgow University Magazine*, 5 December 1928, 110–12.

[27] Whiting, *The University of Durham*, 139; Jones, *University College Durham: A Social History*.

[28] See e.g. 'Notes', *Glasgow University Magazine*, 2 November 1898, 7; 'Editorial', *Glasgow University Magazine*, 1 March 1905, 227–8; 'SRC Minutes', 1913–27, UND/GB1/AA1, DUA.

[29] Patrick Joyce, *The State of Freedom: A Social History of the British State since 1800* (Cambridge: Cambridge University Press, 2013), 265; Helen Sunderland, 'English Girls' Schools and Women's Suffrage', in *The Politics of Women's Suffrage: Local, National and International Dimensions*, ed. Alexandra Hughes-Johnson and Lyndsey Jenkins (London: University of London Press, 2021), 163–90; Helen Sunderland, 'Politics in Schoolgirl Debating Cultures in England, 1886–1914', *The Historical Journal* 63, no. 4 (September 2020): 935–57; Catherine Sloan, 'The School Magazine in Victorian England' (PhD thesis, University of Oxford, 2019).

structures to articulate a gender-integrated vision of student life. In student publications, debates, and political events, men students expressed a genuine desire to
bring women more fully into the corporate body of the university, a view they
tied to support for other causes such as women's suffrage.[30] From the 1890s, most
student societies had women members, and some had women officers.[31] By the
mid-1920s, a woman had held most major student leadership positions at most
universities at least once.[32] Magazines sought actively to recruit women contributors to offer a different perspective from a normative male voice: while this
indicates that the default university student was assumed to be male, it does
mean that editorial meetings were mixed-gender affairs, one of the new gender-
integrated social experiences that both men and women students sought to
negotiate.[33] The turn of the twentieth century saw a shift away from the view that
it was unladylike for women to appear on stage, and more women students took
part in musical and theatrical performances. By 1920, it was sufficiently normative that women *would* take part in performances that the Manchester Musical
Society were obliged to make a public apology when they received criticism for
having inadvertently planned a concert with an all-male programme.[34]

One of the earliest forms of structured cross-gender interaction to be normalized on campuses was the academic subject society. Most departments had a society (the History Society, the Chemistry Society, etc.), run largely by students but
with faculty involvement, that featured visiting speakers, presentations from students on their research, and at-homes and excursions hosted by faculty. The
serious-minded nature of the endeavours meant that they received sanction from
university authorities, and faculty could act as chaperones.[35] In 1904, UCL students
founded the gender-integrated Critical Society, which featured talks by faculty
and discussions of art and current affairs. After the war, it extended its consideration
of subjects outside the curriculum to 'the problems of Sex, or the Decay of
Modern Art, or the Next Religion, or Communist Anarchism', evidently seeking

---

[30] Edith Wilson, 'Scrapbook', 1883–1904, AWS/6/1, MUA; *University College Gazette* 3, no. 48 (11
November 1903), P.P. 6149.fa, British Library; 'The Masculine Mind', *Manchester University Magazine*
6 (February 1910): 97–8, UMP/2/3, MUA; 'Editorial: Public Morals' and letters to the editor, *Glasgow
University Magazine*, 18 November 1908, 72–4; 'Union Committee Minutes', 1902–12, UND/GE1/
AC1, DUA, 179. See also Kelly, *Irish Medical Education*, 182.

[31] See e.g. termcard of Owens College Literary & Debating Society, 1893–4, in Wilson, 'Scrapbook';
Manchester University Magazine 2, no. 9 (November 1905); 'An Unknown (?) Society', *Glasgow
University Magazine*, 24 January 1906, 303–4.

[32] See e.g. 'SRC Minutes', 1913–27, UND/GB1/AA1, DUA. On women magazine editors see *The
Serpent* 14, no. 5 (May 1930), UMP/2/4, MUA, 133. *The Serpent* had its first woman editor in 1923.

[33] 'Editorial', *Manchester University Magazine* 1, no. 1 (November 1904), 9ff.; *Union Magazine*
[UCL] 3, no. 4 (March 1909) and 5, no. 1 (Lent 1911), P.P. 6139.db, BL; *The Sphinx* 6, no. 2 (March
1913), accessed 24 May 2024, http://reed.dur.ac.uk/xtf/view?docId=bookreader/DU_Sphinx/sphinx0602/
sphinx0602.xml;query=sphinx%20volume%206;brand=default#page/4/mode/2up; *Manchester University
Magazine* 9, no. 8 (May 1913); 'Editorial', *The New Durham* 1, no. 4 (Michaelmas 1924), SC+
04523, DUA.

[34] *The Serpent* 5, no. 1 (20 November 1920), 4.   [35] Dyhouse, *No Distinction of Sex?*, 193.

to push the boundaries of what could be discussed by 'advanced' people in mixed company.[36] To some students, mixed societies might benefit both men and women, introducing them to new ways of doing things and challenging preconceptions about how the opposite sex would necessarily behave.[37]

Yet students did not necessarily follow through on these aspirations in practice. In 1912, a cartoonist in the *Manchester University Magazine* offered an astute commentary on the culture of the mixed-gender student society. Captioned 'Social Life in the University—A Society Tea', the cartoon showed a group of men students standing together and drinking tea in the foreground, and some way off in the background a group of women students sitting at tables doing the same (see Figure 3.1).[38] The following autumn, the magazine reprinted the cartoon under the heading 'The Invisible and Impassable Line', warning first-year students, 'Be it known to freshers that there exists...an unwritten law with regard to Society Teas, viz., that the men shall occupy one-half of the room while the women occupy the other, there being an invisible but impassable line dividing the two. This law is inviolable.'[39] The cartoon generated an extensive correspondence in subsequent issues of the magazine. The majority of correspondents, writing under pseudonyms, criticized the social norms with which students of their generation had been raised for inculcating them with anxiety around the opposite sex. They urged their peers to overcome their discomfort with cross-gender interaction.[40]

A few men wrote in to say that the 'invisible and impassable line' was not their fault: they sought to include women students in activities, but it was the women who chose to self-segregate. Indeed, this impression was underscored by a woman correspondent, who suggested that women might be more inclined to participate in mixed events if men truly treated them as equals. '[P]assing over of the women's work in College affairs is quite a usual thing, and when it is not indulged we get on the other hand somewhat fulsome eulogies of their helpfulness, which are several degrees worse than the omission,' she wrote. She suggested that men were disingenuous in claiming that they wished to dissolve gender distinctions in student life, when in fact their overtures to women were still predicated on an assumption of essential distinctions between the sexes.[41]

Yet women students, too, drew on assumptions of essential distinctions when carving out women's-only spaces within gender-integrated universities.

---

[36] 'History of the Critical Society', n.d. (*c.*1925), MEM/III/C/18, UCL, 4. See also Judith R. Walkowitz, 'Science, Feminism and Romance: The Men and Women's Club 1885–1889', *History Workshop* 21 (April 1986): 36–59; Lucy Bland, *Banishing the Beast: Sexuality and the Early Feminists* (New York: The New Press, 1995).

[37] 'College Influence. From a Woman's Point of View', *Glasgow University Magazine*, 5 March 1902, 225–6.

[38] *Manchester University Magazine* 9 (November 1912).

[39] 'The Invisible and Impassable Line', *Manchester University Magazine* 10, no. 1 (25 November 1913), 13.

[40] 'Letters to the Editor', *Manchester University Magazine* 10, no. 3 (23 January 1914), 65–9.

[41] 'Are We a Modern University?', *Manchester University Magazine* 10, no. 5 (10 March 1914), 109.

J. Tynan, 1912.

Social Life in the University—A Society Tea.

Figure 3.1 'Social Life in the University—A Society Tea', *Manchester University Magazine* 9 (November 1912), UMP/2/3, Manchester University Archives. Image provided by the John Rylands Research Institute and Library, University of Manchester.

Frustration with men students often impelled women to invest their time in gender-segregated sociability. Offered greater participation in wider university life, they declined, actively choosing the community of women's unions and halls of residence. In the early years of women's education at Glasgow in the 1890s, for example, women students rejected an invitation from their men colleagues to send representatives to the SRC, assuming that it would not really take any interest in women's issues. They instead formed a separate women's SRC.[42] In the 1900s, women students at Durham created a separate athletics fund to ensure that women students' subscriptions would go to support women's teams.[43] Many women's unions maintained their own debating societies into the interwar period, borne out of members' perception that it was impossible to be heard over the men or to serve as chair in a mixed debate, and that men debaters too often selected risqué, overly politicized, or otherwise undesirable topics.[44]

French lecturer Muriel Dodds, a resident fellow of one of Durham's women's colleges in the 1930s, recalled that both the staff and the students participated enthusiastically in a cloistered, hierarchical 'boarding school' culture that, in her view, contributed to the students' immaturity.[45] Women students did not always, perhaps, live up to others' aspirations that they be models of feminist independence. But they did draw on their experiences of school and on other models of women's civic engagement to engage in student associational culture on their own terms.[46] From the 1890s, as middle-class women increasingly participated in the public sphere and campaigns for women's admission to the national franchise gained momentum, middle-class girls' and young women's education and culture increasingly sought to prepare young women for the responsibilities of citizenship. But as in the women's movement more widely, this was often cast in gender-differentiated terms, focused on women's distinctive ability to contribute to the relief of poverty, children's welfare, and other social issues.[47] Women students were overrepresented in social service-oriented extracurricular activities such as settlement houses, an indication that they may have actively sought out such activities—whether because they seemed purposeful, because they offered an attractive form of intimate gender-segregated community, or because they offered opportunities for professional development in new feminized careers such as social work.[48] By establishing their own governance

---

[42] 'Editorial', *Glasgow University Magazine*, 13 December 1893, 57; 'Queen Margaret Students' Representative Council Meeting Minutes', 1894–8, DC 233/2/16/1, GUA.

[43] 'Women's Union Minutes', 1899–1930, UND/GE2/AA1, DUA.

[44] See e.g. *The Serpent* 12, no. 5 (May 1928), 124; Debates Committee Minute Book, DC 240/2/6/1, GUA.

[45] Marilyn Hird, ed., *Doves and Dons: A History of St Mary's College Durham* (Durham: St Mary's College, 1982); also quoted in Dyhouse, *No Distinction of Sex?*, 113–14.

[46] Oman, *Higher Education and the Gendering of Space*, 96.

[47] Sunderland, 'English Girls' Schools and Women's Suffrage'; Helen Sunderland, '"Politics for Girls": Representations of Political Girlhood in the Girl's Own Paper and the Girl's Realm', *Victorian Periodicals Review* 52, no. 1 (2019): 1–26; Sarah Wiggins, 'Gendered Spaces and Political Identity: Debating Societies in English Women's Colleges, 1890-1914', *Women's History Review* 18, no. 5 (November 2009): 737–52.

[48] Brewis, *Student Volunteering*, 31–2.

structures, debating societies, publications, and sports clubs, women students established that these were such central aspects of the university experience that they did not wish to compromise on access to them. At the same time, in their own eyes and in the eyes of their male peers, women became distinctively associated with aspects of student culture that focused on purposeful social and political engagement with the world outside the university.

To be sure, this culture did not always remain confined to the bounds of respectable femininity, nor appeal to all women students. Activities that prepared young women for active citizenship sometimes offered opportunities for women students to identify with masculine political roles: for example, adopting masculine personas in order to participate in a mock parliament or mock trial in the decades before women MPs, barristers, or judges were conceivable.[49] At the same time, such activities could also serve to uphold the gender order, underscoring the idea that it was impossible for women to participate in national politics or the justice system *as women*. Moreover, while women students' creation of gender-segregated spaces within gender-integrated universities could afford opportunities to escape sexism in wider student culture, women student leaders, concerned to perform respectability and responsibility, often enforced norms of appropriate feminine civic engagement that some women experienced as oppressive or merely uninteresting.[50] As the coming chapters will show, those women who sought to participate in rowdier and more informal forms of student culture that were normatively masculine, or who saw university as an opportunity to socialize, date, and have sex across gender lines, explored alternative possibilities for how women students might conceptualize what university was for.

But the extent to which women students—or, for that matter, men students—could realize such alternatives was limited by the impact of the First World War upon universities, which underscored conceptions of essential gender difference. Both within universities and in the wider culture, the war entrenched a perception that masculine and feminine visions of 'corporate life' were irreconcilable.

The Impact of the First World War

Gender inevitably divided students' experiences of the war and its aftermath. Upon the outbreak of war in summer 1914, many men students volunteered for

---

[49] See e.g. *The Serpent* 2 (9 December 1918) for report of a women's union mock parliament in which students in character as MPs used male names and pronouns. See also Mo Moulton, *The Mutual Admiration Society: How Dorothy L. Sayers and Her Oxford Circle Remade the World for Women* (London: Corsair, 2019), 30.

[50] Oman, *Higher Education and the Gendering of Space*, 100–1; for discussion of similar policing of norms of femininity among American women students see Margaret A. Lowe, *Looking Good: College Women and Body Image, 1875–1930* (Baltimore: Johns Hopkins University Press, 2003).

military, or war-related medical, service.[51] Those who did return at the start of the academic year were exhorted that it was their duty to give all their free time to the Officers' Training Corps.[52] By the advent of conscription in January 1916, virtually all men students were serving. Around 15 per cent of student soldiers were killed in action, a rate slightly higher than the national average.[53] By contrast, government and universities encouraged women to stay in education, arguing that women would be of greatest use to the war effort if they achieved the professional qualifications for which they were studying. Facing a shortage of qualified medical personnel, medical schools that had previously been hostile to women students opened their doors to them.[54] In the absence of men, women assumed more leadership roles in gender-integrated student organizations and student government. Women's unions organized first aid classes and knitting parties, made up Christmas parcels to send to students serving in the armed forces, and donated the proceeds from event ticket sales to hospitals and war relief organizations.[55]

Numbers of men students slowly began to increase again from the 1916–17 academic year, finally returning in large numbers from 1919. By 1922, there were twice as many undergraduate students in England and Wales as there had been in 1914, and almost half of these were ex-servicemen, some of whom qualified for need-based government scholarships for ex-servicemen.[56] Women who had been studying on special war-related courses, in turn, left, meaning that there was only a slight net increase in the proportion of all undergraduates nationally who were women, in keeping with a steady, modest increase in women students over the course of the 1900–20 period.[57] Yet ex-servicemen students widely believed that it was necessary to reclaim their campuses from large feminine invasions. Men's student unions declared their intention, in the words of the Durham Union, to 'get things as far as possible into pre-war condition'.[58] Removing women from university leadership roles and returning them to what were seen as appropriate activities and social roles for their sex seemed an integral part of restoring the pre-war status quo.

---

[51] John Taylor, *The Impact of the First World War on British Universities: Emerging from the Shadows* (Basingstoke: Palgrave Macmillan, 2018), 66.

[52] See e.g. 5 February 1915 in 'SRC Minutes', 1913–27, UND/GB1/AA1, DUA.

[53] J.M. Winter, *The Great War and the British People* (London: Macmillan, 1985), 92–7.

[54] Dyhouse, *No Distinction of Sex?*, 241.

[55] See e.g. 'Women's Union Minute Book', 1913–17, SUA/1/3/5, MUA; 'Women's Union General Meetings Minute Book', 1916–21, SUA/1/3/2/1, MUA; 'Women's Union Society Annual Reports', 1914–16, REC/2005/61/1, UCL.

[56] Georgina Brewis, Sarah Hellawell, and Daniel Laqua, 'Rebuilding the Universities after the Great War: Ex-Service Students, Scholarships and the Reconstruction of Student Life in England', *History* 105, no. 364 (2020): 82–106.

[57] Taylor, *Impact of the First World War*, 67–70; R.D. Anderson, *Universities and Elites in Britain since 1800* (Cambridge: Cambridge University Press, 1992), 23.

[58] 'Union Society Minutes', 1918–35, UND/GE1/AB3, DUA, at 23 January 1919.

This rested not on general conceptions of women's rights or separate spheres, but on a more specific ideal of student life as a protected time and space for men to be themselves and to pursue their preferred leisure activities. In 1920, for example, UCL medical students sent a letter to the management committee of the medical faculty, demanding that it reverse its policy of admitting women—not because they objected to women being doctors, but because, with fewer places available to men, the college rugby team was suffering.[59] Manchester men complained that the increased number of women students meant that there were never seats available in the debating hall and that the tennis courts were always occupied.[60] Refrains that women were losing their womanliness—especially by smoking—were common, as were claims that women students could not write, had no sense of humour, and were ugly.[61] According to these men, women were bad students—bad at the kinds of sociability necessary for participation in student culture, poor sports in their hogging of social and athletic facilities—and should stay in their own sphere rather than trying to compete with men.[62]

Before the war, patronizing attitudes to women students may have been common, but open misogyny was rare. When it was expressed in student publications, editors were careful to frame it as a minority opinion.[63] From 1917, however, there was a marked shift in tone, characterized by resentment that women appeared to have done less than men for the war effort but nevertheless to be getting a better deal out of the war.[64] Nowhere was this more apparent than in the pages of the *Glasgow University Magazine*. In February 1917, an editorial gave the magazine's official sanction to the view that 'the real university is composed only of the men', that it had been a mistake twenty-five years previous to elect women representatives to the SRC or to allow them any place in university life, and that the 'inrush of barbaric hordes' must be stemmed.[65] A 1919 editorial argued that women did not possess 'the university spirit'—which it defined as the kind of originality of thought that might lead to scientific discoveries—and thus would never be full members of the institution.[66] This had been a common refrain from older, more conservative faculty and media commentators twenty or thirty years

[59] Dyhouse, *Students: A Gendered History*, 141.

[60] Letter to the Editor, *The Serpent* 13, no. 5 (May 1929), 168; 13, no. 6 (June 1929), 192.

[61] See e.g. 'Women and Smoke', *The Serpent* 6, no. 3 (December 1921), 74–5; 'Letter to the Editor', *The Serpent* 12, no. 2 (December 1927), 62 (opining that starting a Vegetarian Society was a foolish venture because the group of women who had founded it were ugly); 'Writing Revolutionised', *Glasgow University Magazine*, 23 January 1930, 210–11.

[62] See e.g. *The Serpent* 5, no. 3 (February 1921), 43; and 14, no. 6 (June 1930), 159–60.

[63] See e.g. 'Women as Prize-Winners', *University College Gazette* 3, no. 36 (30 October 1901), 216–17; 'A Monstrous Regiment of Women', *University College Gazette* 3, no. 43 (12 December 1902), 295; *Manchester University Magazine* 2, no. 14 (April 1906), 145–6; 5, no. 35 (February 1909), 74; Dyhouse, *Students: A Gendered History*, 137–54.

[64] See e.g. 'Letters', *Manchester University Magazine* 12 (9 January 1917).

[65] 'Editorial', *Glasgow University Magazine*, 14 February 1917, 160–1.

[66] 'Editorial. Pandora', *Glasgow University Magazine*, 21 February 1919, 104–5.

previous, but it had not typically been expressed by undergraduates before. Similar themes persisted into the 1920s. One columnist informed women students that it was their duty to leave the university so as not to be in direct competition with men for graduate jobs, another that 'women ruin the SRC', and a third expressed optimism that modern science would invent a method of asexual reproduction, allowing for the eventual 'extermination' of women.[67] Editorials held that 'It has never been satisfactorily proved that the intermingling of the sexes has been advantageous', that 'the greatest clubs have all been misogynistic', and that women had no place in university life on the grounds that beer is a superior beverage to tea.[68] At least some of these contributions were intended to be funny. But the sense of humour was a cruel one.

The explosion of misogyny at Glasgow was on the more extreme end, notice-able enough to attract comment from other universities.[69] But a shift in tone was not uncommon. This would appear to map on to broader national patterns, as ex-servicemen faced difficult readjustments to civilian life that could manifest in misogynistic and other violent behaviour.[70] It also took on particular resonance in the context of student life, in which men students could become emotionally invested in a romanticized ideal of studenthood. Men who missed the homosocial camaraderie of wartime may have sought out opportunities to recreate it in gender-segregated student organizations; school-leavers too young to have fought in the war may have seen university as a space where they could enter into a form of adult masculine intimacy that they envied their older peers for having experienced.

In either case, men found such camaraderie in OTC camps, union activities, and the in-group identities forged in especially masculine-coded fields of study such as medicine.[71] OTC membership remained high and enjoyed social cachet.[72] Men's unions continued to host gender-segregated, masculine-coded activities such as smoking concerts in addition to or instead of gender-integrated activities such as dances. 'Smokers', revue concerts featuring 'turns' from students and guest performers, were rowdy, alcohol-fuelled affairs, which might include bawdy songs and even appearances—as in one scandalous incident at Manchester in

---

[67] 'Thoughts on the Present Discontent', Glasgow University Magazine, 17 November 1920, 56; 'SRCs I Have Known', Glasgow University Magazine, 16 December 1931, 134–6; 'Woman: A Timely Warning', Glasgow University Magazine, 20 May 1925, 352.

[68] 'Editorial', Glasgow University Magazine, 4 February 1926, 224; 'Editorial', Glasgow University Magazine, 17 February 1926, 252.

[69] The Serpent 14, no. 3 (February 1930), 80–1.

[70] Jon Lawrence, 'Forging a Peaceable Kingdom: War, Violence, and Fear of Brutalization in Post-First World War Britain', Journal of Modern History 75, no. 3 (September 2003): 557–89, at 562; Susan Kingsley Kent, Making Peace: The Reconstruction of Gender in Interwar Britain (Princeton: Princeton University Press, 1993), 97–8.

[71] On the masculine culture of medicine see Dyhouse, Students: A Gendered History, Ch. 7; Laura Kelly, 'Irish Medical Student Culture and the Performance of Masculinity, c.1880–1930', History of Education 46, no. 1 (January 2017): 39–57.

[72] See 'Letters to the Editor', Glasgow University Magazine, 5 December 1928, 110–12.

1932—from chorus girls.[73] Unions often held an annual 'freshers' smoker', which helped to induct new students into norms of undergraduate masculinity. In 1931, the Manchester Men's Union pre-emptively banned freshers' smoker attendees from bringing fireworks into the venue, an indication of the standard of behaviour at such events.[74] Unions, like other institutions of masculine community, sought to walk a fine line between expressions of masculinity that were raucous, drunken, and destructive and those that associated appropriate masculinity with restraint, chivalry, and good form.[75] But in the immediate postwar period in particular, chivalry seemed less important than an assertion of student masculinity that entailed more permissive attitudes to sexuality, public drunkenness, and the incursion of students upon the broader urban environment. Despite continuity with pre-war forms of masculine sociability, interwar student masculinity was a reinvented formation, evincing new rationales for and practices of gender segregation. It constructed studenthood as an essentially masculine category—as against the forms of gender-integrated sociability that had in fact begun to emerge in the years before 1914—and saw the promotion of this ideal as an essential component of restoring the pre-war status quo.

In 1930, an anonymous male correspondent wrote in to the *Glasgow University Magazine* to argue against the concept of a gender-integrated student union on the grounds that women students were ugly, had no sense of humour, no interest in politics or wider affairs, poor table manners, 'and no wish to escape from their destined and damnable profession, school-teaching'. The magazine subsequently published three responses from women students. Dismissing the author as juvenile and ridiculous, the respondents observed that they would not want a mixed union either, if this was what they would be subjected to therein.[76] Indeed, over the course of the 1920s, members of Glasgow's women's college moved away from supporting full integration of women students into university life, arguing instead for a distinctive 'Queen Margaret *esprit de corps*': a feminine alternative to the vision of masculine university community that men students seemed to be offering.

They were not alone, as women student government leaders at universities across the country, reacting to a wider national perception of backlash against women's wartime gains, protested the misogynistic and domineering attitudes of their male colleagues by refusing to cooperate in gender-integrated student life.[77] This was a countercultural stance: held against men students who did not

[73] *The Serpent* 16, no. 4 (March 1932); see also *The Serpent* 5, no. 2 (December 1920), 36.

[74] 'Men's Union General Committee Book', 1931–2, SUA/1/2/1/4, MUA, 18.

[75] Amy Milne-Smith, *London Clubland: A Cultural History of Gender and Class in Late Victorian Britain* (Basingstoke: Palgrave Macmillan, 2011), 61.

[76] 'Letters to the Editor', *Glasgow University Magazine*, 9 January 1930, 189; and 23 January 1930, 216–17.

[77] On women academics' perception of a wider backlash see Phoebe Sheavyn, 'Higher Education for Women in Great Britain', International Federation of University Women Pamphlet No. 2, 1921, Gerritsen Collection, accessed 24 May 2024, https://www.proquest.com/gerritsen/books/higher-education-women-great-britain/docview/2633988380/sem-2?accountid=13042.

necessarily perceive that there was a problem with their behaviour; against other women students, who despite the challenges still appreciated opportunities for cross-gender social interaction; and against university administrators who hoped that if women took part in university-wide extracurricular activities, they might provide a check on men students' most disruptive inclinations. At Manchester, for example, administrators spent decades unsuccessfully urging the men's and women's unions to integrate for this reason.[78] But in the 1920s, the two unions found it impossible to agree upon the terms of a joint constitution.[79] In spring 1928, the men's union suggested resuming negotiations, but as the proposal came in the middle of a term in which members of the men's union had repeatedly broken into the women's union and destroyed property, the women refused to cooperate. Nor was either union willing to sacrifice any of its own space to the cause of a joint common room.[80]

Finally, in 1932, under administrative pressure, the two unions founded a new Joint Social Sub-Committee—though the men's union continued, with its larger budget, to plan university-wide social functions without involving women in decision-making. Women responded by declining to contribute financially to university societies, and these in turn barred members of the women's union from participating in their activities.[81] The women's union then prohibited men from entering the women's side of the pavilion at the university sports ground, disallowed the renting of union rooms to certain male-dominated university societies, and introduced gender-segregated seating at mixed debates, with a central aisle running down the hall separating men and women attendees.[82] This was animated by real concerns: the university societies that had rented women's union rooms had damaged them; the raucous atmosphere in the debating hall had made women participants and spectators feel unwelcome. Only in 1933, during a large-scale renovation of various university buildings, did university administrators—independent of the two unions—set aside mixed common room space.[83] Asked about what they would like to see in the new space, women students suggested that the men's and women's unions might be laid out so that the two sets of rooms could be merged in the future, but that they had no desire to merge at present.[84]

---

[78] *The Serpent* 2 (December 1918), 45; 'Women's Union Minute Book', 1917–19; 'Women's Union General Meetings Minute Book', 1916–21.

[79] 'Women's Union General Meetings Minute Book', 1921–8, SUA/1/3/2/2, MUA; 'Women's Union Minute Book', 1921–4, SUA/1/3/1/8, MUA.

[80] 'Women's Union Minute Book', 1926–8, SUA/1/3/1/10, MUA; 'Women's Union General Meetings Minute Book', 1929–36, SUA/1/3/2/3, MUA.

[81] 'Women's Union Minute Book', 1931–3, SUA/1/3/1/12, MUA; 'Social Sub-Committee Minute Book', 1930–5, SUA/1/4/2/1, MUA; 'Men's Union General Committee Book', 1931–2, SUA/1/2/1/4, MUA.

[82] 'Rules of the Women's Athletic Union', June 1922, AWS/2/2, MUA; 'Women's Union Minute Book', 1928–31, SUA/1/3/1/11, MUA, 179.

[83] 'Women's Union General Meeting Minute Book', 1929–36.

[84] 'Women's Union Minute Book', 1933–5, SUA/1/3/1/13, MUA, 15.

Previous explanations for the entrenchment of gender segregation in universities after the First World War have pointed to backlash against women's wartime gains, as well as to continuity with pre-war forms of gender segregation.[85] But while these explanations have done justice to the intensity of the vitriol directed at women students in the years after 1918, they have not always examined the reasons for ex-servicemen's investment in a masculine ideal of studenthood, nor the limited extent to which that ideal represented continuity with the pre-war period. Student institutional memory is necessarily short-lived: men who felt that women's presence in the universities impinged upon their aspirations for student life did not remember or care that their forebears twenty years previous had tried (if inadequately) to welcome women into their midst. Indeed, reinforcing masculine cultural norms took a constant effort of rhetoric and ritual: as against the reality of student populations that at some civic universities were as much as one-third women, and as against alternative, gender-neutral visions of 'corporate life'.

Corporate Life

In the years after the First World War, then, there were in fact several competing visions of what a common student culture might look like. A masculine vision sought to thread the needle between valuing chivalry and restraint on the one hand, and according considerable latitude to misbehaviour on the other. A feminine vision sought to prioritize organized, often social service-oriented, activities, while carving out space for women students to feel safe and welcome and make a meaningful contribution to campus life. Although students invested in one or another of these visions could develop them through gender-segregated organizations such as student unions, disagreements could also leave them locked in long-running stalemates. Meanwhile, a large proportion of students had neither the time, the money, nor the inclination to participate in organized student life. Those who saw university primarily as a route to a qualification in a professional occupation that would improve their wider life prospects did not always see the point of joining student societies. Those who commuted home straight after their lectures were less likely to think it financially worthwhile to join the union. Student government officers struggled to convince their commuting peers that it was worthwhile to stay on campus into the evening to participate in extracurricular activities. They pondered how to foster a common sense of what they called 'corporate life'—on any given campus as well as across institutions—that would transcend divides of gender, class, national origin, career aspirations, and other factors that influenced what students hoped to gain from their university experience.

---

[85] Dyhouse, *No Distinction of Sex?*, 240.

Another development in the political culture of the immediate postwar years offered one possible solution to this problem. Students were a prime constituency for the liberal internationalist politics that spread across western Europe after the war. The League of Nations Union was popular among students, as were the internationalist perspectives of many Christian and social service organizations.[86] In 1919, French student activists founded the Confédération Internationale des Étudiants (CIE), whose annual conference British delegates first attended in 1921. One of those British delegates was Ivison Macadam, a distinguished military officer who, upon returning to his studies after the war, had become president of the King's College London Union. In 1922, he founded the National Union of Students (NUS), envisioning it as a member organization of the CIE that would further British students' connections with both internationalist and imperial-unity initiatives.[87]

Though thus positioned with respect to early-1920s politics, the NUS also drew on a longer tradition of inter-university, imperial, and international links. Student representatives from all four Scottish universities had been meeting together annually since the 1890s, and English universities had begun holding regular conferences in 1904.[88] Colleges and universities competed against each other in activities such as sports and debate, and hosted international teams from the United States, the imperial Dominions, and occasionally China or Japan.[89] University magazines printed columns in which they summarized the content of other universities' publications—indicative of a readership interested in goings-on in student life generally, not just on their own campuses. But the NUS offered something different: a new high-minded rationale for bringing students together, and a claim that all students in Britain had a common set of experiences and political interests. While the inter-university conferences of the 1890s and 1900s had been male-dominated—women delegates did not take part in the Scottish Inter-Universities Conference until 1911—women held prominent roles in the NUS.[90] By the 1930s, the organization's official policy was to advocate for increased gender integration of campus life.[91]

---

[86] Helen McCarthy, *British People and the League of Nations: Democracy, Citizenship and Internationalism, c.1918–45* (Manchester: Manchester University Press, 2011); Brewis, *Student Volunteering*, 64.

[87] Ivison S. Macadam, *Youth in the Universities* (London: National Union of Students, 1922); Day, *National Union of Students*, 13–16.

[88] Scottish student newspapers reported regularly on the Inter-Universities Conference. See also Brewis, *Student Volunteering*, 21.

[89] See e.g. the many national and international exchanges of delegates recorded in the 'Joint Debates Sub-Committee Minute Book', 1930–7, SUA/1/4/3/2, MUA.

[90] Day, *National Union of Students*, 17; *Fourth Universities Congress Oxford, March 29th to April 4th, 1928* (London: National Union of Students, 1928).

[91] *The Challenge to the University: A Report of the 1938 Congress of the National Union of Students of England and Wales on University Life and Teaching in Relation to the Needs of Modern Society* (London: The National Union of Students, 1938), 48–9.

This spirit fed back into conversations on individual campuses, as unions and other student groups increasingly used the language of 'corporate life' to describe the ideal for which they were striving. In 1923, for example, the Manchester Women's Union revised its constitution to state that its mission was 'the development of social and corporate life among past and present students of the university'.[92] A correspondence ran in the Glasgow University Magazine over several years in the late 1920s and early 1930s, as students debated what corporate life actually was and how best to engender it. One more cynical view was that corporate life was the preserve of rich students who could afford the cost of a union membership. In February 1928, a correspondent calling himself 'Alcibiades' wrote in to the magazine to argue that 'a great many of the students are too poor to take part in Corporate Life'.[93] But the next issue's editorial chastised Alcibiades for taking so materialist a view. 'Essentially, the Corporate Spirit—like Love—has nothing to do with money; it is the expression of an attitude to life', the editorial claimed. To participate in corporate life, one had to perceive that one had a sense of duty to one's fellow students, regardless of what else one might, or might not, have in common with them. This would help to overcome social divisions and to create a university in which students knew and befriended each other and did not disappear into the suburbs at 5 p.m.[94]

But how to achieve this, beyond vague assertions about 'an attitude to life'? Some students turned to invented tradition, suggesting the establishment of residential colleges on the Oxbridge model and mandatory wearing of academic gowns.[95] The NUS and the University Grants Committee (UGC) shared the sense that civic universities could learn something from the community spirit of fully residential institutions. The UGC's significant financial investment in universities in the interwar period included funding for the construction of halls of residence and student union buildings.[96] They stressed that more needed to be done in urban universities to create the spatial conditions in which informal interpersonal connections might flourish, and highlighted halls of residence as especially important to ensuring that students did not 'remain as isolated units after leaving the class room'.[97] Although halls had long been seen as a necessity for women students who did not live at home with their families, from the early 1930s

[92] 'Women's Union Minute Book', 1921–4, SUA/1/3/1/8, MUA.
[93] 'Letter to the Editor', Glasgow University Magazine, 8 February 1928, 293.
[94] 'Variations on an Ancient Theme', Glasgow University Magazine, 25 April 1928, 283–4.
[95] 'Letter to the Editor', Glasgow University Magazine, 25 April 1928, 293; 'Letters to the Editor', Glasgow University Magazine, 5 December 1928, 110–12; 'Letter to the Editor', Glasgow University Magazine, 23 October 1929, 23; 'Letter to the Editor', Glasgow University Magazine, 15 April 1931, 246–7; 'Women's Union Society', MEM/III/B, UCLRO, 5, 11; 'Women's Union Minutes', 1899–1930, UND/GE2/AA1, DUA.
[96] The Challenge to the University, 48–9.
[97] University Grants Committee, 'Report of the University Grants Committee', 1921, UGC/5/26, TNA, 15; University Grants Committee, 'Report for the Period 1929–30 to 1934–35', UGC/3/16, TNA, 11–16.

universities also started to build halls for men, though these only attracted a small number of students. More expensive than private lodgings and necessarily gender-segregated, halls supported minority, gender-segregated student cultures that were more imitative of the gender-segregated cultures of the Oxford and Cambridge colleges and were less accessible to less affluent students.

Other students sought a higher purpose for corporate life by turning to politics and international affairs. In 1920s Ireland, students fought in the Irish War of Independence and played important roles in the early government of the Free State.[98] After the 1929 economic crash, students volunteered to aid the unemployed—and engaged in mutual aid, as many suffered economic hardship themselves.[99] From 1933, students reacted to Hitler's seizure of power by joining political parties and discussing international political issues in magazines and debating societies. Some student unions and societies ran campaigns to aid student refugees from Germany, Czechoslovakia, and Austria, as well as victims of the Spanish Civil War. But on the whole, students were more interested in how questions of war and peace affected them personally. In the early 1930s, the NUS orchestrated a campaign to encourage university debating societies to pass anti-war motions. The Oxford Union's February 1933 debate of the motion 'This House will under no circumstances fight for its King and country' became notorious, but most unions or debating societies passed analogous motions.[100] The cause of anti-militarism became a rallying cry for students nationwide, something they perceived themselves to have in common with others of their generation and life stage.[101] An editorial in the *Glasgow University Magazine* in October 1934 characterized the students of the day as keen to distinguish themselves from their more frivolous forebears of ten or fifteen years previous. They were anxious about the future and frustrated that politicians and other older people did not take their perspectives into account.[102] Political and international affairs could appeal to more serious-minded women and men students alike. Campaigns to aid refugees drew on the longstanding appeal of social service in women's student culture. But at the same time, the prominence of questions of war and peace reflected the demographic reality that the proportion of students who were women declined somewhat after 1929, as economic pressures led families who could not afford multiple sets of fees to prioritize the higher earning potential of their sons' education.[103] Students primarily framed international affairs in terms of how they

[98] Steven Conlon, 'Rebels and Rustici: Students and the Formation of the Irish State', in *Students in Twentieth Century Britain and Ireland*, ed. Jodi Burkett (Basingstoke: Palgrave Macmillan, 2018), 249–76.

[99] Brewis, *Student Volunteering*, 93.

[100] 'Women's Union Committee Minutes', 1928–45, UND/GE2/AC1, DUA; *The Serpent* 17, no. 4 (March 1933); 'Minutes of Debates', 1933–47, A.32/53, Liverpool University Archives.

[101] William Whyte, *Redbrick: A Social and Architectural History of Britain's Civic Universities* (Oxford: Oxford University Press, 2015), 211–12; Brewis, *Student Volunteering*, 132.

[102] 'Editorial', *Glasgow University Magazine*, 31 October 1934, 46–7.

[103] Dyhouse, *Students: A Gendered History*, 205.

affected the men who, as twenty years previous, would be called up in the event of a European war.

Historians and activists interested in constructing a genealogy of the 'student movement' of the 1960s have gravitated to moments when interwar students seemed collectively interested in leftist politics.[104] It is true that the NUS took a moderately left-wing line throughout the interwar period, that a small number of students joined the Communist Party of Great Britain, and that students who fought for the Republican forces in Spain enjoyed the admiration of their peers. By the mid-1930s, the mainstream of student opinion was squarely anti-fascist.[105] At the same time, a vocal minority of right-wing students sometimes staged disruptions that led to the cancellation of student events featuring left-wing speakers.[106] The Durham Union and SRC voted to disaffiliate from the NUS over its overtly political tone (and, indeed, students' representative bodies at Oxford and Cambridge did not affiliate until the 1960s).[107] Other student unions raised concerns over the high cost of NUS membership: students could see a more immediate return on their union subscriptions were unions to spend their budgets on on-campus activities.[108] Those politically engaged students who urged their peers to support causes often saw those pleas go unheeded.[109]

Indeed, most students simply tended not to view their extracurricular lives in political terms, even when engaging with the world beyond the campus. While there were some students whose earnest political convictions drove them to volunteer as strike breakers during the 1926 General Strike or, conversely, to support the mass marches of the unemployed in the 1930s, there was a larger, apolitical group for whom both events offered the same opportunity to escape from the routine of daily life and participate in something larger than oneself.[110] Similarly, at Manchester in the early 1930s, students grew exasperated with the efforts of a new radical editor of the *Serpent* magazine to turn the publication into a platform for left-wing political causes such as Indian independence, disestablishment of the Church of England, legalization of abortion, and greater gender integration of university social life.[111] After an October 1932 editorial which asserted,

---

[104] Simon, 'The Student Movement'; Eric Ashby and Mary Anderson, *The Rise of the Student Estate in Britain* (London: Macmillan, 1970).

[105] Day, *National Union of Students*, 18–21; Brewis, *Student Volunteering*, 122–9.

[106] See e.g. 'Students Kidnapped. Socialists Sent to Sea. Edinburgh Election "Rag"', *The Scotsman*, 21 October 1926, 8; 'Students' "Rag" at King's College. Smoke Bomb at Socialist Meeting', *The Times*, 9 March 1929, 9.

[107] 'Union Committee Minutes', 1919–31, UND/GE1/AC3, DUA; 'SRC Minutes', 1913–27, UND/GB1/AA1, DUA.

[108] Brewis, *Student Volunteering*, 61–2.

[109] See e.g. an unsuccessful effort to support German Jewish refugees at Liverpool: 'Minutes of Debates', 1933–47, A.32/53, LUA.

[110] Brewis, *Student Volunteering*, 96; on the General Strike see also Rachelle Hope Saltzman, *A Lark for the Sake of Their Country: The 1926 General Strike Volunteers in Folklore and Memory* (Manchester: Manchester University Press, 2012).

[111] See issues of *The Serpent* between October 1931 and October 1932.

'We have reduced purely parochial matter to a minimum, in the belief that a University magazine should aim somewhat higher than making suggestive or insulting remarks about Union personalities', several students wrote in to say that they in fact did read *The Serpent* for the jokes.[112] They may have represented a larger number of their peers for whom student life was a refuge from current events rather than a springboard to them.[113]

It is telling that the radical political programme Manchester students rejected included gender integration. Fifty years previous, a more gender-neutral vision of student 'corporate life' had seemed a positive step forward, part of what it might mean to cast off paternalistic oversight from university administrators and develop a culture of independent young adulthood that moved between the campus and the city. But by the 1930s, backlash to the eradication of gender distinctions seemed entrenched. Later cohorts of men students sustained the ex-service generation's assertion of a romanticized conception of masculine student life; women students, for their own reasons, gravitated to gender-segregated forms of corporate life. Like middle-class Britons more widely, in the late 1920s and early 1930s many, if by no means all, students turned to officially apolitical, but implicitly conservative, forms of civic engagement that seemed to offer reassuring stability at a time of political and social upheaval. Among the forms of stability they sought to uphold was a conception of binary gender difference. It seemed that women could not be students, and participate in student corporate life, on the same basis that men were students. But what were the alternatives? How might students create cohesive community in an urban, gender-integrated university?

In the 1931–2 academic year, the *Glasgow University Magazine* offered two options, neither of them the politically engaged, gender-neutral social service ideal that the NUS sought to promote. In a November 1931 editorial, headlined 'We Are the Hollow Men', the magazine accused students who had played a practical joke on a visiting politician of exhibiting 'a want of elementary manliness'. '[W]hen it amounts to something like the humiliation of a man before women and strangers,' the editorial argued, 'it is time to point out that there is a difference between virility and hooliganism.'[114] In keeping with the message of the T.S. Eliot poem to which the editorial's title alludes, the author articulated a connection between 'manliness' (a word that appears six times in the short editorial) and the moral values a university culture might seek to uphold—and argued that acculturation into this ethos had failed. This, then, was one answer to the 'corporate life' debate's uncertainty about what university life might seek to offer: a revivified masculine public sphere that would overcome the tendency of university masculinity to deteriorate into disruptive, potentially violent, practical jokes.

[112] *The Serpent* 17, no. 1 (October 1932).
[113] 'Letters to the Editor', *The Serpent* 17, no. 5 (May 1933).
[114] 'Editorial', *Glasgow University Magazine*, 4 November 1931, 41–2.

While disengaged from international affairs, it was in some ways continuous with the older idealist tradition of university as a space of acculturation into civic responsibility. Students might demonstrate their subscription to this ideal of masculinity by behaving with dignity 'before women and strangers'—necessarily outside observers of university life.

However, just a few months later, in February 1932, another *GUM* editorial offered an alternative vision. Written in a more light-hearted style, this editorial purported to discourse upon 'Love', claiming that 'no subject [is] more closely entwined among the roots of the Tree of (Corporate) Life'. Undergraduates of opposite sexes falling in love with each other, it suggested, might provide the thread that would tie students together into one body. The students regularly seen embracing at a local nightclub were a sign of the health of corporate life.[115] While the tone of this editorial was tongue-in-cheek, it was not sarcastic—the author thought Love a good thing, perhaps even compatible with the chivalry the November editorial advocated. Yet this vision of university life as constituted and sustained by hedonistic heterosexual dating rituals could not be more different from that which saw it inhering in chivalrous decorum. Both visions expressed the hope that student life might amount to something beyond diligent attendance at lectures and a professional qualification, though they did so by turning away from explicitly political ideals of civic responsibility to consider less formal forms of student sociability. In the process, both offered a vision of university as a space of acculturation into desirable norms of masculinity and femininity, and underscored the centrality of binary gender difference to corporate life. But one lent exalted cast to a homosocial masculinity in which women's role was to serve as a detached and disembodied check on men's morals, while the other delighted in direct social and physical contact between men and women.

The following two chapters explore these two options in turn. As we will see, conflicts both within and outside universities about the kinds of values and behaviours that masculine student culture ought to celebrate contributed to men students' dissatisfaction with a homosocial invented tradition, while the desire of some women students to participate in that culture seemed—both to other women and to men—threatening and unworkable. Women and men students alike flocked instead to heterosexuality as the most practical paradigm through which students might build gender-integrated community without challenging the stability of the gender order, contributing to heterosexuality's dominance and the marginalization of alternative ways of organizing gender and sexuality.

Teaching Gender: The British University and the Rise of Heterosexuality, 1860–1939. Samuel Rutherford,
Oxford University Press. © Samuel Rutherford 2025. DOI: 10.1093/9780198937524.003.0004

[115] 'Editorial', *Glasgow University Magazine*, 2 March 1932, 268–9.

4

Student Masculinities in Public

When the 1931 *Glasgow University Magazine* editorial board identified a student practical joke as antithetical to 'manliness', it marked a striking departure from a longstanding association of student masculinity with misrule, practical jokes, and violence intended to assert the power of 'gown' over 'town'. Since the Middle Ages, Scottish and English students, like their continental European counterparts, had celebrated feast days and university holidays by organizing events such as comedy sports matches and fancy dress processions and pageants, by perpetrating practical jokes on their social superiors, and by thronging city centres to unleash mayhem that, as often as not, descended into drunken violence. From the late nineteenth century, and to an even greater extent after the First World War, men students rediscovered and reinvented these traditions. Associated with the new civic universities, with ex-servicemen's masculinities, and with new styles of performance and technologies of mass media, the form of disruptive student performance that students, the media, and the public referred to as 'ragging' became central to what it meant to embody 'corporate life'.

By the 1920s, rags were wildly popular events, tapping into an enthusiasm for invented tradition characteristic of interwar popular culture. Many northern English and Scottish universities associated their annual rag festivities with collections in aid of local hospitals, which led them to be heralded as evidence of civic pride by city councils proud of their local universities, as a sign of healthy corporate life by new universities eager to stake their claim to student tradition, and simply as entertainment by a nascent but booming mass media interested in the 'human interest' story. Drawing thousands of spectators and grossing tens of thousands of pounds in donations, rags were the primary way that the vast majority of the population who did not go to university, or know anyone who did, gained an impression of student life.

Yet the spectacle of the rag also signified differently in the age of mass media, mass politics, and the gender-integrated university. Media, local politicians, and university administrators celebrated charity rags, sometimes going to great lengths to excuse real violence, as well as looking past the ways that rag rituals constructed the prototypical student as elite, white, and male. But the disruptive hijinks of London, Oxford, and Cambridge students—often associated with major sporting fixtures or other university events, but lacking an altruistic justification—were increasingly condemned by a tabloid press eager to bolster the anti-elite sentiments of its readership and by politicians on both the right and the left eager to seem tough on the 'hooliganism' of an irresponsible postwar generation. Under more pressure to demonstrate the respectability and productivity of their efforts, students who organized charity rags emphasized that their activities, however disruptive, were strictly in the service of social good. They cooperated with police to ensure smoothly run carnivals, self-censored risqué comedy, and developed ever more expansive fundraising schemes.

This shift in the aesthetic and experience of rags also made them less stereotypically masculine events. Rags had helped the media to construct an image of 'the student' as (for good or ill) a misbehaving young man, looking past the more than a quarter of students who, by the late 1920s, were women. Women students themselves had previously characterized rags as men's affairs, either casting themselves in the role of admiring spectators or staying away out of concern for their safety. But by the 1930s, the experience and ideological framing of rags had shifted enough that it became possible for women students to contemplate participating in this most quintessential expression of corporate life: whether on the same terms as men students, or through distinct gender-differentiated activities that also raised money for the hospitals.

But as women increasingly participated in rags in the 1930s, men students' enthusiasm for them declined. Some men offered a left-wing political critique of charitable fundraising; more felt that rags conducted with official approval and cooperation with local law enforcement, and with strict sanctions on dirty jokes, were missing the point. In changing to satisfy the tastes of a wider student body and the public, rags' status as an expression of masculinity appeared under threat. To reassert their own individual masculinities, but also the overarching masculinity of studenthood, men students declared their support not of mayhem, but of chivalry. In the process, they sought to deny both women and insufficiently masculine men a place in corporate life. But although this in some ways appeared to reassert the stability of the gender order, it failed to establish a workable foundation for life in the urban gender-integrated university.

Inventing Tradition

Early-twentieth-century rags shared many elements with a tradition of adolescent and young adult masculinity that had for centuries been an aspect of life in western European cities. Students, like apprentices and journeymen, had long asserted their right to perform an adult, independent masculinity, and to maintain the gender and other aspects of the social order, through ritualized violence and misrule. In the university cities of medieval and early modern Europe, students carried weapons, joined gangs, and intimidated townspeople and those whom they perceived to be their social inferiors.[1] Days associated with 'festival licence', like Carnival or Shrove Tuesday, could institutionalize and legitimate such behaviour.[2] The etymology of the term 'to rag' itself evokes folk tradition: originally an eighteenth-century dialect word meaning 'to scold, to reprove, to dress down', it recalls the traditional ritual of 'rough music' used across western Europe to enforce community moral norms. But by the mid-nineteenth century, the word 'rag' exclusively connoted students' practical jokes or performances of disorder and misrule.[3]

In the mid-nineteenth century, violence was characteristic of student life. Fights among students were a common cause of concern for the Durham University Senate.[4] Students in Oxford in the same period held their tutors hostage, hazed and bullied their peers, and set fire to books and art.[5] But in the late nineteenth century new customs also emerged, connected to the university calendar and to students' pride in their institutional affiliation. In the Scottish universities, the idea of ragging became associated with bi- or triannual elections for the rector, the ceremonial head of the university. Students conducted disruptive and chaotic campaigns on behalf of their chosen candidates. The election period concluded with a torchlight procession in which masses of students, many in fancy dress, escorted the new rector from the railway station to campus. These events were carefully choreographed for maximum theatrical effect, for example ensuring that all students lit their torches simultaneously.[6] Student publications praised large and enthusiastic turnouts for the processions, viewing them as a sign of a robust corporate life.[7] While violence was certainly a feature of rectorial

[1] Ruth Mazo Karras, *From Boys to Men: Formations of Masculinity in Late Medieval Europe* (Philadelphia: University of Pennsylvania Press, 2003), 77, 95–8; Hannah Skoda, *Medieval Violence: Physical Brutality in Northern France, 1270–1330* (Oxford: Oxford University Press, 2013); Carl I. Hammer, 'Patterns of Homicide in a Medieval University Town: Fourteenth-Century Oxford', *Past & Present* 78 (February 1978): 3–23; Alexandra Shepard, *Meanings of Manhood in Early Modern England* (Oxford: Oxford University Press, 2006), 93–6; Natalie Zemon Davis, *Society and Culture in Early Modern France* (Stanford: Stanford University Press, 1975).

[2] Skoda, *Medieval Violence*, 141–2; Keith Thomas, *Rule and Misrule in the Schools of Early Modern England* (Reading: University of Reading, 1976), 33; Robert Darnton, *The Great Cat Massacre and Other Episodes in French Cultural History* (New York: Basic, 1984), 83.

[3] 'rag, v. 3', OED Online, accessed 26 May 2024, http://www.oed.com/view/Entry/157425; 'rag, n. 4', OED Online, accessed 26 May 2024, http://www.oed.com/view/Entry/157421.

[4] 'Senate Minutes', 1869–75, UND/BA1/5, DUA.

[5] M.C. Curthoys, 'The Colleges in the New Era', in *The History of the University of Oxford*, Volume 7: *Nineteenth-Century Oxford, Part 2*, ed. M.G. Brock and M.C. Curthoys (Oxford: Oxford University Press, 2000), 115–58, at 140; J.F.A. Mason and Morton N. Cohen, 'Christ Church', in *The History of the University of Oxford*, Volume 7, 221–36, at 222.

[6] 'Letter to the Editor: Torchlight Procession', *Glasgow University Magazine*, 4 December 1912, DC 198/1, GUA, 164.

[7] 'Record Torchlight Procession', *Glasgow University Magazine*, 2 December 1891, 11–12; 'The Lord Rector's Visit: The Torch-Light Procession', *Glasgow University Magazine*, 10 November 1897, 29; 'Concerning Rectorials', *Glasgow University Magazine*, 5 February 1908, 344; 'Rectorials and Other Matters', *Glasgow University Magazine*, 4 November 1908, 8.

campaigns, there was also a growing concern with order, formal ritual, and appearance.[8] Rectorial elections were an opportunity for a university to show itself off to the city—and, judging by the spectators who lined the streets to watch the processions, they succeeded.

This tradition intersected with one that arose simultaneously in Manchester and Liverpool, in which a local theatre would, as a marketing stunt, designate a 'Students' Night' during its run of a pantomime, comedy, or variety show. Men students would process to the show in fancy dress, and would collaborate with the theatre management and actors to include university-specific songs and jokes in the production.[9] Through the fancy dress procession and audience participation in the show, students asserted their presence as a force to be reckoned with in the city, priding themselves on their parade's ability to stop traffic or the ability of their own alcohol-fuelled singing efforts to drown out the performers onstage. Students' theatre nights were popular both from the point of view of theatre managers, who could sell out a house; and from the point of view of men students, who enjoyed having an occasion that brought the male student body together. They spread throughout England and Scotland, becoming a source both of student-body patriotism and of embarrassing scandals related to drunken misbehaviour.[10] By 1910, Manchester university administrators officially recognized the annual pantomime students' night on Shrove Tuesday as a university holiday, cancelling lectures in an admission that if the event was going to happen anyway, it was better that it be minimally disruptive to academic work.[11]

Ragging took on increased significance in the context of the romanticized masculine vision of university life that ex-servicemen students sought to establish in the aftermath of the First World War. In several Welsh and southern English towns and cities in 1919 and 1920, Armistice Day occasioned disruptions that newspapers characterized as 'rags': students from different London medical schools fought one another for possession of a German machine gun; ex-servicemen students at Cambridge marched through the streets, started bonfires, and rioted at the police station; ex-servicemen students at University College Exeter daubed paint on statues around the city, to the consternation of town officials and the local press.[12] 'Everything is coming back again, even "rags"',

---

[8] For violence see 'Rectorial Agreement, 1925', *Glasgow University Magazine*, 6 May 1925, 334; 'Rectorial Election, 1928', *Glasgow University Magazine*, 9 May 1928, 321; 'Rectorial Agreement', *Glasgow University Magazine*, 21 October 1931, 25.

[9] Carol Dyhouse, *Students: A Gendered History* (London: Routledge, 2006), 188–9.

[10] 'Students' Representative Council. Theatre Night', *Glasgow University Magazine*, 27 February 1901, 190; 'Students' Gallery Night', *University College Gazette* 3, no. 47 (17 June 1903), P.P. 6149.fa, British Library, 347.

[11] *Manchester University Magazine* 6 (February 1910), UMP/2/3, MUA.

[12] 'Frolicsome Students', *Nottingham Evening Post*, 13 November 1919, 3; 'Armistice Day "Rag"', *Cambridge Independent Press*, 14 November 1919, 4; 'Cambridge. The Armistice Night "Rag"', *The Observer*, 16 November 1919, 17; 'Spoliation', *Exeter and Plymouth Gazette*, 13 November 1920, 1;

commented the *Manchester Guardian* in 1919: signalling both expanded media interest in the phenomenon and a tendency to locate rags in the context of the restoration of the *status quo ante bellum*.[13] For the most part, newspapers took a light-hearted approach to these activities, but their reporting nevertheless suggested an undercurrent of real violence. Students who 'ragged' public figures by kidnapping them and parading them through the streets succeeded in intimidating them, preventing them from speaking, and even (as in the case of an American Prohibition activist who lost an eye in a 1919 student rag) seriously injuring them. But the victims (nearly always men) were careful to emphasize their cooperation with this performance of masculinity: they were good sports who could take a joke; the students had meant no harm.[14] In this way, the expectation that non-students would put up with student rags—and even participate in them—became normalized.

At the same time, the war had a different impact upon ragging cultures in Scotland and the North of England. From the early 1920s, students there began to link their fancy dress processions and performances to collections in aid of local hospitals, part of a wider turn to funding voluntary hospitals through community-based philanthropy.[15] Liverpool initiated this custom in 1920, and Manchester followed in 1921.[16] When students processed through the city in fancy dress, they carried collecting tins. Admission charged for pantomimes, carnivals, concerts, and dances could be donated to the hospitals fund. Even real disorder could be subsumed under the charitable impulse, as in Manchester and other cities students threatened to vandalize local businesses that did not pay for an 'immunity badge'. Universities competed with each other to raise the most money, leading to increasingly outrageous publicity stunts. Hospitals were not the only charitable cause rags supported, but they were the primary one, unassailable due to the patriotic connotation of supporting war veterans. Media commentators hailed

---

'Cambridge', *The Observer*, 14 November 1920, 18; 'An Exeter Rag', *Western Gazette*, 19 November 1920, 10.

[13] 'The Revival of the "Rag"', *The Manchester Guardian*, 13 November 1919, 6.

[14] Among several other such incidents that attracted similar press coverage see 'The Very Young Idea', *Daily Express*, 14 November 1919, 6; 'A "Rag" Regretted', *The Manchester Guardian*, 15 November 1919, 10; 'London Students' Raid. "Pussyfoot" Injured', *Daily Telegraph*, 15 November 1919, 11; 'Mr. "Pussyfoot" Still Cheerful. Students' Sympathy', *The Times*, 17 November 1919, 14; 'Students Capture "Mr. Pussyfoot": A "Varsity Rag" in London', *The Illustrated London News*, 22 November 1919, 16; ' "Rag" at Glasgow. Railway Leader's Meeting "Prematurely Closed"', *The Observer*, 23 November 1919, 15; ' "Rag" Enjoyed by Mr. Cramp', *Daily Mail*, 24 November 1919, 7; 'Students Rag Labour Leader', *Daily Telegraph*, 24 November 1919, 12; 'Mr. Asquith's Hat. Hospital Students' Trophy', *Daily Telegraph*, 3 March 1920, 13; 'Mr. Asquith "Ragged": The Ex-Premier on His Way to the House', *The Illustrated London News*, 6 March 1920, 3.

[15] Nick Hayes and Barry M. Doyle, 'Eggs, Rags and Whist Drives: Popular Munificence and the Development of Provincial Medical Voluntarism between the Wars', *Historical Research* 86, no. 234 (November 2013): 712–40.

[16] Dyhouse, *Students: A Gendered History*, 191; *The Serpent* 6, no. 5 (17 February 1922), UMP/2/4, MUA.

students for moving away from 'the destruction of property and the detriment of law and order' to 'constructive' action that would improve society.[17]

In the 1920s, panto days expanded into rag weeks, with planning for a full slate of activities entailing year-round work from student organizers. At Manchester, plans for the Shrove Tuesday rag began at the start of every academic year, with a proliferating programme of student theatre performances and dances alongside the main fancy dress street procession.[18] At its height in the late 1920s, the rag grossed over £10,000 annually in donations.[19] Glasgow organizers, aiming for an efficient collection, put students into teams and assigned each to collect donations and sell special rag magazines in a specific district of the city. By 1935, twelve different student societies sponsored separate dances on the evening of Glasgow's Charities Day.[20] At Liverpool, where the climax of Panto Day was a professional pantomime production, organizers' time was taken up with ensuring good relations with the theatre. They met several times with the actors and stage manager, and gave presents to the cast, orchestra, and theatre staff on the night of the performance. For safety reasons, they requested that the theatre bars be closed, and they came to a seating arrangement that segregated men students in the stalls, away from women students and members of the public in the boxes and balconies.[21] Rags transformed into mass entertainment occasions, reaching beyond men students to take in all members of the university community as well as members of the public. In 1935, Liverpool students sold 80,000 copies of the rag magazine, indicating the scale of their audience.[22] Despite this explosion of mainstream popularity, though, rags remained masculine occasions, with women students cast as spectators to displays of masculine exuberance.

The popularity of charity rags in northern English and Scottish cities attests to how successfully rags conveyed a sense of the spectacular. They were larger-than-life, over-the-top, fantastical, absurdist performances, intended to signal a maximum contrast with daily life. It also speaks to their success at tapping into a wider enthusiasm for invented tradition and folk revival characteristic of regional popular entertainment in the 1920s. In keeping with the 'pageant fever' of the period, rags often featured creative retellings of stories from English and Scottish

---

[17] Columnist from *Birmingham Daily Post*, quoted in *Durham University Journal* 22, no. 7 (December 1920), Per Local DUR, DUA, 223. See also 'A Useful "Rag"', *The Observer*, 21 November 1920, 18; 'The University Rag', *Manchester Guardian*, 18 February 1920, 14.

[18] 'Men's Union General Committee Book', 1931–2, SUA/1/2/1/4, MUA; *The Serpent* 9, no. 3 (16 February 1925), 78.

[19] C.E. Sykes, 'Shrove Tuesday "Rag." Over £11,000 for Medical Charities', *Manchester Guardian*, 6 March 1926, 13.

[20] 'Students' Infirmaries Day', *Glasgow University Magazine*, 20 January 1923, 181–2; 'Charities' Day—Jan. 1925', *Glasgow University Magazine*, 17 December 1924, 120–1; 'Der Tag', *Glasgow University Magazine*, 16 January 1935, 185.

[21] 'Panto Committee Minutes', 1922–31, A.27/27, LUA.

[22] 'Panto Committee Minutes', 1934–52, A.27/28, LUA.

history and folklore.[23] In a 1923 rag at University College Nottingham, for example, students depicting characters from the Robin Hood stories 'captured' the mayor and held him for ransom (to be donated to the hospitals).[24] Rag performances featured folk dancing, drew on the traditions of pantomime and medieval mummers' plays, and commemorated the festivals of a romanticized premodern past, from Bonfire Night to Whitsuntide.

Characteristic of these performances' aesthetic of invented tradition was how they represented gender and racial difference. Female impersonation and blackface had long been staples of British and wider European masculine folk traditions of misrule, rebellion, and carnivalesque performance. Through these costumes, European men tested the boundaries of appropriate white masculinity, while still reasserting the normative gender and racial order.[25] Interwar cross-gender and racist impersonation performances had powerful continuities with the mummers' play and the pantomime, while transposing them into distinctively modern formats that drew on tropes from contemporary theatre, cinema, and popular culture. White men students represented Hollywood starlets, 'cowboys and Indians', and blackface 'jazz musicians'. Newsreel films of rags showcased students dressed as old ladies, dogs and cats, soldiers and sailors of various kinds, clowns, pirates, monks and bishops, babies, 'sheiks' and 'sultans', Vikings, 'Zulu warriors', fishwives, skeletons, Poseidon, Highland clansmen, harlequins, devils, nurses, 'maharajahs', little girls, Crusader knights, and Charlie Chaplin. Cross-gender and racist performances were one part of how students sought to convey to their audiences a sense of the spectacular, the comedic, and the exotic. Audiences likely received such performances as familiar and unremarkable, of a piece with other contemporary forms of popular entertainment.[26] In the process, they accepted the representation of student life that rag parades, pantomimes, and pageants offered: in which white men students might represent gender and racial difference for fantastical or comedic effect, but in which women students and students of colour did not appear on screen or in the streets.

---

[23] Angela Bartie et al., '"History Taught in the Pageant Way": Education and Historical Performance in Twentieth-Century Britain', History of Education 48, no. 2 (March 2019): 156–79; Angela Bartie et al., eds., Restaging the Past: Historical Pageants, Culture and Society in Modern Britain (London: UCL Press, 2020).

[24] 'Robin Hood and His Merry Men', 22 March 1923, British Pathé, accessed 26 May 2024, https://www.britishpathe.com/video/robin-hood-and-his-merry-men.

[25] Michael Pickering, Blackface Minstrelsy in Britain (Aldershot: Ashgate, 2008); Alun Howkins and Linda Merricks, '"Wee Be Black as Hell": Ritual, Disguise and Rebellion', Rural History 4, no. 1 (April 1993): 41–53; Claire Sponsler, 'Outlaw Masculinities: Drag, Blackface, and Late Medieval Laboring-Class Festivities', in, Becoming Male in the Middle Ages, ed. Jeffrey Jerome Cohen and Bonnie Wheeler (New York: Garland Publishing, 2000), 321–48; Zemon Davis, Society and Culture in Early Modern France, 125–50.

[26] Christine Grandy, '"The Show Is Not about Race": Custom, Screen Culture, and the Black and White Minstrel Show', Journal of British Studies 59, no. 4 (October 2020): 857–84, at 865–7.

To both political and cultural elites and the wider public, the representation of rags as invented tradition was appealing in the context of a period that many regarded as exceptionally politically unstable. Newsreels, a form of media especially concerned with presenting a conservative ethos of popular nationalism and political and social consensus, played an important role in framing student rags in these terms. At cinemas nationwide, millions of viewers saw films of rag pageants and processions play alongside films of May Day and harvest celebrations, morris dancing, and other events presented as part of quaint local custom.[27] Yet rag organizers also often made satirical reference to current events and popular culture, choreographed their dance numbers to the rhythms of jazz and swing, and used the BBC and newsreels to advertise their fundraising aims. If rag customs offered a kind of revivified folk nationalism, they also offered a disjointed, kaleidoscopic, technological modernism. Their tone of comic surrealism belied an underlying darkness that, for students and the public alike, raised questions about the gender norms inherent to student life.

The Civic Benefits of Urban Violence

In the English civic and the Scottish universities, university administrators, local politicians, and the press warmly welcomed rags as good for business: celebrating town/gown cooperation, the social responsibility of fundraising for the hospitals, and the flourishing of student life at newer, regional institutions. As the sums rag participants collected swelled, local press from Aberdeen to Bristol expressed pride in the citizenry's beneficence. Civic leaders happily participated in ritualized misrule—often agreeing, for example, to be 'kidnapped' and held for ransom— but also in more decorous proceedings that cemented the status of charity rags as civic occasions. In Manchester, where in the 1920s the Shrove Tuesday rag regularly grossed tens of thousands of pounds, the lord mayor and his wife held an annual reception to thank students for their efforts on behalf of local hospitals.[28] In 1925, the *Times* heralded a Reading rag—in which students at the brand-new university walked out of classes, stopped traffic with a fancy dress procession, and kidnapped a policeman who attempted to restore order—as proof that the fledgling institution was well on its way to being a real university.[29] Overall, the message was one of fun and frivolity. 'Rag Day is … Joy Day!' proclaimed the title card

---

[27] Samuel Rutherford, 'Researching and Teaching with British Newsreels', *Twentieth Century British History* 32, no. 3 (September 2021): 441–61, at 455–6.

[28] 'Court and Personal', *Manchester Guardian*, 10 May 1927, 10.

[29] 'University of Reading. Settled Policy of the College. Residential Character', *The Times*, 3 June 1925, 17.

of a Pathé newsreel film of a 1926 Cardiff rag, which depicted a parade featuring elaborately decorated floats and a comedy rugby match.[30]

This resolutely light-hearted tone belied the frequency and rapidity with which a rag practical joke could turn violent. Comedy sports, such as a football or rugby match in fancy dress with teams in the hundreds, were common rag activities and targets of the newsreel cameras.[31] So were 'flour fights', a ritualized form of mock violence that frequently turned into actual fights. Films of flour fights—which took place regularly at Glasgow between the opposing parties in the rectorial election, on Bonfire Night between UCL and KCL, and occasionally at other universities—have a certain routine. Two large groups of men stand facing each other across a field or quad, often with a mixed-gender group of spectators at a safe distance. At a signal that occurs off-screen, they rush towards each other, throwing flour, soot, and other objects. After an interval or in a subsequent shot, the throwing turns to direct physical contact: men tackle each other, hold each other in headlocks, throw punches. The camera pans across a messy brawl, the field trodden into mud.[32]

Even when allegedly comedic and heavily ritualized, the spectacle of mock violence served to enforce hierarchies of power. Ragging students sometimes burnt effigies of their critics, asserting their right to occupy the city on rag days. In 1922, Edinburgh students burned in effigy a Labour city councillor who had criticized an especially violent rag.[33] In 1926, a comedian who had objected to a rag that had disrupted one of his performances found himself burned in effigy in Liverpool.[34] Students across the country, who, in a nod to the popularity of the 1915 film *Birth of a Nation*, dressed up in the white sheets and pointed hoods of the Ku Klux

---

[30] 'Rag Days Joy Day', 2 March 1926, *British Pathé*, accessed 26 May 2024, http://www.britishpathe.com/video/rag-days-joy-day.

[31] 'Students' Rag—Brighton', n.d. (c.1920s), *British Pathé*, accessed 26 May 2024, https://www.britishpathe.com/video/students-rag-brighton; 'A Joyous Rag', 17 December 1925, *British Pathé*, accessed 26 May 2024, https://www.britishpathe.com/video/a-joyous-rag; '"Rag" Days…Joy Day!', 2 March 1926, *British Pathé*, accessed 26 May 2024, https://www.britishpathe.com/video/rag-days-joy-day.

[32] '20,000 Eggs, Soot and Flour', variously dated 29 October 1925 and 1928, *British Pathé*, accessed 26 May 2024, https://www.britishpathe.com/video/20-000-eggs-soot-and-flour; 'Battle of Gower Street', 14 November 1927, *British Pathé*, accessed 26 May 2024, https://www.britishpathe.com/video/battle-of-gower-street; 'The Panto Rag', 6 January 1930, *British Pathé*, accessed 26 May 2024, https://www.britishpathe.com/video/the-panto-rag-2; 'The Panto Rag', 15 January 1931, accessed 26 May 2024, https://www.britishpathe.com/video/the-panto-rag; 'No Mercy Given or Required', 29 October 1931, *British Pathé*, accessed 26 May 2024, https://www.britishpathe.com/video/no-mercy-given-or-required-1; 'The Battle for "Sister Jane"', 16 January 1933, *British Pathé*, accessed 26 May 2024, https://www.britishpathe.com/video/the-battle-for-sister-jane; 'Glasgow University Poll', 29 October 1934, *British Pathé*, accessed 26 May 2024, https://www.britishpathe.com/video/glasgow-university-poll; 'Students' Rag', 5 December 1935, accessed 26 May 2024, https://www.britishpathe.com/video/students-rag. See also Negley Harte and John North, *The World of UCL, 1828–1990* (London: UCL Press, 1991), 158.

[33] 'Police Batons at Students' "Rag"', *Daily Mail*, 21 June 1922, 7; 'The Fate of a Critic', *The Times*, 24 June 1922, 14.

[34] 'Students' "Revenge"', *Daily Mirror*, 19 February 1926, 12.

Klan to 'raid' neighbourhoods for rag donations, yoked their violence to a universally recognizable symbol of white supremacy, despite media coverage that represented this as light-hearted and inconsequential.[35]

If the threat of racist violence was ubiquitous in rags, so was the threat of violence against women. In Cambridge in 1921, students celebrating after the university senate rejected a proposal to admit women to degrees destroyed the gates of Newnham College, a women's college, with a battering ram, in an event that some newspapers described as a 'rag'.[36] In 1922, at the high tide of postwar misogynistic backlash against women students, London medical students burnt an effigy of a woman medical student during their rag, an episode that the *Observer* newspaper described as being of little significance.[37] The annual rag tradition at Liverpool involved doing violence to a rag doll called 'Sister Jane', whose name and appearance designated her as female. Teams of students from different faculties would fight over Sister Jane, at the end of which, according to the recollections of a student who attended Liverpool in the mid-1930s, 'poor Jane would have been in fragments':

> When all was ready the President of Guild [of Students], formally robed and carrying 'Sister Jane', would walk to the centre of the quadrangle and mount the rostrum...then, after shouting a few words which no-one could ever hear, would hurl the doll high into the air and beat a hasty retreat. Thus began the melée, fought without tactics or plan but with plenty of vigour and enthusiasm. As the doll was torn limb from limb the battle would resolve itself into a series of separate scrums for its component parts. It was reasonable to expect that whoever ended up with the head was the ultimate winner—invariably the engineers, the all-male faculty. To my knowledge there were no serious injuries but I can recollect my hands being lacerated with scratches.[38]

While the 'scrums' the student described seem to have been typical, an undated Pathé film from the early 1920s shows students staging the formal public execution of Sister Jane. A lengthy procession of students carry the larger-than-life effigy, dressed in a white sheet with a cartoonish, heavily made-up, feminine painted face and a paper crown, to a scaffold. After some speeches, cheering, and singing from the crowd of student spectators, and a student dressed as a priest

---

[35] *Durham University Journal* 24, no. 1 (December 1923), 13; see also *Durham University Journal* 25, no. 1 (December 1926), 8–9; 'A Joyous Rag'. On the reception of *Birth of a Nation* in Britain see Michael Hammond, '"A Soul Stirring Appeal to Every Briton": The Reception of "The Birth of a Nation" in Britain (1915–1916)', *Film History* 11, no. 3 (1999): 353–70.

[36] '"Siege" of Newnham College. Miss Clough and the Damaged Gates', *The Times*, 24 October 1921, 7; 'The Newnham Incident. Sex Hatred or Bad Manners? Two Points of View', *The Times*, 25 October 1921, 10; 'Cambridge and the "Sex War"', *Daily Mirror*, 27 October 1921, 5.

[37] 'Women Students at the Hospitals', *The Observer*, 26 March 1922, 7.

[38] James Brophy, letter to Mr Allan, 3 April 1987, D404/2, LUA.

giving a benediction, a bonfire is lit and the effigy is placed on it. For about 45 seconds, the camera dwells in close-up on Sister Jane going up in flames, while students dance hand in hand in a circle around her.[39]

Such a spectacle recalls Guy Fawkes, or any number of similar English folkloric customs. It reads as characteristic of modernist engagement with the iconography of the English pastoral as a site for hauntings, horror, and death.[40] It also, specifically, enacts violence against a woman: year in, year out, as part of a central event in the university calendar. In the early 1920s, about a quarter of the Liverpool student population were women.[41] But no women appear in the film of Sister Jane's execution, the possibility of their presence consumed, instead, by the flames. In the course of staging spectacular stunts—engineered to push the boundaries of the permissible, to assert youthful white masculine power, and to draw spectators and thereby donations—students, and those who filmed and photographed them, sent clear messages about who had a natural place in the university body politic.

Men's unions accepted that property damage, injury, and arrests were an occupational hazard of putting on a rag. In 1921, the Manchester Men's Union preemptively levied all members for a fund to pay for the inevitable property damage the rag would occasion.[42] In 1932, Manchester Union members had to pay medical costs of £13 (over a month of a skilled worker's wages) to a certain Mr Travers, who said that students carousing at the Shrove Tuesday rag had caused him to sustain an injury to his thigh.[43] On one occasion at Liverpool, students set fire to a car that the union had hired for the rag procession, creating both a large bill for the union and a safety hazard as the engine exploded in the crowded city centre.[44] Not only was property damage ritualized in the form of 'immunity badges' that protected businesses from vandalism, there was a real risk of injury if a spectator got in the way while students were asserting their power. By assuming collective responsibility for such acts, men's unions indicated that they understood violence as constitutive of student masculinity.

One might imagine that ragging students' efforts to terrorize the populace might have attracted condemnation, especially in the immediate post-First World War context in which the 'brutalization' of ex-servicemen and the spectre of

---

[39] 'Students' Rag Day', n.d., *British Pathé*, accessed 26 May 2024, https://www.britishpathe.com/video/students-rag-day-liverpool.

[40] Michael Saler, *As If: Modern Enchantment and the Literary Prehistory of Virtual Reality* (Oxford: Oxford University Press, 2012), esp. Ch. 5; Alison Light, *Forever England: Femininity, Literature, and Conservatism between the Wars* (London: Routledge, 1991), Chs. 2 and 4.

[41] Carol Dyhouse, *No Distinction of Sex? Women in British Universities 1870–1939* (London: University College London Press, 1995), 249.

[42] *The Serpent* 5, no. 3 (10 February 1921).

[43] 'Men's Union General Committee Book', 1931–2, SUA/1/2/1/4, MUA, 93–4. Currency equivalency figures come from the National Archives' currency conversion tool, http://www.national-archives.gov.uk/currency-converter/.

[44] Brophy, letter to Mr Allan, 3 April 1987.

political and social unrest were common topics of public concern. But instead, as in other instances in which public discourse asserted 'myths of English peaceableness' against fears of 'brutalization', media and university administrators tended to underscore a message of fun and festivity.[45] Occasional objections to charity rags faded into the background, those who complained seeming like humourless spoilsports who undermined the rags' charitable objectives. There was a sense that, if the public might only be educated about the benevolent purposes of charity rags, they would look at a person taken hostage, a car set alight, or an effigy burned and see not violence but a bit of fun. In 1919, the *Times* reported that the Shah of Iran, touring a Manchester textile mill, was 'disconcerted' when Manchester students greeted him with 'a boisterous welcome'—but this was only because he did 'not quite know…the harmless complexion of a University rag'.[46] In 1926, the registrar of University College Nottingham told the *Nottingham Evening Post* that the college's rag had garnered more proceeds for the hospitals than in the preceding year because 'the general public have now a fuller understanding of the purposes of the "rag," and appreciate the public-spirited motive of the students instead of regarding the affair merely as an inconvenient ebullition of youthful spirits'.[47] Legitimated through the efforts of the press, audiences could be trained to see purpose instead of mayhem, high spirits instead of hooliganism, themselves as participants rather than victims of festival licence. Emptying their pockets for young men in fancy dress with collecting tins, they also invested in the presence of the universities in their cities. In the process, the rags discourse located university students in a long tradition of youthful, rowdy masculinity, deserving of a certain measure of latitude if it did not go too far.

Oxbridge Men and Popular Politics

The licence accorded to charity rags at English redbrick and Scottish universities stood in contrast to how the press and public figures treated the misbehaviour of Oxford, Cambridge, and sometimes London students. Throughout the 1920s, there were numerous episodes when students from Oxford and Cambridge who came to London for an event such as the annual Oxford–Cambridge boat race or rugby match subsequently went out on the town and instigated significant mayhem in the West End theatre and nightlife district. They harassed theatre-goers,

---

[45] Jon Lawrence, 'Forging a Peaceable Kingdom: War, Violence, and Fear of Brutalization in Post–First World War Britain', *The Journal of Modern History* 75, no. 3 (September 2003): 557–89, at 565.
[46] 'The Shah in Manchester. Interest in Manufacturing Processes', *The Times*, 5 November 1919, 14.
[47] 'Students Collect £1,400 for Hospital', *Nottingham Evening Post*, 15 March 1926, 6.

vandalized theatres, and disrupted performances to such an extent that theatres had to be shut down mid-performance.[48]

While these rags lacked the sense of choreographed, ritualized spectacle that characterized charity rags, they nevertheless shared many elements in common: the presence of violence and disorder, the assertion of 'gown' power against 'town', the association with theatre and with sport. But the media and the public responded to them in divergent ways, shaped by the national politics of the 1920s. The decade was characterized by economic instability and a new politics of class that reflected the effects of mass enfranchisement in 1918. Party politics were polarized between an ascendant Labour Party and the Conservatives, who remained in government or coalition for all but three of the interwar years, thanks in large part to long-serving Prime Minister Stanley Baldwin's skilful embrace of new media and his ability to cast the Conservatives as the party of national consensus in contrast to suspiciously socialist Labour. Tensions between the government and trade unions climaxed with a General Strike that ground the country to a halt for two weeks in May 1926. Class and regional divides deepened over the course of the late 1920s, and to an even greater extent after the 1929 stock market crash, the effects of which hit mining and other heavy industries in the North of England especially hard.

In May 1926, 100,000 people responded to the General Strike by engaging in strike-breaking volunteer labour in sectors such as transportation: casting their actions as apolitical and patriotic, but also as light-hearted fun. Some of the most visible and iconic 'volunteers' were wealthy young women and men—the men sometimes students at Oxford or Cambridge—who treated their masquerades as bus drivers or domestic servants as another fancy dress party.[49] Despite its relative brevity, the General Strike was a moment that thrust the elite and unserious Oxbridge man into the public eye, and that helped both to construct wealthy

---

[48] See e.g. A.H. Buckland, 'The Boat Race "Rag"', *Daily Mail*, 29 March 1920, 6; 'Students' "Rag" at Theatre', *Daily Telegraph*, 8 December 1920, 7; 'The Boat Race Revel', *Manchester Guardian*, 3 April 1922, 6; 'West End "Rag." Fun after 'Varsity Rugby Match', *Daily Mail*, 13 December 1922, 7; 'John Blunt, "Rags" in Town. Not to Be Taken Too Seriously. But London Is Not the Place for Them', *Daily Mail*, 14 December 1923, 7; 'Boat Race Night. Oxford President and Police Station Incident', *Daily Mail*, 7 April 1924, 7; 'West End "Rag." Merry Scenes after the 'Varsity Match', *Daily Mail*, 11 December 1925, 9; 'The Talk of London', *Daily Express*, 12 December 1925, 4; "Varsity Man in Court. After the Rugger "Rag"', *Daily Express*, 12 December 1925, 11; 'Boat-Race Night. Sir C. Biron's Warning against "Rags"', *Daily Mail*, 25 March 1926, 7; 'Costly "Rag" in Train. £300 Bill for Undergraduates', *Daily Telegraph*, 2 December 1926, 9; "Varsity Rag Last Night. West End Theatre Invaded. College Songs and Catcalls. Stage Pelted with Streamers', *Daily Mail*, 15 December 1926, 9; 'Students Wreck a London Theatre Show. Rugby Match "Rag." Battle with Fire Extinguishers. Women's Dresses Ruined', *Manchester Guardian*, 14 December 1927, 11; "Varsity Match "Rag." Wild Scenes in the West End. Two Plays Stopped. Police Called in and Men Thrown Out', *Daily Mail*, 14 December 1927, 11; 'University "Rags." Home Secretary's Statement. "Leave the Matter in My Hands"', *Daily Telegraph*, 20 December 1927, 6; 'Students' "Rags" in London. Home Secretary to Discuss Preventative Measures', *Manchester Guardian*, 11 January 1928, 2.

[49] Rachelle Hope Saltzman, *A Lark for the Sake of Their Country: The 1926 General Strike Volunteers in Folklore and Memory* (Manchester: Manchester University Press, 2012).

young urban men as students and to construct the Oxbridge man as the arche-typical university student, despite the fact that the vast majority of both women and men students at this time attended non-Oxbridge institutions.[50] While it was not always clear whether the young men smashing up West End theatres were, in fact, university students, the association of these events with days in the Oxbridge sporting calendar cemented a connection between them, the 'ancient' univer-sities, and the 'Bright Young People' who in the 1920s became known for their purposeless pursuit of fun.[51]

At the same time, Conservative politicians and general moral opprobrium also targeted elite young people's recreational activities. Part of the Conservative elect-oral strategy to cast itself as the party of national consensus was to criticize the excesses of irresponsible young elites who had been too young to participate in the national sacrifices of the First World War and whose frivolous lifestyles posed a threat to the decency and family values of 'ordinary' people. But this was not merely cynical pandering to the electorate: William Joynson-Hicks, the Conservative home secretary from 1924 until 1929, was an evangelical Anglican and right-wing statist who believed that his role as home secretary was to lever-age the power of the state to maintain moral order. His politics spoke to a broader shift in the Conservative Party towards statism and cultural conservatism. While in office, Joynson-Hicks prosecuted suspected communists, sexual deviants, and publishers of obscene books; at his direction, the Metropolitan Police waged a long-running cat-and-mouse war against London's nightclubs and the assumed moral turpitude that occurred therein.[52] Wealthy young people partying in cen-tral London were frequent targets of this moral crusade: young men causing havoc in a West End theatre were more likely than ever to be arrested, to appear in the police court, and to have their names breathlessly reported in the gossip pages of the tabloid press.

Indeed, the press—especially the Conservative donor Lord Rothermere's papers, the *Daily Mail* and the *Daily Mirror*—played an important role in folding student rags in London into a broader moral panic about dissolute privileged youth, to which they presented state intervention, aggressive policing, and a gen-eral atmosphere of law and order as an appropriate response. While in the early 1920s London rags tended to be regarded as 'high spirits' or 'good-natured rough and tumble', by the middle of the decade the press gave column inches to theatre managers who complained that there was no redress for property damage, theatre-goers who asserted that student 'rowdyism' had spoiled their evenings,

---

[50] For student demographics see Dyhouse, *Students: A Gendered History*, 9.

[51] Saltzman, *A Lark for the Sake of Their Country*, 53–6.

[52] James J. Nott, '"The Plague Spots of London": William Joynson-Hicks, the Conservative Party, and the Campaign against London's Nightclubs, 1924–29', in *Classes, Cultures, and Politics: Essays on British History for Ross McKibbin*, ed. Claire V. Griffiths, James J. Nott, and William Whyte (Oxford: Oxford University Press, 2011), 227–46.

and a general sense that West End rags were 'going too far'.[53] After an especially bad outburst of violence at the London Hippodrome theatre on 14 December 1927, following the Oxford–Cambridge Varsity rugby match—during which students smashed glassware in the theatre bar, sprayed each other with fire extinguishers, and rioted in the streets—press condemnation was universal.[54] But university administrators tended to regard student rowdiness that occurred outside the university precinct as beyond their purview. Following the December 1927 incident, it was only after Joynson-Hicks intervened that the vice-chancellors of Oxford and Cambridge threatened disciplinary action against ragging students—further underscoring the media narrative that, if left to their own devices, Oxbridge men of any age would not act to preserve public decency.[55]

For commentators in the regional press, the activities of badly behaved Oxbridge undergraduates in London were an opportunity to draw a contrast with the meritorious activities of charity rags in Scotland and the North of England. In response to the 1927 Varsity match episode, the *Dundee Courier* recommended that English students might 'take a leaf out of the book of our Scottish students, who find adequate expression for their high spirits in their laudable and unconventional efforts on behalf of our infirmaries'.[56] In February 1928 the *Manchester Guardian*, reviewing recent charity rags in Glasgow and Manchester, suggested that rags designed for the serious purpose of fundraising for hospitals were 'commendable', in contrast to the 'hooliganism' of rags prompted by something as frivolous as a sporting victory.[57] A great deal could be subsumed under the charitable impulse, as those in northern cities who raised misgivings about the violence and disorder of charity rags were reminded that it was all in the name of a good cause. When Manchester city councillor Miss Lee wondered in December 1927 if Manchester ought to be trying pre-emptively to avoid violence on the level of that seen in London, her fellow councillor Mrs Simon asserted that the events in London were the work of especially wealthy and entitled students who had

---

[53] Blunt, '"Rags" in Town'; '£70 Damage in Students' Theatre Rag', *Evening Telegraph (Dundee)*, 12 December 1924, 7; 'West End "Rag"'; 'The Talk of London', *Daily Express*, 12 December 1925, 4; '"Raggers" in London. "Undergrads" and the Public', *Daily Mail*, 16 December 1925, 7; "Varsity Rag Last Night'.

[54] 'Students Wreck a London Theatre Show'; 'Varsity Match "Rag." Wild Scenes in the West End. Two Plays Stopped. Police Called in and Men Thrown Out', *Daily Mail*, 14 December 1927, 11; 'A Vice Chancellor on the "Rag." Statement from Cambridge. Theatre Managers Taking Action. How to Deal with Future Disorder', *Manchester Guardian*, 15 December 1927, 15; 'After the Match. Students' Wild Night. Police Court Ending', *The Scotsman*, 15 December 1927, 11; 'London Anger at "Barbaric" University Rag', *Daily Mirror*, 15 December 1927, 3; "Varsity "Rag" Disgrace. Angry Protests. Efforts to Stop Future Scenes', *Daily Mail*, 15 December 1927, 9; 'Young Barbarians', *Daily Mirror*, 15 December 1927, 7.

[55] 'University "Rags"', *Daily Telegraph*, 23 January 1928, 8; "Varsity Rags. Universities Warn Undergraduates', *Daily Mail*, 23 January 1928, 5; 'West End "Rags." A Cambridge Criticism of London Students', *Manchester Guardian*, 24 January 1928, 6.

[56] 'Varsity "Rags"', *Dundee Courier*, 23 January 1928, 4.

[57] 'A Reputable "Rag"', *Manchester Guardian*, 22 February 1928, 10.

'nothing to do with' the more socioeconomically diverse student body of Manchester.[58]

Yet just two years previous, a Manchester University rag prank targeting Manchester College of Technology had led to a brawl between three hundred students, clashes with police, and arrests.[59] Manchester students were not, by and large, Bright Young People. In fact, student 'rowdyism' might have fed into a different source of tension in northern industrial cities, where those praising the 'good cause' of charity rags might implicitly have contrasted them with different kinds of masculine-coded conflict situated within urban space, occasioned for example by industrial action. Yet at the same time, most Oxford and Cambridge students were not extremely wealthy trend-setting nightlife denizens, either. Observers drew on interwar class politics to resignify the violence and disruption common to all student rags, scripting them into an exaggerated North/South and class divide that led to an enduring image of the 'Oxbridge man' as the epitome of elite masculine entitlement.

Remaking the Ragging Gender Order

The emerging critique of men students' entitlement to urban space nevertheless put new pressure on charity rags, leading to subtle but significant changes in their content and aesthetics. University administrators and local governments made new efforts to underscore charity rags' respectability and safety: seeking to scrub rags of their most dangerous, disruptive, and boundary-pushing elements and to recentre their messaging on fundraising, civic responsibility, and family-friendly carnivals. In many cases, this took the form of top-down intervention. In Manchester—home of the nation's largest charity rag—in 1930, the chief constable introduced a wide swathe of new regulations concerning the annual rag, including that 'There must be no undue interference with members of the community' and that 'There must be no form of indecency.'[60] In 1931, responding to what at that point were years of media outrage about exceptionally disruptive central London rags, the constituent colleges of the University of London formed a new board of discipline whose primary role was to adjudicate what was 'legitimate ragging'. The board was empowered to expel 'any student…who breaks the rules of good ragging according to the standards' the board determined.[61]

---

[58] 'College "Rags"', *Manchester Guardian*, 20 December 1927, 13.
[59] 'Police Stop Manchester Students' Rag. Ten Temporarily Detained. Hose Pipes Used against Stink Bombs', *Manchester Guardian*, 14 November 1925, 13.
[60] 'University "Rag." Police and Students at Issue', *Manchester Guardian*, 15 February 1930, 15.
[61] 'Ragging within Limits. London University's New Rules. Board of Discipline', *Manchester Guardian*, 25 June 1931, 9.

Men students had long maintained their own ragging ethics, denouncing 'hooliganism' and jokes in poor taste. In 1894, for example, the editors of Durham magazine *The Critic* wrote that they deplored a student who had played a practical joke on a blind man, making a distinction between ragging in general and ragging a disabled person who, they thought, could not respond in kind.[62] The Manchester Students' Representative Committee made a similar distinction in 1909 between property damage in aid of a funny joke from which others might derive pleasure, and property damage for its own sake.[63] In this way, men students had enforced their own norms of respectable masculinity, while still leaving considerable space for disorder, destruction, and jokes that could be mean or risqué as long as students themselves found them entertaining. But the Manchester chief constable's intervention, and the University of London's suggestion that 'legitimate ragging' might best be determined by an institutional disciplinary process rather than by students themselves, marked a departure from the tradition of self-governance that students had worked to establish before the First World War—speaking to the extent to which student rags placed universities' institutional reputations on the line within their local communities.

University administrators and local governments continued to assume that those who were affected by and would benefit from their actions were the same white men undergraduates who had always participated in rags. But, incidentally, the refashioning of rags as civic occasions created new opportunities for women students to join in the festivities. Since women had entered the universities, men students had assumed that their women peers might serve as a receptive audience for their displays of masculine excess. At both Liverpool and Edinburgh before the First World War, for example, male-led Students' Representative Committees (SRCs) routinely reserved seats for women students at the annual pantomime, at a safe distance from the men sitting in the stalls who might behave in a disorderly and potentially threatening manner.[64] In 1912, a Manchester woman student journalist who reviewed the traditional Shrove Tuesday fancy dress procession underscored this gender divide. Detailing the range of costumes, she took note of the number of participants dressed (in a nod to a major political issue of the moment and its particular importance in Manchester) as militant suffrage activists. She distanced herself and her fellow women students from this performance. '[W]e were not students as the term went that day', she reflected.[65] In making this observation, the author underscored that rags represented an especially masculine vision of corporate life, whose fancy dress costumes mocked women's claims to political equality. She also implicitly gestured to the fact that women students

---

[62] *The Critic*, 23 June 1894, SC12348/7, DUA, 4.
[63] 'Letter to the Editor', *Manchester University Magazine* 5, no. 34 (January 1909), 63.
[64] 'Panto Committee Minutes', 1922–31, A.27/27, LUA; 'SRC Women's Committee Minutes', 1899–1912, EUA/IN20/SRC/d, EUSC.
[65] *Manchester University Magazine* 8 (February 1912), 130.

might find it unpleasant and unsafe to become entangled with crowds of thousands of rowdy young men, many of them intoxicated, primed for violence disguised as a bit of fun.

After the First World War, as charitable fundraising came increasingly to be seen as rags' central purpose, more people began to raise the possibility that women students might like to participate in the fundraising activities. Given the prominence of volunteering and social service in feminized visions of corporate life, this was a natural rationale justifying women's participation in rags.[66] But in the 1920s, women student leaders hesitated to endorse rags' most public-facing aspects, such as fancy dress parades and pageants. In Manchester, for example, the women's union, with the input of the tutor for women, weighed carefully how to respond to men students' invitations to become more involved in the Shrove Tuesday rag. The members of the women's union decided to participate in a range of on-campus student activities, to sell tickets and programmes for the rag revue, and to run a café to raise money for the hospitals fund, but they carefully avoided the fancy dress procession.[67] At Durham and Liverpool, similarly, women increasingly took leading roles in administering the donation-collecting operation, working to maximize efficiency and revenue while steering clear of the signature fancy dress performances, which remained masculine territory.[68]

As in other aspects of student life, men students claimed to welcome women's active involvement in the most traditionally masculine aspects of rags. Manchester men urged 'girls' to 'pull their weight', and regarded the women's union's decision to run separate rag events as 'direct hostility and obstruction' of the procession.[69] In Glasgow in 1925, when—uncharacteristically—a few women students had taken part in the violent 'flour fight' tradition, men students writing in the *Glasgow University Magazine* praised those women for having entered fully into the spirit of corporate life.[70] Another correspondent in the magazine, identifying herself as a woman who had joined in the flour fight, proudly defended her

[66] Georgina Brewis, *A Social History of Student Volunteering: Britain and Beyond, 1880–1980* (Basingstoke: Palgrave Macmillan, 2014), 25–8.

[67] 'Women's Union General Meetings Minute Book', 1921–8, SUA/1/3/2/2, MUA; 'Women's Union Minute Book', 1924–6, SUA/1/3/19, MUA; 'Women's Union Minute Book', 1926–8, SUA/1/3/1/10, MUA; 'Women's Union Minute Book', 1928–31, SUA/1/3/1/11, MUA; letters to and from Phoebe Sheavyn re. rag fancy dress, January–February 1925, AWS/2/4/1, MUA; *The Serpent* 11, no. 4 (March 1927), 94; 'Women's Union Notices', 1927–33, SUA/13/2, MUA; 'Women's Union General Meetings Minute Book', 1929–36, SUA/1/3/2/3, MUA.

[68] 'SRC Minutes', 1927–43, UND/GB1/AA2, DUA; 'Panto Committee Minutes', 1922–31, A.27/27, LUA.

[69] Letters to the editor in *The Serpent* 14, no. 4 (March 1930), 120; and *The Serpent* 15, no. 1 (October 1930), 15; see also a similar discussion in Letters to the Editor, *The Serpent* 11, no. 4 (March 1927), 100–2.

[70] Letters to the editor, *Glasgow University Magazine*, 2 November 1925, 17–18; 11 November 1925, 49–50; 26 November 1925, 85.

involvement in the name of gender equality. 'What mid-Victorian prudery is this...that is going to curtail a woman's enjoyment in University rags?' she wrote.[71]

But the realities of gendered expectations for public life could prove challenging for women students to negotiate. At Manchester in 1931, a scandal arising from the prevalence of sexual innuendo in the annual rag magazine, the *Rag Rag*, put pressure on women's involvement in the rag. Facing outrage from local politicians and civic leaders, the men's union issued a statement to the effect that only those with exceptionally filthy minds could read anything inappropriate into the magazine's innocuous jokes. But the women's union stated that they had no connection with the magazine and would not cooperate in distributing it.[72] In an effort to reassure prospective students and their parents, the tutor for women wrote to every girls' secondary school in Manchester to inform them that women students had not been involved in the magazine.[73] The media and the men's union quickly lost interest in the scandal, and in subsequent years the *Rag Rag* remained packed with double entendre and with blasphemous, sexist, and politically provocative jokes.[74] But in the women's union, the scandal provoked serious consideration of the role women might play in the rag, and the extent to which they might thereby participate fully in corporate life. At the beginning of the 1931–2 academic year, when planning was about to begin for the 1932 rag, the women's union circulated a survey to its members. It asked, 'Do you think that there should be a Rag this year? Do you think that option should be given for Women Students to take part in the Rag Procession? Do you think that all the Past Rag activities should be maintained this year?' and invited respondents to add any further thoughts.[75] 168 women responded, 139 of whom thought that there should be 'some sort of Rag'—though two-thirds of respondents felt 'that it was not desirable for women to take part in the procession.'[76]

The membership decided that the best course of action was for women students to emphasize their respectability and their focus on securing the largest possible quantity of donations for the hospitals. They would not take part in the procession, but would collect donations in the streets and in workplaces while wearing academic dress. They established a rag subcommittee in order to make the logistics of canvassing for donations as efficient as possible. It divided the city into districts and assigned a team to each district that would go door to door

[71] 'Letter to the Editor', *Glasgow University Magazine*, 11 November 1925, 49–50.
[72] *Rag Rag* (1931), SUA/7, MUA; 'YMCA Ban "Rag" Magazine: Copies Returned', *Manchester Guardian*, 16 February 1931, 11; 'The "Rag Rag" Sale Stopped and Copies Called In', *Manchester Guardian*, 17 February 1931, 9; see other newspaper clippings in files of the Adviser to Women Students, AWS/2/4/1, MUA; 'Women's Union Minute Book', 1931–3, SUA/1/3/1/12, MUA.
[73] Newspaper clippings in files of Adviser to Women Students; 'Women's Union Minute Book', 1931–3; Miss Crump, letter to the Vice-Chancellor (16 February 1931), AWS/2/4/1, MUA.
[74] *Rag Rag* (1932) and *Rag Rag* (1933), SUA/7, MUA. Issues from the 1920s are similar in tone.
[75] 'Rag Questionnaire', November 1931, SUA/13/2, MUA.
[76] 'Women's Union Minute Book', 1931–3, SUA/1/3/1/12, MUA.

asking for donations from homes and businesses.[77] Participants in the discussion contrasted women's approach to the rag with men's: for men, they said, 'the primary object of the Rag Day was the Rag itself'—that is, the procession and attendant mayhem—while for women, it was the opportunity to support a charitable cause.[78] In fact, the disorder of the procession might actually detract from the efficiency of the collecting efforts.[79] This viewpoint had a number of implications. Drawing on the decades-long history of women students' charitable extracurricular activities, from settlement house work to war work, it demarcated a space in which participation in some aspects of the rag could be reconciled with social norms for women's university life. But it also suggests that many women students as well as men saw the procession—which in Manchester was the most central and longstanding element of the rag, predating its association with charitable giving—as a quintessentially masculine occasion, and furthermore as an occasion upon which women's respectability, safety, and full equality as students could not necessarily be assured.

This was not mere prudishness, nor instrumental concern about women students' reputations at a time when their place in higher education was still tenuous.[80] Instead, women students, university administrators, and the police expressed implicit, but potent, fears that the ritualized disorder of rags left women students open to sexual harassment during processions and street collections. Women's union officers saw part of their role as student leaders to be to protect their members from this threat. However, these efforts often took the form of contemporary class prejudices: part of the risk of fancy dress, or of women students running a café to benefit the rag fund, was that women students might be conflated with categories of lower-status women perceived to be sexually available, such as actresses or waitresses. To the Manchester chief constable, too, the most troubling aspect of the students' proposed activities from a public-safety perspective was not the procession or its attendant harassment of the public, but the idea that women students might run 'coffee stalls'.[81] Staking a claim for women's safe and equal participation in rags involved creating a carefully gender-differentiated conception of the 'woman student': who was fun, creative, and dedicated to raising the most money possible for the hospitals, but who drew on ideals of middle-class respectability to protect herself from masculine violence. In the process, this occluded the possibility that a woman student, like the Glasgow

---

[77] 'Minutes of the Rag Subcommittee', 1933–41, SUA/1/3/4/1, MUA.
[78] 'Women's Union Minute Book', 1933–5, SUA/1/3/1/13, MUA.
[79] *The Serpent* 17, no. 4 (March 1933), 104.
[80] Cf. Dyhouse, *Students: A Gendered History*, 194–6.
[81] 'University "Rag." Police and Students at Issue. Threat to Abandon the Collection', *Manchester Guardian*, 15 February 1930, 15; 'The Police and the "Rag"', *Manchester Guardian*, 20 February 1930, 13.

student in 1925, might have gained pleasure from joining a violent melee on the same terms as her male peers.

In 1935, then, after the Manchester Men's Union extended a new invitation to women to join that year's procession in fancy dress, the women's union surveyed its members as to their views. Though only twenty-five members claimed that they 'would definitely dress up for the Rag if allowed', and most remained dubious about the wisdom of joining the procession, a majority concluded that it was not appropriate for the Union to restrict members' freedom 'to choose for themselves whether they should wear costume or not'. They voted to allow dressing up, by 123 votes to 85.[82] After meetings with the university vice-chancellor and the Manchester City Police, the women's union drew up further rules: costumes would have to be approved by a committee of women's union members, and women in fancy dress were asked to leave the city centre by 6 p.m. In addition, 'Members are reminded that as this is the first time that women have worn fancy dress in the Rag, attention will be centred on them. As usual Public Opinion and the Press will pounce on individual conduct as representative of the entire Union.'[83] Even within this liberalization of the rules—and despite some women's desire to join fully in such mainstream expressions of corporate life—women students remained attentive to their perceived marginal status as students, to the scrutiny of cameras, and to questions of respectability as implicitly also questions of physical safety. A woman might make her own choice about whether she felt comfortable appearing in public in fancy dress. But to do so after 6 p.m. entailed an intolerable level of risk.

These developments at Manchester were mirrored around the country, as the late 1920s and early 1930s saw changing conceptions of the purpose of rags, and increased interventions from both student and civic leaders that made rags into less exclusionary occasions. In Belfast in 1929, the rag organizers 'banned all kissing in the streets', a step that the press framed as an equal-opportunity crackdown on indecency, but that perhaps also helped to protect women students and other women from sexual assault.[84] Rag performances became still more elaborate, but also more choreographed and controlled: in 1927, the Manchester rag chartered a steamship, decorated it as a pirate ship, and sailed it to Liverpool to promote the rag there; in Glasgow that same year, a rag stunt in which a man student portraying a woman championship swimmer who had swum across the Atlantic drew 30,000 spectators to the banks of the Clyde to watch her ostensibly finish her journey.[85]

---

[82] 'Women's Union General Meetings Minute Book', 1929–36, SUA/1/3/2/3, MUA.

[83] Memo from Women's Union re. Shrove Tuesday Rag, 1935, AWS/2/4/1, MUA.

[84] 'Belfast Students' Rag. A Ban on Kissing', *The Scotsman*, 1 May 1929, 15.

[85] 'Mutiny in the Canal. Drastic Measures on Pirates' Trip. Students' "Rag" Begun', *Manchester Guardian*, 28 February 1927, 11; '"Swimming the Atlantic." Miss Anne Dapenny in the Clyde. 30,000 at a "Rag"', *Daily Mail*, 14 January 1927, 7.

Though police-demarcated procession routes and family-friendly fundraising did not entirely displace more disruptive or offensive rag activities, they did create opportunities for carefully choreographed celebrations of diversity and progress. The 1928 Glasgow rag featured a float that Indian students had decorated to resemble 'an Indian temple complete with gilded dome'.[86] At the University College of North Wales in Bangor in 1932, the procession included Indian and Egyptian students in national dress, in addition to a pageant that celebrated women's rights.[87] This is not to say that charity rags had in fact become less sexist or racist occasions. But by the 1930s, their refashioning by student, university, and civic leaders, with the help of the police and the media, served to associate them with progressive beneficence and good clean family fun. Not only did this over-determine a contrast with the social irresponsibility of the elite men students of Oxford, Cambridge, and London, it shifted the measure of charity rags' success from amount of mayhem caused to number of pounds raised. It was an incidental byproduct of this transformation that it allowed women and other marginalized students to take a greater part in what had once been a more exclusionary tradition.

Ragging's Discontents

In the early hours of 6 November 1930, the Metropolitan Police undertook a violent crackdown on six hundred London students who had gathered in Gower Street in Bloomsbury for a Bonfire Night bonfire and fireworks. Charging the crowd with batons, they arrested several students, whom they charged with 'insulting behaviour'. The same night, police in Oxford and Cambridge also arrested students in similar Bonfire Night circumstances.[88] Meanwhile, later that same week, Manchester dignitaries laid the foundation stone for a new maternity ward at a district hospital in a predominantly working-class area of north Manchester. Paid for through rag donations, the ward was officially named the 'Manchester University Students' Ward', the social responsibility of the students praised by local dignitaries and in the press.[89]

Yet in the early 1930s, as charity rags became more accessible to women students and to the general public, men students, for a variety of reasons, began to lose interest. One line of criticism stemmed from some students' growing interest in left-wing politics amid the context of the Slump, which hit especially hard in

---

[86] 'Glasgow Besieged. University Students Set out to Collect £20,000', *Daily Mail*, 21 January 1928, 2.

[87] 'Bangor Students' "Rag"', *Manchester Guardian*, 26 February 1932, 6.

[88] '600 Students Charged by Police. Bonfire "Rag" Casualties. Eight Arrests', *Daily Mail*, 6 November 1930, 11; 'Many Fines', *The Scotsman*, 7 November 1930, 12.

[89] 'After the "Rag"', *Manchester Guardian*, 10 November 1930, 11.

the northern industrial cities that were home to the largest charity rags. While bringing a fancy dress rag procession to Salford or to the mining villages of County Durham had previously been lauded as a successful form of community engagement, in the early 1930s shaking collecting tins in the faces of unemployed industrial workers came to seem in poor taste.[90] '[W]e are tired of seeing the streets of Manchester lined with throngs of kiddies with starved faces, come to watch and idealise the inane foolings of a crowd of students who ought to know better', the Manchester *Serpent* editorialized in 1933.[91] While fundraising for hospitals had previously seemed socially conscious and patriotic, left-wing students began to ask whether social responsibility might instead lie in advocating for medical services to be centrally funded by the state.[92]

To be sure, the turn to political seriousness in 1930s student life encompassed at most a substantial minority of the student population. But the explicitly left-wing critique was one part of a wider sense of fatigue with the rag machinery. Though the public continued to turn out to enjoy rag festivities, the income they generated was declining. As students put ever more time into inventing ever more schemes to keep takings high, they began to feel that the organizational effort required was unmanageable. Unions and SRCs held debates about whether to continue rags at all. Though no university abolished its rag wholesale in this period, many scaled down the number of related activities, a measure that the National Union of Students' Executive Committee endorsed in 1932.[93] Most students involved in these conversations expressed a desire that fundraising, or at least a general sense of social responsibility, remain rags' core function. But some lamented that rags' anarchic origins had been lost amid the emphasis on social good. Continuing large-scale charity rags—and ensuring that women students would feel comfortable participating in them—had involved close collaboration with police and public officials, and various compromises about where, what, and within what bounds students were permitted to disrupt. Where, wondered the editor of the *Glasgow University Magazine* in 1934, was the fun in 'neatly marching down the main streets of the town shepherded by police'?[94] To at least some

---

[90] Compare 'To-day's "Rag." Tossing the Pancake in Piccadilly. Raid on Salford', *Manchester Guardian*, 1 March 1927, 14, with Durham Women's Union criticism of fundraising in County Durham in 1934, 'Women's Union Committee Minutes', 1928–45, UND/GE2/AC1, DUA; 'Students' Charities' Day Attacked', *Evening Telegraph (Dundee)*, 23 January 1933, 5.

[91] *The Serpent* 17, no. 4 (March 1933), 101.

[92] *The Serpent* 16, no. 4 (March 1932), 114; 'Shrovetide "Rag." "Bolstering up an Obsolete System"', *Manchester Guardian*, 24 December 1932, 4. On the development of a more 'serious' student culture in the 1930s see also Neil Harrington, '"A World Apart": Change in Student Attitudes during the Interwar Period, 1918–1933', *Twentieth Century British History* 34, no. 1 (March 2023): 129–49.

[93] *The Serpent* 12, no. 4 (March 1928), 103; 'Editorial', *Glasgow University Magazine*, 11 February 1931, 173–5; 'Panto Committee Minutes', 1922–31, A.27/27, LUA; 'Men's Union General Committee Book', 1931–2, SUA/1/2/1/4, MUA; 'A "Rag" without "Trimmings"', *Manchester Guardian*, 16 January 1932, 13; Brewis, *Student Volunteering*, 85.

[94] 'Students' Charities Days Attacked', *Dundee Courier*, 25 January 1934, 4.

men students, the Gower Street Bonfire Night rag—spontaneous, anarchic, featuring a confrontation with civic authority rather than cooperation with it—might have better represented what it meant to express an authentically student identity in the midst of the city.

A March 1932 editorial in the Manchester *Serpent* magazine took an especially strident approach to bringing together all of these criticisms. Hospitals should be funded by the state, not by students, it argued; the rag was an 'effete institution…a dead or dying horse from which the vital spark has all but departed'.[95] In framing their criticism in these terms, the *Serpent* editors added a gendered and racialized connotation to their rag fatigue. Implicitly drawing on a wider, typically right-wing, discourse of anxiety about British degeneration and decline as associated with gender and sexual deviance, they represented the rag as an institution that had fallen from its previous heights of (white, imperial) masculine vigour.[96] This editorial can usefully be read alongside the *Glasgow University Magazine* editorial of 1931 that had accused ragging students of 'a want of elementary manliness'.[97] The *GUM* editors abjured a form of 'hooliganism' that many men students would in fact have celebrated and that the wider public would have seen as constitutive of student masculinity. But both the *Serpent* and the *GUM* editors expressed exhaustion and boredom about rags, and both sought to respond to this by re-establishing a masculine norm for student corporate life. In the aftermath of the First World War, rags' ritualized violence had seemed expressive of an authentically virile masculinity. But by the 1930s, by proposing to put rags aside—as juvenile, as politically retrograde, as insufficiently masculine—these men students could craft a vision of corporate life that preserved distinctions: in which women students, students of colour, and members of the public were once again consigned to the role of spectators rather than participants.

The early 1930s did not, in the end, sound the death knell for student rags. In fact, the concept of a 'rag' as a student-run charitable campaign endured throughout the twentieth century.[98] While the excesses of Oxford and Cambridge students continued to come in for criticism, media—especially newsreels—continued to represent provincial rags, whether principally for charity or not, as harmless fun in the vein of an apolitical, classless invented tradition of English folklore.

But the men students who proposed to discard rags as insufficiently masculine at that particular moment indicate how the social and political crises of the interwar period were at once crises about gender and sexuality. The First World War had seemed to pose a fundamental challenge to norms of masculinity and

---

[95] *The Serpent* 16, no. 4 (March 1932), 114.

[96] Matt Houlbrook, '"The Man with the Powder Puff" in Interwar London', *The Historical Journal* 50, no. 1 (2007): 145–71. On the gendered and racialized connotations of 'effete' in the period see 'effete, adj', *OED Online*, accessed 30 December 2021, https://www.oed.com/view/Entry/59728.

[97] 'Editorial', *Glasgow University Magazine*, 4 November 1931, 41–2.

[98] Dyhouse, *Students: A Gendered History*, 197–203.

femininity: as more women accessed public space and traditionally masculine behaviours, jobs, and social roles; and as many men appeared physically and psychologically damaged by their war service. While the brutalized, excessively violent ex-serviceman could seem a harbinger of social unrest, the effeminate man, associated with degeneration and sexual deviance, could also appear as a threat to the body politic.[99] Sensationalist mass media connected students—a highly visible population of middle-class urban young people—to this wider sense of anxiety and instability in the gender order. Women and men students alike responded by asserting norms of feminine and masculine behaviour that emphasized responsibility, dignity, restraint, and gender-differentiated conceptions of studenthood, and by enforcing these norms among each other in homosocial groups. Media and politicians from the centre to the far right widely endorsed the assertion of essentialized binary gender difference among the young as representative of a broader commitment to social and political stability.

To some, these sentiments would tend towards support for fascism. In the early 1930s fascism enjoyed a brief moment of visibility and legitimacy in Britain, endorsed by right-wing elites and by the same tabloid newspapers that preached law and order in the face of the hooliganism of London rags. Indeed, the aesthetic of rag performances like the execution of Liverpool's 'Sister Jane' mascot, which married nostalgia and folk tradition with kaleidoscopic modernism through the medium of ritualized, violent, misogynistic masculinity, had much in common with the iconography of Oswald Mosley's British Union of Fascists.[100] Yet few students became fascists. Among the minority who had avowed political commitments, left-wing views were much more common. Instead, in 1930s Britain, as in other national contexts such as France and the Netherlands, formal fascist political movements were one part of a broader sense of discontent and fear about a decaying social order—one to which anxieties about masculinity, femininity, and

---

[99] Laura Doan, *Disturbing Practices: History, Sexuality, and Women's Experience of Modern War* (Chicago: University of Chicago Press, 2013); Michael Roper, 'Between Manliness and Masculinity: The "War Generation" and the Psychology of Fear in Britain, 1914–1950', *Journal of British Studies* 44, no. 2 (2005): 343–62; Susan Kingsley Kent, *Making Peace: The Reconstruction of Gender in Interwar Britain* (Princeton: Princeton University Press, 1993); Lawrence, 'Forging a Peaceable Kingdom'; Houlbrook, 'Man with the Powder Puff'.

[100] 'Introduction: Building Illiberal Subjects', in *The 'New Man' in Radical Right Ideology and Practice, 1919–45*, ed. Jorge Dagnino, Matthew Feldman, and Paul Stocker (London: Bloomsbury, 2017), 1–16, at 6; Jeannette Baxter, 'Portraits of the New British Fascist Man', in Dagnino, Feldman and Stocker, eds., *The 'New Man'*, 231–52, at 233; Julie Gottlieb, 'Britain's New Fascist Men: The Aestheticization of Brutality in British Fascist Propaganda', in *The Culture of Fascism: Visions of the Far Right in Britain*, ed. Julie Gottlieb and Thomas P. Linehan (London: I.B. Tauris, 2004), 83–99; Julie Gottlieb, 'Body Fascism in Britain: Building the Blackshirt in the Inter-War Period', *Contemporary European History* 20, no. 2 (May 2011): 111–36; Tony Collins, 'Return to Manhood: The Cult of Masculinity and the British Union of Fascists', *The International Journal of the History of Sport* 16, no. 4 (December 1999): 145–62; Martin Pugh, *'Hurrah for the Blackshirts!' Fascists and Fascism in Britain between the Wars* (London: Jonathan Cape, 2005).

the gender order were central.[101] Even as right-wing media leveraged the figure of the student as part of their critique of dissolute modernity, students themselves also partook of this wider cultural climate.

In some ways, students' refashioning of gender difference in the wake of controversies around rags opened up new possibilities. It offered women and men a set of social scripts through which they might connect with each other and participate in the same activities. Women, in particular, might engage in more pleasure-oriented conceptions of student life without their primary concern being how to protect themselves from men. At the same time, it foreclosed challenges to the student gender order, whether from women students who sought to access normatively masculine forms of student life, or from men students who sought to opt out of them. These conditions formed the basis on which heterosexuality emerged as students' most viable avenue of cross-gender interaction: a set of cultural scripts that offered a practical solution to the problem of how to organize life in the urban gender-integrated university, but that also enforced norms of binary gender difference and excluded alternatives.

Teaching Gender: The British University and the Rise of Heterosexuality, 1860–1939. Samuel Rutherford, Oxford University Press. © Samuel Rutherford 2025. DOI: 10.1093/9780198937524.003.0005

---

[101] Joan Tumblety, 'The Fascist New Man in France, 1919–45', in Dagnino, Feldman and Stocker, eds., *The 'New Man'*, 253–74, at 260; Gottlieb, 'Body Fascism in Britain', 118; Pugh, *Hurrah for the Blackshirts*.

5

Staging Heterosexuality

The editorial in the April 1932 issue of the *Glasgow University Magazine* opened with an elaborate metaphor. 'Corporate life' was a tree with many branches, the editors wrote, encompassing intellectual enterprises, feats of athletic prowess, campaigns for social and political causes, religious enthusiasm, and carnivalesque revelry. But if corporate life was a tree, then 'the sap that keeps it alive' was 'the lover': a person to be spotted in lecture halls, coffeehouses, and nightclubs, quickly developing a fervent passion for the nearest body and just as quickly transferring their affections to another. The editors argued that how many and what kind of sexual experiences to pursue was a personal decision that each student would have to make for her- or himself—but that it was incontrovertible that 'necking' was 'essential for the preservation of health', the lifeblood of the community.[1]

In framing sexuality as foundational to student culture, the Glasgow magazine editors reflected a transformation that had occurred in the preceding two decades among middle-class young people in general and on university campuses in particular. With increased social freedom and disposable income, young adults took part in a burgeoning urban youth culture that exploded especially after the First World War and was centred around commercial leisure spaces that emphasized sexualized cross-gender interactions, such as the dance hall, the cinema, the café, and the nightclub.[2] While marriage remained a normative aspiration, most who ultimately married in this period did so in their mid- to late twenties, affording several years of adolescence and young adulthood not necessarily oriented towards securing a future spouse. The expression of complementary opposite-sex sexuality came to be valued as an end in itself, outside of its role in marriage. The rapidly proliferating expert discourses of psychoanalysis, sexology, and self-help that circulated widely in the early twentieth century, especially among the educated middle class, increasingly presented an active opposite-sex sex life as normal, healthy, and necessary.[3]

---

[1] 'The Editorial', *Glasgow University Magazine*, 2 March 1932, DC 198/1, GUA, 268–9.

[2] Claire Langhamer, *Women's Leisure in England 1920–1960* (Manchester: Manchester University Press, 2000), see esp. 127; James Nott, *Going to the Palais: A Social and Cultural History of Dancing and Dance Halls in Britain, 1918–1960* (Oxford: Oxford University Press, 2015).

[3] Laura Doan, 'Marie Stopes's Wonderful Rhythm Charts: Normalizing the Natural', *Journal of the History of Ideas* 78, no. 4 (October 2017): 595–620; Nancy Christie and Michael Gauvreau, *Bodies, Love, and Faith in the First World War: Dardanella and Peter* (Basingstoke: Palgrave Macmillan, 2018);

But student life in large, urban, gender-integrated universities like Glasgow did not merely absorb expert discourses or reflect wider cultural transformations. Instead, students actively innovated new social scripts for how women and men might relate to one another across gender lines. As the Glasgow editorial indicates, interwar students no longer perceived opposite-sex sexual and romantic connection to belong to a later life stage into which students would enter after they left the predominantly homosocial environment of the university and for which their university education might prepare them. As the distinct life stage of studenthood became a time when students might experiment with low-stakes sexual and romantic relationships with the opposite sex, women and men alike saw the ritual of sex and romance as a way to cross the 'invisible and impassable line' that students of an earlier generation had identified as endemic to life on gender-integrated campuses. Both women and men turned eagerly to essentializing narratives that proposed to demystify the feelings and motives of the opposite sex. They sought out extracurricular activities that would facilitate dating and sexual encounters. Students articulated aspirational fantasies for their sexual and romantic lives in fiction, gossip columns, and editorial commentary. But they also lived out real experiences of sex and dating. Although many women, in particular, criticized this dating culture as empty and unsatisfying, they also appreciated that it was governed by a clear-cut set of rules that offered them some sense of agency and control over sexual situations. Extracurricular student life became a space in which middle-class young people were inculcated into, and had the opportunity to practise, a set of cultural scripts that assumed that women and men were complementary opposites who would primarily relate to one another through dating and sex, and that this was healthy, desirable, socially beneficial, and morally correct.

This chapter demonstrates how—through dances and dating, and through student-authored fiction, gossip columns, and editorial commentary— heterosexuality came to seem central to how students imagined the purpose of university life. It also considers what happened to forms of gender and sexual expression that could not be made to fit within this norm. Even as heterosexuality became normative, some students continued to hope that women and men could be 'Platonic' friends. Others found that homosocial campus spaces such as women's halls of residence or the Officers' Training Corps, as well as some gender-integrated activities such as student theatre, offered scope to experiment with gender and sexuality, and perhaps even a basis for self-consciously queer or trans community. Yet mainstream student culture denied the subversive potential of these alternatives. Women who found the behavioural codes of heterosexuality reassuring dismissed 'Platonic friendship' as fake and duplicitous. Cross-gender

Simon Szreter and Kate Fisher, *Sex before the Sexual Revolution* (Cambridge: Cambridge University Press, 2010).

drag performances were central to student life, as to other forms of mainstream interwar popular entertainment. But students, like interwar popular culture more widely, discarded masculine drag performances as incompatible with prevailing gender and sexual norms, while celebrating feminine drag performances as setting standards for heterosexual femininity and upholding the gender binary. Students sought to contain a wider range of possibilities for interpreting, performing, and relating to masculinity and femininity safely within the framework of heterosexuality—in the process, if not always explicitly condemning alternatives as deviant, certainly rendering them less visible and viable.

From Marriage to Heterosexuality

From around 1910, and to an even greater extent after the First World War, several significant social and cultural changes transformed how young people, and students in particular, thought about sex and sexuality. In the first place, for those undergraduates who began their studies after around 1910, the 'woman student' was no longer a category of person who was defined in part by her future as a spinster. While some early women's education activists had imagined that higher education might provide training for a career of marriage, motherhood, and household management, in fact only around 30 per cent of the women who had attended university before 1895 ultimately married, resulting in a wider cultural perception that, for women, there was a relationship between higher education and singleness. By contrast, 67 per cent of women who attended university between the wars married—and of these, a large proportion met their husbands at university.[4] The speed of this generational shift meant that students' lived experience could be at odds with the perceptions that wider society—and, as we shall see in the next chapter, older women faculty and administrators—had of women students and of the purpose of higher education for women. But from the perspective of post-1910 women undergraduates, part of the purpose of higher education was to provide access to suitable partners, alongside or in addition to improving career prospects or facilitating social mobility more widely.

This occurred in the context of a wider cultural shift in favour of new, but in some ways narrower, normative values about marriage.[5] Middle-class readers engaged with the widely popularized work of expert sexological researchers that emphasized good communication, sexual pleasure, and equality between husband and wife while nevertheless preserving sex distinctions. Interventions like

---

[4] Carol Dyhouse, *Students: A Gendered History* (London: Routledge, 2006), 55–7.
[5] Deborah Cohen, *Family Secrets: Shame and Privacy in Modern Britain* (New York: Oxford University Press, 2013), 167; Alison Light, *Forever England: Femininity, Literature, and Conservatism between the Wars* (London: Routledge, 1991).

UCL botanist Marie Stopes's bestselling 1918 book *Married Love* advanced new arguments about what constituted a 'healthy' sexuality, family structure, and life trajectory.[6] One could demonstrate one's normalcy and good health by expressing sexual desire for appropriate objects and in appropriate circumstances; equally, one could be judged abnormal or unhealthy if one failed to do so. This could be liberating for women who found a new language for articulating their entitlement to sexual pleasure and satisfaction within marriage—something that may especially have resonated with those women studying medicine or natural sciences who had the intellectual tools to engage with the background in biology that Stopes and other sexual scientists brought to their arguments.[7] But it could also place new pressure on women to conform to these ideals, as well as on the institution of marriage itself to provide sexual and emotional satisfaction in addition to financial stability and a structure in which to have children.[8] In the process, it contributed to rendering marginal and deviant those women who—like 70 per cent of women graduates a generation earlier—never married and thus were seen not to have an appropriate outlet for their natural sex instinct.

At the same time, the generation who came of age after the First World War understood the life course differently from their predecessors, treating the years between leaving school (between fourteen and eighteen) and marriage (on average in one's mid- to late twenties) as a distinct life stage with its own norms for cross-gender relations. Interwar young people often understood their young adulthood as a time for 'fun, adventure and playful flirtation between the sexes' that would be foreclosed when marriage obliged them to settle down and assume more serious domestic responsibilities.[9] Across region and social class, teenagers and young adults went on dates, socialized as couples, and participated in a culture that centred the public performance of flirtation and sexual rivalry.[10] Though penetrative sex before marriage remained taboo (and contraception was not always freely accessible), it was hardly unheard of, and young people engaged in a wide variety of other sexual behaviour. Middle-class young people had greater access to theoretical, 'book' knowledge about sex than their working-class counterparts, which may have helped them to find the language for more direct conversations about pleasure, consent, and non-procreative sex outside of marriage.[11] In short, in the years from 1910, young adults who arrived at university did so in the context of a new culture of heterosexuality and heteronormativity: one in which opposite-sex sex was understood as a phenomenon in itself beyond its

[6] Szreter and Fisher, *Sex before the Sexual Revolution*, 56.

[7] Doan, 'Marie Stopes's Wonderful Rhythm Charts'; Christie and Gavreau, *Bodies, Love, and Faith*, 7.

[8] Claire Langhamer, *The English in Love: The Intimate Story of an Emotional Revolution* (Oxford: Oxford University Press, 2013), 6.

[9] Szreter and Fisher, *Sex before the Sexual Revolution*, 173.

[10] Langhamer, *Women's Leisure*, 61, 113–29; Langhamer, *English in Love*, 92–5, 111–12.

[11] Szreter and Fisher, *Sex before the Sexual Revolution*, 140–58.

role in marriage and reproduction, and was considered normal, normative, desirable, and central to how young people conceptualized gender-integrated social relations.

It is thus unsurprising that an atmosphere of sexual tension suffused most contexts in which women and men students interacted with one another, from the lecture theatre to the annual Student Christian Movement summer camp.[12] Students had fleeting assignations in corridors and staircases.[13] In 1914, the *Manchester University Magazine* celebrated the library as a place to meet attractive members of the opposite sex.[14] By the late 1920s, off-campus mixed-gender sociability was more normalized, and men and women might go on dates to cafés or to the cinema. These spaces offered a degree of privacy both from administrative oversight and from the prying eyes of fellow students that the Visitors' Room of the Men's or Women's Union did not. Though many students did identify finding a future spouse as their ultimate goal in dating, student publications tended to depict a dating culture that was both relatively casual and increasingly physical and sexualized. For example, the gossip column in one 1925 issue of the Manchester *Serpent* expressed mock surprise that the president of the men's union and the president of the Medical Students' Representative Committee were reported to have 'spent one night in their own digs last week', and another in 1926 archly commented that 'Mr. R—ss—ll and Miss H—rgr—v—s have become enthusiastic imitators of the ju-jitsu expert'.[15] In 1932, the *Glasgow University Magazine* did a series of vox pops on the question 'Do you approve of necking?', delightedly reporting the embarrassment of various club presidents and committee chairs when asked this question out of nowhere—as well as the respondents who elected to view the question as a proposition.[16] In the process, the magazine constructed necking, whether one approved of it or not, as a standard part of the university experience.

Student publications offered not only a space in which to gossip about sexual intrigue, but also a space to spin out fantasies that may not always have mapped on to reality. With their overwhelmingly male editorial staffs, university magazines featured fiction and poetry in which usually pseudonymous male contributors aspirationally cast themselves in the roles of skilful seducers. They set their stories about dating in recognizable campus locations: the magazine office, the canteen, the anatomy lecture theatre. In 1902—nine years after his university had

[12] *The Serpent* 1 (26 June 1917), UMP/2/4, MUA, 204; Christie and Gauvreau, *Bodies, Love, and Faith*, 40.

[13] William Whyte, *Redbrick: A Social and Architectural History of Britain's Civic Universities* (Oxford: Oxford University Press, 2015), 149.

[14] *Manchester University Magazine* 10 (May 1914), UMP/2/3, MUA, 198.

[15] *The Serpent* 10, no. 2 (December 1925), 44; *The Serpent* 10, no. 6 (June 1926), 156.

[16] 'Neck or Nothing', *Glasgow University Magazine*, 30 November 1932, 108–9. See also the similar series, 'Why Do Women Close Their Eyes When They Are Being Kissed?', *Glasgow University Magazine*, 2 March 1932, 274–5.

admitted women to degrees—an anonymous male contributor to the *Glasgow University Magazine* wrote a story in which the narrator, daydreaming during a lecture, thought back on a woman he had met at the previous night's dance:

> With what willingness she retired with me from the dancing hall, and the frank eagerness she displayed in assisting me to find a suitable settee, shielded from draughts, free from prying eyes, and sheltered from the quite unnecessary glare of a small electric light. How coyly she glanced at me when I spoke, and how bewitchingly she accompanied her brilliant sallies with a roll of those blue eyes, causing me such a thrill as I have only experienced when crossing a heavy sea: something akin to a momentary stoppage of the breath, coupled with a most violent throbbing somewhere beneath the left side of the waistcoat! Ah! Everything, every small detail, appears so vividly to my mind's eye. There, the instant when I could not contain myself, and drawing nearer, clasped her little hand in mind, caressing it fondly, while I murmured my warmest breathing of a sudden affection. And she, completely overcome, I'm sure, by my artful wooing, nestled closer still, laid her head upon my shoulders and ——.[17]

Though this sexual fantasy is careful to describe the woman's 'eagerness' to hide with the narrator in a dark corner, it also casts the narrator as an 'artful' manipulator of the situation, whose skill at pushing boundaries in just the right way allows him access to a moment of physical intimacy. The language is breathless, emotionally intense, and heavily sexualized, climaxing with the suggestive dash at the end. The narrator offers little guide to his partner's emotional state: he only asserts (if perhaps sarcastically) that he is 'sure' that she was 'completely overcome…by my artful wooing'. This is in keeping with a culture in which young men and women tended to negotiate sexual boundaries implicitly, though it also suggests the narrator's lack of interest in trying to imagine his partner's point of view.[18] Narrating his conquest in this way allowed the story's author to perform a gallant, but nevertheless persistently sexual, masculinity, regardless of what actual experience with dating and sex he might have had in his own life. Rather than viewing heterosexual relations as something that would occur external to the masculine world of the university, or characterizing women students as ugly, sexless, inappropriate objects for masculine romantic attention, this author brought heterosexuality firmly within the space of the university.[19] He and students like

---

[17] 'A Love-Idyll. Being a Classroom Impression', *Glasgow University Magazine*, Christmas 1902, 123. For a very similar story (from twenty-five years later) see 'Femina', *Glasgow University Magazine*, 13 March 1929, 317–18.

[18] Szreter and Fisher, *Sex before the Sexual Revolution*, 144–5.

[19] Cf. Paul R. Deslandes, *Oxbridge Men: British Masculinity and the Undergraduate Experience* (Bloomington: Indiana University Press, 2005), 142, 165, 171.

him contributed to establishing heterosexuality as the dominant paradigm through which women and men students would relate to one another.

As this example suggests, nowhere was this more apparent than in the sphere of social dancing: one of the most popular leisure activities for students, and young people more generally, across the first half of the twentieth century. In the earlier years of gender-integrated higher education, carefully orchestrated formal dances had been common. Men faculty and their wives chaperoned these dances, modelling appropriate adult behaviour as couples in mixed-gender society. Student humour characterized formal dances as sites of awkward, stilted cross-gender interaction, as students struggled to adjust to an adult world in which cross-gender sociability was more common than it had been at their typically single-sex secondary schools.[20]

But the years after the First World War ushered in a dramatic shift in dancing culture across Britain, with consequences for how women and men students interacted with one another. The period between 1919 and 1926 saw the unprecedented growth of social dancing as a major commercial industry, with dance halls serving as key sites where young people negotiated changing norms around gender and sexuality. Though some young people took dancing seriously as a hobby in itself, many also went dancing explicitly to seek a new kind of casual, fleeting contact with members of the opposite sex. New dances such as the foxtrot and the quickstep were well suited to popular American music styles such as ragtime and jazz. As partnered dances danced in hold, they were also well suited to pursuing physical intimacy—albeit under carefully controlled conditions, something often appreciated by women dancers who used the structure of dancing to exert agency over physical intimacy. By the late 1930s, as many as two million people across Britain—5 per cent of the total population—went dancing at least once per week, with regular dances to be found in every city, town, and village in the country. Social dancing fostered norms of cross-gender interaction that remained heavily ritualized, but also offered new opportunities for casual sexuality.[21]

In many towns and cities, the commercial dance hall was a working-class social space, subject to middle-class moral scrutiny. But the largely middle-class student population embraced social dancing as well, aided by on-campus developments and shifting social norms that made dances cheaper and easier to hold. More student unions had their own space, meaning it was not necessary to rent a hotel

---

[20] *University College Gazette*, 14 March 1896, P.P. 6149.fa, British Library, 14–15; 'The Slade Dance', *Union Magazine* 1, no. 2 (February 1905), P.P. 6139.db, British Library; 'Occasional Notes', *Glasgow University Magazine*, 8 February 1893, 114–15; 'Overheard at the Medical Ball', *Glasgow University Magazine*, 16 February 1898, 175; 'The Liberal Dance', *Glasgow University Magazine*, 19 December 1901, 115; 'The Conference Dance', *Glasgow University Magazine*, 1 February 1906, 323–4; 'The Logic Class Social and Dance', *Glasgow University Magazine*, 15 February 1911, 369.

[21] Nott, *Going to the Palais*; Allison Abra, *Dancing in the English Style: Consumption, Americanisation and National Identity in Britain, 1918–50* (Manchester: Manchester University Press, 2017); Langhamer, *Women's Leisure*, 63–9.

ballroom; phonograph technology became more sophisticated and more afford-able, meaning it was not necessary to hire a live band; and guests did not expect elaborate decorations or a full meal at an informal dance.[22] With a room and a record player all that was required, unions could host informal 'flannel dances' or 'hops' in the lunch hour or in the afternoon as well as in the evening. They did not necessarily have to sell tickets to offset the cost of putting on these cheaper events, meaning that less wealthy students could also participate in the craze. At Manchester, for example, thirty-two dances occurred in the autumn term of 1922 alone, with sponsoring organizations including the French Club, the Economics and Commerce Society, the Science Federation, the Catholic Association, the Rambling Society, and the Vegetarian Society.[23] This frequency persisted through the 1920s and 1930s. Commentators found this explosion remarkable, with fac-ulty and administrators perplexed and sometimes appalled by the younger gen-eration's mania for dancing.[24]

In the absence of joint common rooms or other more quotidian mixed-gender spaces, dances provided students with opportunities to socialize with their opposite-sex friends and boy-/girlfriends. As chaperonage fell out of fashion and the proliferation of dances meant that faculty and administrators could not moni-tor each one, students were able to be physically intimate with less oversight. Dances provided a space for sexual and romantic intimacy, even when the couple in question were not actually moving together around a dance floor. In 1919, one *Glasgow University Magazine* correspondent writing about the Students' Representative Committee Dance observed that the frigid temperature of the ballroom gave him an excuse to sit out the actual dancing and perch atop a radi-ator with his girlfriend.[25] That same year, in evident recognition of the risks that such atmospheres of intimacy could occasion, the Manchester Women's Union installed a new electric lighting system that prevented students from turning out the lights at a wall switch in order to give themselves the opportunity to kiss and touch their dance partners under cover of darkness.[26] As in other circumstances in which women's unions sought to regulate their members' behaviour, this might suggest that the Manchester Women's Union saw it as part of its role to enforce norms of respectable femininity and to preserve its members' reputations.[27] But the incident could also be read as protecting women students from the threat of

---

[22] On the increasing ubiquity of record players see D.L. LeMahieu, *A Culture for Democracy: Mass Communication and the Cultivated Mind in Britain between the Wars* (Oxford: Clarendon Press, 1988), 91–3.

[23] 'Miscellaneous Records of Social Sanctions Committee', 1922–34, AWS/2/1, MUA.

[24] 'Minutes of Discipline Committee', 30 May 1922, AWS/2/1, MUA; Whyte, *Redbrick*, 210.

[25] 'SRC Dance', *Glasgow University Magazine*, 26 February 1919, 135.

[26] 'Women's Union Minute Book', 1919–21, SUA/1/3/1/7, MUA.

[27] On women students regulating each other's engagement with heterosexual femininity (though in the US university context) see also Margaret A. Lowe, *Looking Good: College Women and Body Image, 1875–1930* (Baltimore: Johns Hopkins University Press, 2003), 111–19.

sexual assault and creating a safer, women-controlled environment in which women students could pursue sexual and romantic connections with men on their own terms. At the same time, the women's union minutes do not record *who* was turning out the lights: women as well as men might have sought out the opportunities that darkness afforded.

Students recognized that dancing had significant limitations as the primary venue for cross-gender interaction. The gender ratio at a given dance could be imbalanced, preventing everyone from finding a partner. Dancing was in general a more popular activity among women, yet women's concerns about getting home safely at night sometimes made them less likely to attend late-night events.[28] To maintain gender ratios, men students tended to favour a ticketing system that sold 'double tickets' to men, allowing them to bring a date of their choice. But this contrasted with the one-ticket-per-attendee system preferred by women students. Single ticketing allowed any student who could afford the cost of the ticket to attend a dance without having to have a date, and gave women the ability to choose partners and to move freely between partners during the dance. The Manchester Women's Union, for example, objected repeatedly in the early 1920s to the fact that the men's union (with its significantly larger budget) controlled the ticketing for major university-wide dances, using this power to bring non-university dates who took up space—and dating opportunities—that might instead have gone to women students.[29] Women also complained about men turning up drunk and behaving boorishly, and about systems for matching dance partners akin to 'a prize-cattle show'.[30] Men and women alike observed that people came to dances more to socialize in mixed-gender groups than actually to dance, and wondered if it might not be better to find other spaces, such as the meetings of clubs and societies, in which to meet members of the opposite sex.[31] By the early 1930s, there was a sense that the dancing trend had reached saturation point. In 1930, the weary editors of the Manchester *Serpent* published a desperate plea to contributors not to send in any more fiction submissions 'about a girl, a lecture, and an Informal [dance]. The number of stories we receive about Informals is beyond human credibility.'[32] Yet having become accustomed to the

---

[28] 'Letters to the Editor', *The Serpent* 6, no. 4 (January 1922); 'Letters to the Editor', *Glasgow University Magazine*, 17 December 1930, 133–4. On the popularity of dancing among women see Nott, *Going to the Palais*, 159–78.

[29] 'Women's Union Minute Book', 1921–4, SUA/1/3/1/8, MUA; 'Women's Union General Meetings Minute Book', 1921–8, SUA/1/3/2/2, MUA; Phoebe Sheavyn, untitled notes re. dance ticketing, January 1923, AWS/2/2, MUA.

[30] 'Letters to the Editor', *Glasgow University Magazine*, 13 March 1929 and 30 April 1929, 327, 364; *The Serpent* 5, no. 4 (8 March 1921), 83.

[31] 'On (and against) Dancing', *Glasgow University Magazine*, 14 December 1921, 158; 'Anti-Dancing Society', *Glasgow University Magazine*, 17 March 1920, 224; 'Men's Union Notes', *The Serpent* 7, no. 4 (15 March 1923), 116.

[32] 'Editorial', *The Serpent* 14, no. 5 (May 1930), 135.

structure that dancing provided for negotiating heterosexuality, students struggled to think outside of it.

Heterosexuality's Limits?

Women students were not mere victims of heterosexuality's demands. Instead, those women who engaged in the campus culture of heterosexuality weighed knowledgeably and thoughtfully the opportunities it provided alongside the attendant risks. In educated, radical circles, women had long pointed out that, in a patriarchal society, free love carried risks for women that it did not for men—such as sexual assault, pregnancy, and loss of social standing—and criticized radical men who remained blithely unaware of these pressures.[33] By the early twentieth century, women's critiques of campus heterosexuality, and of the kinds of masculinity it appeared to reward, were part of mainstream student culture. In 1904, an anonymous woman contributor to the *Glasgow University Magazine*, having been given a brief to evaluate 'college men this year' from a woman's perspective, characterized her male peers as self-satisfied and pretentious, given to street harassment of women students and to dating them purely in order to be able to boast to friends about it.[34] Glasgow women in this period also shared information with each other about men whom women should not date because they had a reputation for treating women badly.[35] Decades later, when casual sex had become more normalized, a vociferous correspondence on the subject in the *Glasgow University Magazine* broke down on gendered lines. Men asserted that casual relationships were harmless, while women advised their fellow women students that getting a reputation for promiscuity would, realistically, damage their marriage prospects.[36] In discussions like these, women students demonstrated that they perceived their sexual interactions to be governed by systems of gendered power. They argued that many men dated at best with disregard for women's bodies and feelings, and at worst with active intention to hurt them. Heterosexuality carried risks for women that it did not for men; women had no choice but to operate within a system that was too often defined only on men's terms.

---

[33] Judith Walkowitz, *City of Dreadful Delight: Narratives of Sexual Danger in Late-Victorian London* (Chicago: University of Chicago Press, 1992), 157–9; Lucy Bland, *Banishing the Beast: Sexuality and the Early Feminists* (New York: The New Press, 1995).

[34] 'Happy Notes on College Men by a Q.M. Student', *Glasgow University Magazine*, 9 March 1904, 24.

[35] 'An Unknown Society', *Glasgow University Magazine*, 24 January 1906, 303–4; 'Letters to the Editor', *Glasgow University Magazine*, 1 February 1906, 331.

[36] 'Kissing', *Glasgow University Magazine*, 1 March 1933, 266; 'Letters to the Editor', *Glasgow University Magazine*, 15 March 1933, 304–5.

Yet this analysis did not mean that women students eschewed heterosexuality. Indeed, if women could be perceptive observers of heterosexuality's double standard, they could also be sharp critics of proposed alternatives to it. In the *Glasgow University Magazine* in December 1892, a long article by an anonymous guest columnist took the unusual step of singing the praises of 'Platonic Friendship'. Though the columnist was later identified as a man student, he published the article under the byline 'Madge Wildfire', a stock character from Scottish folklore associated with political rebellion and usually portrayed by a man dressed as a woman.[37] Quoting extensively from Diotima's speech in Plato's *Symposium* (the canonical case of a male writer putting an argument about a higher form of love into a female voice), 'Madge Wildfire' argued—in an apparently earnest tone—that students' rush to secure fiancé(e)s had blinded them to the potential for forms of connection founded on 'purer and juster ideals'. 'Let us sanctify for all humanity some of the sacred fire that has been treasured only for the marriage torch,' the student concluded.[38] It is possible that he assumed a female persona in order to satirize or otherwise to distance himself from the views he was espousing. At the same time, his use of the 'Madge Wildfire' byline and his quotation from Diotima's speech connected 'Platonic Friendship' to gender transgression. 'Platonic Friendship' might offer students not only an escape from the pressures of the marriage market, but also a way to break down gender divides and imagine a form of gender-integrated campus sociability that was not founded on complementarity and essential differences between the sexes.

Indeed, the column's readers appeared to take its arguments at face value—if nearly universally to reject them, in a vociferous series of letters to the editor that appeared in subsequent issues of the magazine.[39] Women, in particular, laughed off the idea of 'Platonic Friendship' as unrealistic and even disingenuous. One woman student wrote a humour piece imagining a 'Platonic Friendship Bureau' as a scheme of interfering older people to desexualize, and therefore take all the fun out of, dating, courtship, and marriage.[40] Another thought 'Platonic Friendship' the invention of pretentious, and perhaps unscrupulous, men who were more interested in promoting their own brilliance than in valuing the ideas and feelings of their women friends.[41] Similarly, a male correspondent also supposed that popularizing the concept of 'Platonic Friendship' would only lead to

---

[37] On Madge Wildfire and the tradition of female impersonation as radical politics see Natalie Zemon Davis, *Society and Culture in Early Modern France* (Stanford: Stanford University Press, 1975), 149. A version of Madge Wildfire features in Walter Scott's *The Heart of Midlothian* and thereby achieved renewed cultural currency in the nineteenth and twentieth centuries. The character appears frequently in Scottish student life sources.

[38] '"Platonic" Friendships', *Glasgow University Magazine*, 18 January 1893, 70–1.

[39] 'Platonic Friendships—A Reply', *Glasgow University Magazine*, 25 January 1893, 86; 'Platonic Friendships', *Glasgow University Magazine*, 15 February 1893, 126–7.

[40] 'The Platonics', *Glasgow University Magazine*, 1 February 1893, 104.

[41] 'My Platonic Friendship', *Glasgow University Magazine*, 25 January 1893, 92.

men using it as a cover to dupe unsuspecting women into romantic entangle-ments.[42] If heterosexuality carried risks for women, so too did discarding its gen-dered conventions.

This debate generated more correspondence in the *Glasgow University Magazine* than any other topic before the Second World War, and popped up again sporadically in the intervening decades. Students continued to evince uncertainty about whether, in the words of a 1930 Glasgow Women's Union debate, 'Platonic Friendship' was 'an unattainable ideal' (the voters were divided on the question).[43] Given students'—especially women students'—cynicism about and fatigue with heterosexual dating culture, one might imagine that they would have welcomed the opportunity to conceive of cross-gender relations outside the paradigm of heterosexuality and to challenge essentialist ideas about gender dif-ference. Yet instead they consistently dismissed the idea from a variety of perspec-tives. Developing a critique of heterosexuality did not lead women students to turn away from cross-gender sex and romance. Instead, it seems to have provided them with the tools to negotiate dating and sex with more awareness of how to manage the attendant risks. In some ways, heterosexual ritual—in which a woman could pursue frivolous fun, but still refuse a man's invitation to dance if she wished—might have offered more scope for feminine agency, and pleasure, than the high-minded aspirations of 'Platonic Friendship'. In the end, despite all the dissatisfaction and complaints from both women and men, student groups more often than not responded to calls for greater cross-gender social interaction simply by organizing yet another dance. In the process, they ensured that an essentialist, complementary idea of the gender binary remained central to how mainstream student life negotiated cross-gender relations.

If the rituals of dances and dating offered some women students a strategy through which to manage their anxieties about and exert control over cross-gender interaction, many men students found a different strategy appealing: the language of romance, as articulated in fiction, memoir, and humour pieces in the pages of student magazines. If the actual lived experience of interwar student life centred on going out dancing—often meeting dance partners whose names one did not know and whom one would never see again—this practice may have been sustained by the hope that one might find on the dance floor not fleeting contact, but true love. Romantic fantasies could also appeal to those who disliked night-life, who felt shy and awkward around the opposite sex, or who had limited sexual experience. Romance and sex could feed off one another; equally, there could be a gulf between a young person's abstracted ideal of the opposite sex (perhaps an ideal sustained through conversation and socialization with others of their own sex) and their practical experience.

---

[42] 'Platonic Friendship', *Glasgow University Magazine*, 1 February 1893, 102.
[43] 'QM Union Annual Non-Political Debate', *Glasgow University Magazine*, 28 April 1930, 310.

Romantic ideals remained present in student culture throughout the late nineteenth and early twentieth centuries, despite significant shifts in norms around dating, sex, and sexuality. Yet they were not equally distributed across the population. In their landmark study of sexual behaviour in Britain in the first half of the twentieth century, Simon Szreter and Kate Fisher observed that middle-class men were most likely to draw on romantic narratives about 'falling in love' when describing their dating and sex lives and their attitudes towards finding a long-term partner. Middle-class women and working-class people were more likely to describe themselves as rejecting 'naïve and unrealistic' ideas about romance in favour of a more pragmatic approach to finding an appropriate life partner, as well as more likely to make a distinction between the recreational dating they pursued before marriage and the more practical task of finding someone with whom one could build a stable household.[44] Middle-class men were significantly overrepresented in student life, and they articulated ideas about romance even as they also participated actively in the culture of casual dating. Their romantic fantasies perpetuated ideas of men and women as abstract archetypes with distinct and essentialized gendered characteristics—helping further to sustain norms of binary gender difference and heterosexuality.

Historians have pointed to cinema, popular music, and popular romantic fiction as sources of tropes that idealized love in this period.[45] But many men students instead drew on an older and more highbrow discourse: medieval romance. Men who attended university at the start of the twentieth century would have come of age in an environment suffused with enthusiasm for an imagined medieval past. Ruskin praised the art and architecture of the Middle Ages, the Pre-Raphaelite painters created new medieval-inspired art, and children grew up reading new illustrated editions of Thomas Malory's fifteenth-century romance *Le Morte d'Arthur* and medieval historical fiction like Walter Scott's *Ivanhoe*.[46] Playacting as knights of the Round Table, men students writing in university magazines—often in a faux-Middle English style—depicted women students as locking themselves in especially tall and removed ivory towers, which citadels men might try to storm. The women were haughty, their favours difficult to win.[47] Men students cast their female peers not as individual people, any of whom a

[44] Szreter and Fisher, *Sex before the Sexual Revolution*, 168.

[45] Langhamer, *English in Love*, 24–38; Stephen Brooke, '"A Certain Amount of Mush": Love, Romance, Celluloid and Wax in the Mid-Twentieth Century', in *Love and Romance in Britain, 1918–1970*, ed. Alana Harris and Timothy Willem Jones (Basingstoke: Palgrave Macmillan, 2014), 81–99.

[46] Angela Bartie et al., 'Historical Pageants and the Medieval Past in Twentieth Century England', *English Historical Review* 133, no. 563 (2018): 866–902, at 871–2; Michael Alexander, *Medievalism: The Middle Ages in Modern England* (New Haven: Yale University Press, 2007).

[47] *The Sphinx* 1, no. 11 (1906), 177–8 and *passim*; 'Afternoon Tea with the Doves', *The Sphinx* 3, no. 5 (1908), 91; 'The Ladies of Queen Margaret (Being Reminiscences of a Court)', *Glasgow University Magazine*, 1 March 1905, 243–4; 'The Queen Margaret Hall "At Home"', *Glasgow University Magazine*, 19 December 1901, 104.

given man might socialize with or date, but as a collective, and mystifying, abstraction around whom men might nevertheless organize their aspirations and their performance of a heroic, dignified masculinity.

It is perhaps not surprising to find this discourse earlier in the period, and at more gender-segregated institutions. In 1880s and 1890s Oxford, where men's colleges were self-consciously constructed as masculine spaces in which cross-gender sociability was proscribed, students developed elaborate rituals around objects sent to them by their female love interests, venerating handkerchiefs and pieces of embroidery as if they were holy relics.[48] But this kind of abstracted adoration was to be found also in institutions where cross-gender interaction was routine, and well into the interwar period. Poetry and fiction continued to use mock Middle English and to draw on neo-medieval romantic tropes from authors such as Scott and Tennyson. A male student journalist at Durham, reporting in 1923 on the year's biggest dance, referred to the women and men present as the archetypical collectives 'Beauty' and 'Chivalry', using the ritualized gendered behaviour of the dance to articulate a neo-medieval, romantic model of gender difference.[49]

That these tropes should reappear after the First World War might in part have been linked to a critique of the quotidian, commercialized heterosexuality that many students seemed to find unsatisfying. But it demands also to be considered in the context of the backlash against gender integration that some ex-servicemen students expressed when returning to university after the war. In the terms of this backlash, 'restoring' a romanticized vision of the pre-war, thoroughly masculine university also entailed 'restoring' norms of binary gender difference against their perceived disintegration. Those men students who, in the 1920s, sought to exclude women from the pleasures of masculine student life also, paradoxically, cast women students themselves as inappropriately, transgressively masculine—for example, through describing women students as ugly or criticizing their participation in conventionally masculine activities such as smoking.[50] Women students, in this schema, could succeed neither at masculinity *nor* at femininity. Their efforts to access activities such as smoking, sports, or rags could only detract from men students' authentic enjoyment of masculine student culture. But locating sex and romance in an abstracted feminine archetype of beauty,

---

[48] Pelican Essay Club Minute Books, 1881–1914, E/5/1–4, Corpus Christi College Archives, discussed in Samuel Rutherford, 'Arthur Sidgwick's *Greek Prose Composition*: Gender, Affect, and Sociability in the Late-Victorian University', *Journal of British Studies* 56, no. 1 (January 2017): 91–116, at 108; see also Deslandes, *Oxbridge Men*, 169.

[49] *The New Durham* 1, no. 2 (March 1923), SC+ 04523, DUA, 21.

[50] See e.g. 'Correspondence', *The Serpent* 1, no. 4 (21 April 1917), 121–3; 'Women and Smoke', *The Serpent* 6, no. 3 (13 December 1921), 74–5. On smoking, women, and gender transgression see Penny Tinkler, 'Sapphic Smokers and English Modernities', in *Sapphic Modernities: Sexuality, Women and National Culture*, ed. Laura Doan and Jane Garrity (Basingstoke: Palgrave Macmillan, 2007), 75–90.

grace, and purity whose power could easily awe its male admirers could also underscore women students' failure to live up to such an exalted ideal.

The pressure that mainstream masculine student culture put on romance, and the way that this was implicated in attitudes to women students, solidified binary conceptions of gender difference. Yet it did so in unexpected ways, creating norms of masculinity and femininity that neither accurately reflected the reality of an active, commercialized heterosexual dating culture, nor straightforwardly mapped onto the bodies and identities of men and women students. This becomes especially clear in the context of one student extracurricular activity in particular: theatre and performance.

Performing Gender

Students had the opportunity to explore narratives of romance and heterosexuality within the context of theatre and other forms of performance. In the first decade of the twentieth century, it became respectable for women students to appear on stage, and performances in which men students played male parts and women students played female parts became a standard feature of campus life. At the same time, performances in which students of one gender played all the parts remained common, as did gender-integrated performances that featured cross-gender casting and other forms of gender experimentation. Whether students played Romeo and Juliet, the lovers in a contemporary drawing-room comedy, or absurd parodies of campus types in original comic revues, they earnestly practised the rituals of—but also satirized and critiqued—sex, dating, romance, marriage, and heterosexuality.[51] Through performance, students had the opportunity to express their own ideals of masculinity, femininity, and what they sought in a sexual or romantic partner. In the context of the changing gender and sexual order of the interwar period, these performances could offer space for experimentation with gender expression. Equally, they could reassert a normative gender order and refuse challenges to it.

While only a minority of women students attended women's colleges or lived in women's halls of residence at coeducational universities, at women's colleges and halls theatre and performance offered students opportunities to experiment with masculine gender expression. Students played masculine roles in plays, but also at fancy-dress parties and (especially in the era before women's admittance to

---

[51] Stephen Brooke has argued that 'the promotion of and resistance to romantic ideals in popular culture occurred simultaneously ....[P]eople could be enchanted, but were, at the same time, well aware of the limitations and, to be fair, the absurdities of those discourses.' Brooke, 'Love, Romance, Celluloid and Wax', 84.

THE DARK LADY OF THE SONNETS

Figure 5.1 'The Dark Lady of the Sonnets'. Masson Hall Photo Album, 1937, Coll-705, Edinburgh University Special Collections. Copyright the University of Edinburgh.

the Bar and women's suffrage) in mock trials and mock parliaments.[52] In 1920s Durham, students at the women's college St Mary's put on William Congreve's 1700 play *The Way of the World*, a racy comedy whose plot turns on a complicated series of sexual intrigues.[53] In mid-1930s Masson Hall, Edinburgh's hall of residence for women, students mounted productions ranging from Chekhov and Shakespeare to original pieces. A photograph of a scene from *The Dark Lady of the Sonnets*, a comedy by George Bernard Shaw, shows a Masson Hall student, clad in Elizabethan breeches and doublet, gallantly embracing another student in a dress and pearls, while a third student in feminine attire looks jealously on (Figure 5.1).[54] In mock trials and mock parliaments, students could access forms of political engagement legally denied them on account of their sex. But in plays, they could also engage with the conventions of sex, romance, and heterosexuality through a masculine lens: embodying the romantic hero, the rake, or the swashbuckling adventurer.[55]

[52] Mo Moulton, *Mutual Admiration Society: How Dorothy L. Sayers and Her Oxford Circle Remade the World for Women* (London: Corsair, 2019), 28–30.

[53] 'Rachel Evans photo album', 1906–40, UND/F8/H10, DUA.

[54] 'The Dark Lady of the Sonnets', Masson Hall Photo Album, 1937, Coll-705, EUSC.

[55] For a similar case from the US women's colleges context see Sarah Parker, 'Elizabethan Lovemaking: College Romance and Queer Anachronism in Edna St Vincent Millay's *The Lamp and the Bell*', in *Interrogating Lesbian Modernism: Histories, Forms, Genres*, ed. Elizabeth English, Jana Funke, and Sarah Parker (Edinburgh: Edinburgh University Press, 2023), 225–47.

Figure 5.2 Actors in *Tilly of Bloomsbury*, Royal Holloway College, 1928. Photo Album of Audrey Baddeley, 1927–9, PH/285/10/1, Archives, Royal Holloway, University of London.

Furthermore, they could also embody more conventional expressions of masculinity. In one photograph (Figure 5.2) from a play staged in 1928 at the residential women's college Royal Holloway—a romantic comedy entitled *Tilly of Bloomsbury*—actors playing a young couple sit together on a box. They gaze into each other's eyes, the masculine actor's right hand on the feminine actor's thigh. They are both dressed in ordinary 1920s fashions: the masculine actor in a tweed jacket and tie, brogues, and a short-back-and-sides haircut parted at the side; the feminine actor in a skirt suit, pumps, and a bobbed haircut. The moment of intimacy, though performed for the camera and the theatre audience, seems quotidian: of a piece with any of the couples who might have embraced each other at dances at coeducational universities.[56]

At the same time, it offers a powerful glimpse into the possibilities of gender crossing in the period. Laura Doan has influentially argued that, in a decade when women's fashion favoured 'boyish' looks, a masculine haircut was as likely to imply trendy, youthful femininity as it was gender transgression. The masculine fashions of the wealthy queer and gender-nonconforming couple Radclyffe Hall and Una Troubridge, for example, signified them as fashion trendsetters rather than sexual deviants. The goal of the fashion was to appear masculine, not

---

[56] 'Second-Year Play: Tilly of Bloomsbury', 1928, in Photo Album of Audrey Baddeley, 1927–9, PH/285/10/1, RHUL.

to pass as a man.[57] But this paradigm does not necessarily describe the gender order at Royal Holloway. Offstage, most of the student actors who played male roles in Royal Holloway plays dressed in more conventionally feminine attire. But they nevertheless occupied a specific position within the college's gender system. Actors who played male roles did so consistently throughout their acting career. Some of them went by chosen masculine first names; when they appeared in male roles, student publications used male pronouns for them when reviewing their performances. They even gravitated to other extracurricular activities together—in the late 1920s, most of the actors who consistently played male roles were also on the college swim team—speaking to a sense of common identity and community beyond theatrical typecasting.[58]

Moreover, in character, with well-fitting men's clothes and fresh haircuts, they consistently appear neither as fashionable women wearing 'boyish' trends, nor as comic actors parodying larger-than-life tropes of masculinity, as had been common in theatrical male impersonation since the late nineteenth century.[59] They demand to be read less in the context of fashionable female masculinity than in that of other contemporary figures who attracted considerable popular interest: 'female husbands', the 'masquerader' Colonel Victor Barker, and, by the 1930s, elite trans men like Michael Dillon and Ewan Forbes who pursued medical transition.[60] Theatrical performances of heterosexuality in the unusual environment of a residential women's college allow us to look beyond the period's sensationalist reporting about masquerades and medical anomalies, seeing not only the isolated, exceptional individual but the possibility of transmasculine community.

Yet in November 1928, at the same time that Royal Holloway's drama society were rehearsing *Tilly of Bloomsbury*, in a courtroom in London Radclyffe Hall's novel *The Well of Loneliness* was being tried for obscenity. The trial brought the expert diagnostic category of the 'invert'—a person whose sense of self and relationship to the world were characterized both by gender nonconformity and by same-sex sexual object choice—into public view.[61] In the context of increasing codification and popular awareness of medicalized definitions of 'healthy' and

---

[57] Doan, *Fashioning Sapphism*, 95–125, esp. 103.

[58] Photo Album of Audrey Baddeley; Photo Album of Margaret Yates, 1923–8, PH/285/4, RHUL; Royal Holloway *College Letter*, 1926–9, AS/902/69–72, RHUL.

[59] Gillian Rodger, '"He Isn't a Marrying Man": Gender and Sexuality in the Repertoire of Male Impersonators, 1870–1930', in *Queer Episodes in Music and Modern Identity*, ed. Sophie Fuller and Lloyd Whitesell (Urbana, IL: University of Illinois Press, 2002), 105–33; Alison Oram, *Her Husband Was a Woman! Women's Gender-Crossing in Modern British Popular Culture* (London: Routledge, 2007).

[60] Oram, *Her Husband Was a Woman!*; Laura Doan, *Fashioning Sapphism: The Origins of a Modern English Lesbian Culture* (New York: Columbia University Press, 2001); Mo Moulton, '"Both Your Sexes": A Non-Binary Approach to Gender History, Trans Studies and the Making of the Self in Modern Britain', *History Workshop Journal* 95 (Spring 2023): 75–100.

[61] Doan, *Fashioning Sapphism*; Christopher Hilliard, *A Matter of Obscenity: The Politics of Censorship in Modern England* (Princeton: Princeton University Press, 2021), 42–8.

'normal' sexuality, female masculinity came to seem like evidence of inability or unwillingness to participate in that normality—and student theatre became implicated in this suspicion. In May 1929, a male student theatre critic, reviewing a recent production at one of Manchester's halls of residence for women, wrote, 'we would advise Ashburne [Hall]...to choose if possible plays written entirely for the sex at hand. Men may often very well take humorous female parts but we doubt whether even a bearded lady tenor could satisfy an audience in any sort of masculine role.'[62] His denial of women students' ability to be sufficiently masculine fits in with a conception of the university as a quintessentially masculine space in which women students could not properly take part. But his dismissive reference to a 'bearded lady tenor' speaks also to increasing sensationalist interest, fuelled by the popular press, in trans and intersex people and in gender transitivity as a scientific phenomenon or medical condition.[63] The critic drew attention to the possibility that actors from a women's hall who played male roles might really belong to an additional, pathologized gender category, while denying them inclusion in the normative gender order that student theatre was supposed to enact. A couple like that in the Royal Holloway play would not be able to portray a convincing romance; only an actor assigned male at birth would have the requisite level of masculinity for the role.

As the critic's comparison to the greater success of 'men [who]...take humorous female parts' suggests, however, this contrasts with how students and wider audiences treated female impersonation, a staple form of mainstream popular entertainment in the period. In the late 1920s and early 1930s, the nexus of male effeminacy, 'inversion', and trans femininity did become an exceptional site of moral panic, subject to extensive policing and persecution. In the eyes of the police and of medical experts, gender nonconformity in those assigned male at birth seemed symptomatic of sexual perversion and social decay.[64] Yet at the same time, female impersonation remained a staple of mainstream popular entertainment that could be cast as upholding, rather than undermining, the gender order. Early-twentieth-century British theatre and film drew on a long, continuous tradition of female impersonation performance that ranged from medieval mummers' plays and commedia dell'arte through to Shakespeare, music hall, and blockbuster nineteenth-century farces like *Charley's Aunt*. In the interwar period, audiences partook of drag entertainment at Christmas-season pantomimes, at the

[62] *The Serpent* 13, no. 5 (May 1929), 63.

[63] Oram, *Her Husband Was a Woman!*; Clare Tebbutt, 'The Spectre of the "Man-Woman Athlete": Mark Weston, Zdenek Koubek, the 1936 Olympics and the Uncertainty of Sex', *Women's History Review* 24, no. 5 (September 2015): 721–38.

[64] Matt Houlbrook, *Queer London: Perils and Pleasures in the Sexual Metropolis, 1918-1957* (Chicago: University of Chicago Press, 2005), 144, 165, 225–7; Matt Houlbrook, '"The Man with the Powder Puff"' in Interwar London', *Historical Journal* 50, no. 1 (2007): 145–71; Emma Heaney, *The New Woman: Literary Modernism, Queer Theory, and the Trans Feminine Allegory* (Evanston, IL: Northwestern University Press, 2017).

'end-of-the-pier' drag shows characteristic of seaside holiday resorts, and at the cinema, which millions attended weekly.[65] After the First World War, female impersonation performance also achieved a new currency in the form of touring stage shows and films featuring ex-servicemen female impersonators. These purported to recreate for a domestic audience the kind of entertainment that soldiers had produced for each other at the front, and became wildly popular as they offered audiences a non-threatening way to process memories of the war.[66]

This mainstream popularity carried into student culture, both in military contexts and more widely. At Officers' Training Corps summer camps in the 1920s, OTC members produced concert parties featuring drag acts—perhaps an instance of returning ex-servicemen students passing down wartime traditions to those men who had been too young to access the mysteries of the Western Front.[67] In fancy-dress parties, parades, pageants, and revues, some student drag mocked femininity. Costumes meant to represent little girls in frilly petticoats or haggard spinsters in black were exaggerated, and sometimes cruel, parodies. The punch lines of the performances often hinged on the contrast between a masculine body and a feminine costume or performance: as in the case of a 1922 mock-historical pageant at Durham depicting the Roman invasion of Britain, in which a tall and thin Boudicca in a large feathered hat towered over a short and stout Julius Caesar; or of a 1925 comic revue at Glasgow, featuring scenes from *Swan Lake* danced by ballerinas whose short hair and men's athletic shirts clashed incongruously with their tutus and pointe shoes (Figure 5.3).[68] Drag costumes—like British popular entertainment more widely in the period—also often drew on racist tropes, using blackface and other forms of racist impersonation to suggest, for allegedly humorous purposes, 'primitive', exoticized, and hypersexualized forms of femininity.[69]

One consequence of drawing on racist and misogynistic tropes to play these performances for laughs was that comedy could neuter the risk that they might be read as homoerotic, queer, or trans. A film that the newsreel company British

[65] Chris O'Rourke, '"What a Pretty Man—or Girl!": Male Cross-Dressing Performances in Early British Cinema, 1898–1918', *Gender & History* 32, no. 1 (2020): 86–107; Jacob Bloomfield, *Drag: A British History* (Berkeley: University of California Press, 2023).

[66] Jacob Bloomfield, 'Splinters: Cross-Dressing Ex-Servicemen on the Interwar Stage', *Twentieth Century British History* 30, no. 1 (March 2019): 1–28; Lisa Z Sigel, '"Best Love": Female Impersonation in the Great War', *Sexualities* 19, nos. 1–2 (February 2016): 98–118; Bloomfield, *Drag: A British History*.

[67] 'OTC Number Photographs', *Glasgow University Magazine*, 9 November 1921, 62–3; 'OTC Number Photographs', *Glasgow University Magazine*, 1 December 1926, 124–5; 'OTC Photographs', *Glasgow University Magazine*, 22 February 1928, 244–5.

[68] 'Invasion of England', 29 June 1922, *British Pathé*, accessed 26 May 2024, http://www.british-pathe.com/video/invasion-of-england; 'College Pudding', *Glasgow University Magazine*, 2 December 1925, 158.

[69] Michael Pickering, *Blackface Minstrelsy in Britain* (Aldershot: Ashgate, 2008), esp. Ch. 8; Christine Grandy, '"The Show Is Not about Race": Custom, Screen Culture, and the Black and White Minstrel Show', *Journal of British Studies* 59, no. 4 (October 2020): 857–84.

THE COLLEGE PUDDINGS.

By courtesy of the " Daily Record."

A touching scene from last week's harrowing melodrama at the Lyric

Figure 5.3 Ballerinas at the University of Glasgow. *Glasgow University Magazine* 37, no. 4 (2 December 1925), 158, DC198/1/32, GUA. By permission of University of Glasgow Archives and Special Collections.

Pathé made of the 1922 Durham pageant includes two sequential takes of a kiss between the actors playing Caesar and Boudicca, intended to symbolize the establishment of harmony between the Romans and the Britons. In the first take, the actors linger on the kiss, to the extent that a third actor hurries into shot to pull their heads apart—and yet the film still offers viewers the opportunity to see the actors kiss a second time.[70] In another British Pathé film, of a 1926 Trinity College Dublin pageant parodying H. Rider Haggard's popular imperialist adventure novel *She*, the actor playing the title character, dressed in an exoticizing, orientalist costume of tunic, wide-legged trousers, and veils, inspects a line of men dressed in athletic wear. Admiring the athletes' muscles, the actor touches them intimately and flirtatiously: squeezing the bicep of one, the thigh of another, the left pectoral muscle of a third; tickling the stomach of a fourth.[71]

As Pathé newsreels, these films would have been viewed by an audience of millions of cinema-goers across the British Isles. Pathé's editorial policy was

[70] 'Invasion of England'.
[71] 'Degree Day Rag by Trinity Students', *British Pathé*, 10 June 1926, accessed 26 May 2024, https://britishpathe.com/video/degree-day-rag-by-trinity-students.

explicitly to shy away from controversy, often choosing to focus on apolitical, light-hearted human interest stories.[72] In both films, the actors' parodic costumes invite the viewer not to take them seriously, an interpretation underscored further by the racism of the Trinity pageant. But if the audience were to view the actors as men in drag, not as women, this therefore also invited a homoerotic interpretation of the performances. As Alison Oram has argued, a 'culture of "knowingness"…innuendo and suggestiveness' prevalent in popular theatrical traditions such as music hall and pantomime may have primed audiences to read more into actors' on-screen physical intimacy.[73] This, too, may have been part of the joke: by adding homophobia to the sexism and racism of the humour, the performance could imply that it mocked queerness rather than embodying it. Nevertheless, decades before the first 'official' same-sex kiss in British cinema, millions of cinema-goers saw two Durham undergraduates kiss on screen, the performance open both to homophobic and to homoerotic interpretations.

In the early twentieth century, comedic or parodic drag sat alongside another popular style that historians have termed 'glamour drag', whose goal was to portray a type of femininity consistent with beauty norms drawn from the stage and Hollywood.[74] In the popular ex-servicemen revues, for example, the ability to craft convincing representations of alluring feminine beauty was key to how critics judged these performances. Reviewers claimed that the performers in these productions were more skilful at embodying femininity than West End actresses. Yet their association with wartime service simultaneously made their masculinity unimpeachable.[75] The same was true in the case of student performance (which, in the early 1920s, likely also included many ex-service performers). When the *Glasgow University Magazine* reviewed the 1925 performance of *Swan Lake*, the critic did not comment on the humorous incongruity of the male ballerinas, but rather celebrated their gracefulness, heralding the prima ballerina, a Mr Stewart, as 'elegance and charm…personified'.[76] In 1923, the same magazine hosted a 'beauty competition', inviting men students to submit photographs of themselves in drag (Figure 5.4). 153 students entered. The magazine published what it judged to be the best photos, criticizing the unsuccessful entrants who had not made enough of an effort. 'Many displayed the most crude conceptions of pose and makeup', the magazine asserted, in contrast praising the winners for their beauty, 'simplicity', and 'complete naturalness'. As in the West End case, the measure of

---

[72] Samuel Rutherford, 'Researching and Teaching with British Newsreels', *Twentieth Century British History* 32, no. 3 (September 2021): 441–61, at 445, 455–7.

[73] Alison Oram, '"A Sudden Orgy of Decadence": Writing about Sex between Women in the Interwar Popular Press', in *Sapphic Modernities: Sexuality, Women and National Culture*, ed. Laura Doan and Jane Garrity (Basingstoke: Palgrave Macmillan, 2007), 165–81, at 175.

[74] Laurence Senelick, 'Boys and Girls Together: Subcultural Origins of Glamour Drag and Male Impersonation on the Nineteenth-Century Stage', in *Crossing the Stage: Controversies on Cross-Dressing*, ed. Lesley Ferris (London: Routledge, 1994), 80–95; Bloomfield, *Drag: A British History*.

[75] Bloomfield, 'Splinters'; Sigel, 'Best Love'.   [76] 'College Pudding'.

Figure 5.4 Entrants in the Glasgow beauty competition. *Glasgow University Magazine* 35, no. 4 (28 November 1923), 97, DC198/1/30, GUA. By permission of University of Glasgow Archives and Special Collections.

the success of these performances was that they were more authentically feminine than the gender expression of women. The magazine suggested that the lessons in femininity the competition winners offered 'ought to be taken to heart by those young ladies of Q[ueen] M[argaret]'—Glasgow's women's college—'who dwell in our midst'.[77]

---

[77] 'A Beauty Competition', *Glasgow University Magazine*, 28 November 1923, 97.

Of course, it is possible to read this assertion as sarcastic. But what if we were to take it seriously? At one level, we might read it as expressive of the moment of postwar backlash against women students. Glamour drag, so strongly associated with ex-servicemen's wartime experiences, afforded men students another opportunity to consign women students to a role as mere outside spectators of traditional student life, and to deride them as so poor at performing sexually desirable femininity that they had to be taught how to do so by men. Like other aspects of interwar student culture, drag performances insistently staged rituals of heterosexual desire, sex, and romance—courtships, weddings, moments of physical intimacy—educating students in these rituals' normalcy and their centrality to adult life.[78]

At the same time, some students who participated in drag ballet performances, beauty competitions, and plays with glamour drag roles may have seen them as opportunities for authentic expressions of femininity in the context of subcultures that accepted gender and sexual nonconformity. Some historians have suggested that, at more gender-segregated Oxford and Cambridge, single-sex male drama societies may have offered a safe haven for queer and gender-nonconforming students. Men students who played glamorous female leads in 1920s Cambridge student theatre were objects of sexual desire for women and men alike.[79] More broadly, in early-twentieth-century theatrical cultures—including in wartime contexts like prisoner-of-war camps—actors who habitually played feminine roles sometimes saw this as an opportunity to express an internal, felt connection with a feminine gender identity; some also lived feminine lives off stage.[80] In a historical moment in which people who lived lives in genders different to those they were assigned at birth were a topic of sensationalist press interest, being able to pass might have read to audiences both as the height of theatrical success and yet also as indicative of substantive trans identification.[81]

Indeed, at the same time that critics lauded female impersonators for creating successful illusions, on campuses some evinced anxiety about whether the

---

[78] See e.g. a mock wedding ceremony staged as part of Manchester's rag carnival in 1922: *The Serpent* 6, no. 6 (10 March 1922), 165.

[79] Dominic Janes, 'The "Curious Effects" of Acting: Homosexuality, Theatre and Female Impersonation at the University of Cambridge, 1900–39', *Twentieth Century British History* 3, no. 2 (June 2022): 169–202; Ross Brooks, 'Beyond Brideshead: The Male Homoerotics of 1930s Oxford', *Journal of British Studies* 59, no. 4 (October 2020): 821–56.

[80] Kit Heyam, *Before We Were Trans: A New History of Gender* (London: Basic Books, 2022), 100–16.

[81] James Vernon, '"For Some Queer Reason": The Trials and Tribulations of Colonel Barker's Masquerade in Interwar Britain', *Signs* 26, no. 1 (2000): 37–62; Oram, *Her Husband Was a Woman!* See also Nadia Ellis's reading of professional dancer Richie Riley's recollections of dancing tango with a male partner in drag in the 1930s. Riley recalled, 'they knew it was a boy doing it, but the makeup was so good, he didn't look like a boy, he didn't look like a boy in drag'. Nadia Ellis, 'Black Migrants, White Queers and the Archive of Inclusion in Postwar London', *Interventions* 17, no. 6 (November 2015): 893–915, at 910–11.

illusions might be *too* convincing. 'I must own that, each year, a fear gets hold of me that someone may mistake a man, in some awful female getup, for a woman student', the tutor for women at the University of Leeds wrote to her counterpart at Manchester in February 1925, referring to the prevalence of female impersonation costumes in annual rag parades and carnivals.[82] The Leeds administrator's concern related to the respectability and safety of the women students in her care. She did not want the newspapers to associate women students with spectacles as outré as, for example, the 'dancing-girls…sold by auction' who featured in a 1926 Durham rag carnival.[83] Nor did she want women students to become a target for violence and sexual harassment because they were assumed to be part of the masculine disorder of the rag festivities. But her fear also speaks to a wider anxiety about the instability of the gender order in the mid-1920s. Perhaps it was the prevalence of 'boyish' fashions among young women that might make it easier for a passerby to 'mistake a man…for a woman student'. Perhaps it was the increasingly widespread use of makeup that might elide the differences between a good girl and a disreputable one, a woman and a 'painted boy'.[84] Or perhaps the 'man' who could pass successfully as 'a woman student' was troubling because she betokened a form of trans existence that was not 'only a rag'.[85]

Students and administrators pursued different strategies for containing this anxiety and shoring up the stability of the gender binary. One strategy was to reaffirm the mainstream popularity of female impersonation performances, their association with unimpeachable wartime masculinities, their expression of sex and romance so successful as to offer a lesson to women and men alike in the norms of heterosexual desire. Another strategy, favoured by administrators like the Leeds tutor for women and some women student government leaders, was to extricate women students from carnivalesque play with gender and sexuality, in the process underscoring one vision of gender difference. At the urging of tutors for women, many women's unions elected to participate in rag festivities while wearing not fancy dress but academic gowns: defining the 'woman student' as indubitably a student, but as a student whose sex meant that she by definition did not participate in a rowdy masculine conception of student life and the gender play that it entailed.[86] Still a third strategy was for women students to participate in gender-complementary, sexualized youth culture themselves. In the 1930s, the

---

[82] Letters to and from Phoebe Sheavyn re. rag fancy dress, January–February 1925, AWS/2/4/1, MUA.
[83] *Durham University Journal* 25, no. 1 (December 1926), 8–9.
[84] Houlbrook, 'Man with the Powder Puff', 167–9.
[85] On the trans femme as a distinctively modern figure who crystallized anxieties about the gender order in the early twentieth century see Heaney, *The New Woman*, 7–8.
[86] Women in gowns appear in several newsreel films of rag processions, especially in the early 1930s: see e.g. 'This Took Place in Aberdeen!', 30 April 1931, *British Pathé*, accessed 26 May 2024, https://www.britishpathe.com/video/this-took-place-in-aberdeen; 'A City Held Up', 21 January 1932, *British Pathé*, accessed 26 May 2024, https://www.britishpathe.com/video/a-city-held-up-aka-glasgow-students-rag; 'The Rag of Rags', 1 February 1932, *British Pathé*, accessed 26 May 2024, https://www.britishpathe.com/video/the-rag-of-rags.

Cambridge Amateur Dramatic Company responded to increasing suspicion of the queerness of its all-male casts by allowing women to play female roles.[87] So, too, did the investment of students at coeducational universities in the rituals of dating, dancing, and sex between women and men assert the stability of binary, complementary gender difference against anxieties about its demise—while also allowing women students an avenue, if a limited one, through which they might participate in a pleasure-oriented young adult leisure culture on their own terms.

Conservative Modernity

The 1920s were an exceptional moment in the history of gender and sexuality in modern Britain. The end of the First World War brought social upheaval, the first moment of true mass democracy and mass politics, a major renegotiation of the legal framework governing the rights of middle-class women, new communication and entertainment technologies, new forms of popular culture and of gender and sexual expression. These developments in turn generated backlash, moral indignation, and a pervasive sense of moral and social crisis whose scapegoats included the fun-loving, promiscuous young woman in the form of the 'flapper'; the cinema, popular music, and dance; and the forms of gender and sexual transgression that scientific and legal experts variously diagnosed as inversion, homosexuality, or transsexuality. Though some far-right voices denounced these deviants in especially strident terms, in the end the response that largely won out was the aesthetic and cultural formation that the literary critic Alison Light has influentially termed 'conservative modernity': concerned with quiet, inward-looking, parochial patriotism; political consensus; and feminine domesticity.[88] Sexual 'normality', 'health', and 'decency', shaped through the collaborative efforts of experts and the public, became important metrics of social integration.[89]

We might understand the gender and sexual expression of interwar students in this context. As the hedonistic pleasures of the new commercial youth leisure culture exerted a tantalizing pull on students, so did the possibility that through them one might arrive at a 'healthy', 'normal', well-adjusted heterosexuality. But for different reasons, both men and women students' engagement with heterosexuality was ambivalent. Women students welcomed the opportunities that new pastimes such as dancing provided to engage with heterosexuality on their own terms; equally, many women became incisive critics of heterosexuality's limitations. Men students, desiring to prove their heterosexuality and masculinity, could evidently do so even when performing as female impersonators or when flirting with those who were. Cultures of cross-gender performance could afford

---

[87] Janes, 'Curious Effects of Acting', 198.   [88] Light, *Forever England*, 10.
[89] Doan, 'Marie Stopes's Wonderful Rhythm Charts', 608–9.

students opportunities to challenge norms of gender and sexuality, and perhaps even to express self-consciously queer or trans identities. But mainstream campus culture often responded to these challenges by seeking anxiously to contain them. Despite its limits, heterosexuality offered both women and men students a promise of pleasure, while also assuring stability, safety, and predictability, foreclosing challenges to the gender order that might have seemed more threatening.

While shoring up the stability of heterosexuality and the gender binary necessitated that female impersonation's respectability and association with hegemonic norms of both masculinity and femininity be consistently reaffirmed, male impersonation disappeared behind the walls of women's colleges and halls. Ever since the women's college had failed to live up to the hopes of some early activists that it prepare women narrowly for marriage and motherhood, these institutions had seemed to offer an alternative, countercultural range of possibilities for gender and sexuality. They contained their own microcosmic spectrums of femininity and masculinity, and allowed academic women to imagine lives outside of heterosexuality, marriage, and the nuclear family. Yet as urban, non-residential, gender-integrated universities became more dominant, and younger generations of women students found heterosexuality more pleasurable, desirable, and reassuring, conceptions of the purpose of higher education for women began to change once again. In the next chapter we will meet women who, in making the mutually exclusive choice of a life in academia rather than a life in marriage, arrived at existences at odds with the categories into which wider society organized gender and sexuality. But we will also see how, over time, the rise of heterosexuality made their life choices less visible and comprehensible: to others, but also to themselves.

Teaching Gender: The British University and the Rise of Heterosexuality, 1860–1939. Samuel Rutherford, Oxford University Press. © Samuel Rutherford 2025. DOI: 10.1093/9780198937524.003.0006

PART III
LOST CAUSES

6

The Single Woman

By 1930, the British higher education sector would have been unrecognizable to the first generation of reformers of the 1860s–70s. The expansion of state funding and oversight for higher education, and the reshaping of the middle-class gender order in British society more widely, had transformed the assumptions that undergirded the structure and culture of universities. As we have seen, one of the major consequences of this transformation was the sidelining of the independent single-sex college, especially the women's college, in favour of large, state-funded, urban, research-oriented, and incidentally coeducational universities, in which students and faculty attempted to work out new paradigms for cross-gender interaction. Yet long after gender-integrated higher education became normative, some women and men still created and sustained gender-segregated educational communities. While they sometimes advanced abstract intellectual arguments for the distinctive value of gender-segregated education, they were just as often drawn to these institutions out of personal affinity. For spinsters and bachelors, the residential college offered a life purpose and a way to forge friendships, community, and family relationships that others found through marriage and children. Over the course of the early twentieth century, as their students—like the wider society of which they were a part—adapted to gender integration and to heterosexuality, these academics came to appear strangely old-fashioned, countercultural, in some cases reactionary, and at times tinged with the suspicion of homosexuality.

Chapters 6 and 7 are about the women and men, respectively, who remained committed to the lost cause of gender-segregated residential higher education, in large part due to the kinds of homosocial bonds that it had the potential to engender. These academics and administrators—unlike many of their colleagues—saw the Oxbridge college as the ideal higher-education model, due to its emphasis on self-development, personal relationships, and extracurricular activities as integral parts of university life. To them, living alongside one another allowed teachers and students to develop a kind of intimacy that was foundational to meaningful higher education, was equivalent to other kinds of familial and romantic relationships, and compared favourably to the possibilities offered by opposite-sex sex, romance, and marriage.

Though both women and men developed such commitments, the connotations of these commitments, and the impact they ultimately had on higher education and on wider society, differed along gender lines. For women, gender-segregated residential higher education became entwined with debates in the feminist movement about equality versus difference feminism, though it also—counterintuitively—fed into a renewed interest in promoting residence and a collegiate culture for both women and men in the wider gender-integrated higher education sector. For men, commitments to the men's college never escaped elitist, reactionary, and misogynistic connotations. But in the process men's colleges became the site, in a way that women's colleges never did, for influential theorizing about the relatively new concept of homosexual identity and community.

The single woman—or 'independent woman', or 'new woman'—was a generationally specific social category, closely identified with the expansion of women's secondary and higher education in the 1860s–90s and the entry that such education provided to new forms of work outside the home. Though there were always some women who never married, in the late nineteenth century this category had a new kind of coherence and visibility. It was a source of meaningful self-identification and also of cultural anxiety. Before the Second World War, in an era of formal marriage bars as well as cultural norms that proscribed married women working outside the home, the single woman's life was structured by the binary, mutually exclusive choice between marriage and career. Many women who did not want to or were not able to marry had no choice but to work for a living in order to provide for themselves. But many also understood themselves to have a profound moral responsibility to dedicate their lives to labouring for the greater good, especially in professions such as teaching, nursing, and social work: using their vocations to contribute to society in the same way, they imagined, that wives and mothers did. And whether through financial exigency or not, women who pursued careers instead of marriage found ways of cultivating networks of intimacy, care, and community beyond the bounds of biological family.[1] They endowed these personal connections with powerful political potential: whether seeking to bring about peace between nations or the Kingdom of Heaven on Earth.[2]

Higher education had opened up possibilities for these women, and many of them in turn opened up possibilities for higher education. This chapter follows the trajectories of a group of women who came of age in the 1890s and 1900s and whose chosen families took shape within the structure and culture of

---

[1] Katherine Holden, *The Shadow of Marriage: Singleness in England, 1914–60* (Manchester: Manchester University Press, 2007); Martha Vicinus, *Independent Women: Work and Community for Single Women, 1850–1920* (London: Virago, 1985); Mo Moulton, *The Mutual Admiration Society: How Dorothy L. Sayers and Her Oxford Circle Remade the World for Women* (London: Corsair, 2019); Gillian Sutherland, *In Search of the New Woman: Middle-Class Women and Work in Britain 1870–1914* (Cambridge: Cambridge University Press, 2015); Carol Dyhouse, *Students: A Gendered History* (London: Routledge, 2006), 55–7.

[2] Seth Koven, *The Match Girl and the Heiress* (Princeton: Princeton University Press, 2014); Moulton, *Mutual Admiration Society*; Ellen Ross, '"Giggling Adolescents" to Refugees, Bullets and Wolves: Francesca Wilson Finds a Profession', in *Precarious Professionals: Gender, Identities and Social Change in Modern Britain*, ed. Heidi Egginton and Zoe Thomas (London: Institute for Historical Research, 2021), 155–80.

gender-segregated residential higher education. It traces the life arc of one particular individual, Margery Fry, who had an exceptional impact upon British
higher education, but also situates Fry within the context of a cohort.[3] These
women were not necessarily research academics. Many, like Fry, pursued careers
in academic administration, enabled by the fact that at the time such roles did not
require specific professional credentials.[4] They used ideas, experiences, and emotions that they had developed within the context of gender-segregated residential
higher education to change the structure and culture of the increasingly gender-
integrated universities in which they worked, but also to craft higher education
policy on a national and international scale. Their commitment to sustaining
women's colleges and halls of residence within formally gender-integrated institutions was undergirded by their commitment to one another, and the story of what
they did for higher education is also a story of how they conceptualized—or
didn't—what it meant to cultivate same-sex dyadic partnerships and chosen family relationships at a time when there were many different, and rapidly changing,
ways to understand the meaning of love between women.

It is sometimes imagined that, in the interwar period, the coalescing spectre
of the 'lesbian' brought women's educational communities under increasing
suspicion.[5] But it would be more accurate to say that the norm of heterosexuality
became too hegemonic to ignore. The academic women of Fry's generation, for
the most part, did not conceptualize themselves as lesbians—nor were they identified as such by others, even implicitly. But they felt increasingly distant from the
experiences of those of their students who actively sought out a student social
life organized around dating and heterosexuality. And as the post-suffrage organized women's movement turned its attention to causes such as social support for
mothers and the removal of barriers to married women's formal paid employment, the paradigmatic academic woman could begin to look rather different: no
longer an exceptional single woman, but a married woman in a two-income
household, often with caring responsibilities for children or for aging parents.
By the mid-1930s, the women who remained invested in gender-segregated residential higher education could seem as old-fashioned as the reactionary men

---

[3] On cohorts of professional women see Laura Carter, 'Women Historians in the Twentieth
Century', in *Precarious Professionals*, 263–85.

[4] On the porousness of professional identity in this period see Egginton and Thomas, *Precarious
Professionals*.

[5] A large literature has discussed this contention, much of it framed in reference to Sheila Jeffreys,
The Spinster and Her Enemies: Feminism and Sexuality, 1880–1930 (London: Pandora Press, 1985):
see e.g. Vicinus, *Independent Women*; Alison Oram, 'Repressed and Thwarted, or Bearer of the New
World? The Spinster in Inter-War Feminist Discourses', *Women's History Review* 1, no. 3 (September
1992): 413–33; Elizabeth Edwards, 'Homoerotic Friendship and College Principals, 1880–1960',
Women's History Review 4, no. 2 (June 1995): 149–63; Laura Doan, *Fashioning Sapphism: The Origins
of a Modern English Lesbian Culture* (New York: Columbia University Press, 2001); Lesley Hall,
'"Sentimental Follies" or "Instruments of Tremendous Uplift"? Reconsidering Women's Same-Sex
Relationships in Interwar Britain', *Women's History Review* 25, no. 1 (January 2016): 124–42.

who continued to advocate for a national women's university or the eugenicist feminists who believed in the imperial strategic importance of a college for domestic science. Still, in often-overlooked but important ways, women who remained committed to the distinctive value of women's colleges left lasting impacts on the structure and culture of British higher education.

Theorizing Women's Community at Somerville

The Oxford and Cambridge women's colleges had been early innovators in the landscape of women's higher education: the first women's institutions to frame their remit in terms of complete equality with the opportunities available to men, and the first—like the men's colleges they emulated—to claim that residence was an integral part of university life. But already by 1894, when Margery Fry arrived at Somerville College, Oxford to study mathematics, events had overtaken these institutions. Women had been admitted to degrees at all of the Scottish universities, the federal University of Wales, and the University of London, and were shortly to be admitted to degrees at several English 'redbrick' universities. Though debates over women's admission to degrees at Oxford and Cambridge raged in the 1890s, the campaigns were resoundingly defeated, not to be taken up again until after the First World War. For the average woman student—the woman who sought a degree in order to acquire a credential that would allow her to enter a stable professional line of work like schoolteaching—an institution that did not grant degrees to women was pointless. And an institution that required full residence of its students was often prohibitively expensive.

Yet for women like Fry, whose affluent families could easily afford the cost of room and board, who had less practical need for a credential, and who wanted to follow their brothers to the ancient universities, an institution like Somerville held inestimable appeal. It also offered enough respectability, especially concerning students' relations with Oxford men students, to put their parents' minds at ease. Fry and her college friends—women like Hilda Oakeley, whom we met in Chapter 2, and the future politician Eleanor Rathbone—came from wealthy, prominent Liberal families, but took haphazard and winding roads to higher education. Neither Fry, Oakeley, nor Rathbone had had a systematic secondary education, and none was well prepared for the mandatory Latin and Greek language study still at the centre of Oxford's curriculum. Fry was twenty when she began her studies, Rathbone was twenty-one, and Oakeley was twenty-seven, having entered college following a first career in the settlement house movement. Fry enjoyed less support from her parents in pursuing educational opportunities than her friends did: worrying about mental strain, her parents forbade her from sitting exams. But Fry and her friends had all been raised with keen awareness of their good fortune and an expectation that they would use their privileges for the greater good of society. They arrived at college prepared to think in serious and open-ended terms about the value of further study and about the value of Somerville in particular.[6]

In the 1890s, Somerville was an especially conducive environment for this kind of contemplation. A new principal, Agnes Maitland, who had taken up office in 1889, had embarked on a programme of expansion and reform: raising the college's academic standards, building better facilities, and relaxing at least some of the strict rules governing students' conduct. In so doing, she indicated a new direction for women's education in Oxford, but she was in keeping with a trend that at the same time was also reshaping the culture of the men's colleges. In the 1870s and 1880s, a new generation of men faculty hired out of 'public' boarding secondary schools after the Oxford colleges had allowed their fellows to marry had brought with them a culture that prized close relations between teachers and students and organized extracurricular activities as an integral part of university life. For more serious-minded students and young tutors, this was further enriched by a fad for British idealist philosophy and its application to social problems. Such students saw the residential college not merely as an institution that enforced curfews and bans on visiting pubs, but as a site for self-development and human flourishing. Though stringent rules about the mixing of the sexes remained in force—men students' cross-gender interaction was as strictly surveilled as women's—in their separate colleges both women and men put into practice new ideas about the particular value of residential community for higher education. One could achieve things, they thought—for oneself and for society writ large—not only by coming top in exams, or even by becoming captain of the boat club, but by staying up late in someone's room, discussing everything under heaven and putting the world to rights. Given prevailing social strictures governing cross-gender social interaction, for many it was precisely the gender segregation of these communities that allowed for their intellectual and personal expansiveness, providing a kind of freedom from social awkwardness and convention not possible in wider mixed-gender society.[7]

---

[6] Hilda D. Oakeley, *My Adventures in Education* (London: Williams and Norgate, 1939); Susan Pedersen, *Eleanor Rathbone and the Politics of Conscience* (New Haven: Yale University Press, 2004), 46–50; Anne Logan, *The Politics of Penal Reform: Margery Fry and the Howard League* (London: Routledge, 2018); Pauline Adams, *Somerville for Women: An Oxford College, 1879–1993* (Oxford: Oxford University Press, 1996); Janet Howarth, '"In Oxford but...Not of Oxford": The Women's Colleges', in *The History of the University of Oxford*, Volume 7: *Nineteenth-Century Oxford, Part 2*, ed. M.G. Brock and M.C. Curthoys (Oxford: Oxford University Press, 2000), 237–307.

[7] Samuel Rutherford, 'Arthur Sidgwick's *Greek Prose Composition*: Gender, Affect, and Sociability in the Late-Victorian University', *Journal of British Studies* 56, no. 1 (January 2017): 91–116, at 108. On the impact of British Idealism see Stefan Collini, *Public Moralists: Political Thought and Intellectual Life in Victorian Britain 1850–1930* (Oxford: Oxford University Press, 1991); Jose Harris, *Private Lives, Public Spirit: Britain 1870–1914* (London: Penguin, 1994); Sandra M. den Otter, *British Idealism and Social Explanation: A Study in Late-Victorian Thought* (Oxford: Clarendon Press, 1996).

At Somerville, Fry and her friends embodied these values and aspirations, in specific ways structured by their gender and class positions. They founded a self-consciously elite discussion society in which they debated practical questions of social reform: the Poor Law, penal reform, factory legislation, agricultural policy, socialism. When their studies came to an end, they pondered what effect they themselves could have on any of these concerns. Rathbone wanted to go into politics, Fry to become a lawyer, and Oakeley to become a schools inspector, but in the 1890s these paths were just barely beginning to open to women, and there was no clear route to establishing a career. Fry had not even taken the exams that could have provided her with an ersatz qualification, if not a degree. Oakeley, a talented philosopher, was interested in graduate study, but worried that was too selfish a path. She felt guilty that, in her view, she lacked the aptitude for practical social work.[8]

Rathbone was, in fact, in due course to go on to a distinguished political career. But for both Oakeley and Fry, the resolution to their dilemmas came in the form of the expanding women's higher education sector itself. Though neither had the correct credentials for research, there were increasingly other jobs in higher education available to women. In 1898, the year after she finished her studies, Fry jumped at an invitation to return to Somerville as librarian, eager to escape a fractious relationship with her parents and the dullness of life in their home.[9] The following year, Oakeley took up a job as warden of a new women's college within McGill University in Montreal. From Oakeley's point of view, the position provided an answer to her fears of selfishness. She could use it to act as a mentor to younger women and to advance the cause of women's education more broadly, something she did throughout her career, at McGill and then in successive roles at Manchester and King's College for Women.[10]

As Somerville librarian, Fry gained important administrative experience, helping to fundraise for and superintending the construction of a new library building. But just as important were decisions that she made at that time about the direction of her personal life. By then in her late twenties, Fry was at the typical age of marriage for women. Some of her friends were marrying, and her parents expected her to do the same. But in 1902, she turned down a proposal from an older Oxford academic and clergyman with whom she shared intellectual and political interests.[11] Instead, she entered another kind of long-term relationship: with her colleague Rose Sidgwick, the daughter of an Oxford classicist who had

[8] Letters between Hilda Oakeley and Margery Fry, 1898–1904, Margery Fry Papers, Box 27 Folder 8, Somerville; Pedersen, *Eleanor Rathbone*, 54; Logan, *Politics of Penal Reform*, 38–9.

[9] Logan, *Politics of Penal Reform*, 41.

[10] Oakeley, *My Adventures in Education*; Carol Dyhouse, *No Distinction of Sex? Women in British Universities 1870–1939* (London: University College London Press, 1995), 108.

[11] Logan, *Politics of Penal Reform*, 46–9.

studied history while living at home with her parents and who became assistant librarian at Somerville in 1903.

Only Sidgwick's love letters to Fry survive, not Fry's letters to Sidgwick. There is much we do not know about the internal content of the two women's relationship and how they made sense of what they were to one another—a question with which Sidgwick herself sought to grapple. In an undated poem, written in honour of Fry's birthday, Sidgwick wrote that she struggled with how to express her feelings for Fry, when 'To talk of love...does not interest you.' The rest of the poem switches back and forth between the language of 'friend' and 'lover': 'take your will', the speaker says about the terminology.[12] Yet in Sidgwick's letters, a picture emerges of the two women's physical and emotional intimacy, and of a bond unlike Sidgwick's connections to other friends and family. Sidgwick's letters address Fry as 'Dearest', expressing pain when they are apart and a desire to be reunited. In one 1906 letter, Sidgwick says that she cannot find the right words to express how she feels about Fry, 'except by saying that 24 hours of you gives me a clearer & wider perception of what is meant by Christianity'.[13] But nor was this only a disembodied, spiritual friendship: in a letter in which Sidgwick told Fry about a time when she went skinny-dipping while on holiday, she wrote, 'I thought at the time that you would like me better if you'd seen me splashing there with nothing on!'[14] Above all, Sidgwick's expressions of love were playful and open-hearted. She signed one letter, 'Yours-that-loves-you-more-every-day-so-that-I-don't-know-where-we-shall-be-in-1950-, R.S.'[15]

There is no evidence that either Fry or Sidgwick ever described herself as having a sexual orientation or identity. Though at the turn of the twentieth century the concept of 'sexual inversion' as popularized by writers such as Havelock Ellis was starting to gain some currency in intellectual circles, it tended to connote primarily gender incongruence: a form of social transgression immediately legible on the body of the 'invert' and pathologized as such.[16] At the time, Fry and Sidgwick's relationship would have been legible within the mode of 'romantic friendship' or domestic partnership available to unmarried professional women, widely assumed by observers to be non-sexual and to be unproblematic provided that it did not detract from women's responsibilities to their work or to their families of origin.[17] Though Fry later in life wrote about her views on sex and relationships, she imagined them to be heterosexual by default, and it is not clear that she felt the same way about Sidgwick as Sidgwick evidently did about her. But the

[12] 'Poems written by Rose Sidgwick for Margery Fry', Margery Fry Papers, Box 29 Folder 3, Somerville.

[13] Rose Sidgwick, letter to Margery Fry, 16 April 1906, Box 29 Folder 5, Somerville.

[14] Rose Sidgwick, letter to Margery Fry, 10 September 1907, Box 30 Folder 6, Somerville.

[15] Rose Sidgwick, letter to Margery Fry, 12 September 1909, Box 29 Folder 6, Somerville.

[16] Havelock Ellis and John Addington Symonds, *Sexual Inversion: A Critical Edition*, ed. Ivan Crozier (London: Palgrave Macmillan, 2008); Doan, *Fashioning Sapphism*, 147–8, 152, 156–8.

[17] Vicinus, *Independent Women*, 35–6, 158–61.

two did not need to articulate self-conscious sexual identities to develop a partnered, familial relationship outside of marriage and the nuclear family. And we
do not need to know whether they saw their relationship as erotic or sexual in
order to view it as significant. Indeed, it clearly proved an anchor in the next stage
of their joint life. In 1904, Fry applied for and received a job as the inaugural
warden of University House, the first women's hall of residence at the University
of Birmingham. Having just turned thirty, she perceived the new job as a fork in
the road: she was leaving behind the possibility of marrying and having children,
instead devoting herself to a life of work that, as she had long hoped, would be
socially useful as well as personally satisfying.[18] The following year, Sidgwick
joined her in Birmingham, having secured a position as a history lecturer. Living
together for the next thirteen years, the two women put into practice the ideas
they had begun to develop at Somerville about the value of residential college life
and of the personal relationships that necessarily undergirded it.

Building Women's Community at Birmingham

Though there had been a technical college in Birmingham for decades, in 1900
work began on a new, planned campus in the leafy suburb of Edgbaston: Britain's
first 'redbrick' university. With its extravagant construction programme under-
written principally by the wealthy politician Joseph Chamberlain, then at the
height of his political prominence, the university had no difficulty in promptly
securing a charter. Its first administrators—especially its principal, Oliver
Lodge—were progressives for whom gender integration was central to their
vision of a modern university. Women were admitted to degrees, and even to a
gender-integrated student union, from the start.[19] But the university's founders
also recognized that women pursuing higher education in this period needed distinct forms of support. Though the university's intake was primarily local and
regional, those women students who could not easily make a daily commute from
their family homes to Edgbaston would need safe, respectable accommodation
designed specifically with them in mind. A committee of women from
Birmingham's prominent industrial families raised funds to build a hall of residence and to hire a warden to run it. The committee's secretary, Charlotte
Chamberlain—a member of the extended Birmingham Chamberlain clan and a
graduate of Newnham College, Cambridge—informed Fry that 'the Hall should

---

[18] Logan, *Politics of Penal Reform*, 45–6; Enid Huws Jones, *Margery Fry: The Essential Amateur*
(London: Oxford University Press, 1966), 67.

[19] William Whyte, *Redbrick: A Social and Architectural History of Britain's Civic Universities*
(Oxford: Oxford University Press, 2015), 166–73.

be managed on similar lines to the Oxford & Cambridge Colleges'.[20] Though the university itself had been founded in self-conscious opposition to the Oxbridge model, when it came to providing for women students, different ideals prevailed.

It is no surprise, then, that Fry and Sidgwick were among a number of women who had passed through the distinctive environment of Somerville in the 1890s who went on to work in women's halls across Britain. In addition to Oakeley, these included Phoebe Sheavyn, the long-serving tutor for women at Manchester; and Fry's friend May Staveley, who was warden of the women's hall at Liverpool and later at Bristol.[21] Together, these women brought about a transformation in the role of the warden and of the women's hall in the ecosystem of the coeducational civic university. The first generation of wardens had secured their respectability by casting their work as philanthropy rather than as a profession, refusing to accept payment and instead using their own private incomes to fund day-to-day expenses. Though they often participated informally in university policy-making, they preferred to emphasize their housekeeping duties.[22] By contrast, Fry only accepted the job at University House on the condition that she would be able to advise students academically. In her hiring negotiations, she secured a higher salary and a seat on the university senate.[23] As the students came, Fry undertook to get to know each one personally, finding out about her academic interests and life aspirations. She treated them as adults: replacing long lists of rules with a general injunction to respect one's fellow residents, and permitting a fairly wide degree of social interaction with men students.[24]

Fry and Sidgwick were joined at University House by other resident administrators and faculty: a philosophy lecturer, two French teaching assistants, a bursar, a deputy warden.[25] Most of these women had been educated in the Oxford and Cambridge women's colleges, and they drew on what they had learned there about how to craft residential educational communities. They prized academic success, and sought to inculcate a democratic culture through organized student politics. But they also sought to foster fun. In her first term, seeking to get what was at that time a chilly and distant community to relate to one another as friends, Fry led the hall's residents in making a snowman in the likeness of Principal Oliver Lodge: an initiative that, she recalled later, set a tone for life in the hall.[26] Fry and Sidgwick both enjoyed amateur dramatics, and there were plays every

---

[20] Charlotte Chamberlain, letter to Margery Fry, 16 June 1904, Margery Fry Papers, Box 31 Folder 1, Somerville.

[21] Dyhouse, *No Distinction of Sex?*, 108.

[22] Dyhouse, *No Distinction of Sex?*, 100. For an example of one such warden see Mrs Robert Jardine, ed., *Janet Galloway: Some Memories & Appreciation* (Glasgow: Glasgow University Press, 1914), DC 240/5/8/2, GUA.

[23] Margery Fry, letter to Charlotte Chamberlain, 16 November 1904, Margery Fry Papers, Box 31 Folder 1, Somerville.

[24] Jones, *Margery Fry*, 69, 82.   [25] Logan, *Politics of Penal Reform*, 55.

[26] Margery Fry, typescript memoir of the early years of University House, n.d. (*c.*1912), UB/HUH/A/9/1, Birmingham.

Figure 6.1 Students at University House, *c.*1910. University House Photo Album, UB/HUH/A/8/1, Cadbury Research Library: Special Collections, University of Birmingham.

term, mostly comedic: Aristophanes, pantomime, 'a suffragette play (given by the staff)'.[27] The style was rough and ready, with homemade costumes and handwritten programmes. Candid photographs from the early years of University House show students posing informally, laughing and smiling (Figure 6.1).[28] A generation previous, Sidgwick's father had leveraged just such controlled silliness, also grounded in large part in amateur dramatics, to create an informal community for the men students in his Oxford college.[29] By adopting the model for University House, Fry and Sidgwick were making a statement about women's entitlement to access this kind of community, despite the challenge it might pose to norms of respectability and propriety. Yet as in the case of men's colleges, the culture of informality at University House was nevertheless premised on a kind of social ease that, in the 1900s, would still have been difficult to achieve in mixed company.

The married fellows of Oxbridge men's colleges moved back and forth between the gender-integrated environment of their home and family lives and the

---

[27] Programmes of University House plays, UB/HUH/A/10/1, Birmingham.
[28] Photo album (n.d.), UB/HUH/A/8/1, Birmingham.
[29] Rutherford, 'Sidgwick's *Greek Prose Composition*', 106–9.

gender-segregated environment of their workplaces.[30] Though the men's college might have been in some sense a domestic space, and one that, as we will see in the next chapter, some faculty and administrators saw as preparatory for the responsibilities of married life, it was distinct from marital and reproductive conceptions of family.[31] Early women's colleges, by contrast, often actually advertised themselves as 'families': a strategic choice designed to affirm bourgeois respectability, but simultaneously a recognition of the ways that pursuing higher education could distance young women from their families of origin and from social expectations that they become wives and mothers.

Historians have tended to dismiss or to undercut the rhetoric of 'family', instead arguing that, in increasingly moving away from finishing school gentility to imitate the structure and culture of the Oxbridge men's colleges, women's colleges and halls offered an 'alternative' to, and perhaps even a 'rejection' of, 'the family model'.[32] But to dismiss talk of 'family' as in some way incompatible with the academic and the feminist ambitions of women's institutions risks obscuring the ways that women's residential higher education innovated *new* conceptions of family. University House was not a normative Victorian nuclear family headed by a patriarch and organized around a male breadwinner ideal. But it was a space of domesticity, informality, friendship, and fun. It had pets (a dog joined the household early on); benevolent uncles, in the form of the university's senior male administrators, who dropped in unannounced for dinner; and a commitment to treating everyone from the domestic staff to distinguished visitors with respect, if not reverence.[33] It had a younger generation, in the form of the students whose personal and professional development Fry, Sidgwick, and their colleagues guided, and it had an older generation, comprising several resident senior members. Fry and Sidgwick's dyadic relationship was one element of a wider ethos of community that flourished on distinct but parallel lines to the normative biological family.

The First World War put University House's familial relationships under unprecedented strain, but these pressures also shed light on their shape and significance. As Fry and Sidgwick negotiated together the challenges of the war, they figured their partnership and their other close relationships within the paradigms of longing and loss that the war made available to those on the home front whose loved ones were performing military service or other types of war work. This began after Britain entered the war in August 1914, when Fry joined the Quaker

---

[30] Rutherford, 'Sidgwick's *Greek Prose Composition*', 115.

[31] On the domesticity of male homosocial environments see John Tosh, *Manliness and Masculinities in Nineteenth-Century Britain: Essays on Gender, Family and Empire* (Harlow: Pearson Longman, 2011); Amy Milne-Smith, *London Clubland: A Cultural History of Gender and Class in Late Victorian Britain* (Basingstoke: Palgrave Macmillan, 2011).

[32] Vicinus, *Independent Women*, 128; Dyhouse, *No Distinction of Sex?*, 112.

[33] Jones, *Margery Fry*, 75–6, 82.

war relief effort: camping just behind the lines of the Western Front, providing food parcels, first aid, and childcare to French refugees. She inspired several University House students to follow her example. But Sidgwick stayed behind, supervising University House's move into rented accommodation after the War Office requisitioned their building.[34]

Sidgwick struggled with guilt at remaining in Birmingham: most of her friends had taken up war work, and her brother Hugh, to whom she was close, was an army captain. Hugh's fiancée, Amphilis Middlemore, lived in Birmingham and was friends with Sidgwick and Fry.[35] The letters that Sidgwick wrote to Fry while the latter was in France explore the parallels between the two women's relationship and a relationship like Hugh and Amphilis's. 'Darling, I am thankful you are not a soldier fighting,' Sidgwick wrote in 1915.[36] But even if Fry was not 'a soldier fighting', she was enduring discomfort and danger close to the front lines. Like other women at home, Sidgwick sent her loved one parcels containing home comforts like powdered shampoo, and she wrote of the difficulty of not being able to talk to each other or to be close to one another, of the limits of what can be said in a letter.[37]

One of Fry's closest friends, a Birmingham maths lecturer, was killed in action in 1916. In 1917, Hugh Sidgwick was also killed. Sidgwick and her sisters adopted Amphilis as part of their family as they mourned together.[38] Fry and Sidgwick were devastated by these losses, and struggled to ascertain what each other were truly feeling and how best to support each other.[39] The tragedies of war could reveal previously unapprehended depths of feeling; equally, they could generate new intimacies and emotional commitments, entangling biological and chosen family.

Sidgwick also sought meaning in the hope that the war might indirectly enact progressive political change. Many academics took up the cause of liberal internationalism during and after the First World War, seeing in the study and teaching of world history, political science, and international relations the opportunity to promote peace and the values of good citizenship in the present.[40] Sidgwick joined this movement, lecturing on internationalism to the Workers' Educational Association and the League of Nations Union in Birmingham. In 1917, she wrote to Fry with a renewed sense of optimism: 'With the suffrage, & Russia on the way

---

[34] Jones, *Margery Fry*, 99, 102; Logan, *Politics of Penal Reform*, 77.

[35] Moulton, *Mutual Admiration Society*, 58–9.

[36] Rose Sidgwick, letter to Margery Fry, 7 August 1914, Box 30 Folder 7, Somerville.

[37] Rose Sidgwick, letter to Margery Fry, 12 February 1917, Box 30 Folder 11, Somerville. For comparisons to soldiers' letters home see Jessica Meyer, *Men of War: Masculinity and the First World War in Britain* (Basingstoke: Palgrave Macmillan, 2009), 14–46; Nancy Christie and Michael Gauvreau, *Bodies, Love, and Faith in the First World War: Dardanella and Peter* (Basingstoke: Palgrave Macmillan, 2018), 191–250.

[38] Moulton, *Mutual Admiration Society*, 59.   [39] Logan, *Politics of Penal Reform*, 84–5.

[40] Helen McCarthy, *The British People and the League of Nations: Democracy, Citizenship and Internationalism, c. 1918–45* (Manchester: Manchester University Press, 2011).

to freedom, & some hope of a League of Nations, one can't help seeing that something has come out of these three black years.'[41] An opportunity came to put theory into practice in summer 1918, when the Foreign Office invited Fry to join a
British Educational Mission that was to tour dozens of US colleges and universities in the final months of the war, using higher education policy and intellectual exchange as a tool to cement geopolitical alliance. Fry had returned from
France, but her father was dying and she was needed to support her family of
origin. She suggested that Sidgwick go to America in her stead.[42]

As we saw at the end of Chapter 2, the British Educational Mission's delegates'
encounters with US higher education informed their visions for gender and the
future direction of British higher education. But the mission also had an enormous personal impact upon Sidgwick and Fry. While Sidgwick and her colleagues were touring the US, a virulent strain of influenza was infecting millions
of Americans, especially those living in densely populated locations like New
York, then the world's largest city. In 1918–20, this strain of influenza would kill as
many as 100 million people worldwide, 6 per cent of the global population.
A disproportionate number of those who died were healthy young adults.

Sidgwick and the mission's other woman delegate, Bedford College English
professor Caroline Spurgeon, both came down with influenza while visiting New
York. Spurgeon recovered quickly, but Sidgwick became critically ill. She was
admitted to the Columbia University Hospital, where she spent over two weeks
before dying on 28 December 1918. No one had thought to tell Fry that Sidgwick
was ill. She learned of her partner's death on 1 January, when Sidgwick's sister
Ethel sent her a telegram—after an obituary had already run in the *New-York
Tribune*.[43] Fry felt consumed with survivor's guilt, blaming herself for having
nominated Sidgwick for the trip. She was also angry that no one had told her, and
that she had therefore been unable to send Sidgwick a telegram saying she loved
her before she died.[44] Though no one from the UK was able to travel to New York
for the funeral, Ethel came a few months later to see Sidgwick's grave and order a
headstone.[45] Fry could only pack up Sidgwick's belongings to send to her family
of origin and vacate their house in Birmingham. She moved to London, asking a
friend to sit with her in the last hours before leaving Birmingham because being
alone in the empty house was 'unbearable'.[46]

Nevertheless, there were paradigms available through which Fry could make
sense of her loss. In 1918, countless people across all levels of society had lost

[41] Rose Sidgwick, letter to Margery Fry, 2 April 1917, Box 30 Folder 2, Somerville; see also 15 June
1915, Folder 8.

[42] Jones, *Margery Fry*, 108.

[43] 'Miss Rose Sidgwick', *New-York Tribune*, 31 December 1918, 11.

[44] Logan, *Politics of Penal Reform*, 88.

[45] Margery Fry Papers, Box 29 Folders 5 and 6, Somerville.

[46] Logan, *Politics of Penal Reform*, 87.

loved ones. Fry and Sidgwick themselves had already lost a friend and a brother respectively. And Sidgwick had, after all, been on a diplomatic mission in aid of the war effort. At the high-church Anglican funeral in the Columbia university chapel, her coffin was draped in a Union Jack, and the pall-bearers included senior diplomats, politicians, and university administrators. The women academics' American host, dean of Barnard College Virginia Gildersleeve, later recalled, 'I felt that she had died as truly in the service of her country as had the thousands of her young countrymen who had fallen on the fields of Flanders and of France.'[47] The University of Birmingham underscored this sentiment by inscribing Sidgwick's name on the university war memorial, one of two women included in the list of the dead. Fry echoed the comparison. Writing to her mother about her regret that she could not have been at Sidgwick's side as she lay ill, she said, 'of course it's what happened to all those soldiers'.[48] If Sidgwick was a soldier, that gave Fry a script through which she could participate in collective mourning alongside those who had also lost lovers and partners in the war—in the process staking a claim to a kind of status as widow. Family, friends, colleagues, and former students who wrote to Fry to express their condolences implicitly recognized the exceptional significance of the two women's relationship.[49] Fry wrote Sidgwick's official obituary, and had printed a collection of Sidgwick's poetry and speeches that she could send to well-wishers.[50] She preserved Sidgwick's personal papers, including Sidgwick's love letters to her—which remain among her own papers in the Somerville archives to this day—and gave University House a donation to establish a memorial garden in honour of Sidgwick. For the rest of her long life, she sent regular payments for the garden's upkeep.[51]

For Fry, Sidgwick, and the other women of their generation who had taken the ideas about the value of residential higher education that they had developed at Somerville and translated them to institutional contexts across Britain, then, the residential hall or college played a foundational role in innovating new models of friendship, family, and intimacy. These models did not draw on a recognizably 'modern' conception of homosexuality as an identity. But like the modern conception of homosexuality figured as parallel to, and mutually constitutive with, heterosexuality, the family that took shape at University House in the years before the war was parallel to the prevailing normative conception of family that inhered in marriage and biological reproduction. Those women who could not or did not want to marry did not reject family. They constructed it anew, in specific ways

---

[47] Virginia C. Gildersleeve, *Many a Good Crusade: Memoirs of Virginia Crocheron Gildersleeve* (New York: Macmillan, 1954), 130.

[48] Logan, *Politics of Penal Reform*, 88.

[49] Margery Fry Papers, Box 27 Folder 2 and Box 29 Folder 6, Somerville.

[50] Margery Fry, 'In Memoriam. Rose Sidgwick', 24 January 1919, MS Eng. misc. c. 706 f. 3, Bodleian; Rose Sidgwick, 'Writings', 1918, UB/HUH/A/10/6, Birmingham.

[51] Charlotte Sidgwick, letter to Beatrice Orange, 28 June 1919, UB/HUH/A/3/2, Birmingham; Margery Fry, letter to Julia Friend, 17 October 1955, UB/HUH/A/3/5/1/14, Birmingham.

that paralleled—to the extent that was possible within prevailing legal and social structures—the affective and the practical, logistical ties of marriage and domestic partnership. They drew on these concepts when seeking the language and emotional resources to process loss, grief, and upheaval. And in leaving their imprint on the built environment, in institutional archives, and in networks, organizations, and policy, they ensured their chosen families remained entangled with the educational institutions they had built.

Choosing Family and Leaving Legacies

These women who did not marry also found ways to have children: that is, to care for, and participate in the upbringing of, younger women, and to leave behind legacies that would survive them. Three legacies arose directly from the affective ties that took shape at Somerville and Birmingham in the years between 1894 and 1918: an internationalist utopian movement that held that women university graduates were integral to the post-First World War effort to promote peace, freedom, and good governance; the personal impact Fry and Sidgwick had on the lives of their own students; and a lasting commitment to the value of university residence that, through Fry's efforts, had profound effects on national higher education policy.

During the British Educational Mission to the US, Sidgwick's colleague Caroline Spurgeon had commented, 'We should have an international association of university women; so that we shall at least have done all we can to prevent another such catastrophe' like the First World War.[52] After the mission's tragic denouement, Spurgeon and Virginia Gildersleeve became determined to found such an association in Sidgwick's memory. Eight months later, British and American women academics and university graduates held the first of what would become annual meetings of the International Federation of University Women (IFUW). Their first act was to establish—thanks to American donors—a Rose Sidgwick Memorial Fellowship for a British woman to pursue an exchange year or graduate study in the US.[53] This responded to practical concerns that had emerged during Spurgeon's and Sidgwick's visits to American women's colleges about the lack of international academic fellowships available to women, by comparison to those available to men.[54] But it also reflected the philosophy that

---

[52] Virginia C. Gildersleeve, 'How It Started', typescript speech, January 1951, Virginia Gildersleeve Papers, Box 47, Columbia RBML.

[53] 'The Rose Sidgwick Memorial Fellowship', Gildersleeve Papers, Box 78, Columbia. The fellowship was widely advertised in student and feminist periodicals throughout the interwar period.

[54] Caroline Spurgeon, 'Supplementary Report on Women's University Education', PP7/6/1/3, RHUL; Rose Sidgwick, 'Diary of US Trip', Margery Fry Papers, Box 30 Folder 3, Somerville; 'Report of Conference on After-War Problems', 6 December 1918, Virginia Gildersleeve Papers, Box 44, Columbia; Tamson Pietsch, 'Commercial Travel and College Culture: The 1920s Transatlantic

animated the IFUW: that meaningful bonds of personal friendship between highly educated women from different countries, sustained through the institutional structures of universities and through the organizational networks of the IFUW, would prove an engine of liberal internationalism and peace. In her speech at the 1919 conference launching the organization, Spurgeon described its mission as 'the enterprise of preparing some portion of human material for the League of Nations that is to be'.[55] Looking back on the IFUW's origins from the vantage point of the 1950s, Gildersleeve recalled, 'Of course our most important aim was world peace', to be achieved through 'get[ting] to know one another as comrades'.[56]

The premise that a transformation in personal relations had the power to bring about world peace was not an uncommon one in the years after the First World War, which saw the blossoming of a number of radical utopian movements.[57] In proposing that highly educated women were uniquely positioned to achieve this, the IFUW was also in dialogue with a pre-war strand of 'avant-garde' feminist thought that had imagined a special role in the women's movement for a new kind of creative and intellectual elite, defined not by social class but by 'genius'. In an era when members of the transatlantic feminist movement were increasingly focusing on making a case for the broader social value of motherhood and for state support of women's domestic and reproductive labour, the promise of a utopia founded on feminine genius may have appealed to single, childless women seeking an alternative meaningful social role.[58] Indeed, the IFUW brought into being a framework for international academic exchange in which a committed relationship between Spurgeon and Gildersleeve could unfold. The two remained partners for twenty-four years, until Spurgeon's death in 1942: they co-owned a holiday cottage in Sussex and, despite professional demands, contrived to spend six months of each year together. Their letters to each other, addressed 'My own Darling', make clear their love, care, and commitment for each other.[59] The philosophy of the IFUW could help women like Gildersleeve and Spurgeon to create a conceptual space for personal relationships that they could perceive as meaningful alternatives to marriage and children at a time when many thought of motherhood as the primary contribution that women might make to the greater good.

Student Market and the Foundations of Mass Tourism', *Diplomatic History* 43, no. 1 (January 2019): 83–106.

[55] Christine von Oertzen, *Science, Gender, and Internationalism: Women's Academic Networks, 1917–1955*, trans. Kate Sturge (New York: Palgrave Macmillan, 2014), 28.

[56] Gildersleeve, 'How It Started'.

[57] Anna Neima, *The Utopians: Six Attempts to Build the Perfect Society* (London: Picador, 2021); Koven, *The Match Girl and the Heiress*.

[58] Lucy Delap, *The Feminist Avant-Garde: Transatlantic Encounters of the Early Twentieth Century* (Cambridge: Cambridge University Press, 2007), 161.

[59] PP7/3/3/10, RHUL; Gildersleeve Papers, Box 4, Box 44, Box 65, Columbia.

Working for a cause like the IFUW also allowed women like Gildersleeve and Spurgeon (and, before she died, Sidgwick) to leave a legacy behind. Though their ambition foundered on the breakdown in international relations brought about by the rise of fascism and the Second World War, before the war the women who worked with the IFUW established a network of thirty national member organizations in Europe and the British Empire; facilitated direct interpersonal exchange among members, including through a membership directory and a network of clubhouses in European capitals; and collected data, published reports, and drafted policy recommendations relating to women, education, and the professions that they placed before national governments and the League of Nations.[60] IFUW campaigning focused on the full gender integration of higher education, the eradication of sex distinction in academic hiring practices, equal pay, and women's 'acknowledged right to the happiness of a family' alongside a career.[61] Although it had its origins in exceptionalist claims for women's gender-segregated academic community, then, the IFUW appeared to be working for a world in which such communities were no longer necessary or desirable.

Arguably more enduring, however, were Fry's and Sidgwick's impact upon their own students and, in part through them, upon how UK universities conceptualized the value of residence to the purpose of higher education. For the majority of University House students, like the majority of undergraduates generally, the hall of residence was a space through which to pass for a few years on the way to the next stage of their lives. But a few, like Marjorie Rackstraw, made lasting commitments to university life. Fourteen years younger than Fry and eleven years younger than Sidgwick, Rackstraw was from a slightly less affluent and less well-networked background, but her father, the owner of an Islington department store, had the resources to send her to a local school and away to university at Birmingham, which he determined would be better for her health than Somerville.[62] When she arrived at University House in 1908 to study history, she developed an especially close relationship with Sidgwick, her tutor, which inspired her to participate enthusiastically in the hall's community life. She adopted Sidgwick and, by extension, Fry as family: while pursuing a postgraduate exchange year at Bryn Mawr College in Pennsylvania, she exchanged letters with them in which she addressed them as her aunts and they addressed her as 'dearest niece.'[63] Rackstraw's relationship with Sidgwick, then, so close that it became familial, in the process also became a way of recognizing Sidgwick and Fry's

---

[60] PP7/6/2, PP7/6/4/1, PP7/6/4/2, PP7/6/5/1, PP7/6/8/1, RHUL; see also generally records of the British Federation of University Women, 5BFW, LSE; von Oertzen, *Science, Gender, and Internationalism*, 35.

[61] von Oertzen, *Science, Gender, and Internationalism*, 30–1.

[62] Enid Huws Jones, 'Rackstraw, Marjorie (1888–1981), Educationist and Social Worker', *Oxford Dictionary of National Biography*, 23 September 2004, accessed 12 March 2022, https://www.oxforddnb.com/view/10.1093/ref:odnb/9780198614128.001.0001/odnb-9780198614128-e-52396.

[63] Letters from Sidgwick to Rackstraw, 1912–18, Coll-705, EUSC.

partnership and of allowing Fry a role in her life as well. In the early twentieth century, commentators sometimes voiced anxieties about 'uncontrolled' or 'unhealthy' passions between women teachers and students.[64] But Rackstraw's relationship with Sidgwick and Fry indicates the need to look beyond the erotic or romantic to more expansive notions of homosocial intimacy and family.

After she returned from Bryn Mawr, Rackstraw took up a role as bursar at University House, to Fry's and Sidgwick's delight. 'I don't think there has ever been a student more heart-whole in the Hostel's cause than you,' Sidgwick wrote to Rackstraw—suggesting her understanding that Rackstraw would as a member of staff help to perpetuate the hall's culture among a new generation.[65] But Rackstraw only spent a little over a year in this position before war broke out. Like other University House residents, she followed Fry's example and joined the Quaker war relief effort. She spent almost ten years supporting refugees in France and then famine victims in Russia, but in 1924 she returned to the UK and to university administration, taking up the position of warden at Masson Hall, the University of Edinburgh's hall of residence for women.

In the immediate postwar years Masson had been the site of heated intergenerational conflict regarding curfews and regulation of cross-gender social contact, over which the previous warden had resigned.[66] At thirty-six, Rackstraw was the hall's youngest warden to date. In addition to her previous experience of university residential life in Birmingham, she brought the broader life experience she had gained in France and Russia. Like Fry twenty years previous, Rackstraw proceeded to revolutionize the role of the warden within the university ecosystem. In her hiring negotiations she secured a higher salary, a promise to hire an assistant warden, and a vote on relevant university committees. Within six months, she developed a new financial plan for the hall that would allow for expansion. She also secured membership for herself in the Federated Superannuation Scheme for Universities, the ten-year-old national pension scheme for university staff—a critical indication of the professionalization of the warden role.[67] She would remain in the position for the next thirteen years. Under her leadership, the proportion of Edinburgh's women students who lived in halls rose from 20 to 27 per cent, though she continually had to urge the university to do more to recognize her expertise in student affairs and grant her a larger role in university-wide decision-making.[68]

---

[64] Vicinus, *Independent Women*, 158, 206–8; Vicinus, 'Distance and Desire: English Boarding-School Friendships', *Signs* 9, no. 4 (Summer 1984): 600–22; Hall, 'Sentimental Follies', 131.

[65] Sidgwick to Rackstraw, 12 July 1912, Coll-705, EUSC; see also Sidgwick to Rackstraw, 13 April 1913, and Fry to Rackstraw, 15 April 1913, Coll-705, EUSC.

[66] Minutes of Masson Hall Committee, 1894–1935, EUA GD58/1, EUSC; see also Dyhouse, *No Distinction of Sex?*, 114–16.

[67] Minutes of Masson Hall Committee, 1894–1935.

[68] Marjorie Rackstraw, 'Report on Women Students', February 1936, Coll-705, EUSC, 23–5.

In a 1936 report on the position of women students at Edinburgh, Rackstraw underscored the importance of residence to women students' welfare. Living on campus, she argued, would prompt students to engage in extracurricular activities that would complement and provide relief from the stress of their studies. And living in a residential community that also included faculty and administrators—especially, she specified, younger ones—would allow women students access to role models who could provide 'sympathy and understanding', 'encouragement', and 'the stimulus of example'.[69] In writing this, Rackstraw may have been drawing on her own experience of the role that Sidgwick and Fry had played in helping her to forge a life path.

University residence had previously been imagined as an option for the affluent. Oxford and Cambridge, with their fully residential models, cost much more than other universities; at civic universities, most less-well-off students lived at home, unable to afford the additional costs of room and board.[70] Even at pre-war University House, the rents had been unaffordable for the average Birmingham student.[71] While scholarships that paid students' tuition fees had become common—by 1930, around half of all British students were receiving some form of financial aid, whether from the Scottish Carnegie Trust, Board of Education scholarships for would-be teachers, local government, or private charitable foundations—outside of Oxford and Cambridge, residence was usually imagined as an optional extra.[72] But Rackstraw perceived that residence had the power to draw into community students who might otherwise be located on opposite sides of intractable social divides. To increase access for lower-income students, Rackstraw campaigned for the university to expand the subsidies it provided to residence halls so that students would not have to cover the full cost of room and board, and she sought to foster a culture of donation among the Masson Hall alumnae network.[73] She also opened up the hall's common rooms to all women students, so that those who could not afford to live at Masson would not necessarily be shut out of the hall's community.[74] For a university administrator of the period, she was unusually cognizant of the obstacles that international students and students of colour faced in participating equally in student social life. She hoped that residence would build social confidence among English language learners, and would prompt

[69] Rackstraw, 'Report on Women Students', 17–18.

[70] Dyhouse, *Students: A Gendered History*, 12.

[71] Anne Logan, 'More than "Bare Walls": The Educational Philosophy of Margery Fry (1874–1958) and Its Impact on University Residential Facilities for Women in the Twentieth Century', *History of Education* 50, no. 3 (2021): 338–58, at 350.

[72] For statistics on financial aid see University Grants Committee, 'Report Including Returns from Universities and University Colleges in Receipt of Treasury Grant Academic Year 1928–1929', 1930, UGC/3/10, TNA.

[73] Masson Association Newsletters, 1931–9, Coll-705, EUSC; 'Masson Hall: Retrospect and Forecast', 1931, Coll-705, EUSC.

[74] Minutes of Masson Hall General Committee, Coll-42/3/1, EUSC; Masson Association Newsletters.

white Scottish students to overcome prejudices and socialize with peers whom they might not otherwise have sought out as friends.[75] For Rackstraw, residence was foundational to making a university a community, fostering students' self-development, and inculcating valuable interpersonal skills that would—as much as any degree course—allow students to become thoughtful members of a democratic society.

Rackstraw preserved in her scrapbook numerous snapshots of daily life at Masson: students lounging outside on blankets reading, sleeping on the roof on summer nights, and arrayed in all kinds of costumes for theatre performances and rag carnivals. But more striking, in some ways, are a set of annual group portraits of the hall's residents, taken in the 1930s. The women appear arranged in rows, but candidly, smiling and laughing with their arms around each other. In every photo, Rackstraw sits at the centre of the crowd: a small middle-aged woman amid a sea of youth. In 1934 (Figure 6.2), a golden retriever sits in the front row, and Rackstraw balances a baby on her knee. It is not clear whose baby it is—perhaps that of the other woman faculty member seated to Rackstraw's left—but baby and dog alike send a powerful message about Masson Hall. Not only an artificial community of young people apart from wider society, or a 'room of one's own' for women students seeking a refuge from family life, Masson was a family home, of which pets, children, and older adults were as much a part as twenty-year-olds.[76] This, as much as a canny attitude to working conditions and institutional politics, was what Rackstraw learned from Fry and Sidgwick and brought with her to Edinburgh. It amounted to a radical claim for what residential collegiate life could be and for the kinds of family and community to which single women living in such environments might be entitled.

While Rackstraw was furthering claims for the distinctive value of residence for women in Edinburgh, though, Fry was putting the ideas about residence she had developed at Somerville and Birmingham into practice on a much wider scale. Having moved to London after Sidgwick's death, Fry became a prominent activist for prison reform, the primary cause that would occupy her for the rest of her life. But the influential role that she played in national higher education policy has often been overlooked. In 1919, Fry became the sole woman member of the University Grants Committee (UGC), a position she held until 1948. Together with her colleagues, she therefore determined the policy direction for the entire national higher education sector.[77]

---

[75] Rackstraw, 'Report on Women Students'.

[76] Photographs, 1930s, EUA GD58/22, EUSC. On the community of Masson Hall between the wars see also Masson Hall Newsletters, EUA GD58/18, EUSC.

[77] On the outsize policy impact of the UGC's members see Christine Helen Shinn, *Paying the Piper: The Development of the University Grants Committee 1919–1946* (London: Falmer Press, 1986), 98.

Figure 6.2 Masson Hall residents, 1934. EUA GD58/22, University of Edinburgh Special Collections. Copyright The University of Edinburgh.

As the woman on the committee, there was an implicit expectation that Fry would take an interest in issues specifically relating to women students, who after the First World War made up 28 per cent of the total undergraduate population. In fact, though, Fry's impact on the UGC was to take issues that had previously been seen as specific to women students and translate them onto a gender-integrated scale.[78] Before the First World War, at non-Oxbridge universities halls of residence had been conceptualized as a solution to a specific need for women students. There was no reason that men students who did not live at home could not simply rent private lodgings, and as *in loco parentis* disciplinary restrictions relaxed, universities did not perceive themselves as responsible for men students' pastoral care beyond their studies. But throughout the interwar period, the UGC insisted that residence for both women and men students was one of the core components of what made a university a university. When new institutions such as Reading, Southampton, and Nottingham were seeking university status in the interwar period, the fact that they had undertaken to build halls was part of how the UGC evaluated their commitment to becoming institutions with national and not just local reach.[79]

---

[78] Logan, 'More than "Bare Walls"', 352.   [79] Shinn, *Paying the Piper*, 97, 125, 159–60.

It was Fry, though, who ensured that the UGC saw in halls not only the capacity to house students, but also the capacity to build a particular understanding of the purpose of university life as inhering in values such as extracurricular intellectual exchange, friendship, student self-governance, and close personal contact between academic staff and students—as much as or more than the discipline-specific content and skills that students might learn in their degrees. She insisted that halls should be purpose-built, that they should include provision for facilities such as common rooms and sports fields, and that they should be run by wardens and also house other academic staff.[80] Throughout the 1920s and 1930s, the UGC's annual reports emphasized these values, in particular commenting on the role that a professional warden could play in setting the right tone for life in a hall. 'The supervision of a fair-sized community of young people, in many respects self-governing, is a difficult and exacting task that calls for rare personal qualities in the Warden, and it is inevitable that the success of the Hall should be largely determined by the selection of the right man or woman to have charge of it,' the committee commented in their 1925 report, a view that they continued to reiterate during the interwar years.[81] Though the committee authored the reports collectively, Fry was the only member to have worked as a warden, and it is not hard to see how her experience at Birmingham may have informed the UGC's policy direction. Indeed, this policy direction went on to have a significant effect upon the higher education sector as a whole. With the benefit of UGC grants, almost every university in Britain erected new purpose-built halls in the interwar period, for men as well as for women.[82] Residence increasingly became a possibility for men students: by 1938, 11.4 per cent of non-Oxbridge men students lived in halls, more than double what the figure had been in 1920.[83]

The UGC's investment in residence therefore arose not only, as previous historians have observed, from the desire of the Oxbridge-educated members of the UGC to make the civic universities conform more closely to the Oxbridge model, but also from the distinct experience that Fry had pioneered at Birmingham of establishing a hall of residence for women at a civic university.[84] In the process of translating this model onto a national scale, however, residence became disconnected from the idea that there was a unique category of person, the university woman, who might require unique personal and professional networks in order

---

[80] Logan, 'More than "Bare Walls"', 354–5.

[81] University Grants Committee, 'Report Including Returns from Universities and University Colleges in Receipt of Treasury Grant Academic Year 1923–1924', UGC/5/27, TNA, 25–6.

[82] See UGC Minutes, UGC/1/1 and UGC/1/2, TNA, for records of grants awarded to colleges and universities for the purpose of building residence halls.

[83] University Grants Committee, 'Returns from Universities and University Colleges in Receipt of Treasury Grant Academic Year 1937–38', UGC/3/19, TNA, 9; University Grants Committee, 'Returns from Universities and University Colleges in Receipt of Treasury Grant 1919–20', UGC/3/1, TNA, 4, 7.

[84] On the influence of the Oxbridge model on UGC policy see Keith Vernon, *Universities and the State in England, 1850–1939* (Abingdon: Routledge, 2004), 193.

to lead a fulfilling life. The residential collegiate community became not an alternative to the nuclear family for a specific group of people who were excluded from its constraints, but a source of intellectual and personal fulfilment from which all students and academics might benefit—and, increasingly, a waystation en route to the nuclear family that most women and men students alike, as well as their teachers, would go on to have.

The Fate of the Single Woman

Indeed, over the course of the interwar period, the world that had made alternative conceptions of family possible for women like Fry, Sidgwick, and Rackstraw was disappearing. As the wardens of Fry's generation entered later middle age, a generation gap began to emerge between them and both their students and younger feminist activists, putting pressure on the idea that the women's hall or college might serve as a refuge for the single woman. As women who lived full-time in gender-segregated halls of residence, wardens remained by definition unmarried—but this was increasingly not the only way for women to make a long-term home in universities. For Fry and her contemporaries, it was an alienating and at times a tragic experience to watch their conception of the possibilities of unmarried life be overtaken by different perspectives.

As we have seen, interwar women students increasingly came to view cross-gender social interaction, heterosexuality, and marriage as part of their aspirations for their time at university. This had direct consequences for the survival of women's colleges and halls as sites of community life. Though it would not be thinkable for women and men students to live in the same building until the 1960s, by the mid-1930s women students tended to reject separate classes, student unions, and extracurricular activities. For example, in 1935, falling student demand contributed to the University of Glasgow's decision to close Queen Margaret College (QMC): retaining it as a hall of residence for women, but ending its social and pastoral functions and transitioning its staff to new roles. In a speech at QMC's closing ceremony in November 1935, the college's sixty-two-year-old warden, Frances Melville, described herself and other women educators of her generation as left behind by a tide of changing opinion that, she argued, it was too soon to unequivocally regard as 'progress'. Echoing the arguments of an earlier generation of women activists who had contested women's formal admission to universities like Glasgow, she worried that a gender-integrated university would lose its ability to safeguard women's distinct educational needs.[85] This

---

[85] Frances H. Melville, 'Presentation Address by Frances Melville on the Occasion of the First Award of the Frances Melville Medal in Philosophy on the Final Closure of the College', November 1935, DC233/2/21/7, GUA.

viewpoint was shared by many of QMC's alumnae, who confessed themselves perplexed by the younger generation of women students who did not perceive that gender segregation would benefit them.[86]

Melville had been warden at QMC since 1909. Her tenure had been progressive: she ended chaperonage requirements, relaxed curfews, and granted the students in her care licence to hold dances, participate in rags, and socialize more freely with men students. For decades, she had crusaded for better educational opportunities for Scottish women, and for allied causes such as suffrage. When the college closed, she retired and moved, alone, to the country, though she continued to work on behalf of women's higher education through involvement with the British Federation of University Women (BFUW). In 1938, she stood unsuccessfully as an independent candidate for the Scottish Universities parliamentary seat. Like the other wardens of her generation, Melville had been an independent-minded professional woman whose commitment to career instead of marriage found expression in her work in higher education and for feminist causes. But the specific life trajectory that she had carved out did not, in her institution at least, survive her.

At the same moment, the conception of academia as the preserve of single women also came into question on a very public national stage. In summer 1932, two women lecturers at the University of Liverpool, Margaret Miller and Jean Wright, married fellow lecturers and announced their intention to remain in their jobs after marriage. While in previous generations there had been a very few women academics who continued with their research after marriage, they were typically only able to do so informally, often working alongside their husbands and publishing under their husbands' names.[87] By the 1930s, many universities had a small handful of married women staff, but it was still sufficiently unusual for a woman academic to retain her job after marriage that no university had thought to introduce a formal marriage bar, unlike other public-sector workplaces such as the civil service, the General Post Office, and the BBC.[88] In direct response

---

[86] 'Special Number of "Pass It On": The Magazine of the Women's Educational Union', Pass It On, November 1935, DC 240/5/8/3, GUA.

[87] For one example, see Mary Paley Marshall: Mary Paley Marshall, What I Remember (Cambridge: Cambridge University Press, 1947); Rita McWilliams-Tullberg, Women at Cambridge: A Men's University–Though of a Mixed Type (London: Victor Gollancz, 1975), 88. For one hypothesis that it was easier for married women academics to continue working on a part-time or casual basis in Oxford and Cambridge than in other universities, see Sutherland, In Search of the New Woman, 36–7. See also Claire G. Jones, 'Women, Science and Professional Identity, c. 1860–1914', in Egginton and Thomas, Precarious Professionals, 63–85.

[88] Helen Glew, Gender, Rhetoric and Regulation: Women's Work in the Civil Service and the London County Council, 1900–55 (Manchester: Manchester University Press, 2016); Kate Murphy, 'A Marriage Bar of Convenience? The BBC and Married Women's Work 1923–39', Twentieth Century British History 25, no. 4 (December 2014): 533–61; Helen McCarthy, Double Lives: A History of Working Motherhood (London: Bloomsbury, 2021). Data collected in 1933 by the Association of University Teachers and the British Federation of University Women showed that no other university in Britain had a marriage bar: D384/1/2/20, LUA.

to Miller's and Wright's announcements, however, the Liverpool University Senate (at the urging of the university's vice-chancellor, H.J.W. Hetherington) instituted a marriage bar. Miller and Wright were informed that their contracts were to come to an end.[89]

Miller, an economist with an expert's understanding of the labour market and with extensive connections within academia, politics, and the feminist movement, led a campaign against the marriage bar that quickly rose to national attention. On a practical level, Miller's household needed her income as well as her husband's: Miller was supporting her aging, unwell mother, and needed to pay for her care. But Miller also pled her case on economic and ideological grounds. She argued that having two highly skilled people in the workforce, doing research of national significance, was better than one; and that employing domestic staff to keep house instead of Miller herself would provide work for other women at a time of high unemployment. She cast her position as in tune with the needs of modern society, and the university's as hopelessly retrograde.[90]

Miller's campaign was perfectly pitched to capture the attention of multiple wings of the feminist movement. Since winning the vote for some women in 1918, the organized feminist movement had been divided. Some feminists continued to advocate for women's formal equality in previously all-male preserves such as the traditional professions, while others campaigned for causes such as family allowances, state-provided childcare, housing reform, and birth control that, they believed, were more urgent for less elite women and better placed to address the nation's most trenchant social inequalities.[91] Miller's campaign to work in a highly skilled occupation while providing materially for her family and managing a household with her husband captured the interests both of feminists who supported women's equal access to the professions and of those who supported women's right to a just and equal family life. The Six Point Group, the equality-feminism campaigning organization, hosted a rally in London on Miller's behalf, with speakers including MP Nancy Astor, suffrage veteran Emmeline Pethick-Lawrence, composer Ethel Smyth conducting the suffrage anthem 'March of the Women', and banners and iconography from the suffrage movement, thereby situating Miller's cause in the tradition of that storied campaign.[92] At the same time, Eleanor Rathbone, by then the MP for the Combined English Universities, who had spent the 1920s on the opposite side of intra-feminist debates from the Six

---

[89] Margaret Miller, 'Statement of events leading to present position', n.d., D384/1/2/11, LUA; 'Council & Senate Report Book 15', 1931–2, S2476, LUA, 383; 'Senate General Purposes Committee, vol. 2', 1932–3, at 16 November 1932, S219, LUA, 61.

[90] Margaret Miller, untitled typescript, December 23, 1932, D384/1/2/1, LUA; letters between Margaret Miller and H.J.W. Hetherington, 20 December 1932, 9 February 1933, 13 February 1933, D384/2/20–24, LUA; Margaret Miller, 'typescript notes of statement by HJ Hetherington', 8 March 1933, D384/1/2/5, LUA.

[91] Pedersen, Eleanor Rathbone, 185–91; see also Delap, Feminist Avant-Garde, 190.

[92] Loose press cuttings re. marriage bar, 1933–5, D384/1/1/3–11, LUA.

Point Group, undertook a deputation to Hetherington and raised Miller's case in Parliament.[93] Miller won the support of her professional association, the Association of University Teachers, and of the BFUW.[94] And public sympathy was on Miller's side: countless journalists and commentators drew a parallel between the Liverpool marriage bar and the new Nazi regime's efforts to remove women from paid employment, appealing to Britain's desire to see itself as a 'civilized' country in favourable contrast to Nazi Germany.[95]

Thanks to the efforts of this campaign, in March 1934 Hetherington recommended that, 'in the face of the organised protest from important sectors of...public opinion', the university council rescind the marriage bar.[96] But it was a pyrrhic victory: Miller's department chair refused to reinstate her, citing his right to manage his own department without university administrative interference. Miller took a job in local government, and six months later, her department hired a man as her replacement.[97] Here, as in so many other cases, the reestablishment of formal equality did not result in real equality of opportunity for women. Yet the Liverpool controversy was exceptional in rallying so many 'important sectors of...public opinion' to a single cause. It indicated an important new direction for feminist campaigning: the eradication of the marriage/career binary that had until then defined the life trajectories of middle-class women. At stake was women's right to personal fulfilment, to be sure, but also the same questions of duty and social purpose that had bedevilled Fry's generation of feminists, reimagined for a new age. In the late nineteenth and early twentieth centuries, feminists had often made common cause with eugenicist activists, arguing for social policies around reproduction and motherhood that would tend towards the 'fittest' people reproducing and the betterment of the 'race'. But highly educated, elite women had sometimes found it difficult to rationalize why they eschewed their responsibility to reproduce in favour of other life paths.[98] Combining marriage and a career offered such women the possibility of contributing to society intellectually, artistically, and administratively, while also contributing biologically.

The organizers of the BFUW campaign on Miller's behalf had written to Margery Fry to ask if she would raise Miller's case to the UGC. Fry was quick to

---

[93] Eleanor Rathbone, letter to HJW Hetherington, 12 December 1932, D384/2/20, LUA; Equal Rights Committee, letter to Margaret Miller, 7 April 1933, D384/2/24, LUA.

[94] Circular letter from the BFUW announcing emergency meeting of the executive committee, 10 January 1933, D384/2/24, LUA; 'Sub-Committee on Employment of Married Women', 1931–4, BFUW, 5BFW/4/20, LSE; 'Resolution Passed at AGM of Liverpool Lecturers' Association', 12 June 1933, D384/2/24, LUA.

[95] Scrapbook of newspaper cuttings about the marriage bar controversy, D384/1, LUA.

[96] H.J.W. Hetherington, 'Memorandum to Special Purposes Committee', 14 March 1934, Council & Senate Report Book 16, S2477, LUA, 384.

[97] 'Statement by Professor Dewsnup upon the Staffing of the Department of Commerce', Council & Senate Report Book 17, 1934–5, S2478, LUA, 16, 334.

[98] Lesley Hall, 'Women, Feminism and Eugenics', in Essays in the History of Eugenics, ed. Robert A. Peel (London: The Galton Institute, 1998), 36–51, at 42; Glew, Gender, Rhetoric and Regulation, 188; Delap, Feminist Avant-Garde, 145–61.

reply that the UGC, as an impartial arm's-length body, could not be seen to take any position that would infringe on universities' independent governance. But she went on to say that she was sympathetic to the Liverpool vice-chancellor's point of view, that she thought the law was on the university's side, that there were 'difficulties' (that she did not enumerate) inherent in 'the employment of a man and wife together in one department of a university', and that she was not inherently opposed to a labour structure in which women circulated through junior, casualized faculty positions before marrying and leaving academia.[99] In the 1930s, Fry, it seems, continued to see professional work as the province of single women, and as incompatible with the competing demands of marriage and family life.

After the Second World War, when she was in her seventies and eighties, Fry became a popular voice on BBC radio and television. While many women worked behind the scenes at the BBC, few women's voices were heard on the airwaves, and so once again Fry occupied an exceptional position in a male-dominated sphere.[100] On the evening of 3 December 1952, Fry gave a talk on the Home Service entitled 'The Single Woman'. Framing herself as speaking 'as a spinster to spinsters', she offered a negative account of life as a single woman, emphasizing experiences of social prejudice and unremitting loneliness whose intensity could only somewhat be leavened by the small compensations of work, friendship, and nieces and nephews. She also commented on the erosion of a special social niche for single women over the previous seventy years, reflecting on how the political, economic, and social gains for women for which so many single women had fought had led to 'a changing pattern of...social life [that] is gradually blurring the boundaries of the special territory of the unmarried women'.[101] Though Fry spoke in general terms, it seems inevitable that when commenting on the social and emotional experience of single womanhood, she was mostly speaking about her personal experience, and about how life had changed over the last several decades specifically for progressive middle-class women of her generation. Looking back from the vantage point of the 1950s—a moment of exceptionally high marriage rates—it seemed that the life path she had entered into when she declined a proposal of marriage in 1902 no longer existed.

In this light, Fry's discussion of marriage and sexuality is especially striking. In her talk, she argued that 'the deepest and most unmanageable of all' difficulties single women faced was '[t]he mere fact of going without mating, physical and mental, of not having the natural satisfaction sought by almost all living

---

[99] Margery Fry, letter to May Campbell, 6 April 1933, BFUW Sub-Committee on Employment of Married Women, 5BFW/4/20, LSE.

[100] Anne Logan, 'Gender, Radio Broadcasting and the Role of the Public Intellectual: The BBC Career of Margery Fry, 1928–1958', *Historical Journal of Film, Radio and Television* 40, no. 2 (April 2020): 389–406.

[101] Margery Fry, 'The Single Woman' (BBC talk MS, 3 December 1952), Margery Fry Papers, Box 41 Folder 3, Somerville.

creatures'. Though she acknowledged that many single women might 'find some relative or friend with whom to make a common life', she framed this as a pale consolation, second-best to the ultimate fulfilment of opposite-sex marriage.[102] Indeed, in a 1956 interview, asked if she had any regrets, she replied, 'Well frankly, I do regret that I never had the life of a married woman with children. I think that's what I really should have preferred doing to anything else but it didn't come my way.'[103] This is in some ways a surprising statement from someone who lived and worked alongside men her whole life, who had several close friendships with men, but whose only known long-term relationship was a thirteen-year domestic partnership with a woman that ended only with that woman's sudden death. Fry's account of her own life evidences how the category of the 'single woman' arose without reference to the concept of sexual orientation—but also how it may, in part, have been the increasing dominance of norms of female heterosexuality that led to the single woman's marginalization and demise. By the 1950s, Fry appeared to view education, work, friendships, relationships, and family not as ends in themselves, as the culture of 1890s Somerville might have urged, but as compensation for the lack of the ultimate form of fulfilment.

Recent literature on spinsters and female homosociality and homoeroticism has challenged and complicated an older (though still oft-invoked) perspective that regarded the spinster as a genealogical ancestor of the lesbian. It is clear that, though episodes of the interwar period such as the *Well of Loneliness* obscenity trial may have contributed to bringing 'the lesbian' into being, they hardly led inexorably to all unmarried women being suspected of scandalous sexual deviance.[104] Rather, as the expression of heterosexuality through marriage came to be seen as a natural and necessary part of women's self-development, it crowded out other ways that a woman might organize her identity, community, and relationships. By 1933, the BFUW was arguing that universities ought to retain married lecturers because they, with their broader life (not least sexual) experience, were better placed than 'quite young women or permanent spinsters' to advise women students about the directions their lives should take.[105] The dominance of the norm of heterosexuality transformed the single woman whose independence had previously allowed her access to a wide variety of life experiences into a 'permanent spinster' who was unqualified to advise the younger generation about the only

---

[102] Fry, 'The Single Woman', 2.

[103] Typescript transcript of interview of Fry on the BBC's Asia Programme, 1956, Margery Fry Papers, Box 41, Folder 4, Somerville.

[104] Hall, '"Sentimental Follies" or "Instruments of Tremendous Uplift"'; Oram, 'Repressed and Thwarted, or Bearer of the New World?'; Doan, *Fashioning Sapphism*; Laura Doan, *Disturbing Practices: History, Sexuality, and Women's Experience of Modern War* (Chicago: University of Chicago Press, 2013); cf. Vicinus, *Independent Women*; Vicinus, *Intimate Friends: Women Who Loved Women, 1778–1928* (Chicago: University of Chicago Press, 2004).

[105] 'Notes on the Marriage Bar', 17 January 1933, BFUW Sub-Committee on the Employment of Married Women, 5BFW/4/20, LSE.

kind of experience that mattered. At the same time, heterosexuality made possible a world that the young Margery Fry could not have imagined, in which marriage and children need not oblige a woman to forsake meaningful work or other kinds of connection.

Dorothy Sayers's 1935 novel *Gaudy Night* uses the plot device of the mystery to dramatize the married/single divide as interwar women graduates experienced it. In the novel, the widow of a lecturer who believes that her husband's academic career was scuppered by a woman PhD examiner vows revenge on the whole class of academic women, whom she equates with a pathological spinsterhood that has led them, unlike her, to neglect their natural role as supporters of husbands. She enacts this revenge by vandalizing, and threatening the fellows and students of, an Oxford women's college: a fictionalized version of Somerville, Sayers's alma mater. After considerable tension between the married and single fellows of the college as they aim to discover the perpetrator of the mysterious vandalism, they vow to put their shared commitment to their profession ahead of their lifestyle differences. The novel has a sympathetic attitude to its single women characters who are married to their work, and offers a way that, through their shared workplace, these women might be able to find common ground with their married colleagues. Yet along the way, the novel is revealing of contemporary prejudices against unmarried women, and of the ease with which the married and the unmarried might come to regard each other with mutual suspicion. It is telling that, in the end, the novel turns out to be not just a mystery, but a marriage plot: its second half traces, in addition to the solution of the mystery, a blossoming romance between its unconventional heroine Harriet Vane and the dashing private detective Lord Peter Wimsey. On the last page, Harriet accepts Peter's proposal. A sequel, *Busman's Honeymoon*, reveals that the characters go on to marry in a conventional Church of England service in which, contra the more liberal form of the marriage service introduced in 1928, Harriet vows to 'obey' her husband.[106]

It is no accident that Sayers's exploration of this theme unfolds within the confines of a fictionalized Somerville. Higher education was at the heart of what it meant for late-nineteenth-century middle-class women to consider 'new', 'independent' life trajectories, imagining a variety of vocations that would afford satisfactions at least as great as marriage and children. Though for Sayers—as for Vera Brittain, Virginia Woolf, and so many other authors then and since—Oxbridge women's colleges epitomized the life of the single woman, single women were in fact to be found in higher education nationwide, and their impact resounded as far afield as Montreal, New York, and Geneva. Yet the brief window in which the educated single woman was a legible and distinct social category ended, in part,

---

[106] Dorothy L. Sayers, *Gaudy Night* (London: Victor Gollancz, 1935); Moulton, *Mutual Admiration Society*, 150–2, 195–6.

because of changes in the higher education sector. From the late nineteenth century, higher education went from being a vocation to being a profession: no longer a lifelong commitment to an institutional community, in which celibacy was sometimes an actual requirement of belonging, it instead became a job for which one earned a salary, its status signified through membership in national professional organizations like the Association of University Teachers, a national pay scale, and a national pension scheme.[107] While the full-time residential component of the warden role meant that wardens remained by definition unmarried, by the 1930s universities like Glasgow were slimming down their dedicated women's pastoral infrastructure, in part in response to declining student demand. As traditional academic careers became more accessible to women, married or not, one's family was not to be found in the college or hall of residence, but rather in the nuclear family to whom the professional academic returned at the end of the work day. To be sure, this meant that, from the mid-1930s, women were increasingly able to combine academic careers with marriage and children. But it foreclosed other possibilities, and it left the single woman invisible and illegible: not normatively married, but not necessarily queer either.

Men academics lived, too, through this realignment of the gender and sexual order and its relationship to the purpose of university life. But because men never faced a social prohibition on combining marriage and career, and because there was no viable progressive, gender-equality-driven case to be made for the preservation of gender-segregated higher education for men, the fate of single academic men unfolded on different lines. Unlike in the case of women, the men's gender-segregated collegiate community remained a formation confined to Oxford and Cambridge, and arguments for its continued importance in the age of gender integration never escaped reactionary and misogynistic connotations. As in the case of women, for men the increasing salience and visibility of the hetero/homo binary edged out a conception of the bachelor that did not merely equate bachelordom with queerness. But if in the case of the women's hall or college, the result was simply to render less visible and more marginalized alternative life trajectories to marriage, the men's college had a rather different response—becoming an important, and hitherto overlooked, site for the theorization of male homosexual identity.

Teaching Gender: The British University and the Rise of Heterosexuality, 1860–1939. Samuel Rutherford, Oxford University Press. © Samuel Rutherford 2025. DOI: 10.1093/9780198937524.003.0007

---

[107] For one influential—though masculine and Oxbridge-centric—account of this transformation, see A.J. Engel, *From Clergyman to Don: The Rise of the Academic Profession in Nineteenth-Century Oxford* (Oxford: Clarendon, 1983).

7

The Higher Sodomy

By the time Oxford admitted women to degrees in 1920, the residential men's college was anomalous and increasingly outmoded, despite the centuries-old endowments and disproportionate cultural cachet that many of the constituent colleges of Oxford and Cambridge enjoyed. Through internal institutional reforms and state intervention, these two idiosyncratic universities increasingly became incorporated into the national higher education system, in which they increasingly engaged *as universities* rather than as federations of colleges. Still, although making a case for the distinctive value of the residential men's college increasingly came to seem a lost cause, to some men in the early twentieth century this type of institution continued to offer an alternative vision of the kinds of knowledge, affect, and community that higher education might engender.

Like women's colleges, men's colleges saw it as their role not only to teach students academic subjects, but to acculturate them into behavioural norms that would lead to them exercising responsible roles as respectable middle-class adults. As colleges abolished longstanding celibacy requirements for fellows in the 1870s and 1880s, the married college fellow and tutor became a new masculine ideal whom students might emulate, for whom the homosocial environment of college and the heterosocial environment of married life might exist in symbiosis. But unlike in the case of women's colleges, this turn to marriage did not occlude a longstanding alternative culture that saw the gender-segregated residential college as a site for the making of meaning about desire and intimacy between men. As non-residential, gender-integrated education became more normative in UK higher education more widely, most men Oxford and Cambridge students sought to engage in heterosexuality and commercial youth leisure culture just as eagerly as their counterparts at urban non-residential universities. But for a minority—students, but also, critically, faculty who made long-term homes in men's colleges—homoerotic intimacy emerged as a new justification for what made the men's college exceptional and worth preserving in the face of the gender integration and ascendant heteronormativity of higher education and of British society more widely. Academics mounted not only negative claims against the admission of women, but positive claims for the distinctive value of the masculine residential educational community of the men's college.

The unique institutional structure of Oxford and Cambridge, and their constituent colleges' historic wealth and prestige, allowed some men to make this case successfully in a way that defenders of women's colleges could not. The men's college could remain not only a refuge from the demands of gender integration and heteronormativity, but, as new ideas about sexual orientation and identity coalesced, increasingly an imagined site of sexual possibility: for 'the higher sodomy', as one set of friends in a Cambridge men's college put it.[1] Moreover, this led to the formulation of newly self-conscious conceptions of *homosexual* identity and community, positioned in explicit opposition to heterosexuality and gender-integrated sociability. The homoerotic subcultures of the men's colleges might not exist only as a forerunner in the life cycle to, or in symbiotic relationship with, married life, but rather as an explicit, mutually exclusive alternative to gender integration and heterosexuality.

In theory, then, the men's college offered radical possibilities: for alternative configurations of sex, sexuality, subjectivity, and the life cycle; for queer formations of home, domesticity, family, and community. But in practice, homoerotic and homosexual defences of the men's college took shape in the context of reaction against the perceived political and social instability of the immediate post-First World War years, entwined with anxieties about democracy, the expansion of the state, the erosion of existing elite privileges, social degeneration, and especially women's social and political gains. The desire to defend the exceptionality of masculine intimacy within the space of the college and as part of the purpose of gender-segregated residential collegiate education was a reaction against the wider gender integration of bourgeois life. This insight can offer greater understanding of at least one aspect of how the hetero/homo binary emerged as the primary paradigm through which middle-class people understood sexuality in modern Britain.[2] Rather than homosexuality first taking shape as an expert medico-legal discourse against which the previously unmarked normal of heterosexuality was subsequently defined, the two paradigms emerged in tandem, each in its own way an unsatisfying norm that crowded out other possibilities for gender and sexuality, intimacy and relationality, community and politics.

But it can also offer one way of understanding the relationship of the exceptional institutions of Oxford and Cambridge to UK higher education as a whole. These two universities were unusual: they had byzantine and idiosyncratic

---

[1]   J.M. Keynes, 'Shall we write filth-packets?', 1903, JMK/UA/19/1, KCC.

[2]   For canonical literature on the invention of the concept of 'homosexuality' in Britain see Jeffrey Weeks, *Coming Out: Homosexual Politics in Britain, from the Nineteenth Century to the Present* (London: Quartet Books, 1977); Jeffrey Weeks, *Sex, Politics and Society: The Regulation of Sexuality since 1800* (London: Longman, 1981); Richard Dellamora, *Masculine Desire: The Sexual Politics of Victorian Aestheticism* (Chapel Hill: UNC Press, 1990); Alan Sinfield, *The Wilde Century: Effeminacy, Oscar Wilde and the Queer Moment* (London: Cassell, 1994); H.G. Cocks, *Nameless Offences: Homosexual Desire in the Nineteenth Century* (London: I.B. Tauris, 2003); Matt Cook, *London and the Culture of Homosexuality, 1885–1914* (Cambridge: Cambridge University Press, 2003); Morris Kaplan, *Sodom on the Thames: Sex, Love, and Scandal in Wilde Times* (Ithaca: Cornell University Press, 2005); Matt Houlbrook, *Queer London: Perils and Pleasures in the Sexual Metropolis, 1918–1957* (Chicago: University of Chicago Press, 2005); Brian Lewis, ed., *British Queer History: New Approaches and Perspectives* (Manchester: Manchester University Press, 2013).

institutional structures that allowed them to resist wider sectoral change, a student body that skewed more affluent than average, and an outsize cultural role in the replication of a national elite. Above all, they uniquely understood residence as definitional of what made a university a university. At the same time, they did not exist in a vacuum, and both women and men students and faculty in Oxford and Cambridge shaped and were shaped by the same changing gender and sexuality norms as students and faculty elsewhere in the country. Previous historians have called attention to the misogyny of Oxford and Cambridge men around conflicts over women's degrees.[3] But in many respects, Oxford and Cambridge students followed the same patterns of gendered politics and sociability that students around the country did: participating in a misogynistic backlash against women students in the 1920s, but otherwise part of a wider middle-class culture of cross-gender sociability that centred on dating and reaffirmed gender difference. What *was* exceptional in the gender order of these two universities, however, was the fertile ground that the space of the gender-segregated men's residential college offered for new conceptions of middle-class male homosexual identity and community to emerge as they did at no other British university—with lasting impact on the gender and sexuality order of twentieth-century Britain.

Marriage and the Regulation of Sexuality

In the second half of the nineteenth century, Oxford and Cambridge underwent a period of substantial and consequential reform. Through the rationalization of college and university governance, the loosening of ties to the established Church, and the raising of academic standards, the universities' constituent colleges went from cloistered clerical communities to outward-facing institutions dedicated to preparing students to excel in competitive examinations and in high-profile careers beyond the university in a variety of fields.[4] One element of these reforms that proved especially consequential for gender and sexuality was the end of requirements that college fellows be celibate. In both universities, the desire to raise academic standards and invest more in undergraduate teaching led to a

---

[3] Paul R. Deslandes, *Oxbridge Men: British Masculinity and the Undergraduate Experience* (Bloomington: Indiana University Press, 2005), 154–83; Rita McWilliams-Tullberg, *Women at Cambridge: A Men's University—Though of a Mixed Type* (London: Victor Gollancz, 1975); Carol Dyhouse, *Students: A Gendered History* (London: Routledge, 2006), 123–6.

[4] A.J. Engel, *From Clergyman to Don: The Rise of the Academic Profession in Nineteenth-Century Oxford* (Oxford: Clarendon, 1983); Sheldon Rothblatt, *The Revolution of the Dons: Cambridge and Society in Victorian England* (Cambridge: Cambridge University Press, 1968); M.C. Curthoys, 'The Colleges in the New Era', in *The History of the University of Oxford*, Volume 7: *Nineteenth-Century Oxford, Part 2*, ed. M.G. Brock and M.C. Curthoys (Oxford: Oxford University Press, 2000) (hereafter *HUO* 7), 115–58; Janet Howarth, 'The Self-Governing University, 1882–1914', in *HUO* 7, 598–643.

greater emphasis on recruiting and retaining faculty who were committed to this project—but this was difficult to do if most faculty were barred from marriage. From the 1860s, colleges began on a case-by-case basis to revise their statutes to abolish celibacy requirements, and to raise and standardize salaries to make it possible for fellows to support families.[5] Colleges were not only able to retain committed and popular teachers who wanted to marry; they also hired new, already married faculty from secondary schools and other universities. This generation of married faculty, alongside their wives and children, transformed the character of middle-class life in the two university towns: they developed new residential neighbourhoods, founded schools for their children and community and voluntary associations, and contributed to mounting pressure for new educational opportunities for the girls and women in their own families.[6]

Some of this new generation of married faculty had started their careers teaching in elite boys' 'public' boarding schools. They brought to the Oxford and Cambridge colleges expertise in and commitment to a distinctive pedagogical philosophy characteristic of the mid-nineteenth-century 'reformed' public school. This centred on the importance of residential educational community as a vehicle for cultivating moral sensibility and 'character' beyond the immediate confines of the classroom.[7] Drawing on the model of the school boarding house, in which schoolboys lived in an approximation of a family home run by a 'housemaster' (often with the aid of his wife, sister, or another female relative, alongside numerous domestic servants), colleges made their domestic arrangements more cloistered and familial. In the mid-nineteenth century, colleges increasingly required students to live in college accommodation, and provided furniture, catering, and cleaning in-house. They assumed an *in loco parentis* disciplinary role: instead of writing to the parents of unruly students to outsource discipline, they instituted their own systems of fines, curfews, and other sanctions, and cracked down assiduously on drinking, vandalism, prostitution, and gambling. They promoted organized extracurricular activities as a distraction from what they saw as more immoral student pastimes. Fellows lived in or near colleges and took an active role in new activities such as sports, debate, and drama, with meetings often

---

[5] Engel, *From Clergyman to Don*, 106–8; Rothblatt, *The Revolution of the Dons*, 227; B. Duckenfield, 'Changes to the Celibacy Rule at the Colleges of Oxford and Cambridge Universities' (PhD thesis, Kingston University, 2008), 192.

[6] Christopher Harvie, 'From the Cleveland Commission to the Statutes of 1882', in *HUO* 7, 67–96; Janet Howarth, '"In Oxford but…Not of Oxford": The Women's Colleges', in *HUO* 7, 237–308; Howarth, 'The Self-Governing University'; Rothblatt, *Revolution of the Dons*, 242; William Whyte, 'The Intellectual Aristocracy Revisited', *Journal of Victorian Culture* 10, no. 1 (2005): 15–45.

[7] David Newsome, *Godliness and Good Learning: Four Studies on a Victorian Ideal* (London: Cassell, 1988); J.R. de S. Honey, *Tom Brown's Universe: The Development of the Public School in the 19th Century* (London: Millington, 1977); T.W. Bamford, *Thomas Arnold on Education* (Cambridge: Cambridge University Press, 1970).

happening late in the evening.[8] When coupled with the simultaneous institution-alization of the tutorial system—a new style of instruction that drew on a Socratic model to imagine an intimate, one-on-one intellectual relationship between the student and his tutor—this amounted to a new conception of the relationships between teachers and students in residential educational community.[9]

Much of this top-down reordering of student—and town—life was intended to regulate undergraduates' contact with townspeople, especially working-class townswomen seen as socially inappropriate objects for middle-class students' sexual desire. Though expectations for student behaviour were similar to those at non-residential universities in the mid-nineteenth century, residence allowed Oxford and Cambridge directly to control students' behaviour to a much greater extent. University officials and private university police forces enforced curfews, banned students from visiting locations such as pubs and theatres, and surveilled students' interactions with women.[10] They also heavily policed the movement in public of working-class townswomen, in a punitive system that perceived any woman alone in public after dark as a potential prostitute liable to tempt under-graduates into sexual liaisons.[11] With curfews confining students to their colleges after 9 p.m. in Oxford and 10 p.m. in Cambridge, and 'gating' a common punish-ment for undergraduate misdemeanours, the college necessarily evolved as a dis-tinct, socially homogeneous space set physically apart from the city. Although students often sought to rebel against these forms of discipline, they also invested their energies in the social and emotional life of the college.

Like the founders of women's colleges, those who in the nineteenth century defended the intimacy of men's colleges sought to characterize them as sites for the cultivation of close, emotionally satisfying friendships as well as moral instruction.[12] But unlike women's colleges, men's colleges did not imagine college family and biological family as distinct or mutually exclusive. Historians have often contrasted the late-Victorian middle-class family home with homosocial institutions like the boarding house, college, gentlemen's club, or officers' mess, arguing that the latter offered middle-class men a 'flight from domesticity'. Homosocial institutions were where elite adult men sought refuge from the

[8] Curthoys, 'Colleges in the New Era'; Patrick Joyce, *The State of Freedom: A Social History of the British State since 1800* (Cambridge: Cambridge University Press, 2013), 240–50; Rothblatt, *Revolution of the Dons*, 227.

[9] Richard Jenkyns and Oswyn Murray, 'The Beginnings of Greats, 1800–1872', in *The History of the University of Oxford*, Volume 6: *The Nineteenth Century, Part 1*, ed. M.G. Brock and M.C. Curthoys (Oxford: Clarendon Press, 1997), 513–42; Linda Dowling, *Hellenism and Homosexuality in Victorian Oxford* (Ithaca: Cornell University Press, 1994), 35, 41.

[10] Deslandes, *Oxbridge Men*, 95–116.

[11] A.J. Engel, '"Immoral Intentions": The University of Oxford and the Problem of Prostitution, 1827–1914', *Victorian Studies* 23, no. 1 (autumn 1979): 79–107; Philip Howell, 'A Private Contagious Diseases Act: Prostitution and Public Space in Victorian Cambridge', *Journal of Historical Geography* 26, no. 3 (July 2000): 376–402.

[12] Dowling, *Hellenism and Homosexuality*, 40.

emotional demands and social pressures of family life, or alternatively where young boys were brutally disciplined out of attachment to the feminizing, maternal influence of home.[13] Yet, as violent as schoolboy hazing rituals and regimes of power were, it is more plausible to think of marriage and family life as functioning in symbiotic relationship to the homosocial environment of the men's college, both for college fellows and for the students who lived in the communities that the fellows created. Although by 1886 only 30 per cent of college fellows were married, a somewhat higher proportion of those fellows engaged actively in undergraduate teaching were, and this was a significant enough number to enact a cultural shift in colleges and in the towns surrounding them.[14] Married faculty commuted daily between their homes and their workplaces. They participated in undergraduate extracurricular activities, but also invited their students to their family homes, acculturating young men into adult bourgeois gender-integrated sociability as well as into masculine homosocial community. They implied by their own lifestyles that the formation of 'good character' that an elite education was supposed to provide necessitated enthusiastic, complementary investment both in homosocial institutions and in the nuclear family.[15]

Married fellows thereby possessed a distinct advantage for colleges: they had the relevant life experience to induct their students into the next stage of the middle-class life cycle, when the boarding school and college would give way to married life. However, even as married fellows became increasingly normal and desirable in college life, a significant minority of Oxford and Cambridge academics and administrators resisted the idea. Some worried that married men would, under the financial pressure of having to support their families, take on excessive quantities of casual teaching, distracting from their research productivity and thus from colleges' intellectual atmosphere. Others thought the best way to create an intimate college community was for most fellows to be 'young, vigorous, and enthusiastic', and that celibacy requirements could ensure that fellows would circulate out of the college as they aged and desired to marry. Still others thought that fellows who resided in college could help to maintain discipline. Some colleges sought to address these concerns by building accommodation for married fellows and their families. But more instituted quotas on numbers of married fellows and created new fixed-term fellowships intended for young, single men.[16] Even as colleges saw the relaxation of celibacy requirements as key to recruiting talented faculty, and perceived the social benefits of married faculty to the college

[13] John Tosh, *A Man's Place: Masculinity and the Middle-Class Home in Victorian England* (New Haven: Yale University Press, 2007), 170–94; Amy Milne-Smith, 'A Flight to Domesticity? Making a Home in the Gentlemen's Clubs of London, 1880–1914', *Journal of British Studies* 45, no. 4 (October 2006): 796–818; Joyce, *State of Freedom*, 290.

[14] Duckinfield, 'Changes to the Celibacy Rule', 233–5.

[15] Samuel Rutherford, 'Arthur Sidgwick's *Greek Prose Composition*: Gender, Affect, and Sociability in the Late-Victorian University', *Journal of British Studies* 56, no. 1 (January 2017): 91–116.

[16] Engel, *From Clergyman to Don*, 108, 160–1.

community, they also imagined that bachelors could play an important role in the college ecosystem.

Indeed, the fact that the colleges provided for a critical mass of bachelors could create the conditions for homoerotic subcultures to flourish. As in other homosocial institutions like schools, prisons, and the military, both sex between men and sexual abuse had been commonplace features of Oxford and Cambridge colleges stretching back to the Middle Ages.[17] Some heads of schools and colleges dedicated themselves to rigorously ferreting out lax morals, but others pursued policies of tacit acceptance—or participated in this culture themselves. While most who engaged in sex within homosocial institutions in the nineteenth century would likely not have understood this to mark them out as a particular kind of person, a minority drew on the resources of their classical educations to make meaning of and give sanction to homoerotic desire and sex. In nineteenth-century Oxford, where Plato was foundational to the curriculum that nearly all undergraduates studied, some men drew on a Platonic framework that idealized 'pederasty', an older man's desire for and appreciation of the beauty of a younger man or adolescent boy. The ideal of pederasty that Plato's character Socrates expressed emphasized abstracted, distanced admiration of beauty, and the pedagogical and morally improving content of pederastic relationships, over physical consummation. Some men who were drawn to this framework as offering a 'higher', 'nobler' model of homoerotic desire called themselves 'Uranians': a word they took from Plato's *Symposium*, in which the character Pausanias described pederastic eros as more *ouranios*, 'celestial', than mere carnal desire for either men or women. They often wrote poetry that gave expression to this idealized form of desire.[18]

Artistically, and sometimes politically, conservative, this subculture was small and strongly associated with the institutional contexts of Oxford and Cambridge. Though some who participated in it also had ties to an urban culture of queer sex and nightlife—most famously, Oscar Wilde and Alfred Douglas—many were academics who remained immersed in their local institutional context. Their pederastic model was distinct from later conceptions of sexual orientation and homosexuality. To a large extent, colleges tolerated fellows who cultivated Uranian social circles and wrote about Uranian love. Yet periodically, scandals, both real and imputed, made their way into the London press, linking 'The Greek

[17] Alan Stewart, *Close Readers: Humanism and Sodomy in Early Modern England* (Princeton: Princeton University Press, 1997); George Rousseau, *Children and Sexuality: From the Greeks to the Great War* (London: Palgrave Macmillan, 2007), Chs. 5–6.

[18] Dowling, *Hellenism and Homosexuality*; Jennifer Ingleheart, *Masculine Plural: Queer Classics, Sex, and Education* (Oxford: Oxford University Press, 2018); Daniel Orrells, *Classical Culture and Modern Masculinity* (Oxford: Oxford University Press, 2011); Samuel Rutherford, 'Impossible Love and Victorian Values: J. A. Symonds and the Intellectual History of Homosexuality', *Journal of the History of Ideas* 75, no. 4 (2014): 605–27.

Spirit in Modern Literature' to sexual immorality.[19] Both commentators who condemned all sex between men and those who sought to distinguish morally blame-
less forms of homosexuality from sexual abuse worried about the risk of sexual
assault on younger men and boys within educational institutions.[20] In this context, some might have welcomed the abolition of celibacy requirements as tending towards an environment in the colleges in which marriage was normal and
desirable. The married tutor had a cast of respectability that his bachelor counterpart did not, both when it came to men students and when it came to the women
students who, from the 1870s, became a small but visible presence in the two university cities.

Yet as the increasing presence of women in Oxford and Cambridge put the
admission of women to degrees on the table, and as other universities around the
country admitted women, the significance of the gender order of the men's college changed. In the face of the gender integration of wider middle-class society, it
became harder to claim that a gender-segregated college would inculcate the
appropriate masculinity to prepare young men for married life. Instead, the
homoerotic subcultures that had long existed within the two universities would
gain new salience as the site of a countercultural opposition to gender integration.
As the political fights around the gender integration of Oxford and Cambridge
became more polarized, those who defended the value of men's colleges in homoerotic terms increasingly came to oppose this vision explicitly to one that privileged heterosexuality.

The Politics of Backlash and Reaction

To understand how the residential college became the site for a new conceptualization of male homosexuality, it is necessary to understand how, at the turn of
the twentieth century, Oxford and Cambridge politics became focused around
two questions—whether women would be admitted to degrees and whether classical languages would remain at the centre of the undergraduate curriculum—
and how a reactionary politics formed in response to both issues. In spring 1895,
activists at Oxford and Cambridge introduced coordinated campaigns in favour
of women's admission to the BA degree: collecting signatures on petitions, circu-
lating campaign literature, and otherwise preparing for votes on the question in
Oxford's Congregation and Cambridge's Senate. At this point, multiple women's
colleges existed in both cities, and most women students studied the same courses

---

[19] Richard St John Tyrwhitt, 'The Greek Spirit in Modern Literature', *Contemporary Review* 29
(March 1877), 552–6.
[20] Jana Funke, '"We Cannot Be Greek Now": Age Difference, Corruption of Youth and the Making
of Sexual Inversion', *English Studies* 94, no. 2 (April 2013): 139–53.

and sat the same exams as men. It was becoming clear nationally that the integration of women into higher education was inevitable.

But unlike at other universities, in Oxford and Cambridge academics formed coordinated campaigns against women's degrees.[21] Like ex-servicemen undergraduates after the First World War, these academics argued that there was something exceptional, and worth safeguarding, about the kinds of masculine community possible only in universities. But they differed from these later, younger reactionaries in the conscious political strategizing that they brought to their arguments, in the particular kinds of masculine intimacy that they sought to protect, and in the exceptional role that they accorded to Oxford and Cambridge's residential colleges in their vision of ideal university life. Their campaigns were careful to state that they supported women's access to higher education generally, women's pursuit of degrees at the several other universities in the UK now open to them, and the idea that Oxford and Cambridge might assume some role in women's education, such as through setting standards for and administering school-leaving exams for girls.[22] But they treated the two universities and their constituent colleges as exceptional institutions whose exceptionality hinged on them remaining men-only.

In Cambridge in particular, rhetoric highlighted the residential college as a uniquely valuable aspect of the university that could only be preserved through continued gender segregation. The chair of the Cambridge anti-women's degrees campaign, provost of King's College Augustus Austen Leigh, grounded his arguments against women's degrees in his experience as the head of a college that had recently undergone a period of reform and cultural change. Previously an extension of the fifteenth-century royal foundation of the secondary school Eton College, King's fellowships had until the 1850s been sinecures for Old Etonians, and King's students had not been required to take exams or degrees. Austen Leigh played a leading role in transforming King's into an educational institution in its own right, which he believed necessitated building a community founded on close association between teachers and students. One of his first acts at King's was to buy a piano, around which he proposed to unite Etonians and non-Etonians, students with scholarships and those without, Anglicans and Nonconformists.[23] Austen Leigh believed that this kind of college community was distinctive to Oxford and Cambridge. Unlike in other universities, in Oxford and Cambridge, awarding a student a BA did not only signify that he had passed a set of exams, it certified that he had kept three years' residence in a college, learning good character and self-reliance through the negotiation of community life. The women's

---

[21] Howarth, 'In Oxford but…Not of Oxford', 256–68; McWilliams-Tullberg, *Women at Cambridge*, 99–101.

[22] See e.g. 'Circular announcing a meeting, on 22 Feb. 1896, of Members of the Senate who are opposed to granting Cambridge Degrees to women', GCPP/Davies/13/2/9/8, Girton.

[23] Rothblatt, *Revolution of the Dons*, 221–4.

colleges, he asserted, were only 'a very faint copy' of the opportunities for personal development available at a college like King's.[24] For Austen Leigh, then, institutional reform and anti-coeducation sentiment were two sides of the same coin: the very flourishing of reformed institutions like King's meant that women could not compete with these institutions' excellence, and might divert attention away from the good work they were trying to do for clever young men.

One of the Cambridge anti campaign's most committed and vocal activists, the economist Alfred Marshall, highlighted his extensive experience with women's higher education as evidence for why Cambridge should remain closed to women. One of the first Cambridge academics to teach women students, he had married a former student, Mary Paley, a talented economist in her own right, with whom he collaborated on research. The Marshalls both taught at University College Bristol, the first higher-education institution in Britain to be founded as coeducational, before returning to Cambridge in 1883. At Bristol, Marshall encountered students with a wider range of backgrounds and abilities than at Cambridge. He came to feel that his wife was an extremely rare exception to a general rule that women were not capable of undertaking the same level of further study as men, and that the average woman was more likely to benefit from a non-residential, part-time course like those offered at Bristol, which would allow her to work at her own pace and balance her studies with her domestic responsibilities. Admitting women to Cambridge degrees would be both bad for women—they could not pursue the courses of study best suited for them and their social roles—and bad for society, which rested on achieving a balance between men's and women's distinct qualities.[25]

But Marshall's arguments against women's admission to Cambridge were also entwined with positive claims about gender-segregated education for men. In an 1897 speech in the university senate, he articulated a relationship between the particularity of the college system and the value of gender segregation:

> The essence of our system lies in the fact that our social life is carried on in our lecture-rooms as well as outside it [*sic*]. The lecturer is not a mere preacher to a congregation; he is a senior student working with and helping junior students. For these and for other reasons the presence of a large number of women is a greater disturbance to our system than to that the seven other teaching

[24] Augustus Austen-Leigh, 'The Question of Granting Degrees to Women', 4 June 1896, GCPP/Davies/13/2/9/13, Girton.

[25] McWilliams-Tullberg, *Women at Cambridge*, 88; Georgia Oman, *Higher Education and the Gendering of Space in England and Wales, 1869–1909* (Basingstoke: Palgrave Macmillan, 2023), 66–9; John Maynard Keynes, 'Memorial of Alfred Marshall', in *Memorials of Alfred Marshall*, ed. A.C. Pigou (London: Macmillan, 1925); John K. Whitaker, ed., *The Correspondence of Alfred Marshall, Economist*, Volume 1: *Climbing, 1868–1890* (Cambridge: Cambridge University Press, 1996); Rita McWilliams-Tullberg, 'Marshall's Contribution to the Women's Higher Education Movement', in *Alfred Marshall's Lectures to Women*, ed. Tiziano Raffaelli, Eugenio F. Biagini, and Rita McWilliams-Tullberg (Aldershot: Edward Elgar, 1995), 47–75.

Universities [in the UK]...Now we have to balance the gain to them [women] of an increase in their numbers here against the loss to us.[26]

Like Austen Leigh, then, Marshall held that gender integration—even if only to the extent of having separate but fully equal men's and women's colleges in the same university—was incompatible with the unique features that made the Cambridge system best for its men students. The arguments that Marshall made in his pages-long campaign circulars played an important role in swaying opinion overwhelmingly against women's degrees in the eventual senate vote in May 1897.[27]

In both Oxford and Cambridge, supporters of women's degrees would not attempt to make their case again until after the First World War. But in the inter-vening years, the question of women's inclusion in both universities became entwined with a wider set of questions about university reform and moderniza-tion, and this in turn had changing significance within the rapidly shifting terrain of national politics in the years before, during, and after the First World War. Amidst fears about mass democracy, the rise of Labour, and the political and social instability of the immediate postwar period, both Conservatives and more old-fashioned Liberals reacted with a sense of intensifying moral panic about the disintegration of the social order, and with suspicion of the expanding state. Some members of the liberal intelligentsia criticized the rise of mass politics and mass culture, advocating cultural hierarchies and forms of critical discernment that were entwined with surprise and fear about Britain's transformation into a mass democracy.[28] Within Oxford and Cambridge, these political views were well rep-resented, and academics and intellectuals who held them found in the men's col-lege a site of resistance to state intervention, modernization, and the degrading effects of mass culture. Though this group can broadly be understood as con-servatives or reactionaries, they also formed unexpected alliances that traversed traditional political divides, as they took different routes to seizing upon the men's college as an exceptional site of intimate community.

This was particularly the case with one issue that loomed as large in Oxbridge politics as it seemed disconnected from the world outside it: 'compulsory Greek', the premise that all undergraduates, regardless of their degree subject, be required to pass an exam in elementary Greek language (as well as Latin, scripture, and, at Cambridge, mathematics) in order to proceed past the first year of their course. As the two universities sought to open up to a wider range of students, it became

---

[26] 'Discussion of the Report of the Degrees for Women Syndicate', *Cambridge University Reporter*, 26 March 1897, 793.

[27] Keynes, 'Memorial of Alfred Marshall', 55.

[28] D.L. LeMahieu, *A Culture for Democracy: Mass Communication and the Cultivated Mind in Britain between the Wars* (Oxford: Clarendon Press, 1988), Ch. 3; Ross McKibbin, *Classes and Cultures: England 1918–1951* (Oxford: Oxford University Press, 1998), 69; Stuart Middleton, 'The Crisis of Democracy in Interwar Britain', *The Historical Journal* 66, no. 1 (February 2023): 186–209.

apparent that men who had attended less prestigious schools, men from overseas, and women (whose gender-differentiated secondary curriculum tended to emphasize modern languages) lacked the necessary preparation to clear this initial hurdle. Academics debated proposals to relax the requirement for students in science subjects, to allow students to substitute a modern language or a classical non-western language, or to drop the requirement altogether. But when these proposals were debated—in Cambridge in 1905 and in Oxford in 1911—they attracted vociferous opposition. Most of this came from the characteristically conservative constituency of non-resident alumni who continued to have a vote in university governance. But some prominent liberal academics, too, expressed vocal support for compulsory Greek, seeing it as a check against a narrowly utilitarian trend in education and as an opportunity to prompt students to encounter great works of literature and important philosophical questions. The politics of compulsory Greek, then, indicated a disjuncture between the two universities and the democratizing nation beyond, as much as a straightforward liberal/conservative political divide. Compulsory Greek was a key issue on which many Oxford and Cambridge academics hoped to preserve their institutional autonomy against the threatened incursions of the state. Moreover, it was a classed, racialized, and gendered question. It implied a connection between the Greek language specifically and the kind of person that Oxford and Cambridge, in contrast to other universities, were for.[29]

No one better exemplifies how compulsory Greek became a political flashpoint—and one with gendered significance—than Thomas Case, an Oxford philosophy professor and, from 1904, president of Corpus Christi College. Intellectually and in institutional politics, Case was a committed conservative.[30] He dedicated himself to opposing institutional change on a host of fronts, including the admission of women and the abolition of compulsory Greek, issues that he saw as intertwined. In numerous public statements on the women's degrees question, he argued that there was something ineffably special about a society of men who resided together in a collegiate environment, and who shared a body of knowledge and cast of mind grounded in the ancient languages. This would be eroded if the university were to admit women to degrees, and doing so would raise untold logistical problems—perhaps even real scandal—about what kinds of subjects men and women would study together and what kinds of spaces they might share. However, he did support a proposal that would have allowed the university to grant a non-degree diploma to certify women students not resident

[29] Christopher Stray, *Classics Transformed: Schools, Universities, and Society in England, 1830–1960* (Oxford: Oxford University Press, 1998), 165–6; Rothblatt, *Revolution of the Dons*, 254; Howarth, 'Self Governing University', 630–1; Rutherford, 'Sidgwick's *Greek Prose Composition*', 110–12.

[30] Sandra M. den Otter, *British Idealism and Social Explanation: A Study in Late-Victorian Thought* (Oxford: Clarendon Press, 1996), 206; G. B. Grundy, *Fifty-Five Years at Oxford: An Unconventional Autobiography* (London: Methuen, 1945), 110.

in Oxford had passed certain university examinations. This indicates how centrally residence loomed in his classically inspired vision of the value and purpose of an Oxford degree for men.[31]

After he became president of Corpus, Case dedicated himself to the cause of compulsory Greek. He chaired the Committee for the Preservation of Greek from 1904 until its ultimate defeat in 1920: hosting meetings in the Corpus president's lodgings, funding its administrative costs, and representing the campaign in the press even as it came increasingly to be seen as out of touch and its initial supporters abandoned it in favour of compromise proposals.[32] To Case, Greek was worth defending because it was the cornerstone of high culture and liberal education. While new universities were free to scrap classical languages if they chose, Oxford and Cambridge were exceptional centres of learning, where the work of scientists and humanists alike would be enriched by a common foundation of Latin and Greek.[33]

Case was a controversial college head among his colleagues, infamous for the doggedness and the eccentricity of his views.[34] But his worldview, and his desire to see it reflected in the college that he ran for twenty years, does indicate how the men's college could use its endowments and its institutional autonomy to maintain its identity as a masculine and a classicizing space against the incursions of modernity. Although decades of steady, moderate campaigning, coupled with recognition of the social transformations wrought by the First World War, led Oxford both to abolish compulsory Greek and to admit women in 1920, the attenuated relationship between the colleges and the central university meant that a college head like Case could leverage collegiate autonomy to resist change. He pursued this aim through a successful fundraising programme, born out of a desire to make the college financially self-sufficient and thus able to insulate itself from demands that might be placed on it either by the university or by the state.[35]

An opportunity for Case to solidify his commitment to gender segregation and the classics came in 1907: a year into the new reformist Liberal government, when external calls for a government inquiry into the governance and finances of Oxford and Cambridge were at their height. Case received an inquiry from Edward Perry Warren, an independently wealthy American art dealer and longtime acquaintance of Case's, who had studied classics at New College, Oxford in the 1880s and who desired to use his wealth to support gender-segregated

---

[31] R.B. Mowat, ed., *Letters to 'The Times' (1884–1922), Written by Thomas Case* (Oxford: Oxford University Press, 1927), 41–4; 'Statements against the Admission of Women to the University', 17 February 1896, MC:F30/N1, f. 7, Magdalen; Thomas Case, 'An Undelivered Speech against Resolution (4)', 29 February 1896, MC:F30/N1, f. 16, Magdalen.

[32] On Case's centrality to the campaign and his dogged commitment to it see C.R.L. Fletcher, letter to F.A. Dixey, 29 October 1911, MS Eng. lett. d. 465, f. 32–3, Bodleian; *Letters to 'The Times'*, 88.

[33] *Letters to 'The Times'*, 58–70, 83–4.   [34] Grundy, *Fifty-Five Years*, 109–11.

[35] Mowat, *Thomas Case's Letters*, 23.

classical teaching and scholarship within Oxford.[36] His generally reactionary political perspective strongly echoed Case's own.[37] Over the next few years, the two men worked out a deal wherein Warren committed a third of the value of his estate to Corpus.[38] In November 1912, he also made over in trust a £2,000 endowment to support classical education. In the deed of trust, he specified that the donation should preferably be used to support the teaching of Greek, and could not be used to support only Latin without Greek; it could not be used to offer tutorials to women; and it could not be used to pay a woman teacher's salary.[39] These stipulations made clear Warren's, and Case's, view of the relationship of Greek to gender segregation. What is more, the fact that Warren had embedded them in a deed of trust meant that the college was legally required to comply with them in perpetuity. In return, the college awarded Warren an honorary fellowship, and in the years prior to his death in 1928 he spent considerable time in residence in the college.[40]

Yet Case never remarked on the fact that there was another layer to Warren's advocacy of the residential college as a site for intimate masculine community. Since his undergraduate years, Warren had been engaged with classicizing ideas of pederastic desire and sex: a theme he pursued in poetry and fiction, in his professional work as an art dealer, in an idiosyncratic treatise about 'Uranian love' at which he worked obsessively towards the end of his life, and in his personal relationships with a long-term romantic partner and with a group of younger men who lived with him and whom he supported financially.[41] None of this was especially secret, and to many heads of educational institutions in the early twentieth century, welcoming someone like Warren into their midst might have seemed to put them at risk of scandal. But Case never expressed the same anxieties about homosex that he did about heterosex in gender-integrated universities. He appears to have perceived Warren as a sufficiently valuable political ally to look past this liability. Case and Warren's collaboration speaks to how a link forged in institutional politics between the Greek language and the remaking of the gender order unintentionally created new avenues along which conceptions of the masculine residential educational community as explicitly homoerotic and homosexual might flourish.

---

[36] E.P. Warren, letter to Mrs Case, 25 August 1911, B/14/8/1, CCC.

[37] Osbert Burdett and E.H. Goddard, *Edward Perry Warren: The Biography of a Connoisseur* (London: Christophers, 1941), collected in Michael Kaylor, ed., *The Collected Works and Commissioned Biography of Edward Perry Warren*, Volume 1 (Brno: Masarykova univerzita, 2015), see esp. 398, 404. Subsequent citations refer to this edition.

[38] E.P. Warren, letter to Thomas Case, n.d., and 'Extract of Proposed Will', 10 January 1911, B/12/4/1, CCC.

[39] E.P. Warren, letter to Thomas Case, 14 November 1912, B/12/4/1, CCC.

[40] The college magazine, the *Pelican Record*, discusses Warren's contributions to college life: see esp. vols. 12–13. Burdett and Goddard, *Edward Perry Warren*, 395–432.

[41] Burdett and Goddard, *Edward Perry Warren*; David Sox, *Bachelors of Art: Edward Perry Warren and the Lewes House Brotherhood* (London: Fourth Estate, 1991).

The College as a Site of Sexual Possibility

Many scholars have suggested that the Hellenizing discourses of Uranian love that had existed in Oxford and Cambridge throughout the nineteenth century climaxed in Oscar Wilde's trials in 1895. Through his testimony about 'the love that dare not speak its name', Wilde brought this discourse out of a cloistered subculture into the public eye. At the same time, his trials connected the subculture's elevated claims about the worship of beautiful boys to a sordid-seeming world of urban sexual degeneracy.[42] The open public discussion of homoerotic desire, identity, and sex certainly became more difficult in the immediate wake of the moral panic that surrounded Wilde's conviction for gross indecency. Yet at the same time, at the turn of the twentieth century, major cities such as London, Berlin, and New York flourished as sites of queer sex, culture, community, and academic theorizing. Owing to factors such as changing conceptions of urban space, new transportation and communication technologies, increasing access to education, and mass media, it had never been more possible to conceptualize oneself as a member of a sexual minority and to connect with others on the basis of that self-identification. But this is not to say that there was a stable, unified conception of 'the homosexual': discourses for making sense of same-sex desire, sex, and relationships remained context-specific and could vary widely. Though some middle-class white British men increasingly came to prefer a conception of congenital, age- and status-equal, masculine 'homosexuality', there was also a great deal of continuity in Uranian and pederastic paradigms, and in paradigms that saw same-sex sex as primarily situational or confined to specific stages in the life cycle. Within sexology, the gendered model of 'inversion' remained popular. Paradigms for making sense of same-sex desire could also vary substantially along lines of class, race, and region.[43]

Indeed, in Oxford and Cambridge in particular, locally specific homoerotic discourses continued to flourish. Homoerotic subcultures never died out within Oxford and Cambridge. Instead, they were reshaped both by their entanglement with the question of women's degrees, and by the growth and visibility of self-consciously homosexual identities and communities beyond the universities. These developments led collegiate homoerotic discourses to become increasingly misogynistic, counterposing separatist homoerotic masculinity to the degrading incursion of gender integration; and at the same time increasingly sexualized,

---

[42] Dowling, *Hellenism and Homosexuality*; Dellamora, *Masculine Desire*; Sinfield, *The Wilde Century*; Kaplan, *Sodom on the Thames*, 226; Orrells, *Classical Culture and Modern Masculinity*, Ch. 4.

[43] Houlbrook, *Queer London*; Cook, *London and the Culture of Homosexuality*; Helen Smith, *Masculinity, Class and Same-Sex Desire in Industrial England, 1895–1957* (Basingstoke: Palgrave Macmillan, 2015); Lewis, ed., *British Queer History*; Laura Doan, *Disturbing Practices: History, Sexuality, and Women's Experience of Modern War* (Chicago: University of Chicago Press, 2013); Anna Clark, 'Twilight Moments', *Journal of the History of Sexuality* 14, no. 1 (2005): 139–60.

imagining sex and not only friendship or aesthetic admiration as an outcome of intimate masculine community. In this specific context, by the 1930s 'homosexuality' emerged as a category that could accommodate both pederastic and age-equal understandings of same-sex desire and sex, and that was positioned in explicit opposition to marriage and heterosexuality.

In Cambridge, the resounding rejection of women's degrees in 1897 may have emboldened university men to assert their preference for gender-segregated homoerotic community. Previous scholars have focused on the misogyny of Oxford and Cambridge students, but avowed gender segregation was not only or even primarily an undergraduate-centric form of sociability. For example, one social circle centred on the University Library and the Baskerville Club, a university society for bibliophiles. One member of the club, librarian A.T. Bartholomew, kept a diary that indicates that he and his friends spent much of their free time visiting each other at home, going for long walks together in the countryside outside Cambridge, and discussing rare books.[44] Even as a librarian, on the outside of the more narrowly academic and more collegiate spheres of the university, living in a 'men's university' town allowed Bartholomew to access a gender-segregated social world that need not come to an end when the student, as he was expected to, left university and entered gender-integrated society.

Another librarian and Baskerville Club member, Charles Sayle, wrote Uranian poetry and socialized with fellow Uranian poets like Charles Kains Jackson, Philip Bainbrigge, and A.E. Housman. But Bartholomew, in addition to teaching himself Greek in order to read the homoerotic Volume 12 of the *Greek Anthology*, met and corresponded with influential queer theorists and activists such as George Ives, Edward Carpenter, and Magnus Hirschfeld. He made a pilgrimage to Venice in 1907 to meet the late John Addington Symonds's literary executor and biographer Horatio Brown, and often discussed Symonds's work with his friend Percy Babington, a fellow Baskerville Club member who later published a book about Symonds.[45] Bartholomew's intellectual and social life did not only centre on the idealized, classicizing homoeroticism specific to Oxford and Cambridge, but reached across national borders to engage with the latest research and activism that conceptualized queer men as a sexual minority entitled to civil rights.

Bartholomew's intellectual interest in homoeroticism needs also to be understood in the context of his misogyny. Throughout his diaries, he implicitly counterposed his masculine, homoerotically oriented community against what he saw as the troubling encroachment of women upon Cambridge society. At the University Library, he had several women colleagues, working in skilled positions

---

[44] A.T. Bartholomew, diaries, 1882–1918, MS Add. 8786/1/1–4, MS Add. 8786/1/11, MS Add. 8786/3, Cambridge University Library.

[45] A.T. Bartholomew, 'Private Journal I', 1904–9, MS Add. 8786/1/3, CUL; 'Private Journal. Vol. 2', 1909–10, MS Add. 8786/1/4, CUL; Percy L. Babington, *Bibliography of the Writings of John Addington Symonds* (London: John Castle, 1925).

equal to his own, but he dismissed them as ugly, shrill, and dull. If a friend married, he viewed the friendship as over.[46] In 1920, when women's admission to Cambridge degrees again came up for a Senate House vote, he voted in opposition.[47] Bartholomew's wholesale rejection of gender integration can thus usefully be contrasted with the perspective of someone like Alfred Marshall, who saw opposition to women's degrees as compatible with marriage and gender-integrated sociability. A generation younger than Marshall, it might make sense to situate Bartholomew and his Baskerville Club friends in the context of a generation of middle-class men who rebelled against Victorian idealizations of marriage and instead invested themselves in homosocial organizations, friendships, and communities.[48] In some ways, he might also be usefully read alongside women like Margery Fry who built homosocial kinship structures in explicit opposition to marriage. Yet Bartholomew's intellectual interests show him to be counterposing not just confirmed bachelorhood, but specifically homosexuality, against marriage and gender-integrated sociability.

Another circle in Edwardian Cambridge who conceptualized homosexuality as entwined with gender-segregated residential educational community was the Apostles discussion society, a self-consciously exclusive and secretive club comprising undergraduates, faculty, and alumni, which met weekly to discuss philosophy and politics in a light-hearted and self-referential way. Like other student societies that gathered in the evening behind college walls, the Apostles fostered the kind of homosocial intimacy unique to Oxford and Cambridge: born of curfews, the regulation of students' movement through the university city, and collegiate values about close association between teachers and students. Founded in 1820, the society had long been preoccupied with cultivating ties of intimacy and 'comradeship', and with debating questions of sexual ethics.[49] But in the 1880s and 1890s, members such as G.L. Dickinson, J.M.E. McTaggart, G.E. Moore, and Bertrand Russell, drawing on new currents in academic philosophy, pushed the group to theorize explicitly the ethics of intimacy and friendship. In 1893, for example, they debated questions including 'Is reciprocity essential to friendship?' and 'What ought Cambridge to give?'—connecting the personal relationships that the Apostles were supposed to engender to the purpose of a university like Cambridge.[50]

---

[46] Bartholomew, 'Private Journal I'.

[47] Cambridge Senate House votes were not anonymous; votes on women's degrees are recorded in the University Registry Guard Books on Higher Education of Women, UA CUR 61–61.1, CUL.

[48] Tosh, *A Man's Place*, Ch. 8; Amy Milne-Smith, *London Clubland: A Cultural History of Gender and Class in Late Victorian Britain* (Basingstoke: Palgrave Macmillan, 2011), 147.

[49] Oscar Browning, *Memories of Sixty Years at Eton, Cambridge, and Elsewhere* (London: John Lane, 1910), 45; Arthur Sidgwick and Eleanor Mildred Sidgwick, *Henry Sidgwick: A Memoir* (London: Macmillan, 1906), 34; Apostles Minute Books, KCAS/39/1, KCC.

[50] Apostles Minute Books, vols. 11–12, KCAS/39/1/11–12, KCC.

The intellectual impact of Apostles philosophers upon the history of philosophy has been well documented.[51] But it was Dickinson who, between the 1890s and 1930s, played the largest role in prompting the group to theorize homosexuality. A polymathic classicist, historian, and political scientist, Dickinson became a fellow of King's College in 1887, at the age of twenty-five, and lived in college until his death in 1932 at the age of seventy. He travelled around the world, was one of the earliest British advocates for a League of Nations, served as a foreign policy adviser to the Labour Party, and publicly advocated for women's rights. At the same time, his social and emotional world remained bounded by the walls of King's, and by his self-conscious understanding of himself as a specific kind of person defined through his experience of congenital same-sex desire.

Unlike many of his peers in the early-twentieth-century intellectual elite, Dickinson used the word 'homosexual' to describe himself.[52] He wrote homoerotic poetry; Platonic-style dialogues that earnestly defended the legitimacy of same-sex desire, sex, and love; and several drafts of an autobiography in which he sought to make meaning of his sexuality. When he explained what same-sex desire meant to him, he espoused a historically transcendent concept of sexual orientation and the hetero/homo binary, in contrast to other paradigms available at the time that understood same-sex desire and sex as more situational or as organized primarily around the age-differentiated structure of pederasty. His historical understanding of congenital love between men began with Plato, but wound its way through Michelangelo and Shakespeare to the present-day bars and brothels of London and Berlin. His writing often sought to obscure the hierarchical aspect of the classical Greek pederastic model, instead giving examples of contexts, such as undergraduate life, in which men might fall in love with their peers. He saw homoerotic desire as sexual, and argued for the moral neutrality, and even the wider social benefit, of men who chose to consummate it.[53]

Though Dickinson never published any of his writing on homosexuality, he shared it widely among his friends, colleagues, and students. The intimate masculine intergenerational context of the Apostles became a key testing ground for the elaboration of new ideas about the meaning of same-sex desire. Dickinson's primary audience was a new generation of undergraduates who joined the Apostles in the first decade of the twentieth century, including E.M. Forster, Lytton and James Strachey, Leonard Woolf, and J.M. Keynes. These young men drew on the discussion society's self-conscious cultivation of intimacy and motto of 'absolute

---

[51] See e.g. Paul Levy, *Moore: G. E. Moore and the Cambridge Apostles* (London: Papermac, 1989); Thomas Dixon, *The Invention of Altruism: Making Moral Meanings in Victorian Britain* (Oxford: Oxford University Press, 2008).

[52] Dickinson uses the word 'homosexual' throughout his manuscript 'Recollections', a memoir written between 1921 and 1931. GLD/1/2, KCC.

[53] Goldsworthy Lowes Dickinson, 'Dialogue between Statues', n.d., GLD/1/8, KCC; 'A Dialogue on Homosexuality', 1918, GLD/1/6, KCC.

candour' to offer a more explicitly sexualized vision of the kind of friendship that groups like the Apostles might engender. Discussion topics engaged with a Platonic ideal of aesthetic appreciation of beauty, but they also admitted the possibility of sex. The first essay Forster read to the society, as an undergraduate in 1904, was titled, 'The Bedroom, Brother?'[54] Keynes, also an undergraduate, coined the phrase 'the higher sodomy' in a 1903 Apostles essay, and discussed 'sodomy' in several of his essays.[55] Keynes's preferred paradigm of homoerotic desire, the phrase 'the higher sodomy' references the Uranian ideal of a 'higher', 'celestial' form of eros that could only exist between men. But by referring not to 'eros' but to 'sodomy', Keynes positioned a sex act as central to the kinds of desire and intimacy that might exist between the young men who sat up late discussing philosophy behind the walls of a Cambridge college.

Though they likely talked about the 'higher sodomy' much more than they practised it, Keynes and Lytton Strachey did imagine the Saturday evening Apostles meetings as sites of flirtation, recruiting new members on the basis of their physical attractiveness.[56] Moreover, despite writing about an age-equal model of homosexuality, Dickinson spent his life in King's romanticizing the beauty of the undergraduates around him. Over decades, he came to the view that, not able to live openly with a male partner, marry, or have children, he might be useful to society by sublimating his desire into the care of his students. He was usually in love from afar with a younger man who did not return his feelings. Just a year before his death, he observed, 'It's really odd...how precisely the mood of Socrates as given in Plato hits my experience.'[57] Once, when he was forty-six, Dickinson aggressively pursued a student, Oscar Eckhard: visiting Eckhard, sending him multiple letters daily, and pressuring him to 'kiss & embrace'. Though Eckhard rejected Dickinson's advances, no one else in their lives, including Eckhard's mother, seemed to think Dickinson's behaviour inappropriate.[58] The context of the gender-segregated residential college and the teacher–student intimacy it might engender offered a script through which Dickinson's desires could flourish, rendered legible and socially unproblematic when detached from the concept of homosexual identity through which he privately understood himself.

Later in life, Dickinson admitted he had made a mistake in his pursuit of Eckhard, though he maintained that his interest as a teacher was stirred by homoerotic

---

[54] Apostles Minute Books, vol. 14 (26 November 1904), KCAS/39/1/14, KCC.

[55] Keynes, 'Shall we write filth-packets?'

[56] Julie Anne Taddeo, 'Plato's Apostles: Edwardian Cambridge and the "New Style of Love"', *Journal of the History of Sexuality* 8, no. 2 (1997): 196–228.

[57] Dickinson, 'Privatissimum', GLD/1/4, KCC; Dickinson, 'Autobiographical Writings', 1916–32, GLD/1/5, KCC.

[58] Dickinson, 'Privatissimum'.

feeling, something not lost on several generations of King's students.[59] 'I still feel an attraction and sympathy with male youth which I have never felt and never shall for female,' he wrote in old age. 'Last night I spent the evening with some undergraduates listening to the gramophone...The subtle charm of them to me pervaded all the atmosphere.'[60] Indeed, though Dickinson explicitly rejected the Uranian claim that love between men was 'higher' than any emotion of which women were capable, his writing about his sublimated passions for his students tended to undermine his commitment to that assertion. Following a 1909 visit to the University of Wisconsin, he wrote of the mixed-gender sociability that he observed there, 'of course there's no real sentiment in it, nothing beautiful or passionate—only this eternal barbarian girl and boy game.'[61] He explicitly counterposed the sexual possibilities of the men's college to the 'barbarian... game' of heterosexuality in the coeducational university.

Dickinson had several meaningful friendships with women, advocated publicly for women's suffrage, and consistently voted in favour of women's admission to Cambridge degrees. Yet, as Forster would later write, Dickinson advocated for women's equality only mechanically, out of a sense of duty: '[H]e was not a really creditable feminist. He did think that men on the whole are superior.'[62] Members of the Apostles, who tended to understand their politics as self-consciously progressive, typically supported expanded political and social rights for women. In both 1897 and in 1920, they voted in support of women's degrees in much larger numbers than Cambridge faculty and alumni as a whole.[63] At the same time, the masculine residential college and the discussion society offered them a refuge from the gender integration of the university and of middle-class life more widely, and their sense of themselves as intellectual elites in some ways challenged their political commitment to democracy. In the years before the First World War, one topic to which the group returned frequently was whether women were capable of being Apostles, a discussion that unfolded in the context of the controversy around women's inclusion in the university. Bertrand Russell was the first to propose the question, in March 1896, at the start of the first campaign for women's admission to the BA. Nearly all the members present voted yes, though no action was taken.[64] But as the question came up again on several occasions in the ensuing years, progressively fewer members voted in favour. By October 1908, members doubted that, if they were to open the society to women, any would meet its exacting standards of brilliance and beauty.[65] As this particular group of writers

---

[59] Dennis Proctor, ed., *The Autobiography of G. Lowes Dickinson and Other Unpublished Writings* (London: Duckworth, 1973), 6–8.

[60] Dickinson, 'Recollections', c.1921–31, GLD/1/2, 139–40, KCC.

[61] Dickinson, 'Recollections', 139–40.

[62] E.M. Forster, *Goldsworthy Lowes Dickinson* (London: Edward Arnold, 1934), 106.

[63] University Registry Guard Books.   [64] Apostles Minute Books, vol. 12.

[65] Apostles Minute Books, vol. 14.

and philosophers worked in their discussions with each other to define a masculine, homoerotic, and explicitly sexual ideal of collegiate intimacy, they, like their contemporaries in the University Library circle, positioned it as necessarily opposed to the wider gender integration of university life.

Like other student societies, the Apostles fell into abeyance during the First World War. At the end of the war, alumni—especially Dickinson and Keynes—revived it, selecting new members and transmitting their ideals of what intimate collegiate student life should be to a new generation.[66] At the same time, the university at large reopened the question of women's admission to degrees. While Oxford had decided to admit women to degrees in 1920, faculty and administrators in Cambridge were unable to agree upon a path to admitting women. Many were wary of women faculty's greater participation in university governance, expressed their own social anxiety about teaching women students, and doubted that the gender integration of student life was beneficial.[67] Some argued that admitting women to degrees was a slippery slope to gender integration of the colleges (though no one was arguing in favour of this), and would thus erode Cambridge's most special qualities.[68]

Ultimately, fearing intervention from the University Grants Committee and from the Royal Commission into Oxford and Cambridge then collecting evidence, in 1921 members of the university senate rushed to assemble a compromise proposal that would admit women to the BA but to no further status in the university or say in university governance. Representatives of the women's colleges could attend university committee meetings but not vote, and a quota was imposed on women students. This proposal passed in October 1921 by a substantial majority. But undergraduates rioted in response, threatening women they encountered in the streets and taking a battering ram to the gates of Newnham College. When the Royal Commission reported the following year, it expressed its support of the compromise: 'We desire strongly that Cambridge should remain mainly and predominantly a "men's University" though of a mixed type as it is already.'[69] The women's colleges had established their place within the university city, but as the last 'men's University' left in Britain, Cambridge nevertheless had a unique role to play in the wider national higher education landscape.

Cambridge's conflict over women's degrees in 1919–21 fits within the wider moment of panic around the instability of the gender order, misogynistic backlash against women's wartime gains, and remaking of the relationship between the universities and the state, that characterized the immediate postwar years. The men students who asserted a particular masculine conception of the

---

[66] J.M. Keynes, 'Presidential Address to the Society of Apostles', June 1921, JMK/UA/36, KCC.
[67] 'Discussion of a Report', *Cambridge University Reporter*, 28 October 1920, 206.
[68] McWilliams-Tullberg, *Women at Cambridge*, 130–46.
[69] McWilliams-Tullberg, *Women at Cambridge*, 157, 164–71.

university by rioting in 1921 were not especially different from peers at universities like Glasgow or Manchester who made similar statements. But what set Cambridge, and Oxford, apart was the conception of an exceptional role for the men's college as a bulwark against both the encroachment of the state and the encroachment of gender integration and heterosexuality. Despite the differences in how the women's degrees debates unfolded in Oxford and Cambridge, in both universities in the interwar period the college became increasingly not a site situated in symbiotic relationship to gender integration and heterosexuality, but rather a site of resistance—and a site where a homosexual sexual culture might flourish instead.

We can see this shift taking shape through the development of E.P. Warren's thought, and the changing nature of his bequest to Corpus Christi College, Oxford, after the First World War. While in residence as an honorary fellow at Corpus during and after the war, Warren worked obsessively at a polemic, *A Defence of Uranian Love*, that drew on a variety of textual and visual evidence to present a grand unified theory of the role of pederasty in Greek culture and its continuing value in the present. Warren criticized theorizations of 'Greek love' focused on a Platonic framework that conceptualized pederastic desire as a stage through which a would-be philosopher might pass in order to access more abstract, idealized conceptions of the beautiful and the good.[70] Instead, drawing on material evidence such as sculpture, he argued that ancient Greek culture revered the 'hard', athletic, youthful male body as a good in itself, from which it developed a hierarchical value system that prioritized physical strength and toughness as central to virtue. Moreover, he argued that cultivating pederastic desire in the present would ineluctably lead to the wider revivification of a more masculine, more robust society opposed to degenerate, effeminate modernity. 'To fortify ourselves we must turn back to Greece,' he insisted; '[I]n Greece is found the severe beauty, the exacting ideal, of manhood.'[71]

Warren's argument for the civilizational benefits of a physical, sexualized model of pederastic desire was universalizing rather than minoritizing: it held that all of western society stood to gain from the eroticization of the youthful, athletic male body. At the same time, he sought to make claims about the nature of pederastic desire specifically. Throughout the *Defence*, Warren was at pains to insist that 'Uranian love' was essentially masculine: 'the love of the very root and

---

[70] E.P. Warren, *A Defence of Uranian Love. Part the Second: The Uranian Eros* (privately printed, 1930), 151–2.

[71] E.P. Warren, *A Defence of Uranian Love. Part the Third: The Heavenly Wisdom and Conclusion* (privately printed, 1928), 80; see also Jen Grove, '"Firm Outlines and Hard Muscles Immortalised": Ancient Statuary and E.P. Warren's "Uranian Ideal"', in *Sculpture, Sexuality and History: Encounters in Literature, Culture and the Arts from the Eighteenth Century to the Present*, ed. Jana Funke and Jen Grove (Cham: Springer, 2019), 171–94, at 185–90.

fibre of manhood'.[72] It was therefore categorically different both from what he termed the 'effeminacy' of Plato's more chaste, spiritual vision of pederastic desire, and from men's desire for women. Warren thus implicitly rebutted other contemporary paradigms for understanding same-sex desire: such as the 'inversion' model, popular among some sexual scientists, that held that men who desired other men had female souls; the idea that homosexual relationships between equals were homologous with and parallel to opposite-sex marriage; or that, in certain situations, a man otherwise attracted to women would find adolescent boys to be an acceptable substitute. 'From the beginning I have dealt with paiderastia as a passion for the masculine...and not as if a masculine object had been merely substituted for a feminine,' he wrote.[73]

This assertion of masculinity, when coupled with ideas about the transmission of knowledge and spiritual development that might occur within an age-differentiated pederastic relationship, allowed Warren to offer a vision of a society in which intellectual, spiritual, and moral reproduction might occur homosocially and asexually, without reference to women, sexual reproduction, and the family. Such a society would be more robust and less degenerate than one founded on the feminizing influences of marriage, gender-integrated society, and Christian charity.[74] Over the course of the 1910s and 1920s, then, and even more so once he came into residence at Corpus, Warren became strongly committed to a theory of homoerotic desire, sex, and relationships as a defence against the incursion of gender-integrated, heterosexualized modernity, and as entwined with a right-wing politics that opposed equality and democracy in politics, ethics, and civil society.

In this, Warren had much in common with contemporaries in the masculinist wing of the nascent German gay rights movement such as Adolf Brand, Benedict Friedländer, and Hans Blüher.[75] It is also possible to situate him in the context of a slightly older English masculinist imperialist tradition exemplified by figures such as Robert Baden Powell or Cecil Rhodes. Indeed, Rhodes—a relative outsider to the English elite who also sought to use his personal wealth and the instrument of English charities law to make Oxford the foundation for a distinctive racist and masculinist political vision—offers striking parallels to Warren.[76]

---

[72] Warren, *A Defence of Uranian Love, Part the Second*, 165; Edward Perry Warren, *A Defence of Uranian Love. Part the First: The Boy-Lover* (privately printed: 1928), 40.

[73] Warren, *Defence of Uranian Love, Part the First*, 98.

[74] Warren, *Defence of Uranian Love, Part the Second*, 16.

[75] Javier Samper Vendrell, *The Seduction of Youth: Print Culture and Homosexual Rights in the Weimar Republic* (Toronto: University of Toronto Press, 2020), 116–21; Laurie Marhoefer, *Sex and the Weimar Republic: German Homosexual Emancipation and the Rise of the Nazis* (Toronto: University of Toronto Press, 2015), 150–5; Jason Crouthamel, '"Comradeship" and "Friendship": Masculinity and Militarisation in Germany's Homosexual Emancipation Movement after the First World War', *Gender & History* 23, no. 1 (2011): 111–29.

[76] Philip Ziegler, *Legacy: Cecil Rhodes, the Rhodes Trust and Rhodes Scholarships* (New Haven: Yale University Press, 2008); W.T. Stead, *The Last Will and Testament of Cecil John Rhodes, with Elucidatory Notes* (London: Review of Reviews Office, 1902).

Yet Warren eschewed the 'muscular Christianity' that served as a basis for ideals of masculinity for English imperialists like Baden Powell. Moreover, unlike his German counterparts, or indeed some British contemporaries who turned to fascism as a source for new, self-consciously modern ideals of virile masculinity, Warren's status as an older, wealthy American expatriate meant that his own life and his ideas about masculinity remained relatively untouched by the experience of the First World War. Instead, what set Warren apart was his investment in the space of the residential college as a site of intimacy, his desire to use the college to offer a critique of the degenerative effects of gender integration and heterosexuality, and his commitment to a pederastic ideal as the preferable future for Oxford's men's colleges.

Reflecting these developments in his thought and the wider political context of the 1920s, in 1927, a year before he died, Warren made a new will that doubled down on, but also more narrowly specified, the terms of his donation to Corpus. He offered a bequest of £30,000 to endow a lectureship in classics. The terms of the bequest required the lecturer to live and to teach within the college precinct, and forbade him from teaching 'in the presence of any woman'. Warren also outlined a fund for the construction of an underground tunnel connecting the college's sixteenth-century main quad to a set of newer buildings across the street. He specified that the lecturer could only be housed in the new buildings if they were linked to the main site by the tunnel, and that the entire bequest would lapse if the college did not undertake to construct it.[77] In subsequent conversations with Case's successor as president, Percy Allen, Warren expressed that, while he would countenance a married man being appointed to the lectureship, he would prefer the college to hire a bachelor; and he would prefer the lecturer to devote most of his attention to providing one-on-one tutorials. He also insisted repeatedly on the centrality of the tunnel to his vision, despite Allen expressing misgivings about cost and engineering challenges. 'It is one thing to know that you can reach your keeper, if you have permission to go over the road and ring a bell. It is another, if his rooms are connected with yours by an open passage,' Warren wrote.[78] The evidence does not indicate whether Warren imputed an explicitly sexual connotation to the lecturer's accessibility via tunnel. But in the context of a 9 p.m. curfew after which the college's front gates were locked and students would have to request permission to enter and exit them, his insistence on the importance of the tunnel does speak to a fantasy of an intimate masculine residential community, segregated from the rest of the city, that might flourish after dark.

---

[77] Draft will codicil, October 1927, B/12/4/1, CCC.
[78] E.P. Warren, letter to P.S. Allen, 4 January 1927, B/12/4/1, CCC; P.S. Allen, 'Notes on Conversation with Edward Perry Warren', 2 May 1928, B/12/4/1, CCC.

In some ways, then, Warren's vision was continuous with an older tradition, reaching back into Oxford's medieval and early modern history, of the college as a celibate community that fostered close relationships between individual teachers and students.[79] But it was also modern and reactionary: responding directly to the institutional political questions of women and compulsory Greek, and entwined with Warren's larger masculinist, homoerotic worldview. Warren's biographers wrote of the lectureship that its 'object...was to have in Oxford a man who would be a Socrates to the Undergraduates, a lover both of hardness and of beauty'.[80] Moreover, the instrument of the will made Corpus's commitment to Warren's detailed vision legally binding.

To be sure, some practicalities got in the way: the city council refused to grant planning permission for the tunnel, citing engineering challenges; and Warren's funds lost so much value in the US stock market crash of 1929 that the college was not able to establish the lectureship until after the Second World War.[81] Ultimately, in the 1960s, the college undertook a four-year legal process to challenge Warren's ban on the lecturer teaching women, and the Sex Discrimination Act 1975 meant that women could no longer be barred from applying for the position.[82] In the long term, Warren was not successful in remaking Corpus Christi College in the likeness of his vision of a masculinist, separatist, homoerotic ideal that would restore the robustness of degenerate modern western society. But in the 1920s, Warren's vision, like Dickinson's, evidently seemed one possible response to the gender integration and heterosexualization of university life and of middle-class society more broadly. Dickinson, Warren, A.T. Bartholomew, and many other men like them made comfortable long-term homes in Oxford and Cambridge, despite the transformation in the university gender order wrought by the end of celibacy requirements and the admission of women to degrees. Even when, like Dickinson, they pushed the boundaries of permissible behaviour towards students, their proclivities went relatively unremarked. Their voluminous archives certainly tell us more about what they thought about homosexuality than about whether they gave practical expression to their ideas. But whether advancing minoritizing (in the case of Dickinson and the Apostles) or universalizing (in the case of Warren) views about the meaning and cultural significance of desire, sex, and love between men, they situated homoerotic intimacy within the distinctive institutional context of the Oxbridge men's college. They conceptualized that institutionally specific intimacy as a more ennobling alternative to the 'eternal

---

[79] On relations between teachers and students and intimate masculine community in Corpus Christi's early years see Julian Reid, 'Living in a Sixteenth-Century College', in *Renaissance College: Corpus Christi College, Oxford in Context, 1450–1600*, ed. Mordechai Feingold and John Watts (Oxford: Oxford University Press, 2019), 183–99.

[80] Burdett and Goddard, *Edward Perry Warren*, 411.

[81] P.S. Allen, letter to unknown recipient, 20 February 1931, B/12/4/1, CCC; Burdett and Goddard, *Edward Perry Warren*, 402.

[82] Ewen Bowie (E.P. Warren Praelector emeritus), email correspondence, 17 April 2019.

barbarian girl and boy game': a reaction against heterosexuality (especially student heterosexuality) that might offer wider civilizational benefits.

Inventing the Hetero/Homo Binary

Warren's biographers wrote that, in the 1920s, 'the Post-War men did not seem quite to know what to make' of the eccentric American living in their college who wanted to talk only about sex and Greek literature.[83] Oxford and Cambridge undergraduates were no different from students at universities around the country in, after the war, turning increasingly to gender integration and heterosexuality. The admission of women to degrees at Oxford and the 1921 compromise at Cambridge led to greater gender integration of student social and extracurricular life. Chaperonage requirements for women students disappeared. Both women and men students also increasingly participated in urban nightlife, whether in Oxford and Cambridge or in London, despite the best efforts of their colleges to regulate their conduct.[84] Changing social mores and students' experiences of the social dislocation of wartime, when coupled with new technologies such as the automobile, called into question the idea of the residential collegiate university as a world apart where different, lifecycle-specific and gender-specific, cultural norms pertained; where colleges were *in loco parentis*; and where curfews and a heavily policed divide between town and gown defined student life for residents of both women's and men's colleges.

If, by the 1920s, the conceptual distance between Oxford or Cambridge and London seemed shorter for those students who, as we saw in Chapter 4, laid waste to West End theatres after the Varsity match, so must it have done for those students who could find in that same West End bars, restaurants, and nightclubs that catered to a queer clientele. Admittedly in part as a result of increased policing and media attention, spaces of queer sex, leisure, and community were, in London and many other cities, more visible than ever before.[85] Though students across the country may have accessed such spaces, what sets Oxford and Cambridge apart is the connections that their proximity to the metropolis and their social cachet allowed them to establish between intramural queer subcultures and queer London. Oxford and Cambridge students who participated in self-consciously queer subcultures through extracurricular activities such as theatre or creative writing interacted with queer professionals in those fields, and could enter into London-based careers upon graduation. Conversely, older men

---

[83] Burdett and Goddard, *Edward Perry Warren*, 412.

[84] Brian Harrison, 'College Life, 1918–1939', in *The History of the University of Oxford*, Volume 8: *The Twentieth Century*, ed. Brian Harrison (Oxford: Oxford University Press, 1994), 80–108, at 97–8, 101; McWilliams-Tullberg, *Women at Cambridge*, 143–6.

[85] Houlbrook, *Queer London*.

resident in London with connections to Oxford and Cambridge could travel easily to visit the two universities, remaining connected to the spaces of gender-segregated intimacy and sexuality they fostered.[86]

There is some evidence to suggest that, in the interwar period, self-consciously queer subcultures existed in Oxford and Cambridge to an extent that they did not in gender-integrated, urban, non-residential universities, with homosexuality discussed as openly in the Oxford and Cambridge student press as heterosexuality was in the student magazines of other universities.[87] By the interwar period, these cultures were not understood (and sometimes excused) as a stage in the life cycle that young men would ultimately outgrow, or viewed as a symptom of wider cultural decay, but rather linked to more fixed, minoritized, pathologized conceptions of gender and sexual deviance.[88] Importantly, some commentators did identify Oxford's and Cambridge's continuing gender segregation as a factor that allowed homoerotic cultures to take root. The author of a 1930 book about 'degenerate Oxford', for example, recommended full coeducation of the university as a strategy for arresting effeminacy and romantic friendships among undergraduates.[89] Media panic about sexual degeneracy at Oxford and Cambridge may have created a self-reinforcing narrative, drawing more men—students and not—to the queer subcultures of these university towns that linked the relatively open discussion and pursuit of sex and relationships between men to cultures of aestheticism and camp.

In some ways, all this was a far cry from Warren's or Dickinson's careful articulation of conceptions of 'Uranian love' or the 'higher sodomy'. But the theorizations that Warren, Dickinson, and others like them offered of the men's college as a site of sexual possibility as against the incursions of heterosexuality were an equally important part of the story of the invention of homosexuality in the early twentieth century. The historian Ross Brooks has characterized the homoerotic subculture of interwar Oxford as 'queer modernism'. But if queer, it was also *conservative* modernism: borne of a desire to resist what many perceived as the inexorable trend towards gender integration of middle-class sociability and the breakdown of gender norms that would necessarily ensue; and of the concomitant impulse to assert segregationist and robustly masculine visions of comradeship, intimacy, and desire in response. Some, like Warren and others aligned with

[86] Ryan Linkof, '"These Young Men Who Come down from Oxford and Write Gossip": Society Gossip, Homosexuality and the Logic of Revelation in the Interwar Popular Press', in *British Queer History*, ed. Lewis, 109–33; Ross Brooks, 'Beyond Brideshead: The Male Homoerotics of 1930s Oxford', *Journal of British Studies* 59, no. 4 (October 2020): 821–56; Dominic Janes, 'The "Curious Effects" of Acting: Homosexuality, Theatre and Female Impersonation at the University of Cambridge, 1900–39', *Twentieth Century British History* 33, no. 2 (June 2022): 169–202.

[87] Brooks, 'Beyond Brideshead'; Janes, 'Curious Effects'.

[88] Brooks, 'Beyond Brideshead', 825.

[89] Terence Greenidge, *Degenerate Oxford? A Critical Study of Modern University Life* (London: Chapman & Hall, 1930), 113.

pederastic or Uranian conceptions of homoerotic desire, resisted or simply chose not to engage with 'modern', 'scientific', minoritizing conceptions of congenital homosexual identity. But others, such as Dickinson and his Apostles friends and colleagues, synthesized older Uranian ideas with newer conceptions of sexual orientation. Despite their differences, however, all these men drew on the intellectual and cultural resources of the men's residential collegiate community to construct a conception of the man-desiring man as securely masculine, conforming in most respects to norms of educated middle-class masculinity.

It is telling that, while the men's residential college gave someone like Dickinson a set of resources with which to come to an understanding of congenital, minoritizing homosexual identity and its wider social and cultural value, the changing fortunes of gender-segregated women's colleges foreclosed such a possibility for someone like Margery Fry. While queer women's cultures and communities undoubtedly became more visible in the interwar period, too, and queer women's identities and relationships were relatively acceptable within the Oxford and Cambridge women's colleges and within a wider world of intellectual and artistic, educated middle-class women, the women's college did not become the basis for a cultural politics of opposition to gender integration that the men's college or university did.

But the 'men's university' could offer other, unintended, resources. Michael Dillon, who in the 1940s became one of the first British people to access medical transition, attended Oxford as a member of the women's Society of Home Students (meaning that he lived not in a college, but in private lodgings) in 1934–8. In his autobiography, Dillon wrote that he found it impossible to participate in undergraduate gender-integrated social life, which necessitated wearing a dress and interacting with 'politely condescending' men. Though he spent most of his time outside his studies captaining the Oxford University Women's Boat Club, he also engaged in male homosocial Oxford life, passing as a man in order to attend men's boxing matches and to take martial arts lessons. He took up riding a motorcycle and smoking a pipe.[90] Dillon's experiences in masculine community at Oxford helped him to begin to construct a middle-class masculine identity.

Dillon—who rejected the well-meaning suggestions of friends and mentors that his gender nonconformity might be due to his being a lesbian—illustrates how the interwar period did offer some possibilities for making sense of gender and sexual diversity outside of the paradigm of homosexuality. At the same time, his story also speaks to the centrality of a binary conception of gender difference and a norm of respectable, productive masculinity to the social order of mid-twentieth-century Britain. Dillon could find social belonging through conformity

---

[90] Michael Dillon/Lobzang Jivaka, ed. Jacob Lau and Cameron Partridge, *Out of the Ordinary: A Life of Gender and Spiritual Transitions* (New York: Fordham University Press, 2016), 74–87.

to ideals of middle-class masculinity.[91] Similarly, men like Warren and Dickinson could articulate what they perceived as respectable and socially valuable ideals of male homoeroticism by positioning them in opposition to gender integration and femininity—while it was men students playing women's parts who, as we saw in Chapter 5, were in the 1930s increasingly being banned from Oxford's and Cambridge's stages.[92]

The idiosyncratic institutional structure and culture of Oxford's and Cambridge's constituent colleges, and the political conflicts that unfolded therein, thus had unintended consequences for the gender and sexuality order of twentieth-century Britain. The 'men's university' could offer a space for the assertion and performance of a range of elite and middle-class separatist masculinities—even those that the law formally proscribed—at the expense of femininity and of paradigms for gender-integrated sociability. Scholars who have in recent years returned to renewed critical engagement with the narrative of the making of the modern homosexual have shown that, in the late nineteenth and early twentieth centuries, not all forms of queer sexuality were equally marginalized and condemned. Elite white English homosexuality constructed itself in opposition to cultures of gender and sexual diversity associated with working-class men; men of colour, immigrants, and imperial subjects; and 'inversion', gender nonconformity, and trans femininity.[93] It therefore carved out a space associated with normative masculinities and with prestigious institutions like England's two oldest universities—at the expense of other forms of gender and sexual diversity that could not be rehabilitated into the normative gender order.

In 1957, a Home Office committee on Homosexual Offences and Prostitution recommended the decriminalization of sex between two men over twenty-one in private, alongside the increased regulation and policing of street sex work. The committee's recommendations thus drew a clear line between sexual behaviour that could be deemed respectable (because it involved only two people, in private, without the exchange of money, even if the two people were men) and behaviour that could not and thus needed to be subjected to state surveillance.

[91] Alison Oram, *Her Husband Was a Woman! Women's Gender-Crossing in Modern British Popular Culture* (London: Routledge, 2007), 17, 24, 38; Adrian Kane-Galbraith, 'Male Breadwinners of "Doubtful Sex": Trans Men and the Welfare State, 1954–1970', in *Men and Masculinities in Modern Britain: A History for the Present*, ed. Matt Houlbrook, Katie Jones, and Ben Mechen (Manchester: Manchester University Press, 2024), 49–66.

[92] Janes, 'Curious Effects of Acting', 198.

[93] Smith, *Masculinity, Class, and Same-Sex Desire*; Nadia Ellis, 'Black Migrants, White Queers and the Archive of Inclusion in Postwar London', *Interventions* 17, no. 6 (November 2015): 893–915; Emma Heaney, *The New Woman: Literary Modernism, Queer Theory, and the Trans Feminine Allegory* (Evanston: Northwestern University Press, 2017). Scholars have also explored this topic in the German context: see e.g. Laurie Marhoefer, 'Was the Homosexual Made White? Race, Empire, and Analogy in Gay and Trans Thought in Twentieth-Century Germany', *Gender & History* 31, no. 1 (2019): 91–114; Laurie Marhoefer, *Racism and the Making of Gay Rights: A Sexologist, His Student, and the Empire of Queer Love* (Toronto: University of Toronto Press, 2022).

This reflected the successful efforts of campaigners—many associated with Oxford and Cambridge—who had for decades sought to delineate a concept of the respectable homosexual who upheld rather than undermined the prevailing gender and social order.[94] It seems not incidental that the chair of this committee, John Wolfenden, an experienced educational administrator, was at the time the vice-chancellor of the University of Reading. A few years later, he would become chair of the University Grants Committee. Some of the most pivotal moments in the history of sexuality in twentieth-century Britain were entwined with the history of university administration. And thinking about this university story can help us to understand both the idiosyncratic role of Oxford and Cambridge within UK higher education and the idiosyncratic role of male homosexuality within the gender and sexuality order of twentieth-century Britain. If, across most of the UK higher education sector, the relatively uncontested reorganization of the sector around a norm of gender integration led to the rise of heterosexuality, the more fraught contestation over gender integration in Oxford and Cambridge can help us to understand how middle-class, masculine, male homosexuality, too, became part of twentieth-century Britain's structures of classed, racialized, and gendered power.

Teaching Gender: The British University and the Rise of Heterosexuality, 1860–1939. Samuel Rutherford, Oxford University Press. © Samuel Rutherford 2025. DOI: 10.1093/9780198937524.003.0008

[94] Brian Lewis, *Wolfenden's Witnesses: Homosexuality in Postwar Britain* (London: Palgrave Macmillan, 2016).

Epilogue

Sex on Campus

As they responded to the everyday challenges of negotiating cross-gender relations in the gender-integrated university, faculty, students, and other historical actors fostered visions of the gender order and of the purpose of higher education that would continue to hold sway throughout the twentieth century. The era of postwar social democracy saw the wider dissemination of the norms for gender and sexuality that interwar young people had begun to innovate, and these norms' solidification in the institutions of the welfare state. Though social change from the 1960s put pressure both on the structure of UK higher education and on gender and sexuality, these transformations—as they had a few decades previous—could affirm the existing gender and sexuality order as much as challenge it. The story this book has told about everyday life and the making of norms at the turn of the twentieth century might cause us to see the changes of the later twentieth century in a different light—and to reflect on how universities might still be key sites for the production of norms about gender and sexuality today.

The period after the Second World War represented the apex of the male breadwinner ideal, the gender binary, and heteronormativity. The welfare state that the 1945 Labour government brought into being built on a longer tradition of social policy that located the exercise of citizenship and definitions of who was deserving of its benefits in productive and reproductive masculinity. The postwar government enshrined these assumptions in policies such as their approach to National Insurance, in which men paid higher taxes and received higher benefits on the assumption that they were earning higher wages and supporting families. The culture of social democracy also placed increased emphasis on women's value as nurturing mothers and effective household managers, imagining the nuclear family as the primary and privileged site of emotional intimacy and well-being. Though these ideals were not necessarily borne out in practice, they had a pervasive impact upon individuals' senses of self and their assumptions about social cohesion, as well as influencing party politics and the outcome of elections.[1]

---

[1] Adrian Kane-Galbraith, 'Male Breadwinners of "Doubtful Sex": Trans Men and the Welfare State, 1954–1970', in *Men and Masculinities in Modern Britain: A History for the Present*, ed. Matt Houlbrook, Katie Jones, and Ben Mechen (Manchester: Manchester University Press, 2024), 49–66; Teri Chettiar, *The Intimate State: How Emotional Life Became Political in Welfare-State Britain* (Oxford: Oxford University Press, 2022); Carolyn Steedman, *Landscape for a Good Woman: A Story*

In this context, postwar mainstream cultural norms about sexual behaviour and identity also built on trends that had been in place before the war. Historians working in several national contexts have identified the Second World War as a watershed in the rise of heterosexuality.[2] But in the British case, at least, the norms that governed individuals' negotiation of sex and relationships in the post-war period evinced continuity with the 1930s. As before the war, norms varied according to one's stage in the life cycle, but continued to uphold the stability of the gender binary. An ideal of companionate marriage grounded in complementary gender roles, in which sex was accepted (not least for its reproductive role) but rarely openly discussed, existed alongside an ever-burgeoning culture of teenage and young adult premarital heterosexuality in which having a boy- or girl-friend was an important element of social currency that affirmed young people's appropriate femininity or masculinity.[3]

What did differ in the postwar period was the wider circulation of psychological discourses and the extent to which expertise in the medical and human sciences influenced policy around gender and sexuality in a significantly expanded state. Psychological discourses contributed to increased popular perception of heterosexual sexual expression as 'normal', 'healthy', and 'well-adjusted' for both women and men. These same discourses also increasingly diagnosed homosexuality as both an individual psychological and a wider social problem that could be addressed through expert intervention.[4] Values of social cohesion and integration loomed large in expert conceptions of how to respond to gender and sexual diversity. 'Bachelor uncles' and 'spinster aunts' could be tolerated, if not fully accepted, provided that they exercised discretion and did not disrupt the stability of the nuclear family.[5] Trans people's access to legal and medical transition was premised on expert evaluation of their ability to conform to normative

of Two Lives (New Brunswick: Rutgers University Press, 1986); Ina Zweiniger-Bargielowska, 'Rationing, Austerity and the Conservative Party Recovery after 1945', The Historical Journal 37, no. 1 (March 1994): 173–97; Susan Pedersen, Family, Dependence, and the Origins of the Welfare State: Britain and France, 1914–1945 (Cambridge: Cambridge University Press, 1993).

[2] See e.g., for North America, Mary Louise Adams, The Trouble with Normal: Postwar Youth and the Making of Heterosexuality (Toronto: University of Toronto Press, 1997); Rebecca L. Davis and Michele Mitchell, eds., Heterosexual Histories (New York: New York University Press, 2021); Stephen Vider, The Queerness of Home: Gender, Sexuality and the Politics of Domesticity after World War II (Chicago: University of Chicago Press, 2021). Cf. Margot Canaday, The Straight State: Sexuality and Citizenship in Twentieth-Century America (Princeton: Princeton University Press, 2009), which highlights continuities before and after the Second World War.

[3] Simon Szreter and Kate Fisher, Sex before the Sexual Revolution (Cambridge: Cambridge University Press, 2010); Hannah Charnock, 'Teenage Girls, Female Friendship and the Making of the Sexual Revolution in England, 1950–1980', The Historical Journal 63, no. 4 (September 2020): 1032–53.

[4] Chris Waters, 'The Homosexual as a Social Being in Britain, 1945–1968', Journal of British Studies 51, no. 3 (July 2012): 685–710.

[5] Deborah Cohen, Family Secrets: Shame and Privacy in Modern Britain (New York: Oxford University Press, 2013), 156–92; Matt Cook, Queer Domesticities: Homosexuality and Home Life in Twentieth Century London (Basingstoke: Palgrave Macmillan, 2014).

standards of heterosexual masculinity and femininity.[6] The coupling of psychology with the welfare state could put new pressure on the life cycle and on the acculturative powers of state institutions. How might state education, for example, ensure that children were socialized into appropriate roles of gender and sexuality, preparing them for psychologically and socially well-adjusted adulthoods?

Yet the postwar state stopped short of imagining academic secondary education, much less higher education, as a universal public good. The Education Act 1944 mandated universal secondary education for the first time, but divided this between selective grammar schools and the secondary modern schools attended by the majority of the population. Advanced academic education was conceptualized as reserved for the most talented who would make the best use of it. The University Grants Committee (UGC) continued to direct national higher education policy: its grants increasingly funded nearly the whole of universities' operating costs, and it developed other centralizing policies such as a firmer commitment to a single national pay scale for academic staff. But through the 1950s and into the 1960s, national higher education participation remained at approximately 3 per cent of the eighteen-to-twenty-five age cohort nationally, with a quarter of those students women. In the postwar period, average age of marriage and first childbirth dropped substantially for women. Many women left school at the minimum age of fifteen and dropped out of the labour market. Despite work by progressive feminist activists in the 1930s and 1940s both to challenge the binary between marriage and career and to decouple ideas about the purpose of higher education from vocational training, women tended either to eschew higher education in favour of marriage or to pursue forms of non-university further education oriented towards feminized professions. For example, between 1938 and 1974, the number of students enrolled at teacher-training colleges increased tenfold, of whom 70 per cent were women.[7]

Women academics and administrators, meanwhile, especially but not only those at women's colleges, contributed in some ways to erecting barriers to widening women's higher education participation. Like the Newnham College chemist Ida Freund a generation previous, they sought to identify the most talented minority who would not 'waste' the educational resources that had been invested in them, but would instead dedicate themselves to lives in academe. Some such women academics, like their nineteenth-century forebears, continued to defend women's colleges as offering exceptionally talented students the most conducive environment to their intellectual flourishing, and worried that increased gender integration would make this impossible. Women university

---

[6] Adrian Kane-Galbraith, 'Public Bodies: "Sex Change" and the State in Postwar Britain' (PhD thesis, University of Washington, 2024).

[7] William Whyte, *Redbrick: A Social and Architectural History of Britain's Civic Universities* (Oxford: Oxford University Press, 2015), 226–7; Carol Dyhouse, *Students: A Gendered History* (London: Routledge, 2006), 79–96.

students in the 1950s and 1960s, however, struggled to establish themselves in careers that used their degrees, resented the artificial segregation of women's colleges and halls, and evinced uncertainty about the purpose of their education and its relationship to their future lives. Given all this, it seems unsurprising both that women's higher education participation did not immediately increase after the Second World War and that social life at postwar universities was similar to that in the 1920s and 1930s, with cross-gender interaction grounded in a fairly sexualized dating culture that, through heterosexuality, affirmed ideas of gender difference.[8]

The gender order of British higher education began to change in the 1960s, however, owing once again both to changes in the institutional structure of the sector and to how students and academics responded to wider social changes regarding gender and sexuality. In 1963, a new national government inquiry, chaired by economist Lionel Robbins, recommended the expansion of higher education such that places might be available to all qualified applicants, alongside full state financial support for institutions and for students. In addition to prompting the UGC to fund the expansion of existing institutions, this inquiry led to the foundation of several new universities, and brought some forms of non-degree further education such as teacher training into the fold of universities. By 1970, 14 per cent of eighteen-to-twenty-five-year-olds attended university, 31 per cent of whom were women. Both overall higher education participation and women's participation would continue to rise steadily for the rest of the twentieth century.[9]

Government and the UGC rationalized increased higher education funding on practical economic grounds. University degrees could prepare young people for new kinds of careers—in engineering, business, information sciences—that would allow Britain to remain competitive in the global economy amidst fears of decline.[10] But as in the interwar period, this had consequences for how students were perceived as social and political actors beyond their degree courses. In an era when nearly all undergraduates attended university for free, students had the time and resources to devote themselves to new political and social causes. In the eyes of the public, this generationally specific category of person became associated with the political and social change of the 1960s–70s, whether in terms of global issues such as anticolonial and anti-apartheid activism or in terms of the domestic women's and gay liberation movements.[11] The first official conference of

---

[8] Dyhouse, *Students: A Gendered History*, 79–96.

[9] Whyte, *Redbrick*, 235–7; Dyhouse, *Students: A Gendered History*.

[10] Whyte, *Redbrick*, 232–3.

[11] Marc Matera, *Black London: The Imperial Metropolis and Decolonization in the Twentieth Century* (Oakland: University of California Press, 2015); Jodi Burkett, '"Don't Bank on Apartheid": The National Union of Students and the Boycott Barclays Campaign', in *Students in Twentieth-Century Britain and Ireland*, ed. Jodi Burkett (Basingstoke: Palgrave Macmillan, 2018), 225–45; Margaret Jolly, *Sisterhood and After: An Oral History of the UK Women's Liberation Movement*,

the Women's Liberation Movement took place at Ruskin College, a further education college in Oxford; the London Gay Liberation Front first met in a lecture theatre at the London School of Economics. Both movements drew involvement from large numbers of academics as well as students. Feminist and gay student societies, with the backing of local student unions and the National Union of Students, played important roles in fostering new styles of political consciousness and organizing. These identity-political movements gave new significance to ideas of university as a site for self-development and for the making of an adult self beyond one's formal studies. University could be a space in which a student might come out and come into new kinds of community.

At the same time, as in the interwar period, political activities only ever drew in a minority of students, and norms of heterosexuality that affirmed essential differences between the sexes continued to structure many students' experiences of cross-gender interaction. On campuses as in British society more widely, the 'permissive society' of the 1960s–70s promised sexual liberation in terms that scandalized conservative Christians, but also objectified women for the pleasure of a heterosexual male gaze.[12] Frustration with the restrictions that gender-segregated halls of residence placed on cross-gender interaction led students who had increasingly flocked to halls in the 1930s and 1940s to desert them in favour of private lodgings, while at some universities halls quietly and relatively uncontroversially amended their policies to allow for gender integration. At the University of Swansea in the 1970s, for example, women students successfully challenged curfews and bans on male visitors in women's halls. Yet feminist protest had little impact upon a dominant student culture that valued women for their physical attractiveness and sexual availability.[13] As in the period before the Second World War, many students negotiated new forms of cross-gender interaction through paradigms that affirmed heterosexuality and the gender binary.

What has led some previous historians to highlight the 1970s as a 'tipping point' is not changing relations between young women and men more broadly, but the end of gender-segregated institutional spaces, especially the independent women's college, as a meaningful presence in the UK higher education

---

1968–Present (Oxford: Oxford University Press, 2019); Jeffrey Weeks, *Between Worlds: A Queer Boy from the Valleys* (Cardigan: Parthian, 2021), 59.

[12] Jane O'Neill, '"Education Not Fornication?" Sexual Morality among Students in Scotland', in *Students in Twentieth-Century Britain and Ireland*, 77–98; Frank Mort, 'The Permissive Society Revisited', *Twentieth Century British History* 22, no. 2 (June 2011): 269–98; Frank Mort, *Capital Affairs: London and the Making of the Permissive Society* (New Haven: Yale University Press, 2010); Marcus Collins, ed., *The Permissive Society and Its Enemies: Sixties British Culture* (London: Rivers Oram, 2007).

[13] Jay Rees, 'Student Experience at Swansea University, 1920–1990' (PhD thesis, University of Swansea, 2020). See also Sarah Browne, '"Women Are Far Too Sweet for This Kind of Game": Women, Feminism and Student Politics in Scotland, c. 1968–c. 1979', in *Students in Twentieth-Century Britain and Ireland*, 277–95.

landscape.[14] Narratives with this periodization focus overwhelmingly on the gender integration of Oxford's and Cambridge's constituent colleges. The London women's colleges had already admitted men between 1944 and 1963, owing largely to declining demand for gender-segregated women's education in London, albeit over the protests of an older generation of women faculty and administrators who saw gender integration as a betrayal of their colleges' founding principles. Administrators also sometimes expressed that gender-integrated institutions better prepared students for the realities of twentieth-century adulthood. The male chair of Westfield College's Council even suggested that a gender-integrated Westfield would lead to fewer 'moral problems' than a women's-only college, echoing those a generation previous who had been suspicious of gender-segregated colleges as sites of homoeroticism and who perceived the gender-integrated university as a space where students could be socialized into healthy, normal heterosexuality.[15]

When Oxford and Cambridge men's colleges began to discuss the admission of women in the early 1970s, they reflected some of these considerations, citing the desire to attract a more competitive applicant pool (including of men students who preferred to attend a gender-integrated institution, as well as women) and generally to keep up to date amid changing times. The Sex Discrimination Act 1975 meant that the fellowships of these colleges could also no longer be all-male, and invalidated gender restrictions on many longstanding scholarships and endowments, such as the Rhodes Scholarships. The first men's colleges in Cambridge admitted women in 1972, and most of the rest of Oxford and Cambridge followed quickly in the ensuing years, though a few held out into the 1980s. Magdalene College, Cambridge became the last men's college to admit women, in 1988.[16] At other universities, too, men's-only spaces disappeared. The Glasgow University Union, for example, admitted women in 1980, when university administrators observed that it was becoming untenable to grant university (and thus taxpayer) funds to a men-only organization.[17] Most of the Oxford and Cambridge women's colleges admitted men in the 1980s and 1990s, albeit at times reluctantly and accompanied by a sense of loss from older faculty and alumnae.[18] The last women's college in Oxford, St Hilda's, admitted men in 2008, while as of 2024 Cambridge still has two women's colleges, Newnham and Murray Edwards, the only gender-segregated higher-education institutions left in the UK.

---

[14] Recent accounts that have offered this periodization include Dyhouse, *Students: A Gendered History* and Nancy Weiss Malkiel, *Keep the Damned Women Out: The Struggle for Coeducation* (Princeton: Princeton University Press, 2017).

[15] Dyhouse, *Students: A Gendered History*, 156–9.

[16] Dyhouse, *Students: A Gendered History*, 163–9; Malkiel, *Keep the Damned Women Out*, 491–594.

[17] James Riddell, letter to Mr Wallace (president, Glasgow University Union), n.d., c.1979, DC 94/1/7, GUA.

[18] Dyhouse, *Students: A Gendered History*, 107–12, 177–8.

Although these developments loomed large in the press at the time and in popular memory since, residential colleges remained marginal and anomalous in the context of a higher education system that, as it continued to expand in the late twentieth century, continued to treat the large, urban, non-residential university as paradigmatic. In numerical terms, a far more consequential structural transformation for the gender order of UK higher education was the 1992 conversion of the 'polytechnic' system of further education institutions into full-fledged universities. Like the former teacher-training colleges, polytechnics—more accessible to mature students and those studying part-time—had heavily female student populations. When they became universities, the number of women university students equalled that of men for the first time in British history.[19] By the early twenty-first century, at which point (despite declining government investment in higher education and significant increases in tuition fees) half of all Britons were likely to participate in some form of higher education by age thirty, significantly more women than men would apply to university, though there were sometimes large gender gaps in subject choice.[20] At the same time, women remained underrepresented among academic staff, especially at more senior levels, and often experienced gender pay gaps.[21] The casualization of academic labour in the UK, as in other national contexts, reinforced existing inequalities.

*

In an era when increasingly many careers require a university degree, the importance of higher education for vocational training and social mobility has never seemed greater, and a wider range of students from different backgrounds and at different life stages access higher education. At the same time, university has retained substantial cultural significance as a young adult rite of passage: a stage in the life cycle when, whether they live 'on campus' or not, young adults leave home for the first time, experience new geographies of home, campus, and university city, often encounter some kind of communal living with other young adults, and confront the challenges of new kinds of interpersonal relationships. Students navigate between cultural norms and their own desires, come into new understandings of their gender and sexual identities, make mistakes, and learn things about themselves. Though today's students are likelier than ever to have full-time jobs, to be parents, or to study part-time, a cultural ideal of studenthood

---

[19] Dyhouse, *Students: A Gendered History*, 82.

[20] 'UCAS Undergraduate End of Cycle Data Resources 2022', accessed 20 August 2023, https://www.ucas.com/data-and-analysis/undergraduate-statistics-and-reports/ucas-undergraduate-end-cycle-data-resources-2022; 'Participation Rates in Higher Education: Academic Years 2006/2007–2017/2018', Office for National Statistics, 26 September 2019, accessed 7 March 2020, https://www.gov.uk/government/statistics/participation-rates-in-higher-education-2006-to-2018.

[21] For statistics on gender equality among academic historians, for example, see Nicola Miller et al., 'Promoting Gender Equality in UK History: A Second Report and Recommendations for Good Practice', Royal Historical Society, November 2018.

as a distinctive time in the life cycle has shaped the expectations of young adults (and their parents) about university and the cultural norms they reproduce while they are there, as well as the experiences and attitudes of faculty and administrators and the assumptions underlying government higher education policy.

Not least of these assumptions is the idea that university might acculturate young adults into appropriate norms for gender and sexuality. In recent years, this theme has been especially prevalent in scholarship and cultural commentary in the United States, where debates about federal Title IX sex discrimination legislation have contributed to a perception that universities have a moral as well as a legal responsibility to respond to gender-based misconduct, sexual harassment, and sexual assault among students and of students by faculty. While American conservative commentators have long decried student life at gender-integrated residential universities for fostering 'hookup culture', liberal commentators have also integrated sex education into a broader vision of university as a site for self-development and orientation into community and civic life. For example, in a social-scientific study of primarily heterosexual behaviour and mores at 2010s Columbia University, public health scholar Jennifer Hirsch and sociologist Shamus Khan describe campus sexual assault as a structural problem, shaped by campus geographies, cultures of substance abuse, and normative scripts for heterosexual sexual behaviour in which students feel trapped. Yet they also characterize sexual assault as a failure of liberal self-development. '[W]hat consistently separated interactions that verged on or constituted assault from those that did not', they argue, 'was [a] moment of recognition about the other person's equivalent humanity.'[22] As a solution, they propose a model of 'sexual citizenship' in which universities might instruct students not in legalistic models of 'affirmative consent', but in autonomy, self-determination, and equity.

Similarly, the philosopher Amia Srinivasan has argued that what is wrong with teacher–student sexual relationships is not primarily a power differential that necessarily implies an absence of consent, but rather a 'pedagogical failure': a teacher's failure to exercise their ethical responsibility as a teacher; a misapprehension of the kinds of intimate connections between teachers and students that a responsible university community should foster.[23] In Srinivasan's normative case, male teachers harass female students: teacher–student sex is, if a matter of pedagogical ethics, also definitionally entwined with patriarchy and constitutive of sex discrimination under US law. Like Hirsch's and Khan's university, Srinivasan's university is an ethical community, part of whose role is to disseminate sexual mores that are representative of broader precepts about what constitutes human flourishing and common life. These scholars are heirs to a longer

---

[22] Jennifer S. Hirsch and Shamus Khan, *Sexual Citizens: A Landmark Study of Sex, Power, and Assault on Campus* (New York: W.W. Norton, 2020), 111.

[23] Amia Srinivasan, 'Sex as a Pedagogical Failure', *The Yale Law Journal* 129, no. 4 (February 2020): 1100–46; see also her *The Right to Sex* (London: Bloomsbury, 2021).

tradition of liberal thought about education, self-development, and the purpose of the university that—as I have sought to show throughout this book—has in other times and places also been refracted through norms of gender and sexuality.

In the process of advancing claims about the kinds of education in sexual mores that universities might provide, these scholars also show how the university has been a site for the making of meaning about *heterosexuality* in particular. Both Hirsch and Khan and Srinivasan imagine the ethical problem of sex on campus to be one of managing cross-gender relations under patriarchy. Their analyses demonstrate how students and teachers alike may turn to the conventions of heterosexuality as a tactic for navigating interpersonal relationships across gender lines—often to their detriment and the detriment of others who are in community with them. Yet the solutions these scholars propose, if in some ways liberating, in other ways reinscribe fairly narrow conceptions of the possibilities for gender and sexuality as facets of self-development and community life.

Other voices, however, offer alternatives. One great achievement of second-wave feminism was to firmly establish women's, and, later, gender and sexuality studies as an academic field of study. Within higher education across national contexts, there is now a fifty-year tradition of formally 'teaching gender' in the classroom as well as outside it. Scholars across academic disciplines have integrated the insights of women's, gender, and sexuality studies into their research and teaching. At the same time, in several national contexts, the teaching of gender studies in universities has become a highly visible target of the global far-right 'anti-gender' movement, which imagines reproductive justice and LGBTQ+ rights as threats to the stability of an essential, biological sex binary and of the heteronormative nuclear family. To such activists, for whom famous gender studies academics like Judith Butler are symbols of 'gender's excesses, the university classroom looms large as a dangerous site where young people risk being seduced into 'gender ideology'.[24]

These views are conspiracist and extremist, but they are in some sense on to something. After all, students often do develop new ways of thinking about gender and sexuality while at university, whether in the classroom or not. Traditional-age students who leave home to go to university may question the values and senses of self with which they were raised. They may experiment with and adopt new gender and sexual identities, and have new sexual experiences. They may find that what they learn in their studies does challenge their preconceived notions about the kinds of sex and sexuality, or the expectations for the trajectory of their adult lives, that are 'normal' or 'good'. Importantly, while far-right activists might imagine the university classroom as a site of top-down transmission of nefarious 'gender ideology', gender studies academics themselves often emphasize the dialogic nature of teaching gender studies. Through peer groups, popular

---

[24] Judith Butler, *Who's Afraid of Gender?* (London: Farrar, Straus & Giroux, 2024).

culture, and personal experience, students develop their own conceptions of how gender and sexuality work, which can sometimes clash with academic frameworks, leading to tension and conflict in the classroom.[25] The trans studies scholar Nicholas Clarkson has called for gender studies instructors to 'model emotional maturity' in the course of such difficult exchanges: resisting the temptation to dismiss students as immature or excessively fragile, and instead creating space in which students can work through challenges to their preconceived views and take their thinking further.[26] Like Srinivasan, Clarkson identifies a robust pedagogical ethics as central to what it means to think and to do gender and sexuality in the space of the university campus. But, further, he imagines intergenerational exchanges about gender and sexuality as dialogic and productive, opening up avenues along which new possibilities for doing gender and sexuality can flourish— one imagines, in academic work, but also in students' and faculty's own lives.

*

Throughout *Teaching Gender*, I have sought to show that none of this is new. Among students and faculty alike, both a conception of campus life as inhering in cross-gender relations facilitated by heterosexuality, and challenges or alternatives to that paradigm, have had long and contingent histories. Out of a need to make sense of the lived experience of cross-gender relations in newly gender-integrated universities, early-twentieth-century British students developed a new paradigm of heterosexual sex, dating, and desire that quickly became central to how many conceptualized the purpose of their time at university. The rise of this paradigm could marginalize or resignify some alternatives, like the queer and trans possibilities of student theatre or the homosocial intimacies available to those who made careers in women's higher education. And it could lead directly to the rise of others, like the paradigm of male homosexuality that emerged in Oxford and Cambridge men's colleges in reaction to gender integration. Through generational conflict, interaction between the university and the city, and wider political and cultural shifts and moments of crisis, students, faculty, and others continued iteratively to remake the campus gender order as they lived out everyday life in the space of the university.

I have also sought to show that new ways of thinking and doing gender and sexuality developed within specific institutional constraints. From the mid-nineteenth century, the expansion and reform of British higher education was shaped by abstract conceptions of for what and for whom higher education ought

---

[25] Kadji Amin, 'We Are All Nonbinary: A Brief History of Accidents', *Representations* 158, no. 1 (May 2022): 106–19; Kadji Amin, 'Taxonomically Queer? Sexology and New Queer, Trans, and Asexual Identities', *GLQ: A Journal of Lesbian and Gay Studies* 29, no. 1 (January 2023): 91–107; Nicholas L. Clarkson, 'Teaching Trans Students, Teaching Trans Studies', *Feminist Teacher* 27, nos 2–3 (2017): 233–52.

[26] Clarkson, 'Teaching Trans Students', 243.

to be—but also by the availability of funds, whether from private donors or the state, and by the relative political power that different higher-education reformers, activists, and administrators wielded. Small, independent institutions designed with women in mind became in relatively short order subsumed into large, urban, non-residential, incidentally gender-integrated universities, for reasons of efficiency and not of commitment to gender equality. This process was not foreordained, but happened as a consequence of larger changes in conceptualizations of the role of the state and the national and imperial strategic value of university teaching and research. Though not centrally *about* gender and sexuality, however, this process fundamentally shaped the conditions within which faculty, students, administrators, and other inhabitants of university cities lived gendered lives. It led to the construction of the laboratories, libraries, student unions, and halls of residence, but also the cinemas, coffeehouses, and private homes in new middle-class residential districts, in which individuals worked out how to relate to one another within and across gendered lines. Through the interactions of everyday life—faculty meetings, dances, chance encounters on the street—abstract ideas about gender, sexuality, and the purpose of higher education ran up against realities. And through this process of encounter between students, faculty, administrators, donors, politicians, the media, and the public, new norms were made.

In the decades since the Second World War, higher education in Britain, as in other national contexts, has in some sense changed beyond recognition. Yet in another sense, we still live in the world that the inhabitants of early-twentieth-century universities made. Both those of us who live and work in higher education, and those of us who do not, continue to take an interest in what higher education is for and what its relationship to the nation is, what it means to be a student, what students do when they are not studying, how university might prepare students for future life, what the relationship is between faculty and students and between town and gown, and how students' encounters with higher education might, for good or ill, prompt new ways of living and of making sense of one's life choices. To be sure, we ought to be wary of idealism. Not only, as we have seen, is the remaking of gender and sexuality in universities as likely to affirm norms as to subvert them, in Britain and in many other national contexts, universities have in recent years been eviscerated by chronic underfunding, the casualization of academic labour, and attacks on academic freedom, once again shaping the structural conditions in which academics and students alike live and work. Yet the promise that university education might prove transformative of worldviews and of personal relationships endures. We would do well to fight for its survival.

Teaching Gender: The British University and the Rise of Heterosexuality, 1860–1939. Samuel Rutherford,
Oxford University Press. © Samuel Rutherford 2025. DOI: 10.1093/9780198937524.003.0009

Bibliography

Primary Sources

Archives

Bodleian Library, University of Oxford

Archive of the Dixey Family
    MS Eng. lett. d. 465: Letters to F.A. Dixey concerning the study of Greek at Oxford
Archive of Ethel Sidgwick
    MS Eng. misc. *c.* 704–706: Archive of Ethel Sidgwick

British Library

P.P. 6139.db: *UCL Union Magazine*
P.P. 6149.fa: *University College Gazette*

Cadbury Research Library, University of Birmingham

University House
    UB/HUH/A/3: Correspondence
    UB/HUH/A/8: Photographs
    UB/HUH/A/9: History of University House
    UB/HUH/A/10: Miscellaneous Files

Cambridge University Library

A.T. Bartholomew Papers
    MS Add. 8786/1–3: Diaries
University Archives
    UA/CUR/61–61.1 University Registry Guard Books on the Higher Education of Women
    UA/Min.VI.23: Degrees for Women Syndicate Minutes
    UA/Synd.II: Papers of the Degrees for Women Syndicate

Christ's College, Cambridge

Papers of A.E. Shipley
    Box 196: Scrapbook concerning Christ's College and A.E. Shipley

Columbia University Rare Books and Manuscripts Library

Virginia Gildersleeve Papers
    Box 4: Miscellaneous biographical material
    Box 44: International Federation of University Women
    Box 65: Manuscripts
    Box 78: Organizations

Corpus Christi College, Oxford

Papers of Edward Perry Warren
    B/12–B/14: Papers regarding Warren's donation to Corpus
Student Societies
    E/5/1–4: Pelican Essay Club Minute Books
    The Pelican Record

Durham University

Student Publications
  Per Local DUR: *Durham University Journal*
  SC12348/3: *The Undergrad*
  SC12348/7: *The Critic*
  SC+04522: *The Palatine*
  SC+04523: *The New Durham*
University Archives
  UND/BA1: Senate Minutes
  UND/F8: Photographs
  UND/GB1: Students' Representative Committee
  UND/GE1: Durham University Union
  UND/GE2: Women's Union Society

University of Edinburgh

Edinburgh Association for the University Education of Women
  Coll-42/1: Calendars and Reports
  Coll-42/3: Meeting Minutes
  Coll-42/5: Correspondence of Mrs Mary Crudelius
Papers of Marjorie Rackstraw
  Coll-705: Uncatalogued personal papers
Papers of Sir John Smith Flett
  Coll-100: 'My Student Days at Edinburgh University, 1886–1894'
Edinburgh University Students' Association
  EUA/IN20/SRC/d: SRC Women's Committee Minutes
Records of Masson Hall of Residence
  EUA GD58/1: Minutes of Masson Hall Committee
  EUA GD58/18: Masson Hall Newsletters
  EUA GD58/22: Photographs

Girton College, Cambridge

Emily Davies Papers
  GCPP/Davies/11: Pamphlets and letters to the press
  GCPP/Davies/13: Cambridge Degrees for Women
  GCPP/Davies/15: Girton College: Foundation, Hitchin and Girton

University of Glasgow

University Publications
  DC 198/1: *Glasgow University Magazine*
University Archives
  GUA 62398: Correspondence between John Caird and Isabella Elder
  GUA 62445: Correspondence concerning Queen Margaret College
Glasgow University Union
  DC 94/1: Correspondence
  DC 94/2: Minutes
Records of Queen Margaret College
  DC 233/2/3: Annual Reports
  DC 233/2/4: Establishment and Affiliation to Glasgow University
  DC 233/2/16: Student Societies
  DC 233/2/21: History of Queen Margaret College
Queen Margaret Union
  DC 240/2: Minutes
  DC 240/5: Publications

King's College, Cambridge

G.L. Dickinson Papers
  GLD/1: Prose, 1904–33
John Maynard Keynes Papers
  JMK/UA: University affairs, 1874–1946
Cambridge Apostles
  KCAS/39/1: Minute Books

King's College London

Archives of King's College for Women
  KW/M: Minute Books
  K/HOS: King's College Hostel records
  KW/LECT: Lecture Notes
  KW/SYL: Syllabuses and Prospectuses
  KWA/GPF: General and Policy Files
Archives of Queen Elizabeth College (formerly King's College for Household and Social Sciences)
  Q/EPH/SYL: Syllabuses and Prospectuses
  Q/PP1: Papers of Sir John Adkins
  QA/C: Minutes of Council
  QA/CS: Special Investigation Sub-Committee on Future of KCHSS
  QAP/GPF: Administrative Records

University of Liverpool

University Council and Senate
  S2476–8: Council and Senate Report Books
  S219–20: Senate General Purposes Committee
Student Union
  A.27: Entertainments Committee
  A.32: Debating Society
  D404: Papers regarding Rag
Margaret Miller Papers
  D384/1/1: Scrapbook of press cuttings
  D384/1/2: Material relating to marriage bar controversy
  D384/2: Correspondence

London School of Economics

British Federation of University Women
  5BFW/4/20: Sub-committee on Employment of Married Women
  5BFW/5/2: BFUW Committee on Standards

Magdalen College, Oxford

Papers of Thomas Case
  MC:F30/N1: Ephemera on the Admission of Women

University of Manchester

Student Publications
  UMP/2/1: *Owens College Magazine*
  UMP/2/3: *Manchester University Magazine*
  UMP/2/4: *The Serpent*
Women's Union
  AWS/2: Files of the Adviser to Women Students
  AWS/6: Department for Women Records

University of Manchester Students' Union
  SUA/1: Committee Minutes
  SUA/7: Rag Magazines
  SUA/13: Women's Union Notices

Royal Holloway, University of London

Papers of the Royal Holloway College Association
  AS/902: Royal Holloway *College Letter*
Royal Holloway College Papers
  RHC/1: Records of the Board of Governors
  RHC/2: Records of Thomas Holloway
Photograph albums and scrapbooks
  PH/285/4: Photographs donated by Margaret Yates
  PH/285/10: Photographs donated by Audrey Baddeley
Caroline Spurgeon Papers
  PP7/3: Records of Teaching
  PP7/6: International Federation of University Women

Somerville College, Oxford

Margery Fry Papers
  Box 27: Letters re. Somerville College
  Box 29: Papers relating to Rose Sidgwick and Margery Fry
  Box 30: Letters between Rose Sidgwick and Margery Fry
  Box 31: Letters to Margery Fry re. University of Birmingham
  Box 41: Lectures and Broadcasts

The National Archives

University Grants Committee
  UGC/1: Minutes
  UGC/3: Returns from universities and university colleges in receipt of grant
  UGC/5: Reports

University College London

University Archives
  UCLCA/CC: Council Minutes
Women's Union
  REC/2005/61/1: Annual Reports
  REC/2005/61/2: Minutes
Miscellaneous University Files
  MEM/III/B: Women's Union Society

Newspapers, Magazines, and Newsreels

British Pathé
Cambridge Independent Press
Cambridge University Reporter
Common Cause
Daily Express
Daily Mail
Daily Mirror
Daily Telegraph
Dundee Courier
Education
The Englishwoman
Evening Telegraph (Dundee)
Exeter and Plymouth Gazette

The Illustrated London News
Manchester Guardian
New-York Tribune
Nottingham Evening Post
The Observer
The Scotsman
The Sphinx
The Times
Western Gazette

Published Primary Sources

The Challenge to the University: A Report of the 1938 Congress of the National Union of Students of England and Wales on University Life and Teaching in Relation to the Needs of Modern Society (London: The National Union of Students, 1938).

Essays and Reviews (London: John W. Parker and Son, 1860).

'Fourth Universities Congress Oxford, March 29th to April 4th, 1928' (London: National Union of Students, 1928).

Babington, Percy L. *Bibliography of the Writings of John Addington Symonds* (London: John Castle, 1925).

Browning, Oscar. *Memories of Sixty Years at Eton, Cambridge, and Elsewhere* (London: John Lane, 1910).

Burdett, Osbert and E.H. Goddard. *Edward Perry Warren: The Biography of a Connoisseur* (London: Christophers, 1941).

Davies, Emily. *The Higher Education of Women* (London: Alexander Strahan, 1866).

Dillon, Michael/Lobzang Jivaka, ed. Jacob Lau and Cameron Partridge. *Out of the Ordinary: A Life of Gender and Spiritual Transitions* (New York: Fordham University Press, 2016).

Ellis, Havelock and John Addington Symonds. *Sexual Inversion: A Critical Edition*, ed. Ivan Crozier (London: Palgrave Macmillan, 2008).

Farrar, F.W., ed. *Essays on a Liberal Education* (London: Macmillan, 1867).

Forster, E.M. *Goldsworthy Lowes Dickinson* (London: Edward Arnold, 1934).

Fry, Margery. 'The University Grants Committee: An Experiment in Administration', *Universities Quarterly* 2, no. 3 (May 1948): 221–30.

Fry, Margery. *The Single Woman* (London: Delisle, 1953).

Gildersleeve, Virginia C. *Many a Good Crusade: Memoirs of Virginia Crocheron Gildersleeve* (New York: Macmillan, 1954).

Greenidge, Terence. *Degenerate Oxford? A Critical Study of Modern University Life* (London: Chapman & Hall, 1930).

Grundy, G.B. *Fifty-Five Years at Oxford: An Unconventional Autobiography* (London: Methuen, 1945).

Kaylor, Michael, ed. *The Collected Works and Commissioned Biography of Edward Perry Warren*, Volume 1 (Brno: Masarykova univerzita, 2015).

Macadam, Ivison S. *Youth in the Universities* (London: National Union of Students, 1922).

Marchant, Sir James, ed. *What Life Has Taught Me: By Twenty-Five Distinguished Men & Women* (Long Acre & London: Odhams Press, 1948).

Marshall, Mary Paley. *What I Remember* (Cambridge: Cambridge University Press, 1947).

Mill, J.S. *Inaugural Address Delivered to the University of St Andrews* (London: Longmans, Green, Reader, and Dyer, 1867).

Mill, J.S. 'Considerations on Representative Government', in J.S. Mill, *On Liberty, Utilitarianism and Other Essays*, ed. Mark Philp and Frederick Rosen (Oxford: Oxford University Press, 2015), 181–405.

Mitcheson, Richard Edmund. *Charitable Trusts: The Jurisdiction of the Charity Commission, Being the Acts Conferring Such Jurisdiction, 1853–1883* (London: Stevens and Sons, 1887).

Mowat, R.B., ed. *Letters to 'The Times' (1884–1922), Written by Thomas Case* (Oxford: Oxford University Press, 1927).

Oakeley, Hilda. *History & Progress, and Other Essays and Addresses* (London: George Allen & Unwin, 1923).

Oakeley, Hilda. *My Adventures in Education* (London: Williams and Northgate, 1939).

Pigou, A.C., ed. *Memorials of Alfred Marshall* (London: Macmillan, 1925).

Proctor, Dennis, ed. *The Autobiography of G. Lowes Dickinson and Other Unpublished Writings* (London: Duckworth, 1973).

Sayers, Dorothy L. *Gaudy Night* (London: Victor Gollancz, 1935).

Sheavyn, Phoebe. 'Higher Education for Women in Great Britain', International Federation of University Women Pamphlet No. 2, 1921.

Shipley, Arthur Everett. *The Voyage of a Vice-Chancellor* (Cambridge: Cambridge University Press, 1919).

Sidgwick, Arthur and Eleanor Mildred Sidgwick. *Henry Sidgwick: A Memoir* (London: Macmillan, 1906).

Stead, W.T. *The Last Will and Testament of Cecil John Rhodes, with Elucidatory Notes* (London: Review of Reviews Office, 1902).

Tyrwhitt, Richard St John. 'The Greek Spirit in Modern Literature', *Contemporary Review* 29 (March 1877), 552–6.

Warren, Edward Perry. *A Defence of Uranian Love* (privately printed, 1928–30).

Government Reports

Charitable Trusts Acts, 1853–1894. Analytically Arranged. (London: Charity Commission, 1896).

Royal Commission on University Education in London. First Report of the Commissioners, 1910. Cmnd 5165.

Royal Commission on University Education in London. Appendix to First Report of the Commissioners, 1910. Cmnd 5166.

Royal Commission on University Education in London. Appendix to Second Report of the Commissioners, 1911. Cmnd 5528.

Royal Commission on University Education in London. Appendix to Third Report of the Commissioners, 1911. Cmnd 5911.

Royal Commission on University Education in London. Final Report of the Commissioners, 1913. Cmnd 6717.

Royal Commission on University Education in London. Appendix to Final Report of the Commissioners, 1913. Cmnd 6718.

Secondary Sources

Published

Abra, Allison. *Dancing in the English Style: Consumption, Americanisation and National Identity in Britain, 1918–50* (Manchester: Manchester University Press, 2017).

Adams, Mary Louise. *The Trouble with Normal: Postwar Youth and the Making of Heterosexuality* (Toronto: University of Toronto Press, 1997).

Adams, Pauline. *Somerville for Women: An Oxford College, 1879–1993* (Oxford: Oxford University Press, 1996).

Alexander, Michael. *Medievalism: The Middle Ages in Modern England* (New Haven: Yale University Press, 2007).

Amin, Kadji. 'We Are All Nonbinary: A Brief History of Accidents', *Representations* 158, no. 1 (May 2022): 106–19.

Amin, Kadji. 'Taxonomically Queer? Sexology and New Queer, Trans, and Asexual Identities', *GLQ: A Journal of Lesbian and Gay Studies* 29, no. 1 (January 2023): 91–107.

Anderson, R.D. *Education and Opportunity in Victorian Scotland* (Edinburgh: Edinburgh University Press, 1989).

Anderson, R.D. *Universities and Elites in Britain since 1800* (Cambridge: Cambridge University Press, 1992).

Anderson, R.D. *European Universities from the Enlightenment to 1914* (Oxford: Oxford University Press, 2004).

Anderson, Robert. 'Professors and Examinations: Ideas of the University in Nineteenth-Century Scotland', *History of Education* 46, no. 1 (January 2017): 21–38.

Anderson, Robert and Stuart Wallace. 'The Universities and National Identity in the Long Nineteenth Century, c. 1830–1914', in *The Edinburgh History of Education in Scotland*, ed. Robert Anderson, Mark Freeman, and Lindsay Paterson (Edinburgh: Edinburgh University Press, 2015), 265–85.

Andrews, Matthew. *Universities in the Age of Reform: Durham, London and King's College, 1800–1870* (Cham: Palgrave Macmillan, 2018).

Ashby, Eric and Mary Anderson. *The Rise of the Student Estate in Britain* (London: Macmillan, 1970).

Ashby, Eric and Mary Anderson. *Portrait of Haldane at Work on Education* (London: Macmillan, 1974).

Axelrod, Paul. *Making a Middle Class: Student Life in English Canada during the Thirties* (Montreal & Kingston: McGill–Queen's University Press, 1990).

Bailkin, Jordanna. *The Afterlife of Empire* (Berkeley: University of California Press, 2012).

Bamford, T.W. *Thomas Arnold on Education* (Cambridge: Cambridge University Press, 1970).

Barron, Caroline M. and Joel T. Rosenthal, eds. *Thomas Frederick Tout (1855–1929): Refashioning History for the Twentieth Century* (London: Institute of Historical Research, 2019).

Bartie, Angela et al. 'Historical Pageants and the Medieval Past in Twentieth Century England', *English Historical Review* 133, no. 563 (2018): 866–902.

Bartie, Angela et al. '"History Taught the Pageant Way": Education and Historical Performance in Twentieth-Century Britain', *History of Education* 48, no. 2 (March 2019): 156–79.

Bartie, Angela et al., eds. *Restaging the Past: Historical Pageants, Culture and Society in Modern Britain* (London: UCL Press, 2020).

Biagini, Eugenio F. *Liberty, Retrenchment and Reform: Popular Liberalism in the Age of Gladstone, 1860–1880* (Cambridge: Cambridge University Press, 1992).

Bingham, Caroline. *The History of Royal Holloway College, 1886–1986* (London: Constable, 1987).

Bland, Lucy. *Banishing the Beast: Sexuality and the Early Feminists* (New York: The New Press, 1995).

Bland, Lucy. 'White Women and Men of Colour: Miscegenation Fears in Britain after the Great War', *Gender & History* 17, no. 1 (2005): 29–61.

Bloomfield, Jacob. 'Splinters: Cross-Dressing Ex-Servicemen on the Interwar Stage', *Twentieth Century British History* 30, no. 1 (March 2019): 1–28.

Bloomfield, Jacob. *Drag: A British History* (Berkeley: University of California Press, 2023).

Brewis, Georgina. *A Social History of Student Volunteering: Britain and Beyond, 1880–1980* (Basingstoke: Palgrave Macmillan, 2014).

Brewis, Georgina, Sarah Hellawell, and Daniel Laqua. 'Rebuilding the Universities after the Great War: Ex-Service Students, Scholarships and the Reconstruction of Student Life in England', *History* 105, no. 364 (2020): 82–106.

Brittain, Vera. *The Women at Oxford: A Fragment of History* (London: Harrap, 1960).

Brock, M.G. and M.C. Curthoys, eds. *The History of the University of Oxford*, Volume 6: *The Nineteenth Century, Part 1* (Oxford: Oxford University Press, 1997).

Brock, M.G. and M.C. Curthoys, eds. *The History of the University of Oxford*, Volume 7: *Nineteenth-Century Oxford, Part 2* (Oxford: Oxford University Press, 2000).

Brooks, Ross. 'Beyond Brideshead: The Male Homoerotics of 1930s Oxford', *Journal of British Studies* 59, no. 4 (October 2020): 821–56.

Burkett, Jodi, ed. *Students in Twentieth-Century Britain and Ireland* (Basingstoke: Palgrave Macmillan, 2018).

Bush, Julia. *Women against the Vote: Female Anti-Suffragism in Britain* (Oxford: Oxford University Press, 2007).

Butler, Judith. *Who's Afraid of Gender?* (London: Farrar, Straus & Giroux, 2024).

Canaday, Margot. *The Straight State: Sexuality and Citizenship in Twentieth-Century America* (Princeton: Princeton University Press, 2009).

Canaday, Margot, Nancy F. Cott, and Robert O. Self, eds. *Intimate States: Gender, Sexuality, and Governance in Modern US History* (Chicago: University of Chicago Press, 2021).

Carter, Jennifer J. and Donald J. Withrington, eds. *Scottish Universities: Distinctiveness and Diversity* (Edinburgh: John Donald, 1992).

Charnock, Hannah. 'Teenage Girls, Female Friendship and the Making of the Sexual Revolution in England, 1950–1980', *The Historical Journal* 63, no. 4 (September 2020): 1032–53.

Chauncey, George. *Gay New York: Gender, Urban Culture, and the Making of the Gay Male World 1890–1940* (New York: Basic, 1994).

Chettiar, Teri. *The Intimate State: How Emotional Life Became Political in Welfare-State Britain* (Oxford: Oxford University Press, 2022).

Christie, Nancy and Michael Gauvreau. *Bodies, Love, and Faith in the First World War: Dardanella and Peter* (Basingstoke: Palgrave Macmillan, 2018).

Clark, Anna. *The Struggle for the Breeches: Gender and the Making of the British Working Class* (Berkeley: University of California Press, 1995).

Clark, Anna. 'Twilight Moments', *Journal of the History of Sexuality* 14, no. 1 (2005): 139–60.

Clark, Anna. *Alternative Histories of the Self: A Cultural History of Sexuality and Secrets* (New York: Bloomsbury, 2017).

Clarkson, Nicholas L. 'Teaching Trans Students, Teaching Trans Studies', *Feminist Teacher* 27, nos. 2–3 (2017): 233–52.

Cocks, H.G. *Nameless Offences: Homosexual Desire in the Nineteenth Century* (London: I.B. Tauris, 2003).

Cohen, Deborah. *Family Secrets: Shame and Privacy in Modern Britain* (New York: Oxford University Press, 2013).

Collini, Stefan. *Public Moralists: Political Thought and Intellectual Life in Victorian Britain 1850–1930* (Oxford: Oxford University Press, 1991).

Collini, Stefan. *What Are Universities For?* (London: Penguin, 2012).

Collins, Marcus, ed. *The Permissive Society and Its Enemies: Sixties British Culture* (London: Rivers Oram, 2007).

Collins, Tony. 'Return to Manhood: The Cult of Masculinity and the British Union of Fascists', *The International Journal of the History of Sport* 16, no. 4 (December 1999): 145–62.

Cook, Matt. *London and the Culture of Homosexuality, 1885–1914* (Cambridge: Cambridge University Press, 2003).

Cook, Matt. *Queer Domesticities: Homosexuality and Home Life in Twentieth Century London* (Basingstoke: Palgrave Macmillan, 2014).

Cook, Matt and Alison Oram. *Queer beyond London* (Manchester: Manchester University Press, 2022).

Corley, T.A.B. 'Holloway, Thomas (1800–1883), Manufacturer of Patent Medicines and Philanthropist', *Oxford Dictionary of National Biography*, 23 September 2004, accessed 12 July 2022, https://www.oxforddnb.com/display/10.1093/ref:odnb/9780198614128.001.0001/odnb-9780198614128-e-13577.

Crouthamel, Jason. '"Comradeship" and "Friendship": Masculinity and Militarisation in Germany's Homosexual Emancipation Movement after the First World War', *Gender & History* 23, no. 1 (2011): 111–29.

Dagnino, Jorge, Matthew Feldman, and Paul Stocker, eds. *The 'New Man' in Radical Right Ideology and Practice, 1919–45* (London: Bloomsbury, 2017).

Darnton, Robert. *The Great Cat Massacre and Other Episodes in French Cultural History* (New York: Basic, 1984).

Davin, Anna. 'Imperialism and Motherhood', *History Workshop*, no. 5 (April 1978): 9–65.

Davis, Natalie Zemon. *Society and Culture in Early Modern France* (Stanford: Stanford University Press, 1975).

Davis, Rebecca and Michele Mitchell, eds. *Heterosexual Histories* (New York: New York University Press, 2021).

Day, Mike. *National Union of Students, 1922–2012* (London: Regal Press, 2012).

De Bellaigue, Christina. *Educating Women: Schooling and Identity in England and France, 1800–1867* (Oxford: Oxford University Press, 2007).

De Coninck-Smith, Ning. 'Gender Encounters University—University Encounters Gender: Affective Archives, Aarhus University, Denmark, 1928–1953', *Women's History Review* 29, no. 3 (2020): 413–28.

Delamont, Sarah. 'Davies, (Sarah) Emily (1830–1921), Suffragist and Promoter of Higher Education for Women', *Oxford Dictionary of National Biography*, 23 September 2004, accessed 10 July 2022, https://www.oxforddnb.com/view/10.1093/ref:odnb/9780198614128.001.0001/odnb-9780198614128-e-32741.

Delaney, Samuel. *Times Square Red, Times Square Blue* (New York: New York University Press, 1999).

Delap, Lucy. *The Feminist Avant-Garde: Transatlantic Encounters of the Early Twentieth Century* (Cambridge: Cambridge University Press, 2007).

Dellamora, Richard. *Masculine Desire: The Sexual Politics of Victorian Aestheticism* (Chapel Hill: UNC Press, 1990).

D'Emilio, John. 'Capitalism and Gay Identity', in *The Lesbian and Gay Studies Reader*, ed. Henry Abelove, Michèle Aina Barale, and David M. Halperin (New York: Routledge, 1993), 467–76.

Den Otter, Sandra M. *British Idealism and Social Explanation: A Study in Late-Victorian Thought* (Oxford: Clarendon Press, 1996).

Deslandes, Paul R. *Oxbridge Men: British Masculinity and the Undergraduate Experience* (Bloomington: Indiana University Press, 2005).

Dixon, Thomas. *The Invention of Altruism: Making Moral Meanings in Victorian Britain* (Oxford: Oxford University Press, 2008).

Doan, Laura. *Fashioning Sapphism: The Origins of a Modern English Lesbian Culture* (New York: Columbia University Press, 2001).

Doan, Laura. *Disturbing Practices: History, Sexuality, and Women's Experience of Modern War* (Chicago: University of Chicago Press, 2013).

Doan, Laura. 'Marie Stopes's Wonderful Rhythm Charts: Normalizing the Natural', *Journal of the History of Ideas* 78, no. 4 (October 2017): 595–620.

Doan, Laura and Jane Garrity, eds. *Sapphic Modernities: Sexuality, Women and National Culture* (Basingstoke: Palgrave Macmillan, 2007).

Dowling, Linda. *Hellenism and Homosexuality in Victorian Oxford* (Ithaca: Cornell University Press, 1994).

Dyhouse, Carol. *Girls Growing up in Late Victorian and Edwardian England* (London: Routledge, 1981).

Dyhouse, Carol. *No Distinction of Sex? Women in British Universities 1870–1930* (London: University College London Press, 1995).

Dyhouse, Carol. *Students: A Gendered History* (London: Routledge, 2006).

Edgerton, David. *Warfare State: Britain, 1920–1970* (Cambridge: Cambridge University Press, 2006).

Edwards, Elizabeth. 'Homoerotic Friendship and College Principals, 1880–1960', *Women's History Review* 4, no. 2 (June 1995): 149–63.

Egginton, Heidi and Zoe Thomas, eds. *Precarious Professionals: Gender, Identities and Social Change in Modern Britain* (London: Institute for Historical Research, 2021).

Ellis, Ieuan. *Seven against Christ: A Study of 'Essays and Reviews'* (Leiden: Brill, 1980).

Ellis, Nadia. 'Black Migrants, White Queers and the Archive of Inclusion in Postwar London', *Interventions* 17, no. 6 (November 2015): 893–915.

Elwick, James. *Making a Grade: Victorian Examinations and the Rise of Standardized Testing* (Toronto: University of Toronto Press, 2021).

Engel, A.J. '"Immoral Intentions": The University of Oxford and the Problem of Prostitution, 1827–1914', *Victorian Studies* 23, no. 1 (autumn 1979): 79–107.

Engel, A.J. *From Clergyman to Don: The Rise of the Academic Profession in Nineteenth-Century Oxford* (Oxford: Clarendon, 1983).

Funke, Jana. '"We Cannot Be Greek Now": Age Difference, Corruption of Youth and the Making of Sexual Inversion', *English Studies* 94, no. 2 (April 2013): 139–53.

Ghosh, Peter and Lawrence Goldman, eds. *Politics and Culture in Victorian Britain: Essays in Memory of Colin Matthew* (Oxford: Oxford University Press, 2006).

Gibert, Julie S. 'Women Students and Student Life at England's Civic Universities before the First World War', *History of Education* 23, no. 4 (December 1994): 405–22.

Gleadle, Kathryn. *Borderline Citizens: Women, Gender, and Political Culture in Britain 1815–1867* (Oxford: Oxford University Press, 2009).

Glew, Helen. *Gender, Rhetoric and Regulation: Women's Work in the Civil Service and the London County Council, 1900–55* (Manchester: Manchester University Press, 2016).

Gordon, Lynn D. *Gender and Higher Education in the Progressive Era* (New Haven: Yale University Press, 1990).

Gottlieb, Julie and Thomas P. Linehan, eds. *The Culture of Fascism: Visions of the Far Right in Britain* (London: I.B. Tauris, 2004).

Gottlieb, Julie. 'Body Fascism in Britain: Building the Blackshirt in the Inter-War Period', *Contemporary European History* 20, no. 2 (May 2011): 111–36.

Grandy, Christine. '"The Show Is Not about Race": Custom, Screen Culture, and the Black and White Minstrel Show', *Journal of British Studies* 59, no. 4 (October 2020): 857–84.

Griffin, Ben. *The Politics of Gender in Victorian Britain: Masculinity, Political Culture and the Struggle for Women's Rights* (Cambridge: Cambridge University Press, 2012).

Griffin, Ben. 'Paternal Rights, Child Welfare and the Law in Nineteenth-Century Britain and Ireland', *Past & Present* 246, no. 1 (February 2020): 109–47.

Grove, Jen. '"Firm Outlines and Hard Muscles Immortalised": Ancient Statuary and E.P. Warren's "Uranian Ideal"', in *Sculpture, Sexuality and History: Encounters in Literature, Culture and the Arts from the Eighteenth Century to the Present*, ed. Jana Funke and Jen Grove (Cham: Springer, 2019), 171–94.

Gullace, Nicoletta F. *'The Blood of Our Sons': Men, Women, and the Renegotiation of British Citizenship during the Great War* (Basingstoke: Palgrave Macmillan, 2002).

Hadley, Elaine. *Living Liberalism: Practical Citizenship in Mid-Victorian Britain* (Chicago: University of Chicago Press, 2010).

Hall, Catherine, Keith McClelland, and Jane Rendall. *Defining the Victorian Nation: Class, Race, Gender and the British Reform Act of 1857* (Cambridge: Cambridge University Press, 2000).

Hall, Lesley. 'Women, Feminism and Eugenics', in *Essays in the History of Eugenics*, ed. Robert A. Peel (London: The Galton Institute, 1998), 36–51.

Hall, Lesley. '"Sentimental Follies" or "Instruments of Tremendous Uplift"? Reconsidering Women's Same-Sex Relationships in Interwar Britain', *Women's History Review* 25, no. 1 (January 2016): 124–42.

Halperin, David. 'How to Do the History of Male Homosexuality', *GLQ: A Journal of Lesbian and Gay Studies* 6, no. 1 (2000): 87–121.

Hammer, Carl I. 'Patterns of Homicide in a Medieval University Town: Fourteenth-Century Oxford', *Past & Present* 78 (February 1978): 3–23.

Hammond, Michael. '"A Soul Stirring Appeal to Every Briton": The Reception of "The Birth of a Nation" in Britain (1915–1916)', *Film History* 11, no. 3 (1999): 353–70.

Harrington, Neil. '"A World Apart": Change in Student Attitudes during the Interwar Period, 1918–1933', *Twentieth Century British History* 34, no. 1 (March 2023): 129–49.

Harris, Alana and Timothy Willem Jones, eds. *Love and Romance in Britain, 1918–1970* (Basingstoke: Palgrave Macmillan, 2014).

Harris, Jose. *Private Lives, Public Spirit: Britain 1870–1914* (London: Penguin, 1994).

Harrison, Brian, ed. *The History of the University of Oxford*, Volume 8: *The Twentieth Century* (Oxford: Oxford University Press, 1994).

Harte, Negley, John North, and Georgina Brewis. *The World of UCL* (London: University College London Press, 2018).

Harvie, Christopher. *The Lights of Liberalism: University Liberals and the Challenge of Democracy 1860–86* (London: Allen Lane, 1976).

Hayes, Nick and Barry M. Doyle. 'Eggs, Rags and Whist Drives: Popular Munificence and the Development of Provincial Medical Voluntarism between the Wars', *Historical Research* 86, no. 234 (November 2013): 712–40.

Heaney, Emma. *The New Woman: Literary Modernism, Queer Theory, and the Trans Feminine Allegory* (Evanston: Northwestern University Press, 2017).

Hearnshaw, F.J.C., ed. *The Centenary History of King's College London, 1828–1928* (London: George G. Harrap & Co., 1929).

Heyam, Kit. *Before We Were Trans: A New History of Gender* (London: Basic, 2022).

Hilliard, Christopher. *A Matter of Obscenity: The Politics of Censorship in Modern England* (Princeton: Princeton University Press, 2021).

Hilton, Boyd. *The Age of Atonement: The Influence of Evangelicalism on Social and Economic Thought, 1795–1865* (Oxford: Clarendon Press, 1988).

Hindmarch-Watson, Katie. 'Sex, Services, and Surveillance: The Cleveland Street Scandal Revisited', *History Compass* 14, no. 6 (June 2016): 283–91.

Hird, Marilyn, ed. *Doves and Dons: A History of St Mary's College Durham* (Durham: St Mary's College, 1982).

Hirsch, Jennifer S. and Shamus Khan. *Sexual Citizens: A Landmark Study of Sex, Power, and Assault on Campus* (New York: W.W. Norton, 2020).

Holden, Katherine. *The Shadow of Marriage: Singleness in England, 1914–60* (Manchester: Manchester University Press, 2007).

Holton, Sandra Stanley. *Feminism and Democracy: Women's Suffrage and Reform Politics in Britain 1900–1918* (Cambridge: Cambridge University Press, 1986).

Honey, J.R. de S. *Tom Brown's Universe: The Development of the Public School in the 19th Century* (London: Millington, 1977).

Houlbrook, Matt. *Queer London: Perils and Pleasures in the Sexual Metropolis, 1918–1957* (Chicago: University of Chicago Press, 2005).

Houlbrook, Matt. '"The Man with the Powder Puff" in Interwar London', *The Historical Journal* 50, no. 1 (2007): 145–71.

Howarth, Janet. 'Oakeley, Hilda Diana (1867–1950), Educationist and Author', *Oxford Dictionary of National Biography*, 23 September 2004, accessed 6 August 2022, https://www.oxforddnb.com/display/10.1093/ref:odnb/9780198614128.001.0001/odnb-9780198614128-e-48502.

Howell, Philip. 'A Private Contagious Diseases Act: Prostitution and Public Space in Victorian Cambridge', *Journal of Historical Geography* 26, no. 3 (July 2000): 376–402.

Howkins, Alun and Linda Merricks. '"Wee Be Black as Hell": Ritual, Disguise and Rebellion', *Rural History* 4, no. 1 (April 1993): 41–53.

Ingleheart, Jennifer. *Masculine Plural: Queer Classics, Sex, and Education* (Oxford: Oxford University Press, 2018).

Janes, Dominic. 'The "Curious Effects" of Acting: Homosexuality, Theatre and Female Impersonation at the University of Cambridge, 1900–39', *Twentieth Century British History* 3, no. 2 (June 2022): 169–202.

Jarvis, David. 'Mrs Maggs and Betty: The Conservative Appeal to Women Voters in the 1920s', *Twentieth Century British History* 5, no. 2 (January 1994): 129–52.

Jeffreys, Sheila. *The Spinster and Her Enemies: Feminism and Sexuality, 1880–1930* (London: Pandora Press, 1985).

Jolly, Margaret. *Sisterhood and After: An Oral History of the UK Women's Liberation Movement, 1968–Present* (Oxford: Oxford University Press, 2019).

Jones, Edgar. *University College Durham: A Social History* (Aberystwyth: self-published, 1996).

Jones, Enid Huws. *Margery Fry: The Essential Amateur* (London: Oxford University Press, 1966).

Jones, Enid Huws. 'Rackstraw, Marjorie (1888–1981), Educationist and Social Worker', *Oxford Dictionary of National Biography*, 23 September 2004, accessed 12 March 2022, https://www.oxforddnb.com/view/10.1093/ref:odnb/9780198614128.001.0001/odnb-9780198614128-e-52396.

Jones, H.S. *Intellect and Character in Victorian England: Mark Pattison and the Invention of the Don* (Cambridge: Cambridge University Press, 2007).

Joyce, Patrick. *The State of Freedom: A Social History of the British State since 1800* (Cambridge: Cambridge University Press, 2013).

Kalenak, Maggie. '"Consider Yourself Kissed": Intimacy, Engagement, and Material Culture in Nineteenth-Century Middle-Class English Love Letters', *Journal of Victorian Culture* 28, no. 2 (April 2023): 243–62.

Kane-Galbraith, Adrian. 'Male Breadwinners of "Doubtful Sex": Trans Men and the Welfare State, 1954–1970', in *Men and Masculinities in Modern Britain: A History for the Present*, ed. Matt Houlbrook, Katie Jones, and Ben Mechen (Manchester: Manchester University Press, 2024), 49–66.

Kaplan, Morris. *Sodom on the Thames: Sex, Love, and Scandal in Wilde Times* (Ithaca: Cornell University Press, 2005).

Katz, Jonathan Ned. *The Invention of Heterosexuality* (New York: Penguin, 1995).

Kaye, Hilda. *A History of Queen's College, London, 1848–1972* (London: Chatto and Windus, 1972).

Kelly, Laura. 'Irish Medical Student Culture and the Performance of Masculinity, c. 1880–1930', *History of Education* 46, no. 1 (January 2017): 39–57.

Kelly, Laura. *Irish Medical Education and Student Culture, c. 1850–1950* (Liverpool: Liverpool University Press, 2018).

Kelly, Thomas. *For Advancement of Learning: The University of Liverpool, 1881–1981* (Liverpool: Liverpool University Press, 1981).

Kent, Susan Kingsley. *Making Peace: The Reconstruction of Gender in Interwar Britain* (Princeton: Princeton University Press, 1993).

Koven, Seth. *The Match Girl and the Heiress* (Princeton: Princeton University Press, 2014).

Langhamer, Claire. *Women's Leisure in England 1920–1960* (Manchester: Manchester University Press, 2000).

Langhamer, Claire. *The English in Love: The Intimate Story of an Emotional Revolution* (Oxford: Oxford University Press, 2013).

Lawrence, Jon. 'Forging a Peaceable Kingdom: War, Violence, and Fear of Brutalization in Post-First World War Britain', *Journal of Modern History* 75, no. 3 (September 2003): 557–89.

Lefkowitz Horowitz, Helen. *Alma Mater: Design and Experience in the Women's Colleges from Their Nineteenth-Century Beginnings to the 1930s* (New York: Knopf, 1984).

LeMahieu, D.L. *A Culture for Democracy: Mass Communication and the Cultivated Mind in Britain between the Wars* (Oxford: Clarendon Press, 1988).

Levine, Emily J. *Allies and Rivals: German–American Exchange and the Rise of the Modern Research University* (Chicago: University of Chicago Press, 2021).

Levsen, Sonja. 'Constructing Elite Identities: University Students, Military Masculinity and the Consequences of the Great War in Britain and Germany', *Past & Present*, no. 198 (2008): 147–83.

Levy, Paul. *Moore: G.E. Moore and the Cambridge Apostles* (London: Papermac, 1989).

Lewis, Brian, ed. *British Queer History: New Approaches and Perspectives* (Manchester: Manchester University Press, 2013).

Lewis, Brian. *Wolfenden's Witnesses: Homosexuality in Postwar Britain* (London: Palgrave Macmillan, 2016).

Light, Alison. *Forever England: Femininity, Literature, and Conservatism between the Wars* (London: Routledge, 1991).

Logan, Anne. *The Politics of Penal Reform: Margery Fry and the Howard League* (London: Routledge, 2018).

Logan, Anne. 'Gender, Radio Broadcasting and the Role of the Public Intellectual: The BBC Career of Margery Fry, 1928–1958', *Historical Journal of Film, Radio and Television* 40, no. 2 (April 2020): 389–406.

Logan, Anne. 'More than "Bare Walls": The Educational Philosophy of Margery Fry (1874–1958) and Its Impact on University Residential Facilities for Women in the Twentieth Century', *History of Education* 50, no. 3 (2021): 338–58.

Lowe, Margaret A. *Looking Good: College Women and Body Image, 1875–1930* (Baltimore: Johns Hopkins University Press, 2003).

Macdonald, Catriona M.M. '"To Form Citizens": Scottish Students, Governance and Politics, 1884–1948', *History of Education* 38, no. 3 (May 2009): 383–402.

Malkiel, Nancy Weiss. *Keep the Damned Women Out: The Struggle for Coeducation* (Princeton: Princeton University Press, 2017).

Mandler, Peter, ed. *Liberty and Authority in Victorian Britain* (Oxford: Oxford University Press, 2006).

Marcus, Sharon. *Between Women: Friendship, Desire, and Marriage in Victorian England* (Princeton: Princeton University Press, 2007).

Marhoefer, Laurie. *Sex and the Weimar Republic: German Homosexual Emancipation and the Rise of the Nazis* (Toronto: University of Toronto Press, 2015).

Marhoefer, Laurie. 'Was the Homosexual Made White? Race, Empire, and Analogy in Gay and Trans Thought in Twentieth-Century Germany', *Gender & History* 31, no. 1 (2019): 91–114.

Marhoefer, Laurie. *Racism and the Making of Gay Rights: A Sexologist, His Student, and the Empire of Queer Love* (Toronto: University of Toronto Press, 2022).

Matera, Marc. *Black London: The Imperial Metropolis and Decolonization in the Twentieth Century* (Oakland: University of California Press, 2015).

Matthew, H.C.G. 'Haldane, Richard Burdon, Viscount Haldane (1856–1928), Politician, Educationist, and Lord Chancellor', *Oxford Dictionary of National Biography*, 6 January 2011, accessed 24 May 2024, https://www.oxforddnb.com/view/10.1093/ref:odnb/9780198614128. 001.0001/odnb-9780198614128-e-33643?rskey=FNmqOG&result=3.

Mazo Karras, Ruth. *From Boys to Men: Formations of Masculinity in Late Medieval Europe* (Philadelphia: University of Pennsylvania Press, 2003).

Mazón, Patricia M. *Gender and the Modern Research University: The Admission of Women to German Higher Education, 1865–1914* (Stanford: Stanford University Press, 2003).

McCarthy, Helen. *The British People and the League of Nations: Democracy, Citizenship and Internationalism, c. 1918–45* (Manchester: Manchester University Press, 2011).

McCarthy, Helen. 'Whose Democracy? Histories of British Political Culture between the Wars', *The Historical Journal* 55, no. 1 (March 2012): 221–38.

McCarthy, Helen. *Double Lives: A History of Working Motherhood* (London: Bloomsbury, 2021).

McKibbin, Ross. *Classes and Cultures: England 1918–1951* (Oxford: Oxford University Press, 1998).

McKibbin, Ross. *Parties and People: England, 1914–1951* (Oxford: Oxford University Press, 2010).

McWilliams-Tullberg, Rita. *Women at Cambridge: A Men's University—Though of a Mixed Type* (London: Victor Gollancz, 1975).

McWilliams-Tullberg, Rita. 'Marshall's Contribution to the Women's Higher Education Movement', in *Alfred Marshall's Lectures to Women*, ed. Tiziano Raffaelli, Eugenio F. Biagini, and Rita McWilliams-Tullberg (Aldershot: Edward Elgar, 1995), 47–75.

Meyer, Jessica. *Men of War: Masculinity and the First World War in Britain* (Basingstoke: Palgrave Macmillan, 2009).

Middleton, Stuart. 'The Crisis of Democracy in Interwar Britain', *The Historical Journal* 66, no. 1 (February 2023): 186–209.

Milne-Smith, Amy. 'A Flight to Domesticity? Making a Home in the Gentlemen's Clubs of London, 1880–1914', *Journal of British Studies* 45, no. 4 (October 2006): 796–818.

Milne-Smith, Amy. *London Clubland: A Cultural History of Gender and Class in Late Victorian Britain* (Basingstoke: Palgrave Macmillan, 2011).

Morris, George. 'Intimacy in Modern British History', *The Historical Journal* 64, no. 3 (June 2021): 796–811.

Mort, Frank. *Capital Affairs: London and the Making of the Permissive Society* (New Haven: Yale University Press, 2010).

Mort, Frank. 'The Permissive Society Revisited', *Twentieth Century British History* 22, no. 2 (June 2011): 269–98.

Moss, Michael, J. Forbes Munro, and Richard H. Trainor. *University, City and State: The University of Glasgow since 1870* (Edinburgh: Edinburgh University Press, 2000).

Moulton, Mo. *The Mutual Admiration Society: How Dorothy L. Sayers and her Oxford Circle Remade the World for Women* (London: Corsair, 2019).

Moulton, Mo. '"Both Your Sexes": A Non-Binary Approach to Gender History, Trans Studies and the Making of the Self in Modern Britain', *History Workshop Journal*, no. 95 (Spring 2023): 75–100.

Murphy, Kate. 'A Marriage Bar of Convenience? The BBC and Married Women's Work 1923–39', *Twentieth Century British History* 25, no. 4 (December 2014): 533–61.

Myers, Christine D. *University Coeducation in the Victorian Era: Inclusion in the United States and the United Kingdom* (Basingstoke: Palgrave Macmillan, 2010).

Neima, Anna. *The Utopians: Six Attempts to Build the Perfect Society* (London: Picador, 2021).

Newsome, David. *Godliness and Good Learning: Four Studies on a Victorian Ideal* (London: Cassell, 1988).

Nott, James J. '"The Plague Spots of London": William Joynson-Hicks, the Conservative Party, and the Campaign against London's Nightclubs, 1924–29', in *Classes, Cultures, and Politics: Essays on British History for Ross McKibbin*, ed. Claire V. Griffiths, James J. Nott, and William Whyte (Oxford: Oxford University Press, 2011), 227–46.

Nott, James. *Going to the Palais: A Social and Cultural History of Dancing and Dance Halls in Britain, 1918–1960* (Oxford: Oxford University Press, 2015).

Oertzen, Christine von. *Science, Gender, and Internationalism: Women's Academic Networks, 1917–1955*, trans. Kate Sturge (New York: Palgrave Macmillan, 2014).

Oman, Georgia. *Higher Education and the Gendering of Space in England and Wales, 1869–1909* (Basingstoke: Palgrave Macmillan, 2023).

Oram, Alison. 'Repressed and Thwarted, or Bearer of the New World? The Spinster in Inter-War Feminist Discourses', *Women's History Review* 1, no. 3 (September 1992): 413–33.

Oram, Alison. *Her Husband Was a Woman! Women's Gender-Crossing in Modern British Popular Culture* (London: Routledge, 2007).

O'Rourke, Chris. '"What a Pretty Man—Or Girl!": Male Cross-Dressing Performances in Early British Cinema, 1898–1918', *Gender & History* 32, no. 1 (2020): 86–107.

Orrells, Daniel. *Classical Culture and Modern Masculinity* (Oxford: Oxford University Press, 2011).

Pedersen, Susan. *Family, Dependence, and the Origins of the Welfare State: Britain and France, 1914–1945* (Cambridge: Cambridge University Press, 1993).

Pedersen, Susan. *Eleanor Rathbone and the Politics of Conscience* (New Haven: Yale University Press, 2004).

Pedersen, Susan. 'A Knife to the Heart', *London Review of Books* 40, no. 16 (30 August 2018).

Pellew, Jill and Lawrence Goldman, eds. *Dethroning Historical Reputations: Universities, Museums and the Commemoration of Benefactors* (London: Institute of Historical Research, 2018).

Perraton, Hilary. *A History of Foreign Students in Britain* (Basingstoke: Palgrave Macmillan, 2014).

Pickering, Michael. *Blackface Minstrelsy in Britain* (Aldershot: Ashgate, 2008).

Pietsch, Tamson. *Empire of Scholars: Universities, Networks and the British Academic World, 1850–1939* (Manchester: Manchester University Press, 2013).

Pietsch, Tamson. 'Commercial Travel and College Culture: The 1920s Transatlantic Student Market and the Foundations of Mass Tourism', *Diplomatic History* 43, no. 1 (January 2019): 83–106.

Pugh, Martin. *'Hurrah for the Blackshirts!' Fascists and Fascism in Britain between the Wars* (London: Jonathan Cape, 2005).

Raftery, Deirdre. 'The Opening of Higher Education to Women in Nineteenth Century England: "Unexpected Revolution" or Inevitable Change?', *Higher Education Quarterly* 56, no. 4 (2002): 331–46.

Reid, Julian. 'Living in a Sixteenth-Century College', in *Renaissance College: Corpus Christi College, Oxford in Context, 1450–1600*, ed. Mordechai Feingold and John Watts (Oxford: Oxford University Press, 2019), 183–99.

Richmond, Marsha L. '"A Lab of One's Own": The Balfour Biological Laboratory for Women at Cambridge University, 1884–1914', *Isis* 88, no. 3 (1997): 422–55.

Roberts, Mary Louise. *Civilization without Sexes: Reconstructing Gender in Postwar France, 1917–1927* (Chicago: University of Chicago Press, 1994).

Rodger, Gillian. '"He Isn't a Marrying Man": Gender and Sexuality in the Repertoire of Male Impersonators, 1870–1930', in *Queer Episodes in Music and Modern Identity*, ed. Sophie Fuller and Lloyd Whitesell (Urbana: University of Illinois Press, 2002), 105–33.

Rogers, Annie M.A.H. *Degrees by Degrees: The Story of the Admission of Oxford Women Students to Membership of the University* (Oxford: Oxford University Press, 1938).

Roper, Michael. 'Between Manliness and Masculinity: The "War Generation" and the Psychology of Fear in Britain, 1914–1950', *Journal of British Studies* 44, no. 2 (2005): 343–62.

Rothblatt, Sheldon. *The Revolution of the Dons: Cambridge and Society in Victorian England* (Cambridge: Cambridge University Press, 1968).

Rothblatt, Sheldon. 'Historical and Comparative Remarks on the Federal Principle in Higher Education', *History of Education* 16, no. 3 (1987): 151–80.

Rothblatt, Sheldon. *The Modern University and Its Discontents: The Fate of Newman's Legacies in Britain and America* (Cambridge: Cambridge University Press, 1997).

Rousseau, George. *Children and Sexuality: From the Greeks to the Great War* (London: Palgrave Macmillan, 2007).

Rutherford, Samuel. 'Impossible Love and Victorian Values: J.A. Symonds and the Intellectual History of Homosexuality', *Journal of the History of Ideas* 75, no. 4 (2014): 605–27.

Rutherford, Samuel. 'Arthur Sidgwick's *Greek Prose Composition*: Gender, Affect, and Sociability in the Late-Victorian University', *Journal of British Studies* 56, no. 1 (January 2017): 91–116.

Rutherford, Samuel. 'Researching and Teaching with British Newsreels', *Twentieth Century British History* 32, no. 3 (September 2021): 441–61.

Rutherford, Samuel. 'Higher Learning and Contestations', in *The Cultural History of Higher Learning in the Age of Industry*, ed. Heather Ellis and Tamson Pietsch (London: Bloomsbury, 2025).

Saler, Michael. *As If: Modern Enchantment and the Literary Prehistory of Virtual Reality* (Oxford: Oxford University Press, 2012).

Saltzman, Rachelle Hope. *A Lark for the Sake of Their Country: The 1926 General Strike Volunteers in Folklore and Memory* (Manchester: Manchester University Press, 2012).

Samper Vendrell, Javier. *The Seduction of Youth: Print Culture and Homosexual Rights in the Weimar Republic* (Toronto: University of Toronto Press, 2020).

Schwartz, Laura. 'Feminist Thinking on Education in Victorian England', *Oxford Review of Education* 37, no. 5 (October 2011): 669–82.

Searle, G.R. *The Quest for National Efficiency: A Study in British Politics and Political Thought, 1899–1914* (Berkeley: University of California Press, 1971).

Sedgwick, Eve Kosofsky. *Epistemology of the Closet* (Berkeley: University of California Press, 1990).

Semmel, Bernard. *Imperialism and Social Reform: English Social-Imperial Thought, 1895–1914* (London: Allen & Unwin, 1960).

Senelick, Laurence. 'Boys and Girls Together: Subcultural Origins of Glamour Drag and Male Impersonation on the Nineteenth-Century Stage', in *Crossing the Stage: Controversies on Cross-Dressing*, ed. Lesley Ferris (London: Routledge, 1994), 80–95.

Shepard, Alexandra. *Meanings of Manhood in Early Modern England* (Oxford: Oxford University Press, 2006).

Shinn, Christine Helen. *Paying the Piper: The Development of the University Grants Committee 1919–1946* (London: Falmer Press, 1986).

Shrosbree, Colin. *Public Schools and Private Education: The Clarendon Commission, 1861–1864, and the Public Schools Acts* (Manchester: Manchester University Press, 1988).

Sigel, Lisa Z. '"Best Love": Female Impersonation in the Great War', *Sexualities* 19, nos. 1–2 (February 2016): 98–118.

Simon, Brian. 'The Student Movement in England and Wales during the 1930s', *History of Education* 16, no. 3 (September 1987): 189–203.

Sinfield, Alan. *The Wilde Century: Effeminacy, Oscar Wilde and the Queer Moment* (London: Cassell, 1994).

Skoda, Hannah. *Medieval Violence: Physical Brutality in Northern France, 1270–1330* (Oxford: Oxford University Press, 2013).

Smith, Helen. *Masculinity, Class and Same-Sex Desire in Industrial England, 1895–1957* (Basingstoke: Palgrave Macmillan, 2015).

Sondheimer, Janet. *Castle Adamant in Hampstead: A History of Westfield College, 1882–1982* (London: Westfield College, 1983).

Sox, David. *Bachelors of Art: Edward Perry Warren and the Lewes House Brotherhood* (London: Fourth Estate, 1991).

Sponsler, Claire. 'Outlaw Masculinities: Drag, Blackface, and Late Medieval Laboring-Class Festivities', in *Becoming Male in the Middle Ages*, ed. Jeffrey Jerome Cohen and Bonnie Wheeler (New York: Garland Publishing, 2000), 321–48.

Srinivasan, Amia. 'Sex as a Pedagogical Failure', *The Yale Law Journal* 129, no. 4 (February 2020): 1100–46.

Srinivasan, Amia. *The Right to Sex* (London: Bloomsbury, 2021).

Steedman, Carolyn. *Landscape for a Good Woman: A Story of Two Lives* (New Brunswick: Rutgers University Press, 1986).

Stewart, Alan. *Close Readers: Humanism and Sodomy in Early Modern England* (Princeton: Princeton University Press, 1997).

Stray, Christopher. *Classics Transformed: Schools, Universities, and Society in England, 1830–1960* (Oxford: Oxford University Press, 1998).

Sunderland, Helen. '"Politics for Girls": Representations of Political Girlhood in the Girl's Own Paper and the Girl's Realm', *Victorian Periodicals Review* 52, no. 1 (2019): 1–26.

Sunderland, Helen. 'Politics in Schoolgirl Debating Cultures in England, 1886–1914', *The Historical Journal* 63, no. 4 (September 2020): 935–57.

Sunderland, Helen. 'English Girls' Schools and Women's Suffrage', in *The Politics of Women's Suffrage: Local, National and International Dimensions*, ed. Alexandra Hughes-Johnson and Lyndsey Jenkins (London: University of London Press, 2021), 163–90.

Surkis, Judith. *Sexing the Citizen: Morality and Masculinity in France, 1870–1920* (Ithaca: Cornell University Press, 2006).

Sutherland, Gillian. 'The Movement for the Higher Education of Women: Its Social and Intellectual Context in England, c. 1840–80', in *Politics and Social Change in Modern Britain: Essays Presented to A.F. Thompson*, ed. P.J. Waller (Sussex: The Harvester Press, 1987), 91–116.

Sutherland, Gillian. 'Education', in *The Cambridge Social History of Britain, 1750–1950*, Volume 3, ed. F.M.L. Thompson (Cambridge: Cambridge University Press, 2000), 119–69.

Sutherland, Gillian. *Faith, Duty and the Power of Mind: The Cloughs and Their Circle* (Cambridge: Cambridge University Press, 2006).

Sutherland, Gillian. *In Search of the New Woman: Middle-Class Women and Work in Britain 1870–1914* (Cambridge: Cambridge University Press, 2015).

Syrett, Nicholas. *The Company He Keeps: A History of White College Fraternities* (Chapel Hill: University of North Carolina Press, 2009).

Szreter, Simon and Kate Fisher. *Sex before the Sexual Revolution* (Cambridge: Cambridge University Press, 2010).

Taddeo, Julie Anne. 'Plato's Apostles: Edwardian Cambridge and the "New Style of Love"', *Journal of the History of Sexuality* 8, no. 2 (1997): 196–228.

Taylor, John. *The Impact of the First World War on British Universities: Emerging from the Shadows* (Basingstoke: Palgrave Macmillan, 2018).

Tebbutt, Clare. 'The Spectre of the "Man-Woman Athlete": Mark Weston, Zdenek Koubek, the 1936 Olympics and the Uncertainty of Sex', *Women's History Review* 24, no. 5 (September 2015): 721–38.

Thelin, John R. *A History of American Higher Education*, 3rd edition (Baltimore: Johns Hopkins University Press, 2019).

Thomas, Keith. *Rule and Misrule in the Schools of Early Modern England* (Reading: University of Reading, 1976).

Thompson, F.M.L. *The University of London and the World of Learning, 1836–1986* (London: Hambledon, 1990).

Todd, Selina. 'Young Women, Work, and Leisure in Interwar England', *The Historical Journal* 48, no. 3 (2005): 789–809.

Tosh, John. *A Man's Place: Masculinity and the Middle-Class Home in Victorian England* (New Haven: Yale University Press, 2007).

Tosh, John. *Manliness and Masculinities in Nineteenth-Century Britain: Essays on Gender, Family and Empire* (Harlow: Pearson Longman, 2011).

Tuke, Margaret J. *A History of Bedford College for Women, 1849–1937* (London: Oxford University Press, 1939).

Turpin, Andrea L. *A New Moral Vision: Gender, Religion, and the Changing Purposes of American Higher Education, 1837–1917* (Ithaca: Cornell University Press, 2016).

Vernon, James. '"For Some Queer Reason": The Trials and Tribulations of Colonel Barker's Masquerade in Interwar Britain', *Signs* 26, no. 1 (2000): 37–62.

Vernon, Keith. *Universities and the State in England, 1850–1939* (Abingdon: Routledge, 2004).

Vicinus, Martha. 'Distance and Desire: English Boarding-School Friendships', *Signs* 9, no. 4 (Summer 1984): 600–22.

Vicinus, Martha. *Independent Women: Work and Community for Single Women, 1850–1920* (London: Virago, 1985).

Vicinus, Martha. *Intimate Friends: Women Who Loved Women, 1778–1928* (Chicago: University of Chicago Press, 2004).

Vider, Stephen. *The Queerness of Home: Gender, Sexuality and the Politics of Domesticity after World War II* (Chicago: University of Chicago Press, 2021).

Walkowitz, Judith R. 'Science, Feminism and Romance: The Men's and Women's Club 1885–1889', *History Workshop*, no. 21 (April 1986): 36–59.

Walkowitz, Judith R. *City of Dreadful Delight: Narratives of Sexual Danger in Late-Victorian London* (Chicago: University of Chicago Press, 1992).

Walkowitz, Judith R. 'Going Public: Shopping, Street Harassment, and Streetwalking in Late Victorian London', *Representations*, no. 62 (April 1998): 1–30.

Waters, Chris. 'Distance and Desire in the New British Queer History', *GLQ: A Journal of Lesbian and Gay Studies* 14, no. 1 (December 2007): 139–55.

Waters, Chris. 'The Homosexual as a Social Being in Britain, 1945–1968', *Journal of British Studies* 51, no. 3 (July 2012): 685–710.

Weber, Thomas. *Our Friend 'The Enemy': Elite Education in Britain and Germany before World War I* (Stanford: Stanford University Press, 2008).

Weeks, Jeffrey. *Coming Out: Homosexual Politics in Britain from the Nineteenth Century to the Present* (London: Quartet Books, 1977).

Weeks, Jeffrey. *Sex, Politics and Society: The Regulation of Sexuality since 1800* (London: Longman, 1981).

Weeks, Jeffrey. *Between Worlds: A Queer Boy from the Valleys* (Cardigan: Parthian, 2021).

Weisz, George. *The Emergence of Modern Universities in France, 1863–1914* (Princeton: Princeton University Press, 1983).

Whitaker, John K., ed. *The Correspondence of Alfred Marshall, Economist*, Volume 1: *Climbing, 1868–1890* (Cambridge: Cambridge University Press, 1996).

Whiting, C.E. *The University of Durham, 1832–1932* (London: The Sheldon Press, 1932).

Whyte, William. 'The Intellectual Aristocracy Revisited', *Journal of Victorian Culture* 10, no. 1 (2005): 15–45.

Whyte, William. *Redbrick: A Social and Architectural History of Britain's Civic Universities* (Oxford: Oxford University Press, 2015).

Wiggins, Sarah. 'Gendered Spaces and Political Identity: Debating Societies in English Women's Colleges, 1890–1914', *Women's History Review* 18, no. 5 (November 2009): 737–52.

Williamson, Philip. *Stanley Baldwin: Conservative Leadership and National Values* (Cambridge: Cambridge University Press, 1999).

Winter, J.M. *The Great War and the British People* (London: Macmillan, 1985).

Ziegler, Philip. *Legacy: Cecil Rhodes, the Rhodes Trust and Rhodes Scholarships* (New Haven: Yale University Press, 2008).

Zweiniger-Bargielowska, Ina. 'Rationing, Austerity and the Conservative Party Recovery after 1945', *The Historical Journal* 37, no. 1 (March 1994): 173–97.

Unpublished

'Participation Rates in Higher Education: Academic Years 2006/2007–2017/2018', Office for National Statistics, 26 September 2019, accessed 7 March 2020, https://www.gov.uk/government/statistics/participation-rates-in-higher-education-2006-to-2018.

'UCAS Undergraduate End of Cycle Data Resources 2022', accessed 20 August 2023, https://www.ucas.com/data-and-analysis/undergraduate-statistics-and-reports/ucas-undergraduate-end-cycle-data-resources-2022.

Blakestad, Nancy L. 'King's College of Household and Social Science and the Household Science Movement in English Higher Education, c. 1908–1939', PhD thesis, University of Oxford, 1994.

Duckenfield, B. 'Changes to the Celibacy Rule at the Colleges of Oxford and Cambridge Universities', PhD thesis, Kingston University, 2008.

Kane-Galbraith, Adrian. 'Public Bodies: "Sex Change" and the State in Postwar Britain', PhD thesis, University of Washington, 2024.

Lees, Lynton. 'Democracy's Children: Education, Childhood, and Citizenship in Britain and the Empire, c. 1918–1955', PhD thesis, Columbia University, 2024.

Miller, Nicola, et al. 'Promoting Gender Equality in UK History: A Second Report and Recommendations for Good Practice', Royal Historical Society, November 2018.

Rees, Jay. 'Student Experience at Swansea University, 1920–1990', PhD thesis, University of Swansea, 2020.

Sloan, Catherine. 'The School Magazine in Victorian England', PhD thesis, University of Oxford, 2019.

Index

Note: Tables are indicated by an italic *t*, respectively, following the page number.

Since the index has been created to work across multiple formats, indexed terms for which a page range is given (e.g., 52–53, 66–70, etc.) may occasionally appear only on some, but not all, of the pages within the range.